Reconstructing Public Housing

Liverpool's hidden history of collective alternatives

Contents

List of Figures ix
List of Abbreviations x
Acknowledgements xi

Prologue xv

Part I Introduction

1 Introducing Collective Housing Alternatives 3
Why Collective Housing Alternatives? 9
Articulating Our Housing Commons 14
Bringing the State Back In 21
2 Why Liverpool of All Places? 27
A City of Radicals and Reformists 29
A City on (the) Edge? 34
A City Playing the Urban Regeneration Game 36
Structure of the Book 39

Part II The Housing Question

3 Revisiting the Housing Question 45
Nouns and Verbs: On the Nature of Value 48
Exploitation and Alienation: On the Contradictions of Capitalism 50
Ends and Means: The Point Is to Change It! 55

4 Liverpool's Co-operative Revolution 60

Rehabilitating Housing in a SNAP 65

You Hold the Pen, We'll Tell You What to Draw! 76

Competition: The Counterintuitive Component of Cooperativism 85

5 Liberal Compromises: Diluting the Cooperative Revolution? 89

You Can Have Any House You Like So Long as It's a New-Build Co-op 92

Utalitarianism (Utilitarian plus Totalitarian): On Form Following Function 97

Contradictions of Choice: Defensive Urbanism or (Extra)Ordinary Sub-urbanism? 99

6 Municipalisation: A Militant Response to the Housing Question 103

A Tory–Liberal Plot: The Gravedigger of Municipal Housing? 107

Defensible Principles and (Policy) Design Disadvantagement 110

Keeping the Cooperative Spirit Alive: The Movement Migrates to Knowsley 114

Part III The Neighbourhood Question

7 Locating the Neighbourhood Question 123

Liverpool's Second Blitz 124

How to Make Water Flow Uphill 128

Can Collective Housing Save the City? 135

8 The Eldonians: From Parish Politics to Global Exemplar 140

Militant Tactics, Boss Politics, Tribal Loyalties, Friends in High Places 144

We Do It Better Together: Towards a Self-Regenerating Community 147

Eldonia: An Independent Micro-State? 151

9 Cooperative by Name If Not by Nature 158

Singing the Post-Development Blues: On Revolutionaries Retiring 160

Third Sector Empire-Building 161

The Story So Far: How Self-Regenerating, Really? 167

Part IV The Urban Question

10 Grappling with the Urban Question 177

Weapons Wielded against Enclosure of the Commons 178

Grounding Capitalism in the Land Question 185

Housing Market Renewal, Neo-Haussmannisation and the New Urban Enclosures 189

11 Growing Granby from the Grassroots: A (Plant) Potted History 201

Living through Hell: On the Violence of Managed Decline 208

Putting the T into CLT; Finishing the Work that SNAP Started 213

From Success to Failure: A Great British Property Scandal 228

12 Technocratic Experiment or Experimental Utopia? 232

Dereliction-by-Design and Transatlantic Knowledge Transfer 237

Homebaked: Brick by Brick, Loaf by Loaf, We Build Ourselves 242

Seeing Liverpool's Housing History through a Bifocal Verb–Noun Lens 251

Part V Conclusion

13 Reconstructing Public Housing (History) 263

In, Against and Beyond Public Housing 268

How to Answer the Housing, Neighbourhood and Urban Questions? 275

Using the Master's Tools to Dismantle the Master's House 285

14 On (Myth) Making History 289

From Heroic Event to Boring Bureaucratic Process 294

The Myth of Liverpool Exceptionalism 300

Recipes for Revolution: From Cultivating Local Delicacies to Sourcing Essential Ingredients 303

15 Building a Bureaucracy from Below 311

Dormant, Not Defunct: Self-Funding the Next Co-Op Spring 313

Realising Municipal Dreams 318

Recoding the DNA of Collective Alternatives 323

Epilogue: Translating Between Inward, Upward and Outward Languages 327

Artificial Hells, Social Practice and Artistic Spectacle: Who (or What) Is All This For? 335

Bibliography 345

Index 363

Figures

1 Dilapidated dwellings and neighbourhood abandonment in Liverpool 8 in 2015. 38

2 "Utalitarian" community architecture of the Weller Street Co-op. 84

3 Typical Eldonian Village streetscape, overshadowed by the world's largest brick warehouse at Stanley Dock. 100

4 Subverting "target hardening" with artistic symbols of hope. 211

5 Granby Street Market relocated to Ducie Street during Cairns Street renovation, 2015. 217

6 Dereliction by design: irreverent Scouse wit on display in Anfield. 240

All figures are photographs taken by the author.

Abbreviations

CDP	Community Development Project
CDS	Co-operative Development Services (Liverpool agency)
CIC	Community Interest Company
CLT	Community Land Trust
CPO	Compulsory Purchase Order
EGL	Eldonian Group Ltd
HAG	Housing Association Grant
HMR	Housing Market Renewal
KTP	Knowledge Transfer Partnership
LHT	Liverpool Housing Trust
LIFE	Lead–Influence–Follow–Exit (Council policy for Housing Associations)
MHOS	Mutual Home Ownership Society
MIH	Merseyside Improved Houses
NDC	New Deal for Communities
NWHS	North West Housing Services (formerly CDS)
RIBA	Royal Institute of British Architects
SNAP	Shelter Neighbourhood Action Project
URBED	Urbanism Environment Design (planning consultancy)
URS	Urban Regeneration Strategy (Council policy programme)
ZOO	Zone of Opportunity

Acknowledgements

This book could not have been written without the people of Liverpool, past and present. It is a story about their history—albeit one strand in a colourful tapestry—woven out of oral testimony and multiple personal reflections. A large part of the narrative has been composed through conversations with numerous insightful participants who each, in one way or another, helped make history in Liverpool. They include Jane Corbett, Chris Davies, John Earnshaw, Juliet Edgar, George Evans, Ed Gommon, Bill Halsall, Jackie Harris, George Howarth, Richard Kemp, Eleanor Lee, Rob MacDonald, Tony McGann, Erika Rushton, Max Steinberg, Bill Taylor and many others who wish to remain anonymous. I am especially indebted to Paul Lusk, whose first-hand account of the co-op movement helped frame my own, for guiding me, step by step, through the potted history of cooperative development on Merseyside. To Jack McBane, for his hospitality and enthusiasm for my project, in many ways extending his own on the Eldonians, who he worked so closely with to construct and materialise their vision. To Jonathan Brown (of Share the City and SAVE Britain's Heritage) who introduced me to Liverpool's urbanism and its controversial politics of housing regeneration through his excellent tours. And also to (the late) Des McConaghy, former director of the Shelter Neighbourhood Action Project (and the first person I interviewed for my doctoral research upon which this book is broadly based) for his take on the early period of experimentation in Granby.

I would especially like to thank Ronnie Hughes, Granby's own unofficial urban historian and photojournalist, who has been a brilliant help in piecing together the history since SNAP. And Gemma Jerome, a Terrace 21 cooperator and Granby CLT collaborator, who first introduced me to the neighbourhood and its emerging CLT campaign. Likewise, her Terrace 21 comrade, Marianne Heaslip, has generously imparted critical insights into both Granby and Homebaked. To Ronnie, Gemma and Marianne, I am grateful for the dialogue we have continued on and off over the years since we first met in 2013. More recently, the Homebaked collective have been a real inspiration to me. I would like to thank them all for their warm welcome in bringing me into the fold for an all too brief period in 2017 and 2018, when I served as a participant-observer on the CLT board. Alongside Angela McKay, Sue Humphreys, Ralph Bullivant, Peter Colby, Andrew Beattie, Sam Jones, Paul

Kelly, Sally Anne-Watkiss and (the late) Cal Starr, Britt Jurgensen in particular has been an amazing critical friend in helping me get the narrative right, as someone so passionately committed to crafting and realising Homebaked's collective vision. In (re)constructing Liverpool's hidden history of collective housing alternatives, I have drawn upon, and been influenced by, the testimony of all these participant-contributors. What follows, however, is not a direct, unmediated representation of their views but wholly my own, distinct take on events, one triangulated with multiple secondary sources and alternative analyses and refracted through a theoretical lens that I feel illuminates this history most clearly—a necessarily partial interpretation which, no doubt, will be seen in a different light by others.

Writing this book has been a long, meandering journey that began back in 2011 when I started my PhD at the University of Manchester. I am forever grateful to Graham Haughton and Ste Hincks for showing me the way—in equal measure encouraging and challenging in their tireless (and tirelessly entertaining) supervision. I want to thank Graham for introducing me to the work of Colin Ward (Graham's own unique brand of radicalism is not unlike Ward's: modest, respectable, scholarly). And Ste (born and bred on Merseyside) for persuading me to study the history of collective housing alternatives in Liverpool rather than in Manchester or London. Neil McInroy and Alex Lord, too, my third and fourth supervisors, for bringing fresh perspectives and making connections. Manchester's PhD programme and cohort within the geography, planning, international development and architecture departments—and politics, too—was a hotbed of radical intellectual activity; the extraordinary richness of which I have only come to appreciate since moving on to pastures not quite so green. In reading groups and seminars—often degenerating into long, ale-fuelled sessions at Sandbar—I made so many friends and comrades whose energies have, each in their own way, fed into the conception and writing of this book (not least Abby Gilbert, Ben Sessions, Craig Thomas, Chris Foster, Dan Slade, Esther Meininghaus, Gareth Price-Thomas, Gemma Sou, Jess Hope, Jon Las Heras, Nadim Mirshak, Natalie Langford, Paul James, Phil Horn, Purnima Purohit, Rachel Alexander, Roisin Read, Sally Cawood, Sam Hayes, Shamel Azmeh, Simon Chin-Yee, Soma Laha, Tomas Maltby and, through association, Charlie Winstanley and Dale Lately). The Urban Rights Reading Group organised by Melanie Lombard was really constructive. Through working (and playing) with the OpenSpace collective—Maria Kaika, Erik Swyngedouw, Lazaros Karaliotas, Ioanna Tantanasi, Nadim Mirshak and Caglar Koksal—and organising a number of critical urban studies events together, I was introduced to Andy Merrifield and Japhy Wilson, whose work on Henri Lefebvre and the production of space has been a major inspiration. Andy's passion in articulating a Lefebvrean perspective on the city, and on his home town of Liverpool, has been a guiding light throughout. My interest in Marxist and critical urbanism was first piqued whilst studying for a Masters in Urban Planning at UCL—particularly by Michael Edwards' enlivening teaching and a reading group on David Harvey's *Limits to Capital* convened by Louis Moreno. Whilst at UCL, my knowledge of community land trusts, which were to become the main subject of my PhD, was initiated through conversations with fellow students, Daniel Fitzpatrick and Dan Durrant especially.

My understanding of CLTs has been honed over the years not only through engaged research in Liverpool but also discussion at conferences and other events with a number of practitioners and scholars, not least Tom Moore, whose pioneering efforts at bringing together a network of CLT researchers from the across the UK has been instrumental to the development of my own research. Catherine Harrington and Tom Chance at the National CLT Network, as well as action-researcher Tom Archer, have each helped me get to grips with the complex policy landscape and technicalities of CLTs. Similarly, David Rodgers (formerly CDS Cooperatives) was a fount of wisdom on co-ops; Hugh Ellis (Town and Country Planning Association) on utopian planning alternatives; and David Ireland (World Habitat) on self-help housing and bringing empty homes back into use. I owe an intellectual debt to countless scholars and theorists of capitalism, cooperativism, housing and the commons who have helped me see many of the conceptual connections I make in what follows—too many to list here but whose names can be gleaned from glancing at the bibliography.

Many of the theoretical arguments I make in the book were first tested out at various academic conferences through dialogue with comrades I met along the way, not least Michele Vianello, Hamish Kallin and Jessie Brennan. Conferences proving particularly formative include the 9th International Social Innovation Research Conference in Melbourne, Australia, in 2017, the 7th International Conference of Critical Geography in Ramallah, Palestine, in 2015 and the Association of European Schools of Planning (AESOP) Young Academics Network conference in Gothenburg, Sweden, in 2014. Melissa García Lamarca and Philipp Horn were frequent fellow travellers from Manchester to such conferences and astute critical friends in shaping my arguments. At an AESOP PhD workshop in Belfast in 2013, Ben Davy pushed me to develop my ideas further. Since first meeting her at the 2013 RGS-IBG conference in London, Antonia Layard has always been really supportive. David Mullins was particularly encouraging when I first met him at the Housing Studies Association Conference in York in 2012; I thank David, and also Quintin Bradley, for such generous critical feedback as peer reviewers of the first draft submitted to Liverpool University Press (LUP). I am grateful to Alison Welsby, my editor at LUP, for her encouragement and patience with continual deadline extension requests; and for backing this book to be made open access online as part of a demonstration project in open access academic publishing funded by the University of Liverpool

Library. I can only hope the finished product lives up to these expectations placed in it.

I would like to thank Alan Southern for all his support and sage advice over an exciting, if rather unstable and precarious period marked by informal short-term postdoctoral contracts during which he has been my mentor as well as comrade. So too Pete North, who had the unenviable task of examining my PhD thesis in 2015 and who has since provided great guidance, particularly in our recent work together, with Alan and others such as Vicky Nowak and Helen Heap, on researching and cultivating the social and solidarity economy in Liverpool and beyond. The planning academics at Liverpool University—particularly Alex Lord, Olivier Sykes, John Sturzaker and Bertie Dockerill—invited me to give a number of guest lectures around 2016 and then welcomed me as one of their own while I was writing up the book, or trying to. I would also like to thank Len Gibbs for putting his faith in me, inviting me onto the board of EPIC Housing Association (Empowering People, Inspiring Communities) in Stoke-on-Trent in 2016. My few years there volunteering as a board member taught me a great deal about the practical and policy challenges—and ethical dilemmas—facing community-based housing associations in this difficult era of commercialisation and ratcheting austerity.

This book has been (almost) completely rewritten and reconstituted from its embryonic form as my PhD thesis. I am grateful to my good friends Will Wheeler and George Hoare for reading and reviewing in great depth the new introductory and concluding parts which has certainly sharpened up my analysis; and to Matt Ingleby for coming up with the title, amongst other imaginative alternatives. I am indebted to the Leverhulme Trust for providing the financial support enabling me to dedicate much of my time to writing and editing during the first year of my early career fellowship. The majority of the writing, however, took place while I was unemployed, between postdocs, living back in my home town with my mum and dad, Chris and Brian, over the summer of 2018—long, productive days bookended by beautiful bike rides into the South Downs or runs on Bognor beach. Being unemployed has never been so much fun; but it was only because of mum and dad that this was made possible. I am grateful for all their love and support over the years. Finally, none of this would ever have seen the light of day were it not for Abby—she is an unstoppable force of ruthless critique and joyful inspiration. Doubtless I could not have remained so energised about the radical potential residing in the everyday life of collective housing activism were it not for Abby's loving spirit and unwavering faith in the actual as well as the possible.

Prologue

In 2015, a long-neglected neighbourhood on the south side of inner-city Liverpool, Granby, was thrust into the media spotlight when a small resident-led experiment to bring empty homes back into community use, the Granby Four Streets Community Land Trust, became the first ever architectural or housing project in the Turner Prize's controversy-punctuated history to be nominated for and indeed win Britain's coveted national art award. The community land trust (CLT) and their architects Assemble were up against the usual (dis)array of avant-garde nominees and were bemused to be shortlisted by the judges for a prize that recognises cutting-edge interventions in the visual and material arts—not so much architecture, and certainly not so-called 'community architecture' associated with vernacular housing (and for many decades derided by the architecture establishment). What had regenerating housing in a self-consciously amateur 'do-it-together' approach that decentred the role of the architect and, by the same token, foregrounded residents as the collective 'artist' got to do with art? Thus ensued a debate in the national press about the function of art and the merits of an award that continually sought to push the boundaries—beyond breaking point for many critics—of the very concept it celebrates. Some commentators rolled their eyes; others pointed to the way in which these four streets, saved from demolition by their few remaining inhabitants (the majority having been forced out years ago by urban decline and state-led demolition threats), had been turned into a work of art through spontaneous acts of guerrilla gardening, street planting and wall murals. Tricky questions were raised over the changing role of art in society; over why the prize had been awarded to Assemble rather than the residents who had been working hard to transform the streets for years before the trendy architectural collective arrived on the scene from London; and why it had been left to citizens and artists—however (re)defined—to regenerate public space and renovate housing, much of it ex-council and now owned by housing associations, more obviously the responsibility of the state.

When the news broke of Granby Four Streets' Turner Prize victory, I was fortunate enough to have been observing the project for a number of years as part of my doctoral research. I was based nearby in Manchester at the time and, in seeking to study alternative approaches to public housing and urban regeneration, I had been seduced by Liverpool's rich history of cooperative housing as well as the city's two CLT campaigns, Granby Four Streets and Homebaked. Both projects were pioneering in their application of the CLT model—originally developed out of the American Civil Rights movement and imported to Britain in the 1990s to tackle rural affordability issues—to an urban context suffering disinvestment and decline. They aimed to demonstrate how housing and neighbourhood governance could be done differently, more imaginatively and democratically, by drawing people together around a common project of breathing life back into urban spaces long left to rot by public authorities and private landlords alike.

My involvement with Granby was only ever very partial. I was an outsider looking in—and there were many of us. Those community activists that I met in the early days of my research were understandably reticent to give me much of their time. They complained of 'researcher fatigue'—referring to the growing number of students, researchers and journalists who were each asking for a little of their time. It soon adds up of course. Trying to find the extra time and energy outside of their day jobs and family and personal lives to give to the CLT campaign, let alone deal with research requests, was challenging to say the least. I intended to make my approach as participatory and reciprocal as I could; in return for access and information, I wanted to get involved and offer up my skills in whatever way might be helpful. An opportunity arose to do just that when Assemble asked me to write a short reflective piece on the theoretical and historical background of the CLT model as a chapter in the catalogue they were putting together to present to the Turner Prize judges at the exhibition of the nominations in Glasgow.[1] I was incredibly honoured to be invited to play a part, however small; that was where my formal involvement began and ended.

By 2016, having defended my dissertation, I moved to Liverpool and found myself getting more involved with Homebaked as part of new research I was undertaking on the city region's social economy at the University of Liverpool. I was invited onto the CLT board as a participant-observer and so I began working closely with activists, residents and other board members on how to turn their vision for a revitalised local high street of community-owned enterprise and housing into a reality. Witnessing at first hand the travails of a small community project to bring creative ideas to fruition, I was impressed by the energy and commitment invested but so too exasperated by the barriers imposed by policy and bureaucracy at various levels and the sheer complexity of coordinating so many actors and interests towards a common goal. It was an insight into a slow collective learning process—a steep curve no doubt scaled by countless others before Homebaked and many others still to come. There was a sense among activists that they were reinventing the wheel; that surely all this had been done before and it was merely a matter of finding out how.

1 "What Exactly is a CLT?", in Assemble, eds, *Granby Workshop Catalogue 2015*, pp. 56–59.

That was one impetus for writing this book. I wanted to show how similar things had been done in the not too distant past, in the same city, often in the very same street, by other collective housing movements that shared so much, if not their name, with Liverpool's budding community land trust movement. In the 1970s, fuelled by tenant protests over poor conditions and the displacement entailed by the council's 'slum clearance programme', one of the largest and most imaginative housing co-operative movements in Britain if not Europe was born—Liverpool's so-called 'Co-op Spring'[2] or 'Co-operative Revolution'.[3] With unprecedented levels of resident participation and democratic decision-making in all aspects of housing, the new-build co-op movement was heralded at the time as a possible—but ultimately unworkable—paradigm shift towards Public Housing 2.0. Nonetheless, some 50 housing co-ops can still be found across Merseyside to this day—a not insignificant sum for a British city. This book aims to bring the historical development of Liverpool's co-op movement into conversation with the presently unfolding CLT campaigns through tracing historical, geographical and conceptual connections.

In excavating Liverpool's role in Britain's 'hidden history'[4] of housing co-ops, I found other important experiments that seem to have been largely forgotten or else overlooked by activists and policymakers as well as scholars. The co-ops came out of a time in which voluntary associations were beginning to vie with municipal authorities in the provision of public housing and the governance of neighbourhoods. Liverpool proved especially fertile ground to grow housing associations and, as I dug deeper, it seemed to me that these associations had grown out of a radical era of activism against council-led demolition of inner-city 'slums' in the 1960s and 1970s—an era in which the homelessness charity Shelter was founded and which experimented with an innovative approach to rehabilitate rather than demolish run-down housing in Granby called the Shelter Neighbourhood Action Project or, quite simply, SNAP. In the policy switch SNAP initiated, Liverpool City Council supported the growth of old and new housing associations, which took on municipal stock precisely in order to rehabilitate it, helping develop the city's burgeoning co-operative movement. SNAP also saved from demolition the four streets that would later become the site of Granby CLT. In the intervening years, as society has been reshaped by the tightening grip of neoliberalism, these same housing associations have become bureaucratic behemoths with large-scale for-profit development arms and instrumental roles in the latest round of clearance and redevelopment that has in turn provoked new waves of housing

2 José Ospina, *Housing Ourselves* (Hilary Shipman Ltd, 1987).

3 CDS, *Building Democracy: Housing Cooperatives on Merseyside. Update '94* (Cooperative Development Services (Liverpool) Ltd, 1994).

4 Johnston Birchall, "The Hidden History of Co-operative Housing in Britain", *Department of Government Working Papers* 17 (1991).

activism, leading to the contemporary CLT movement, which includes several failed campaigns as well as the two success stories. This book, then, is also about how collective housing activism has influenced the direction of neighbourhood renewal policy and demonstrated a more sensitive way of doing urban regeneration as an alternative to the large-scale redevelopments that all too often befall our cities.

In reconstructing Liverpool's history of collective housing alternatives, it became clear that the movements came in waves and that the force of these waves was heightened by the swell created by the last. Historical waves deposited resources for activists of the future to salvage from the beached wreckage of past struggles and use afresh. Local cultural practices of cooperation and community organising developed by the co-op movement provided just such a depository of stored energy and practical wisdom for contemporary CLT campaigns. Collective memory of cooperative campaigning implanted in place the seeds that would eventually flower when the climatic conditions were once again favourable. After a long dormancy, from the 1980s through to the 2000s, collective housing was reactivated when Granby and Homebaked CLTs were established in 2011—the year in which 'the political' erupted back onto the world stage after decades of neoliberal inertia and technocratic tinkering with redoubled force in global urban occupations; *the year of dreaming dangerously*, as Slavoj Žižek has put it.[5] The critical geographer Don Mitchell goes so far as to position the embryonic Liverpool CLT movement alongside the 'movements of the squares', as part of a radical tradition of anti-capitalist struggle and experimentation that had its last pivotal moment in the events around May 1968. "Homebaked Community Land Trust and Co-operative Bakery Anfield", writes Mitchell, "are just as thrilling as the example of the neighbourhood park forums that developed across Turkey after Taksim Square was cleared out. They show that urban space can be collectively taken and collectively remade, that use can dominate exchange, that our fate is not necessarily a fate written by the tendency towards abstract space in capitalism".[6] Whilst Homebaked and Granby CLTs are clearly not so dramatic or disruptive events as, say, Occupy Wall Street or the Arab Spring, they nonetheless seem to reignite the political possibilities and creative transformation latent in Liverpool's own 'Co-op Spring', its housing cooperative revolution in the 1970s. The co-op and CLT movements are each the product of particular openings in the ideological fabric that wraps our world with a veneer of stability and certainty, but which blinds us from seeing political alternatives. These movements represent two such alternatives—what I call collective housing alternatives—to the bipolar status quo, the public–private,

5 Slavoj Žižek, *The Year of Dreaming Dangerously* (Verso Books, 2012).
6 Don Mitchell, "Taking Space", *Stages: Liverpool Biennial* #2, Homebaked: A Perfect Recipe (2014).

state–capitalist system of owning and managing housing that has dominated our political economy for over a century.

But what caused these collective alternatives to flourish when they did? Was it just a sign of the times, or a factor of political, economic and cultural conditions embedded in a particular geography? Or, does it have something to do with the specific legal and institutional designs of the co-op and CLT models themselves? This book tells the stories of the people and movements involved in bringing these abstract models to life in Liverpool and how those models in turn shaped their social and urban environments as and after they were instituted. It is thus a tale of the dialectical interplay between collective actions and institutional forms, which, like skeletons, give strength and structure yet contort the muscle tissue that animates collective alternatives.

What hope do we have for institutionalising collective housing alternatives without compromising their radical political intentions? What changes occur in the transition from the excitement of political campaigning to the procedural task, once the campaign is won, of developing governance mechanisms for the ongoing practical management and maintenance of housing? Why have the most experimental and radical ideas for developing public housing gradually shifted outside the purview of the local state and into the hands of professional and community groups in civil society? Why has what was once deemed public housing provision delivered by the state become the subject of art? What does this categorisation as art say about how our approach to providing shelter for everyone has changed over time? Can collective housing alternatives become a mainstream tenure as part of a revitalised municipalism or are they fated to remain marginal, bespoke solutions to specific urban problems? What distinguishes the 'common' and the 'public' in housing? Can we rethink these two categories together? Is there something in the co-op and CLT models tried and tested out in Liverpool that could provide a real utopian vision for the future renewal of public housing and the expansion of our housing commons? Why did all this happen here, in Liverpool, of all places? Can it be replicated elsewhere? These are some of the critical questions to which this book seeks answers.

Part I
Introduction

CHAPTER 1

Introducing Collective Housing Alternatives

> As long as the capitalist mode of production continues to exist, it is folly to hope for an isolated solution of the housing question or of any other social question affecting the fate of the workers. The solution lies in the abolition of the capitalist mode of production and the appropriation of all the means of life and labour by the working class itself.[1]

These words, written in 1872 in *The Housing Question* by Karl Marx's comrade and collaborator Friedrich Engels, distil the problem of the housing crisis down to its essence: as one of the capitalist modes of production, initiated by state-enforced enclosure of the commons and only ever resolvable through its abolition and transformation. Engels does not offer us any intermediate solutions and, moreover, derides the 'bourgeois reformists', utopian-socialists and anarchists, who all in different ways sought to combat the housing crisis wrought by capitalism through some form of alternative: common or state ownership. A debate ensued—over the nature of revolutionary social change, over the value of housing, over the place housing occupies within the capitalist economy—which has never really been fully resolved. It is no accident that, after many decades of relative obscurity, *The Housing Question* is once again commonly cited in critical commentaries—some even proclaiming the 'return of the housing question'—revealing startling parallels between Engels' and our own age of capitalist urbanisation.[2] Even in a globalised process of capital

1 Friedrich Engels, *The Housing Question* (Progress Publishers, 1972), pp. 73–74.

2 Manuel B. Aalbers and Brett Christophers, "The Housing Question under Capitalist Political Economies", *Housing, Theory and Society* 31.4 (2014): 422–428; Stuart Hodkinson, "The Return of the Housing Question", *Ephemera: Theory and Politics in Organization* 12.4 (2012): 423–444; Danny Dorling, *All That Is Solid: How the Great Housing Disaster*

accumulation increasingly predicated on speculative investment in (fictitious) financial, land and property assets rather than production of (real) commodities, it seems we cannot escape Engels' devastating logic in his original formulation. This book is one attempt to find possible pathways beyond this impasse and to outline some cursory, necessarily partial answers to the housing question through a political and social history of Liverpool's unique experiment with precisely those 'isolated solutions' dismissed by Engels. This is a book about finding collective alternatives to public housing and urban regeneration in, against and beyond capital and the state.

Public housing—like all things public—has been under threat for a number of decades. The market fundamentalists who have occupied the upper echelons of power in Britain, and increasingly the rest of the world, since the ascendance of what has become known (perhaps all too well) as neoliberalism, have set about the near total destruction of the 'municipal dream' of housing everyone in decent homes, designed and delivered by local councils with a democratic mandate.[3] Whilst not all the housing built by the state was of good quality, or always that responsive to all residents' needs, it nonetheless represented a dignified alternative to the often inhumane slum conditions that went before it. Of those council homes built in the heyday of mass municipal housing that are still standing today, many have been sold off into private ownership through populist policies such as the Right to Buy, which offered tenants a leg up onto the property ladder but, through passing into the wrong hands, effectively offered handouts to speculative buy-to-let landlords who profit from public subsidy. Thatcher's promise of a property-owning democracy has failed to materialise; its failure confirmed by the rise of Generation Rent and the return of a private rental sector to levels not witnessed since the 1970s. At the same time, privatisations have occurred through the transfer of council stock to housing associations—part of a neoliberal project to privatise public land, assets and services[4]—whilst councils have come under mounting pressure to outsource, streamline and marketise what is left of their own much diminished housing service in the face of neoliberal reforms and austerity-driven public budget cuts. The confluence of these trends is, tragically, all too visible in the Grenfell Tower fire disaster of 2017 in which 72 people lost their lives.

Defines Our Times, and What We Can Do About It (Allen Lane, 2014); Neil Gray, "Spatial Composition and the Urbanization of Capital: The 1915 Glasgow Rent Strikes and the Housing Question Reconsidered", in Neil Gray, ed., *Rent and Its Discontents: A Century of Housing Struggle* (Rowman & Littlefield, 2018), pp. 49–67.

3 John Boughton, *Municipal Dreams: The Rise and Fall of Council Housing* (Verso, 2018).

4 Brett Christophers, *The New Enclosure: The Appropriation of Public Land in Neoliberal Britain* (Verso, 2018); James Meek, *Private Island: Why Britain Now Belongs to Someone Else* (Verso Books, 2014).

If the state was once harnessed to provide public homes for those neglected by the market, as a better quality and more affordable alternative to private renting, but has since become embroiled in a neoliberal project of dismantling council housing—housing which has, moreover, often been found wanting by inhabitants and designers alike—then what is the non-state public alternative? One alternative already tried and tested is the voluntary housing association model. Today they manage most of what is now known as 'social housing' in the UK. This shift in language—from public (or council) to social—reflects the fact that housing associations are neither public nor private but something else entirely. Whilst many are becoming increasingly market-oriented for-profit organisations, housing associations are historically rooted in a distinctive and oft-forgotten heritage of voluntary association within civil society, mutual aid, philanthropy and solidarity. Emerging neither out of the state (public sector) nor the market (private sector), they have thus been labelled part of the 'third sector'. Such language reflects their co-optation by neoliberal policy agendas (such as the 'Third Way' championed by the Democrats in the USA and New Labour in the UK in the late 1990s) but so too does it point to historical origins, and a potential future, in an alternative system—neither state-socialism nor market-capitalism—for organising the development, allocation and management of shelter. Unfortunately, housing associations have (so far at least) failed to live up to this potential—as the following history of their development in Liverpool attests.

Another alternative—gestured at by housing associations—seems to suggest something 'social' or 'common' that now only exists in the interstices between technocratic state management and property-based market exchange, even if it pre-existed both. One way to answer this question—what alternative to state-led public housing?—is thus to look back at what went before both the state and market. If the capitalist market was socially constructed through the state-enforced enclosure of previously common land, how did those commoners once provide for themselves before they faced the encroachment of private property and their dispossession? Such questions conjure up romantic images of the commons, an ancient, pre-modern code of collective rights—or *rites* as in customs—to share in the resources of common land, managed through cooperative relations and mutual aid, increasingly understood as practices of what Marxist historian Peter Linebaugh terms 'commoning'.[5]

In our modern era of state-regulated capitalism, the commons appears a long way away in the distant past, despite growing empirical evidence that commons continue to flourish in the present,[6] and can point the way

5 Peter Linebaugh, *The Magna Carta Manifesto: Liberties and Commons for All* (University of California Press, 2009).

6 Elinor Ostrom, Thomas Dietz, Nives Dolšak et al., eds, *The Drama of the Commons* (National Academy Press, 2002).

towards—and, perhaps, prefigure in present practices—a potential post-capitalist future.[7] Over the past century or so, activists and advocates have innovated a number of different models that attempt to articulate in some form or another our common right to housing—making the most out of the legal materials and institutional frameworks they have to hand. These models have a variety of names—from co-operatives and co-housing to mutual homeownership societies, common ownership societies and community land trusts—all coalescing around the conceptual kernel of solidarity, reciprocity, co-operation and mutuality. What they all have in common—the principle of the 'common' over private or public—is an eschewal of possessive individualism and private property in favour of collective ownership; and an emphasis on cooperative relations, shared responsibilities and democratic governance over top-down, hierarchical and bureaucratic management. This book is about bringing to life some of these models—specifically co-operatives and community land trusts—by tracing their historical genesis and evolution in one particular city with a rich history of experiments in collective alternatives—Liverpool, England. Before delving into Liverpool's history, it is worth considering why collective housing alternatives can help us understand—and move beyond—our present conjuncture, defined as it is by housing crisis.

The prevailing system for providing shelter under advanced capitalism is, quite simply, broken—and collective housing alternatives might just provide a way to mend it. Co-ops and CLTs may be marginal models now, in these inimical conditions, but they point towards another way of housing ourselves that is not so dependent on volatile markets or on distant bureaucracies. The way in which we have, for over a century now in the UK as in many capitalist liberal democracies, sought to provide shelter is through a dual system of state and market, of public and private ownership and management. This broadly correlates with the time in which we have as a society generally lived out our lives under an urban-industrial system. The dawn of industrial capitalism created what many still see as an ongoing housing crisis—rising costs, declining quality, shortage of access, homelessness, physical dilapidation, tenant exploitation and alienation—and, despite state intervention and rising prosperity during the post-war decades, the crisis has arguably been with us ever since. Indeed, as critical urbanists David Madden and Peter Marcuse argue in their 2016 polemic, *In Defense of Housing*, 'crisis'—despite semantically implying a temporary moment of emergency—has been invoked by anti-capitalist activists and social reformers for over a century precisely because capitalism makes crisis conditions a norm, especially for working-class communities.[8] In the grand scheme of things, however, this characterisation as crisis may not

7 J.K. Gibson-Graham, *A Postcapitalist Politics* (University of Minnesota Press, 2006).

8 David Madden and Peter Marcuse, *In Defense of Housing: The Politics of Crisis* (Verso, 2016).

seem so contradictory after all: the anarchist writer Colin Ward (a significant protagonist in Liverpool's co-operative history) conjectures that for 90 per cent of human history people have housed themselves through subsistence—only denied this 'freedom' (or, depending on your perspective, saved from this cruel fate) once state-capitalist enclosures began forcing people from the land and into mass housing to work the factories in burgeoning industrial cities, "because by that time the space, the materials and the means of subsistence all belonged to someone else".[9]

That capitalism continually reproduces the housing crisis anew—despite admirable attempts to use the state to legislate against it—should be of no surprise. The capitalist system of commodity production is necessarily predicated upon scarcity—either 'natural' or socially created—in order to realise value for exchange. The artificial creation of scarcity amidst relative plenty and abundance is the central mechanism driving a commodified housing system as a profitable sector of capital accumulation. This raises some serious questions about the nature of value—an issue that informs a great deal of this book. What is the real value of housing? How is it valued? What form does that value take? Who dictates how value is conceived, produced and utilised; and who benefits from it? At the root of these questions is a fundamental tension: value in housing understood as a commodity to be traded for financial gain versus that understood as the use of a space for people to inhabit now and in the future—the dichotomy intrinsic to capitalism between exchange value and use value. Treating housing as a commodity over a basic need may optimise the production of exchange value but in so doing leads to a poor or suboptimal distribution of housing as an essential use value. This presents an intractable contradiction between capital accumulation based on exchange value and social reproduction based on use. The phenomenon of swathes of empty homes across the country amidst worsening housing shortages and a homelessness epidemic is just one peculiar outcome of the dominance of exchange over use value. Taking housing out of the market so that it is relatively free from the logic of capital and governing it through alternative mechanisms—either through some sort of public ownership by the state or through a more decentralised and citizen-led form of common ownership that protects and enhances use values—is the challenge, and choice, we now face if we wish to tackle the housing crisis.

So what can the state do in this regard? Although the state was of course complicit in enforcing the acts of enclosure that were responsible for the dispossession and displacement entailed in the process Marx identified as 'primitive accumulation'—thereby complicit in the very creation of the housing crisis—the state has also been harnessed by reformists to ameliorate the worst

9 Colin Ward, *Welcome, Thinner City: Urban Survival in the 1990s* (NCVO Publications, 1989), p. 101.

excesses of this crisis and, at its most ambitious and utopian, to inaugurate a universal social system of good quality housing provision intended as one of the material foundations for the socialist transformation of society. That was—and perhaps still is—the promise of municipal housing in Britain and beyond. But that promise has long been broken—or at least has not lived up to our hopes placed in it. The history of municipal housing and its renewal in Liverpool, as I sketch out towards the end of this introduction, provides a clear account in this regard. There are two broad reasons why. First, the social-democratic project of universal municipal housing has been thwarted, hijacked even, by stronger political forces which have hollowed out public ownership through privatisations, outsourcing and market disciplining. From Margaret Thatcher's Right to Buy and stock transfer policies in the 1980s to the intensifying marketisation and financialisation of the housing associations that have replaced councils as the primary providers of a much diminished and renamed 'social housing' sector—it is clear that the dream of universal housing provision has been trumped by neoliberalism.[10] What many of us, until relatively recently, have taken for granted—a right of citizenship to decent affordable shelter guaranteed by the state—is actually a historical abnormality. Housing theorist Michael Harloe has described what is known as the 'residualisation' of council housing[11] (its demise from a mainstream tenure of choice for the skilled working class to an increasingly residual part of provision only for the most marginalised in society) not as some aberration but as a return, awful as it may seem, to the 'normal' or default mode under capitalism; a climb down from a seemingly stable but brief and abnormal golden age in European history where in the wake of two world wars the state, aspiring to universal welfare provision and responding to market failure, had to step in to restructure capitalist society and meet new demands for housing and other public goods and services. That era is now well and truly over.

Secondly, for all its good intentions, there were inherent problems with this state project—even when delivered at the municipal scale by local authorities (as is all too evident in Liverpool's history)—to do with the way in which housing was done *to* and *for* people rather than *by* them. Participation in the process of dwelling is argued by some[12] to be an important part of being human—it informs our relationship with ourselves (our self-identity), with our immediate environments, the people around us and with wider society. Housing delivered by the state has often succumbed to impersonal bureaucratic

10 Boughton, *Municipal Dreams: The Rise and Fall of Council Housing.*

11 Michael Harloe, *The People's Home? Social Rented Housing in Europe and America* (Wiley-Blackwell, 1995).

12 Peter King, *Private Dwelling: Contemplating the Use of Housing* (Routledge, 2004); John F.C. Turner and Robert Fichter, eds, *Freedom to Build* (Collier Macmillan, 1972); Martin Heidegger, "Building Dwelling Thinking", in David Farrell Krell, ed., *Basic Writings* (Routledge, 1978), pp. 347–363.

procedures that prevent people from shaping these relationships to mutually beneficial ends and alienates them from the deeply personal and sociable process of dwelling. Moreover, when the state controls housing decisions the democratic distance between citizens and the bureaucratic machinery that implements decision-making, via elected representatives, is often too wide a gap to bridge. Bad decisions are made. Slum clearance policies destroy people's homes without due consideration of their affective bonds to place. Communities are broken up needlessly, along with the collective cultures of social provisioning that they sustained. Architecture is designed by experts that, however impressive aesthetically, proves too monolithic or inflexible to meet the everyday needs of residents. The tendency towards abstraction and alienation from everyday life inhering in elite expertise and professionalisation—cutting across public and private domains—is a theme that will recur throughout this book. Collective housing alternatives are in many ways about healing these divisions—between the producer and consumer of housing; between the physical object of the house and the act of living in it; between those who make decisions about dwelling and those who have to live with them—that were first cracked open by enclosure and carved deeper by the abstractions of state-capitalist modernity. Whether these models can be any more than a sticking plaster in this regard—whether they are mere symptoms of capitalism or prefigurations of something else entirely—is a key question I want to consider.

Why Collective Housing Alternatives?

At this point it would be useful to explain some terminology. Precise technical definitions of housing cooperatives and community land trusts—my main focus in the book—will be delineated as the narrative unfolds. For now, suffice to say that they are not-for-profit, democratically governed voluntary associations for the development, ownership and management principally of affordable housing but also of other local assets. They exemplify what I define as collective housing alternatives. What precisely do I mean by this? First, co-ops and CLTs can be characterised as *alternatives* by offering another option to the mainstream. Indeed, they remain a marginal, bespoke form of housing provision, especially in Britain. At the time of writing, the National CLT Network reports on its website around 300 CLTs in total in England and Wales and only 935 homes built to date—but the sector is expanding rapidly, having grown six-fold in the last six years, with 16,000 homes in the pipeline. The larger, more established (and slower growing) co-op housing sector had by 2012 over 600 co-ops in England alone and an estimated total of over 45,000 dwellings across the UK.[13]

13 Housing Europe, *Profiles of a Movement: Co-operative Housing around the World*, CECODHAS Housing Europe ICA Housing, 2012: www.housingeurope.eu/resource-115/profiles-of-a-movement.

This likewise remains marginal in the broader national housing context—under 0.2 per cent of total housing stock—especially in comparison with European counterparts, such as Germany (5 per cent of total national stock in 2012), Spain (6 per cent), Belgium (7 per cent), Austria (8 per cent) and Sweden (17 per cent). Britain's—but more specifically England's—exceptionally low levels of cooperative housing might be explained by cultural factors: the enduring national obsession with private homeownership, wrapped up with an anti-urban, individualistic privatism (expressed in the problematic proverb 'an Englishman's home is his castle') and a subtle reverence for feudal and aristocratic forms of bucolic (sub)urbanism (captured in the image of the English country garden or village green) over any bourgeois or socialist or cooperative forms of urbanism.[14] On this point, Scotland for one is a different story, arguably sharing more with continental Europe than England. The reasons may also be political: Britain has been the subject of a brutal experiment in neoliberalism, penetrating faster and deeper into everyday life than anywhere else. Yet Britain also pioneered the cooperative movement in the nineteenth century and, in the aftermath of war, established a national health service as a collectivist form of public provision based on experiments in cooperative social care in Welsh mining villages. Set against this ambiguous context, the potential for co-ops and CLTs to become more mainstream sectors—and grow into an alternative system of owning and managing housing and neighbourhood assets that can challenge the hegemony of private property—is a background concern animating this book.

Collective housing alternatives are named just that—*alternatives*—as they speak to the relatively hidden traditions of utopian socialism, libertarian communism and democratic socialism (as opposed to social democracy) that share many of the same overall goals of state-socialism and public ownership—that is, providing a collective alternative to private property and the individualism of the market—but, in light of the latter's historical difficulties, point us in a different direction towards achieving them. Collective alternatives also speak to the more ancient tradition of the commons. As political economist Massimo De Angelis states, the commons stand at the beginning—and at the end—of capitalist history.[15] The state played an intrinsic, complicit part in that capitalist history and cannot, therefore, at least in its current form, hope to resolve it. What it can do, though, is help support the flourishing of new forms of commons that exist in the here and now and

14 Patrick Keiller, "The Dilapidated Dwelling", in *The View from the Train: Cities and Other Landscapes* (Verso Books, 2013), pp. 51–63; Dorling, *All That Is Solid: How the Great Housing Disaster Defines Our Times, and What We Can Do About It*; Owen Hatherley, *A Guide to the New Ruins of Great Britain* (Verso Books, 2011).

15 Massimo De Angelis, *The Beginning of History: Value Struggles and Global Capital* (Pluto Press, 2006).

could potentially become the cell structure of a new, post-capitalist state and society. A rich academic debate on the meaning and potency of political and economic alternatives, including co-ops and CLTs, and their variously oppositional and ambiguous relationships to the state and capital—captured by the term 'alterity'[16]—informs my approach here.

But why have I chosen to use this term when there are already plenty of other—perhaps too many—similar concepts all jostling to describe roughly the same thing? For instance, for some time now in the UK, the group of housing models that I have been referring to as collective alternatives—co-ops, CLTs, self-build, co-housing, mutual homeownership, community self-help etc.—has come to be called 'community-led housing'. This emphasises that it is the community—not the state or the market—that controls the decisions regarding housing and seems to derive from particular British traditions of community organising and voluntary association in civil society as well as, perhaps, more recent neoliberal and Third Way trends towards centring community in public policy as part of a new localism.[17] In continental Europe, particularly central and northern European countries such as Austria, Germany and the Netherlands, there is an emerging consensus around the term 'collaborative housing'.[18] This draws attention to the more partnership-based approach towards building cooperative housing in collaboration with housing associations, professional organisations and the state, stemming from traditions of corporatism in these countries. Another concept gaining currency, originating in Australia, is 'self-organised housing'[19] which emphasises the autonomous nature of these movements, drawing connections with the 'community economies' research of feminist political economists J.K. Gibson-Graham and their concern with cultivating prefigurative practices of a post-capitalist future.[20]

16 Duncan Fuller, Andrew Jonas and Roger Lee, eds, *Interrogating Alterity: Alternative Economic and Political Spaces* (Ashgate, 2010); Andrew Leyshon, Roger Lee and Colin C. Williams, *Alternative Economic Spaces* (SAGE, 2003). In particular, see Stuart Hodkinson, "Housing in Common: In Search of Strategy for Housing Alterity in England in the 21st Century", in Fuller, Jonas and Lee, *Interrogating Alterity*, pp. 241–258.

17 David Mullins and Tom Moore, "Self-Organised and Civil Society Participation in Housing Provision", *International Journal of Housing Policy* 18.1 (2018): 1–14.

18 Darinka Czischke, "Collaborative Housing and Housing Providers: Towards an Analytical Framework of Multi-Stakeholder Collaboration in Housing Co-Production", *International Journal of Housing Policy* 18.1 (2018): 55–81; Richard Lang and Harald Stoeger, "The Role of the Local Institutional Context in Understanding Collaborative Housing Models: Empirical Evidence from Austria", *International Journal of Housing Policy* 18.1 (2018): 35–54.

19 Louise Crabtree, "Self-Organised Housing in Australia: Housing Diversity in an Age of Market Heat", *International Journal of Housing Policy* 18.1 (2018): 15–34.

20 Gibson-Graham, *A Postcapitalist Politics*.

Fundamentally, the concept of collective housing alternatives attempts to draw out an important relationship with the state and the notion of the public that I think is missing from the more familiar terms outlined above. First, Community-led, collaborative and self-organised each describe—with different inflections on community, autonomy and partnership—the actors involved in organising this kind of housing, but they do not adequately convey the wider state–market nexus within which they necessarily develop. Secondly, each descriptor conjures images that run against the grain of what many in these movements are attempting to achieve. 'Collaborative' is too acquiescent, too caught up in existing institutional relations to inspire much meaningful social change. 'Self-organised' puts the stress on *self* and thus fails to capture notions of collectivity, solidarity and cooperation. 'Community' suggests a parochialism and exclusivity that does not sit well with notions of the common or public good. Instead, I use collective as a simple descriptor to infer that decisions are made collectively—at various scales—rather than individually and that outcomes are achieved with collective benefits in mind rather than just self-interest. This is intended to reappropriate the language of collectivism from the collectivist scale of the state and reinvigorate interest in alternative forms of collective organisation that are more democratic than bureaucratic. In this way, it speaks to renewed discourses around collective or alternative forms of public ownership of the economy and economic democracy.[21] Housing is just as much a part of the economy as manufacturing and we should do more to make that connection rather than maintain a silo. If we drop the 'housing' in the concept we could be talking about any other part of the economy—and many of the arguments made in this book are intended in this generalist spirit.

By focusing on collectivity and commons over community, I wish to draw attention to certain facets of collective alternatives that the term community-led housing tends to obfuscate. Whereas community suggests members are bound together by a shared identity or homogeneous culture, commons transcends identitarian concerns and points towards common interests in owning, governing and maintaining a set of shared resources.[22] This entails bringing people together from across traditional cleavages in new formations, which, rather than look inwards to define a bounded community, connect outwards towards the public sphere or the 'common' in ways which may

21 Andrew Cumbers, *Reclaiming Public Ownership: Making Space for Economic Democracy* (Zed Books, 2012); Robin Murray, Jeremy Gilbert and Andrew Goffey, "Post-Post-Fordism in the Era of Platforms: Robin Murray Talks to Jeremy Gilbert and Andrew Goffey", *New Formations* 84/85 (2015): 184–208.

22 Jeremy Gilbert, *Common Ground: Democracy and Collectivity in an Age of Individualism* (London: Pluto Press, 2013).

prefigure a post-capitalist future.[23] By associating collective alternatives with the commons I invoke their as yet unrealised potential as an alternative, democratised form of public housing—part of a reformed, decentralised state that enables and protects commons.

The commons is becoming increasingly relevant in contemporary movements fighting for social justice the world over: as the domain that broadly describes all social activity and circuits of value that remain or, more often, are fought free from the capitalist logic of exchange relations and private property—especially in the domain of the city and urban space.[24] Applying this perspective to housing, critical geographer Stuart Hodkinson contrasts intensifying 'new urban enclosures' threatening to reverse the post-war progress made with public housing—such as attempts to regenerate ex-council estates through private finance initiatives which so often lead to dispossession and displacement—with efforts to reclaim our 'housing commons' with collective alternatives such as cooperatives and CLTs.[25] In the commons–enclosure debate, therefore, public ownership can be aligned in solidarity with common ownership as a (partial, imperfect) shelter from the full force of exchange relations.

Collective housing alternatives play a part in this struggle as institutional articulations of a housing commons that has at once been lost and is, perhaps, still yet to come. Encompassing a broad range of different organisational designs—from more informal and oppositional interventions like squatting through more institutionalised initiatives like cooperatives and co-housing to more politically pragmatic models such as co-ownership societies, self-help, community land trusts and community development trusts, all with variations on bespoke legal devices and organisational covenants—collective housing models attempt to articulate in existing political and legal terms the kinds of relationships and practices that might one day constitute a new kind of post-capitalist society. More immediately, they inculcate ways of living in the present that are beneficial to individual and collective well-being and help heal some of the division and deprivation wrought by capitalist markets.

Specifically, collective housing alternatives—as an 'ideal type'—can be seen to do three things to combat the deleterious effects of treating housing as a commodity rather than a home. First, they attempt to resolve *exploitation*—the unproductive (and often parasitic) extraction of rent by landlords or of mortgage interest by banks which is in itself a moral problem

23 Michael Hardt and Antonio Negri, *Commonwealth* (Harvard University Press, 2009).

24 Stavros Stavrides, *Common Space: The City as Commons* (Zed Books, 2016).

25 Hodkinson, "The Return of the Housing Question"; Hodkinson, "Housing in Common: In Search of Strategy for Housing Alterity in England in the 21st Century"; Stuart Hodkinson, "The New Urban Enclosures", *City: Analysis of Urban Trends, Culture, Theory, Policy, Action* 16.5 (2012): 500–518.

but also, when coupled with speculation in land and property treated as a financial commodity, creates crisis conditions in affordability, thereby socially constructing exclusion from one of life's most fundamental needs. Second, they attempt to tackle *alienation*—the disconnection of residents from their homes and the spiritually fulfilling act of dwelling by the mediations of capital (banks, neo-feudal landowners and buy-to-let property speculators) or of distant bureaucracies (be they private, public, or quasi-public absentee landlords). Third, they attempt to protect against *displacement*—the increasingly common experience of being 'dis-placed' that occurs through market-led speculation and gentrification or through state-backed regeneration projects that forcibly relocate residents against their will, dislodged from their lodgings.

How do collective housing alternatives go about doing this? In short, they protect land from the market by holding it in common, through alternative forms of ownership that are neither private nor public, that are collective but not collectivist. Taking land or property off the market and into some form of collective ownership—be that through a mutual, a co-operative or a charitable trust—works via three mechanisms in relation to the problems identified above. First, in response to exploitation, they provide a legal asset lock which protects that land from being bought out, sold off or bet upon. This prevents the extraction of the value of land and property such that any surpluses from rent or rising land values are 'locked in' and recycled for community benefit rather than being siphoned off as profit. Strictly speaking, co-operatives do not do this, but may create an effective lock through a cooperative ownership structure and ethos. Second, in answer to alienation, they seek to reconnect the consumer and producer of housing through participation in design, development and management decisions. This brings residents together in the governance of a shared resource in ways which are small enough in scale—collective rather than collectivist—that enable more proximate and directly democratic forms of engagement than could possibly be achieved at greater scales, by the state. Third, in response to displacement, they provide a counterpower to both market and state—guaranteed, perhaps paradoxically, by (state-enforced) law—that protects residents' rights to dwell in place.

Articulating Our Housing Commons

These three powers of collective housing alternatives position them as torch-bearers of a housing commons. We can see this in the way that a commons is commonly defined in a similar tripartite fashion: as a shared resource pool (the housing that has been taken off the market into common ownership, to prevent exploitation and extraction); as a 'public sphere' of encounter, interaction and democratic deliberation that is collective but not collectivist in character (as a salve to alienation); and as a collective rights claim over a specific place of dwelling by its inhabitants (to protect against displacement). The third of these aspects, the issue of rights, is a thorny one that I will consider in some depth below. The first two—resource pool and public sphere—reveal the dialectical nature of the commons as a domain which is both simultaneously a material resource with spatial dimensions and a set of embodied practices enacted through time. This reflects anarchist architect John F.C. Turner's dualistic characterisation of housing as both a noun (material object) and a verb (lived process).[26] The changing relationship between housing seen as a noun and as a verb is a major theme of this book, one which will inform our understanding of how collective housing alternatives differ from public and private forms of ownership; how within housing activism there is always a tension between the verb-like social practices that are the lifeblood of collective alternatives and the noun-like legal models and organisational forms which codify creative experiments as enduring structures. One of the arguments I wish to make is that whilst noun-like models are essential to the sustenance of collective housing alternatives they also risk calcifying as brittle bones the dynamic energy that first inspired them as campaigns. There is always a trade-off to be made between these forces and tendencies.

Another, related background argument of this book is that state and capitalist forms of housing provision, ownership and management all too often fall into this trap of freezing verb-like practices into noun-like abstractions; while, to the contrary, collective housing alternatives attempt to resist this tendency towards objectification and abstraction by foregrounding the embodied practices and lived experiences of commoning. Commoning best describes those verb-like social practices that are analytically distinct from (though dialectically embedded within) the material resource pool of the commons. Collective housing alternatives embody and encourage acts of commoning, in differential degrees, through the organisational form they take and the governance arrangements that this entails. Why can they only be articulations—proxies at best—of a housing commons? Because they are, by legal definition, forms of property—albeit common or collective or mutual or co-operative property but property nonetheless—and property is antithetical to the very idea of a commons.[27] Private property was, after all, the very technology by which the commons, at the beginning of capitalist history, were enclosed by the state. Enclosure is in many ways an act of transforming verb-like lived reality into a noun-like object, a commodity, which can then be divorced from its embedded social context to be owned, accumulated and traded as the property holder sees fit. Since original acts of enclosure, the

26 John F.C. Turner, "Housing as a Verb", in John F.C. Turner and Robert Fichter, eds, *Freedom to Build* (Collier Macmillan, 1972), pp. 148–175.
27 Nicholas Blomley, *Unsettling the City* (Routledge, 2004).

capitalist economy has increasingly become, as Karl Polanyi famously argued, 'dis-embedded' from society and ecology.[28]

This process of dis-embedding and abstracting from lived processes is inscribed in the very logic of ownership and private property rights. No study into the changing nature of housing can ignore ownership and property rights as foundational concepts. When it comes to property, the state and the market form a nexus—the public–private dualism. The twentieth century can in many respects be seen as a sustained though unstable flirtation with the domain of the public as a means to organise the ownership of land and the provision of goods and services, not least housing, which appears to be in stark contradistinction to the domain of the private so often portrayed, for instance, in studies of privatisation of the welfare state, as the enemy of the public. Yet the public–private dichotomy is not best characterised as two distinct ways of doing things but as dialectically related poles of one essential view, which property theorists, following Joseph William Singer, call the 'ownership model'.[29] This dominant conception of property rights as distinct, individualised, separable, exclusive and clearly bounded—that is, abstracted and objectified from the flow of lived experience—is the legal foundation for the successful development of capitalism and neoliberalism, a political discourse founded on the liberal institution of private property. In its ideal type expression, the ownership model invests absolute control over a clearly delineated space or thing in a single identifiable owner, who therefore enjoys certain rights and entitlements to use the property as they wish, including the power to exclude all others as well as the power to pass on all powers of ownership to another through transfer of rights, which are protected by determinate boundaries that mark ownership off from non-ownership, simply by virtue of being identified in formal legal title. As Singer surmises: title bestows entitlement. The powerful protection of exchange rights under the ownership model allows the enclosure of our housing commons into an alienable object, and the extraction of its socially produced surplus value through exchange on the global market. It is the state that enforces this institution, through legally binding property rights.

Property rights, then, seem antithetical to the very concept of the commons and commoning. Yet the latter have nonetheless been expressed in various ways in the language of rights. For instance, in describing the city as a kind of urban commons, Colin Ward has this to say: "the city is the common property of its inhabitants. It is, in the economic sense, a public good".[30] This is 'common property' and 'public good' meant in the more expansive sense of

28 Karl Polanyi, *The Great Transformation: The Political and Economic Origins of Our Time* (Beacon Press, 1944).

29 Joseph William Singer, *Entitlement: The Paradoxes of Property* (Yale University Press, 2000).

30 Ward, *Welcome, Thinner City*, p. 1.

these terms. We can see the concept of rights mobilised in the mantra of the global social movement for the Right to the City—first articulated by Marxist philosopher Henri Lefebvre—which "like a cry and a demand" agitates for "a transformed and renewed 'right to urban life'".[31] Radical planning theorist Mark Purcell delineates two fundamental components of the right to the city: the right to *appropriate* urban space for its social use value and the right to *participate* centrally in the political decision-making that produces space.[32] Rather than rights of citizenship being founded on passive membership of a nation-state and abstract entitlement to property, they derive from the active contribution of each inhabitant to the creation of a complex urban ecology as well as their necessary embeddedness within the web of social relations that make up the city. At its heart, then, argues Marxist urbanist Andy Merrifield, is a radical reconception of citizenship in which the tragically disconnected city-dweller and citizen are reconciled as one.[33] So too are rights here reconfigured away from the formal entitlements of private property towards more expansive rights of social citizenship. Lefebvre's image of the city as an *oeuvre*—a collective work of art created by the daily rituals and practices of its inhabitants, and therefore justly governed by them—turns on its head the justifications for private property and relocates rights to urban space to the citizens that breathe life into them. This has important implications for housing, that is, if we see housing, in a microcosmic relation to the city, as an urban commons whose use value—and, by extension, exchange value—is produced by its inhabitants and all those who engage in productive and socially reproductive activities in its environs.

The notion of rights hailed by the commons and the right to the city is a very different one from that instituted by the ownership model. Rights talk assumes from the outset that there is some sovereign institution in which ultimate authority is invested and to which rights claims can be made and in turn legitimated and upheld. As political philosopher Todd May has argued, this moves the responsibility for fulfilling such rights from citizen to that institutional body and focuses attention on "what people are owed, on what they should receive" from the state, which therefore renders what can be an active process of political empowerment into a "matter of passive recipiency".[34]

31 Henri Lefebvre, *Writings on Cities* (Wiley-Blackwell, 1995), p. 168.

32 Mark Purcell, "Excavating Lefebvre: The Right to the City and Its Urban Politics of the Inhabitant", *GeoJournal* 58.2–3 (2002): 99–108; Mark Purcell, "Citizenship and the Right to the Global City: Reimagining the Capitalist World Order", *International Journal of Urban and Regional Research* 27.3 (2003): 564–590.

33 Andy Merrifield, "The Right to the City and Beyond: Notes on a Lefebvrian Re-Conceptualization", *City* 15.3–4 (2011): 468–476.

34 Todd May, *The Political Thought of Jacques Rancière: Creating Equality* (Edinburgh University Press, 2008), p. 34.

Exemplifying what cultural theorist Jeremy Gilbert calls 'Leviathan logic'[35]—referring to the dark shadow cast by Hobbes over all subsequent (neo)liberal political thought—private property rights invest authority in a sovereign source supporting a hierarchical structure of individual rights-bearers who are related to each other only by their shared vertical relationship with the ultimate authority, the state. But collectivism need not be synonymous with the state and there is a missing mediating horizontal link to be (re)discovered in the commons. Where Hobbes saw the state of nature as a nasty, brutish world, red in tooth and claw, from which humans needed protecting by means of the state, the Leviathan, anarchists such as Peter Kropotkin have conversely seen the state of nature as a sort of primordial commons defined more by cooperation and mutual aid than by violence, competition and hierarchy. In seeking to break free from the Leviathan logic of liberal thought the notion of the commons speaks to this anarchist perspective on human nature and envisages a world where (to borrow a Marxist idea) the state one day withers away—however impossible that appears today.

The common right, in contrast to the private, is a highly contextual and interactive claim to shared space originating immanently through negotiation among users, not transcendentally from some abstract deed of entitlement authorised by the state. In its fullest expression, the commons represents a break with Leviathan logic, in that members are related in a collective structure where rights are legitimated through the very act of their mutual negotiation. In principle, a commons perspective refutes the very idea of a predetermined right that can be passively owed to someone; insisting instead on the active cooperative justification of rights between members based on the self-legitimating authority of democracy. In practice, however, as I argue below, we cannot so simply free ourselves from Leviathan logic but must engage with rights as they currently are if we wish ever to bring about actually existing commons. Moreover, if the state withers away, who or what is left to adjudicate between the self-legitimating authorities of individual commons?

Seeing the city as an *oeuvre* and housing as a commons highlights property as essentially relational—its verb-like qualities—against the abstract, noun-like concept of property conceived by the ownership model (the public–private dualism). In the latter, property is presented in a highly simplified model that emphasises simplicity, certainty, security, clarity and legibility. In attempting to 'unsettle' the conceptual certainties of the ownership model, critical geographer Nick Blomley acknowledges one of its greatest strengths: that it appears 'settled' (in the spatial legibility of its visible boundaries, such as walls and fences, for instance, or in the legal legibility of title deeds) and therefore acts to 'settle' the complexities, ambiguities, disputes and conflicts

35 Gilbert, *Common Ground: Democracy and Collectivity in an Age of Individualism.*

in property claims into an ordered, coherent and uncontested settlement.[36] But this also acts to obscure the inherently messy multiplicity of uses and claims that constitute property—its verb-like nature as a relational set of practices—in favour of an abstract, mono-typological noun-like concept. It also obscures the fact that property more accurately reflects a set of relationships between people in terms of the things they can access, and not simply, as the ownership model implies, an isolated relation between a single owner and a thing. Property is perhaps better understood as an unfinished, embodied act of 'doing' than as an abstract enacted state of 'having'. It only really gains any value—either for use or exchange—through the social relations that construct it as a meaningful and respected power to do certain things with certain objects in relation to other people. The aspects which make housing at all valuable or worth owning are mostly socially produced, through a complex web of relations that stretch out through society. For instance, private property remains protected and valuable on the market only insofar as people respect its boundaries, desist from vandalism and actively valorise the surrounding public space and the wider territory through spending money in local shops, paying taxes for the upkeep of public services, valuing its spaces as attractive places, expending energy interacting with others or just simply walking through it so as to produce and reproduce its social vitality. In short, private ownership depends upon the collective and the locality: in terms of both tacit assent in its recognition and also its relational co-production as a product of social conditions actively created by inhabitants.

Such a relational understanding of property provides the intuitive and moral foundation for collective housing alternatives and the particular common property rights they attempt to articulate. Ebenezer Howard, one of the founding fathers of modern common property regimes, built into his original vision of the Garden City model at the turn of the twentieth century a legal device, a trust structure, for capturing what he called the 'unearned increment' of land and property value[37]—that which is socially produced and therefore not strictly earned by the individual property owner. This has been adapted down the decades as the basis for a number of different collective housing alternatives, especially the CLT model. On the ethical understanding of 'just deserts' based on proportionality, the American CLT advocate and theorist John Emmeus Davis has called for a reallocation of the equity value of property so that "to the individual goes the fruits of individual labour; to the community goes the social increment".[38] This is the ethical principle

36 Blomley, *Unsettling the City*.

37 Ebenezer Howard, *To-Morrow: A Peaceful Path to Real Reform, Town And Country Planning* (Cambridge University Press, 1898).

38 John Emmeus Davis, ed., *The Community Land Trust Reader* (Lincoln Institute of Land Policy, 2010), p. 363.

underpinning the CLT model's rejection of the ownership model's preference for individual exchange rights—specifically to transfer and to speculate—over common use rights. By specifically blocking the rights of individuals to speculate or profit on their share of the equity, the CLT model enables the realisation of use values usually suppressed by the power of accumulative interests.

Articulating the commons through a language of legal rights may well be a dangerously slippery slope down into private property terrain, yet it is clear that there is no getting away from it, at least any time soon. It is a game that is worth playing if we seek to make any headway with combating the dominance of the ownership model in the current conjuncture. A property right is an enforceable claim to use or benefit from a particular property, enforced by the sovereign authority of the state. In other words, rights are claims made upon the state to recognise, grant, protect or provide some particular entitlement to space, privileges or resources. It is only through their translation into property *rights* that property *relations* gain the necessary legitimacy and enforceability of 'proper' proprietorship. Property theorist Carol Rose highlights the striking etymological ties between property, proprietorship (the private ownership of property) and propriety (the proper ordering or correct conformity to conventional values and usages).[39] Property makes invisible those claims that are not deemed proper or legitimate by legal authority; it obfuscates moral claims to land (and housing) and the full scope of rights and responsibilities deriving from social stakes in ownership. Here opens up an important distinction between a mere rights claim, an appeal awaiting legal sanction, and a right itself, which is a legitimate claim enforced by the state. It is in this gap, this traverse—converting claim into right—wherein the lines of political and social inclusion are drawn. Collective housing alternatives can be seen as tools for attempting to bridge that gap; they are means for the commons being deemed a proper—that is, legitimate and visible—form of ownership under a system that otherwise maintains the fiction of its invisibility. Indeed, we will never get anywhere with trying to defend our housing commons in practical ways—for instance, resisting displacement and dispossession—without some kind of legal protection and state-recognised entitlement to that space we seek to defend. This means engaging with the language of property rights and articulating housing commons as common property institutions.

The governance structures that dictate the rules, membership and the associational relations of various collective housing models (CLTs, co-ops etc.) are the institutionalised forms of common rights. But, of course,

39 Carol Rose, "The Comedy of the Commons: Commerce, Custom, and Inherently Public Property of Chicago Law Review", *University of Chicago Law Review* 53.3 (1986): 711–781; Carol Rose, *Property and Persuasion: Essays on the History, Theory and Rhetoric of Ownership* (Westview Press, 1994).

many tensions, contradictions and inevitable compromises are entailed in any attempt to translate collective user rights into private property rights. Collective housing alternatives can thus never be fully realised embodiments of a commons by virtue of being expressed as property. In reality, they are messy hybrids of various property forms and tenure types. Common property regimes such as CLTs and co-ops are perhaps closer to being what alternative property theorists call "collective private ownership"[40] than common property per se; more accurately understood, in Carol Rose's term, as 'limited common property'—that is, "property held as a commons among the members of a group, but exclusively vis-à-vis the outside world".[41] Co-ops, for instance, can be seen to embody the commons internally—sharing resources through mutual aid and cooperation—but must inevitably act externally like collective private property: excluding all non-members and thereby threatening to reproduce the social exclusion of private property only at a higher scale than the individual. By the same token, this exposes collective housing alternatives to the very real and present danger of co-optation, incorporation and colonisation by neoliberal forces, which thrive through the language of property rights.

Bringing the State Back In

The state, therefore, is important for a number of reasons: for giving legal legitimacy to the tools used to support the ongoing growth and sustenance of collective housing alternatives; for providing institutional shelter from neoliberal incursions; and for providing the scalar coordination and connection to the notion of the public that so many small-scale commons, as micro-enclosures, lack the capacity for or, for reasons of self-preservation, sometimes turn their backs upon. Indeed, by positioning collective housing alternatives in an antagonistic relationship to both the market and the state, I do not wish to overemphasise any supposed fundamental opposition to them, especially the state. The state is crucial and is potentially an ally, as it has been in the not too distant past, at the dawn of municipal socialism and then, again, at the birth of the welfare state. Following neo-Marxist state theory,[42] the state should not be seen as a fixed entity, an agent with a particular agenda or simply the offices of government, even though its institutional design seems to prescribe certain bureaucratic tendencies in favour of capitalist class interests above all others. The state is an arena of social forces, a set of competing

40 Charles Geisler and Gail Daneker, *Property and Values: Alternatives to Public and Private Ownership* (Island Press, 2000), p. 72.

41 Carol Rose, "The Several Futures of Property: Of Cyberspace and Folk Tales, Emission Trades and Ecosystems", *Minnesota Law Review* 83.129 (1998): 129–182 (p. 132).

42 Bob Jessop, *State Theory: Putting the Capitalist State in Its Place* (Polity Press, 1990).

political interests and class alliances, a multi-scalar and far-reaching apparatus of central and local state institutions (from government departments to local authorities) and a diverse range of governmental, quasi- and non-governmental agencies (including housing associations) through which the invested capacities of the public are implemented as public policy. It is therefore highly contingent upon the social, political and ideological forces of the historical juncture—or certainly seems to be so in the UK. Here, under a highly adversarial, first-past-the-post system of parliamentary democracy, we see the state being geared in different directions depending on political circumstances with a rough pattern of distinct approaches emerging every thirty years or so. In the post-war period we saw the Fordist settlement produce a relatively well-funded welfare state that invested in council housing and to some degree delivered on the municipal dream of providing shelter for all citizens—which also created new circuits of capital accumulation through infrastructure for collective consumption, the contradiction animating the Urban Question.[43] Following the crisis of Fordism in the 1970s, we saw neoliberalism retool the state towards the dismantling of public housing provision in favour of the market. Thus the state can, at different times and contexts, be co-opted as an ally or an enemy of the democratic-socialist project for a housing commons.

Moreover, the public is not incompatible with the commons; it is its essential counterpart. Just because the state has delivered public housing in the past in ways which run counter to the participatory principles of the commons does not mean we should dismiss the importance of the state in bringing the housing commons to fruition. One way in which this can be seen clearly is through the concept of the 'foundational economy'—another domain to which collective housing alternatives belong. The term itself was first conceived and popularised by a collective of researchers who sought to draw attention to those materially and socially important aspects of the economy that have in the past been taken for granted and conceptualised lazily as public services or civic infrastructure delivered by the state and therefore not strictly economic.[44] The foundational economy comprises two components: material infrastructure (the pipes and cables, utilities and networks of everyday life, such as transport, food and retail banking) and what the foundational economy collective call 'providential' services (referring to the providence—the benevolent care and guidance—to be found in health, education and welfare provision). In being "welfare-critical for users because limited material and providential access stunts lives and limits possibilities",[45]

43 Manuel Castells, *The Urban Question: A Marxist Approach* (MIT Press, 1977).

44 Justin Bentham, Andrew Bowman, Marta De Cuesta et al., *Manifesto for the Foundational Economy*, CRESC Working Paper 131 (Centre for Research on Socio-Cultural Change, 2013).

45 Foundational Economy Collective, *Foundational Economy: The Infrastructure of Everyday Life* (Manchester University Press, 2018), p. 22.

the foundational economy is bound up with notions of citizenship and the common good and therefore demands greater care and accountability in its delivery, through some form of public ownership or scrutiny (leading, ironically, to its undervaluation, under neoliberalism's privileging of the private realm, as not strictly part of the productive or so-called 'real' economy).

Interestingly, housing occupies a central though ambiguous position within the foundational economy, identifying fully neither with the material nor providential but straddling both. It is arguably the very foundation of the foundational economy itself—for housing provides the minimum underlying basis for households to enjoy access to all other material and providential goods. The Foundational Economy Collective make much of the household as the nexus through which material infrastructures—all the pipes, cables and networks—flow to provide our daily essentials, such as water, power, food, care and information. One of the central defining features of the foundational economy is that it is composed of a 'branch and network structure' whereby multi-scalar systems of access and provision determine individual consumption of a good or service. For instance, you can buy a bathroom tap on the open market but without integrating it with the regional water utility network there is no chance of receiving any water from it. Similarly, though perhaps less obviously, when it comes to housing, house-builders (or, for instance, communities seeking to take empty homes into co-operative ownership) need to comply with planning regulations at the municipal and national levels and also make sure their plans fit with requirements for all the material and providential services that connect with households via local, regional and national infrastructures. The need for a branch and network structure in housing is enough to show that the state plays an important role in its provision. A point underlined by the abject policy failure of outsourcing to profit-hungry private companies much of the branch and network foundational economy of the UK, notably water, gas, electricity and the railways—representing a kind of privatisation of taxation.[46] A housing commons requires a supportive state infrastructure if it is ever to flourish on any significant scale.

The foundational economy is part of a recent rediscovery of the moral economists R.H. Tawney, G.D.H. Cole and Karl Polanyi, amongst others. According to Polanyi, the economy is composed of four elements each operating according to different logics: householding, according to self-provisioning; the market, by a logic of exchange; the state, by a logic of redistribution; and civil society, by a logic of reciprocity.[47] Polanyi's fundamental insight—the double movement—was to show how the tendency under capitalism was to 'dis-embed' and abstract the market economy from the social relations,

46 Meek, *Private Island: Why Britain Now Belongs to Someone Else.*
47 Polanyi, *The Great Transformation.*

cultural practices and material environments that produce and sustain it and to elevate exchange as the primary principle governing economic relations; in turn producing a counter-movement for re-embedding the economy into society through the reassertion of the principle of reciprocity, often by way of state redistribution. Indeed, on this reading of the state, the Leviathan is not just a force of hierarchical control, physical violence and abstract power wielded over subjects but also the overarching arbiter of justice, through which redistribution is possible. Actors from within both the state and civil society, then, are to be seen as (potential) allies in the counter-movement of reclaiming the commons.

Since the 1970s, however, the state has been in retreat, consumed by the logic of exchange, leaving the counter-movement solely in the hands of collective alternatives. The "recognition of housing as a foundational need", argue the Foundational Economy Collective, "depends on political struggle which does not have an inevitable outcome".[48] Of all the foundational economy, it is housing, perhaps, that has been subject to the most political contestation. This is partly due to its ambiguous relationship with economic value—limited employment, mostly taken up with construction, yet astounding asset value. In countries such as the UK, property value has increasingly replaced state welfare provision as the primary source of social security, particularly income in retirement. In a context in which state capacity, and appetite, for universal welfare has been systematically eroded, private debt-fuelled investments in property assets appeared sensible. This has created political pressure to inflate the housing market in ever-expanding bubbles that cannot but eventually burst. Collective housing models offer an alternative that may one day prove politically popular, after the bubble bursts, but in the meantime may struggle to gain adherents who are pressured to 'buy in' to this unsustainable model in the absence of an adequate publicly owned foundational economy.

With this in mind, the question then becomes how to re-engineer the state to work for, rather than against, the housing commons. How can we re-scale the state towards more decentralised and networked institutions that enable us to engage in democratic decision-making over the material and providential services that underpin our lives? How can we reform the monolithic, centralised and hierarchical versions of public ownership of the post-war past into more collective and participatory forms of common ownership? How can we bring the state into closer conversation and engagement with that third domain of economic ownership and management often referred to as the social economy? Like the commons, the social economy is an alternative to the public and private domains and a historical tradition from which collective housing alternatives can be seen to derive. But whereas the commons stands in

48 Foundational Economy Collective, *Foundational Economy: The Infrastructure of Everyday Life*, p. 28.

a more antagonistic opposition to the public–private dualism constituted under capitalism, the social economy can be seen to emerge alongside, and often in cooperation with, the state to provide an alternative to capitalism that in some way mediates the public and the private without discarding it completely.[49] The social economy thus emerges from within modernity and its notions of property and economic ownership but seeks to transform these according to non-profit, co-operative and democratic values.

The original co-operative movement of the nineteenth century in Britain, sparked by the Rochdale Pioneers in northern England but drawing on older, medieval traditions of mutualism and guild socialism, is perhaps the quintessential historical figure of the social economy, from an era when this concept was only just beginning to be articulated. Co-operatives were at first organised to democratise the relations of production, in worker-owned co-ops, then consumption, with the rise of retail co-ops and, more recently, areas more associated with social reproduction, such as housing co-ops. The argument implicit in the concept of the foundational economy—that domains conventionally conceived as parts of social reproduction rather than production are actually an intrinsic, foundational part of the productive economy—helps us see that non-profit forms of ownership, such as state and co-operative activities, are just as much a part of the economy as are for-profit sectors. It also helps us see that housing co-ops are just as much a part of the social economy as the worker co-ops that more immediately come to mind.

Social economy traditions such as the co-op movement provided much of the inspiration and impetus for the involvement of the state in the production and provision of the foundational economy. Granted, the original so-called 'gas and water' municipal socialism of the 1880s and 1890s in which European municipalities pioneered the provision of basic material infrastructure may have drawn on a different intellectual hinterland. But the state provision of providential services, such as social care and housing, brought to life in the 1940s, owed much to earlier experiments in co-operative practices at more localised scales in the social economy. Thus we see the public sector and the social economy developing together through imitation, competition, conflict and mutual support, over the past century or so. This book charts one particular period of their co-evolution in Liverpool, where a budding co-operative housing movement was brought to life by central and local state support, in ways which proved at least partially mutually beneficial. But this alliance between the state and Liverpool's co-op movement proved fragile and ultimately precarious upon political circumstance. The question remains whether any such relationship can be rekindled for the development of a

49 Frank Moulaert and Oana Ailenei, "Social Economy, Third Sector and Solidarity Relations: A Conceptual Synthesis from History to Present", *Urban Studies* 42.11 (2005): 2037–2054.

publicly minded housing commons in the future, building on the lessons learnt from this history. Having defined collective housing alternatives and suggested why they are of interest in understanding how to move beyond our present housing crisis, in the remainder of this introduction I want to do two things: to outline the structure of the book but, first of all, to introduce Liverpool and explain why this city, of all places, provides an important case study into the historical and ongoing development of collective housing alternatives.

CHAPTER 2

Why Liverpool of All Places?

> If there were to be a revolution in England it would start in Liverpool.[1]

Liverpool has long been a leading light in public housing and its alternatives—one of the first cities to build municipal housing in Europe and home to one of the continent's most inventive and intensive housing cooperative movements as well as, later, a pioneer of British urban community land trusts. This inventiveness extends beyond housing into civic and social domains. During its heyday as England's second city and a primary port of the British Empire, Liverpool was an innovator of inter-city rail as well as underground, overhead and overwater metro railways, integrated sewerage systems, cast iron churches, electric trams and the longest underwater road tunnel at the time—the list goes on.[2] Animating its knack for innovation is an 'edginess'[3] that still shines through its culture today. The global trading links connecting Liverpool with far-flung places have been vital conduits for the transmission and cross-pollination of radical new ideas and cultures—leading to a perception of Liverpool as a cosmopolitan 'city on the edge'.[4] Quite literally on the edge of the British Isles and Europe, at the intersection with other continents, this edgy city full of edgy people experimenting with cutting-edge ideas is said to have more in common with Atlantic port counterparts—Naples, Marseilles, Istanbul, New York, New Orleans, Kingston—than with other British cities: "the tides carry the rhythm" of these 'mari-time' cities.[5] Liverpool's temperament seems to reflect the estuary that defines its urban landscape, the River Mersey—one of the

1 Jim Allen, quoted by Ken Loach in Dave Sinclair, *Dockers: The '95 to '98 Liverpool Lockout* (2015), p. 19.

2 Olivier Sykes, Jonathan Brown, Matthew Cocks et al., "A City Profile of Liverpool", *Cities* 35 (2013): 299–318.

3 Steve Higginson and Tony Wailey, *Edgy Cities* (Northern Lights, 2006).

4 John Davies, *Cities on the Edge* (Liverpool University Press, 2008).

5 Davies, *Cities on the Edge*, p. 14.

most extreme tidal ranges in the UK. Movement is essential to Liverpool: expressed in the rhythms of the popular music that has come to define it and the maritime flows of people and ideas, making it a hotbed of effervescent energy, creativity and cultural movements, as it has evolved from 'world city to the world in one city'.[6] Yet at the same time it is a city with a very distinct identity—of Scouse and Scousers[7]—paradoxically dissociated from other places and turned inward towards its own unique culture as much as it can be said to be outwardly connected to others.

Its historical evolution as a place made up of migrants and intersections of ideas from elsewhere, but which have grown into their own, is tinged with a certain political flavour, distinctly radical, democratic and anti-authoritarian. It has been a hotbed of radicalism over the decades, experimenting with new forms of revolt and resistance leading, in turn, to new forms of social organisation. The "foundational myth" of Liverpool's radical identity is the 1911 strike.[8] What began as a strike by transport workers escalated into one of the most significant moments of working-class agitation in British history, involving some seventy thousand workers from across a wide range of industries in direct action led by syndicalists. The city came, the *Liverpool Daily Post* reported at the time, "near to revolution"—a phrase borrowed for the title of labour historian Eric Taplin's book on the subject—prompting then Home Secretary Winston Churchill, anticipating insurrection, to deploy troops into Liverpool and a gunboat up the Mersey.[9] That such extreme actions by the state were taken twice more to pre-empt further strikes in the early twentieth century confirms Liverpool's identity as a revolutionary city in the minds of the ruling and working classes alike. A recent edited collection commemorating this distinctive history is subtitled: 'city of radicals'.[10] Perhaps it is no surprise, then, that Liverpool has over the years produced some truly *radical* movements and innovations—in the original sense of the term, getting to the structural root of the issue—and not least in the domain of public housing and its alternatives long after its economic power faded.

6 Tim Bunnell, *From World City to the World in One City: Liverpool through Malay Lives* (Wiley-Blackwell, 2016).

7 Philip Boland, "The Construction of Images of People and Place: Labelling Liverpool and Stereotyping Scousers", *Cities* 25.6 (2008): 355–369.

8 Mark O'Brien, "Liverpool 1911 and Its Era: Foundational Myth or Authentic Tradition", in John Belchem and Bryan Biggs, eds, *Liverpool: City of Radicals* (Liverpool University Press, 2011), pp. 140–158.

9 Eric Taplin, *Near to Revolution: The Liverpool General Transport Strike of 1911* (Bluecoat, 1994).

10 Belchem and Biggs, *Liverpool: City of Radicals*.

A City of Radicals and Reformists

One such radical attracted to Liverpool's streets was Friedrich Engels—but for very different reasons. Engels came to Liverpool to document the terrible conditions that industrial capitalism presented for the new urban proletariat in his 1844 work *The Condition of the Working Class in England.* This was based on field studies of the rapidly industrialising cities of northern England, including Liverpool:

> Liverpool, with all its commerce, wealth, and grandeur ... treats its workers with the same barbarity. A full fifth of the population, more than 45,000 human beings, live in narrow, dark, damp, badly ventilated cellar dwellings, of which there are 7,862 in the city. Besides these cellar dwellings there are 2,270 courts, small spaces built up on all four sides and having but one entrance, a narrow, covered passage-way, the whole ordinarily very dirty and inhabited exclusively by proletarians.[11]

What Engels' early observations reveal is that Liverpool's radical innovations in housing are only partly explicable by its revolutionary inventiveness; the large part was driven by sheer necessity—a response to the horrendous conditions wrought by colonial-capitalist urbanisation. As Britain's leading slave port between 1699 and 1807—although no slave as such ever set foot there—slaving profits continued to enrich the city long after the British Empire as a whole abolished slavery in the 1830s. Its great wealth is still evident in the legacy of monumental architecture, with more listed buildings than anywhere else in Britain outside London, now protected by UNESCO World Heritage status. Such wealth and power was paid for with severe social and housing problems: inexcusable side-effects of the accumulation of capital, in which the bare minimum of surplus value produced by the exploitation of workers was allocated to the construction and maintenance of their dwellings. Liverpool's maritime economy was driven by working-class labour, comprised largely of poor migrants drawn from across the UK and beyond through its far-reaching trade connections. The city has, for instance, the most established black community in Britain and the oldest Chinatown in Europe. Economic migrants settled in the waterfront districts in north and south Liverpool that developed behind the working docks, which became incredibly dense and overcrowded, constituting "a city within a city" the size of Bristol or Newcastle in itself.[12]

As a result, Liverpool was regarded as the most unhealthy English city, with 34 per cent of the city's population in 1841 living in filthy overcrowded

11 Friedrich Engels, *The Condition of the Working Class in England* (Penguin Classics, 1992).
12 Tony Lane, *Liverpool: City of the Sea*, 2nd ed. (Liverpool University Press, 1997).

cellars without light, ventilation, sanitation or fresh water; 25 per cent living in back-to-back tenement courthouses housing the growing numbers drawn to work on the docks.[13] As urban historian Bertie Dockerill has highlighted, Liverpool's housing conditions compared unfavourably with counterparts such as Manchester or Leeds by the excessive if not unique prevalence of cellar accommodation owing to the city's more mercantile than industrial heritage.[14] All this was made worse by the sudden arrival of Irish migrants escaping the Potato Famine of 1845–47, a disaster largely attributable to British colonial-capitalist practices—practices to which Liverpool's fortunes were inextricably linked. Liverpool was the first port of call for refugees, with some two million travelling through the city over the following decade. Over half were designated by the authorities as 'paupers', and tens of thousands stayed, many settling in slum areas in the north end of the inner city, built behind the docks that provided much of the employment on offer. Housing conditions were hardly improved by new purpose-built tenements thrown up by speculative builders, from which the phrase 'Jerry-built houses' is said to have originated.[15]

Liverpool was the first city in Britain to legislate against the dire urban conditions created by capitalism. The 1842 Liverpool Building Act, Dockerill demonstrates, challenged laissez-faire attitudes of the time to municipal intervention—enforcing minimum space and hygiene standards in newly constructed privately rented courts across Liverpool. In 1846, the Liverpool Sanitary Act—the first comprehensive health legislation in England, two years ahead of the national Public Health Act, which likewise made local authorities responsible for drainage, sewerage and water supply—inaugurated the world's first Medical Officer of Health and Borough Engineer in 1847 so as to begin to ameliorate some of the worst conditions through public improvements such as sewers. In *Municipal Dreams*, charting the rise and fall of council housing in Britain, housing historian John Boughton describes how "Liverpool led the way" in the design and delivery of these early reforms: the only local authority, significantly, to make use of the 1866 Labouring Classes Dwellings Act that permitted councils to purchase sites and build or improve homes for people who would otherwise remain at the mercy of unscrupulous private landlords.[16] Dockerill goes further to suggest that "Liverpool

13 José Ospina, *Housing Ourselves* (Hilary Shipman Ltd, 1987), p. 66.

14 Bertie Dockerill, "Liverpool Corporation and the Origins of Municipal Social Housing, 1842–1890", *Transactions of the Historic Society of Lancashire and Cheshire* 165 (2016): 39–56.

15 Robert Cowan, P. Hannay and R. Owens, "The Light on Top of the Tunnel, in Vauxhall Victors: Eldonians Special Issue", *Architects' Journal* (23 Mar. 1988): 37–66.

16 John Boughton, *Municipal Dreams: The Rise and Fall of Council Housing* (Verso, 2018), pp. 12–13.

Corporation did not merely foreshadow central government guidelines, but set a socio-political agenda that was a model which other local authorities would eventually emulate".[17]

Liverpool Corporation—as the city council was then called, known by its tenants as the 'Corpy'—built Europe's first municipal housing scheme, St Martin's Cottages in Vauxhall, in 1869, to replace back-to-back slums. These were not cottages as the name suggested but tenements—six blocks over five storeys (including basements)—which failed to make much progress in answering working-class housing needs but nonetheless began a trend for council tenement-building that would only decease in the 1980s. Even by 1880, some 70,000 people still lived in courthouses condemned as unfit for human habitation, in dockside districts, which, as the new Medical Officer of Health remarked in 1882, were as "plagued as the cholera-smitten cities".[18] Two decades later, a successor Medical Officer reported that "there was not a city in this country, nay in Europe, which could produce anything like the squalor … found in some of Liverpool's back streets".

In response, Liverpool has delivered amongst the most intensive programmes of slum clearances and municipal house building the world over. The city has given birth to a number of innovations in council housing construction and provision, including pioneering the use of prefabricated concrete housing. These municipal interventions to replace terraced housing with modernist tenements were embarked upon in distinct phases. The first wave of pre-war tenements included experiments such as one of the first prefabricated concrete housing blocks in the world, at Eldon Street. Prior to the First World War, with a total of 2,747 flats and houses, Liverpool was the only city in England to build proportionately more municipal housing than London.[19] The second, inter-war period saw the Conservative City Council—motivated by a mix of Tory paternalism and electoral tactics—construct monumental art deco 'garden' tenement blocks, arranged around a central communal courtyard or garden, and inspired by the municipal socialist schemes of Vienna, such as Karl Marx-Hof, following site visits made by Liverpool's city architect and housing director to Austria. For Marxist sociologist and Liverpool historian Tony Lane, "the best council housing ever built in Liverpool went up under the aegis of a Tory council":

> In the 1930s, apart from the Labour-controlled London County Council, Liverpool was comfortably the most progressive housing authority in Britain. The monolithic tenements of the inner city were

17 Dockerill, "Liverpool Corporation and the Origins of Municipal Social Housing, 1842–1890", p. 45.

18 Lane, *Liverpool: City of the Sea*, p. 66.

19 Boughton, *Municipal Dreams: The Rise and Fall of Council Housing.*

> modelled on the Karl Marx Stadt blocks of socialist Vienna and the suburban estates were borrowed from Welwyn Garden City.[20]

Liverpool stood alone with London amongst English cities—Scotland was a different story—to embrace the continental European trend for large-scale multi-storey urban architecture, as opposed to the taste for more quintessentially English garden suburb designs, which disavow the urban. Indeed, it has often been said that Liverpool is *in* but not *of* England; "an English city", remarks the 'militant modernist' architectural critic Owen Hatherley, "as honest about its urbanity as a Scottish or European one".[21] Following the post-war birth of the welfare state, the third phase produced three-storey 'walk-up' tenements—built in the 1940s and 1950s in infill sites left over by war damage or pre-war clearances. The appetite for municipal intervention did not get into full swing until 1955, when the Labour Party was elected to the council for the first time in the city's history—unusually late for a northern industrial city with strong working-class traditions. Liverpool was unusual among northern industrial cities with strong working-class traditions for electing Liberal and Tory council administrations when others voted in Labour—partly due to the religious sectarianism that had divided the city since the Irish in-migration in the nineteenth century: Protestants tended to vote Tory; Catholics Labour. This fourth phase, from the mid-1950s and through the 1960s, was more ambitious and embraced the systems-built prefab concrete tower block as its emblem. In the modernist and often utopian fervour of the period, city planners rebuilt much of Liverpool and its housing stock—large parts having been destroyed in Second World War bomb damage—and designed and constructed on the urban periphery entire new towns and outer estates to which many inner-city communities were relocated in the slum clearance programme. Due to numerous interlocking factors—alienating designs, poor quality construction techniques and building materials, bureaucratic mismanagement, political choices and socioeconomic decline—much post-war municipal housing built in Liverpool quickly deteriorated and became increasingly unpopular. Tony Lane remarks:

> Who would have dreamt in the 1950s that a housing dept. would have to invent the term "hard-to-let"? Who would have dreamt that some tenants would have been driven to a systematic destruction of their own housing as a means of forcing a change in policy? Who could have imagined a situation where tenants would have complained of the state of repair of their buildings—and then said that they didn't want repairs

20 Lane, *Liverpool: City of the Sea*, p. 340.

21 Owen Hatherley, *A Guide to the New Ruins of Great Britain* (Verso Books, 2011), p. 336.

> carried out because they wanted the place to deteriorate to the point where they would have to be re-housed?[22]

A more sympathetic view of municipal housing would contend that it was not only its failure that caused the alienation and resistance of tenants but also its success. It was only through the universal provision of warm, dry, light, spacious, hygienic housing with all the mod cons that residents had the minimum satisfaction of basic needs met required for more complex needs and desires to seem at all attainable. Whether it was due to its success or failure—or both—by the 1970s, campaigns for better council housing were becoming commonplace among Corpy tenants, who were gaining in confidence and collective organisation. This was Liverpool's late 'Indian Summer' before the long winter fell; a time when unemployment was only 5 per cent, residual wealth accrued through colonialism was still circulating and the working classes had gained the confidence to challenge the cultural authority of the ruling elite. It was the era of rock 'n' roll and Beat poetry—the Beatles, Mersey Beat and the Mersey poets were Liverpool's own home-grown talents—the era when the American Beat poet Allen Ginsberg arrived in Liverpool (in 1965) and famously declared the city to be "at the present moment, the centre of consciousness of the human universe" whilst psychoanalyst Carl Jung had visited Liverpool previously and recorded a dream about it that "Liverpool is the pool of life".[23] Tony Lane again:

> In the 1960s Liverpool became the working class capital of the UK. No city could have been better equipped to express the brash self-confidence of young working people; the anarchic solidarism of the seafarer was just perfect for the temper of the times. This was also the decade of shop floor liberation. The yoke of the old autocracy in the trade union movement was being lifted and a belief in the virtues of local self-government and direct action rippled out into the sleepiest quarters of the labour markets.[24]

In the 1960s, Liverpool gained a reputation for trade union militancy, for a distinctively bolshie, anarchic and spontaneous style, an independent-mindedness and 'swagger'—gestures that were in many respects inherited from the traditional seafaring lifestyle, the casualised nature of work on the docks and the influence of anarcho-syndicalism—seeded by Spanish and American seafarers during the time of the Spanish Civil War—over more

22 Tony Lane, "Liverpool—City of Harder Times to Come", *Marxism Today* (Nov. 1978): 336–343 (pp. 338–339).

23 Carl Jung, *Memories, Dreams, Reflections* (Random House, 1961).

24 Lane, "Liverpool—City of Harder Times to Come", p. 11.

traditionally socialist labour movement ideologies. These specific forms of labour empowerment in the realm of production rippled out to influence the community activism that was beginning to emerge in the sphere of social reproduction, notably housing. Various rent strikes and marches were organised by council tenants angry at the terrible condition of their homes, culminating in the intensive strike actions of 1972. Other communities protested against being rehoused in the council's so-called 'slum clearance programme'; not only protecting themselves from displacement to outer estates but also from the threat of being split up as a community.

Some of these protests fuelled what was to become one of the largest and most imaginative housing co-operative movements in Britain if not Europe—setting in motion an alternative process, led by working-class tenants themselves, of building, owning and managing municipal homes. In 1974, Colin Ward's book *Tenants Take Over* was published and, a few years later, his call for 'collective dweller control'[25] was answered by the Weller Street Co-op, the country's first ever new-build housing co-op to be designed, owned and managed by its tenants. Whilst the early cooperative movement was focused on the rehabilitation of terraced housing and was led largely by idealistic middle class professionals, the later waves were focused on new build and were led by tenants who worked with professionals, such as architects and development managers, in ways which reversed the conventional balance of power between these two groups. The historical development of Liverpool's rehab and the new-build co-op movements is the subject of Part II.

A City on (the) Edge?

Liverpool is radical or edgy in another sense, too. It has often been characterised as a 'city on the edge'[26] or 'on the brink'[27] of economic collapse and political disaster. Liverpool's rise to major global port and leading cultural light is matched only by its swift and brutal decline. As the British Empire rescinded and the UK turned away from the Atlantic towards Europe, Liverpool found itself on the wrong side of the British Isles to benefit from the growing trade with the European Community. Coupled with automation of port activities, thousands of jobs on the docks were lost, with huge knock-on effects for ancillary industries. From a peak of some 870,000 people at the turn of the twentieth century, the city had, by the century's close, lost over half its population. Unemployment was high for those left behind. Capital flight and public divestment blighted

25 Colin Ward, *Tenants Take Over* (Architectural Press, 1974).

26 Diane Frost and Peter North, *Militant Liverpool: A City on the Edge* (Liverpool University Press, 2013).

27 Michael Parkinson, *Liverpool on the Brink: One City's Struggle against Government Cuts* (Policy Journals Ltd, 1985).

housing and the general urban environment. All this was compounded by the council's 'slum clearance programme'—a policy conceived in Liverpool's late 'Indian Summer' period of growth and optimism in which impending socioeconomic decline seemed incredible. By removing thousands of the city's working-age population from the inner city to outer estates and new towns, city planners unintentionally exacerbated this decline. This created the conditions for social unrest and political upheaval. The Toxteth Riots of 1981—sparked by up to 90 per cent unemployment rates for young black men coupled with racial discrimination against the local black community—were amongst the most significant in living memory and suffered one of the most violent repressions by police witnessed on mainland Britain.[28] All these various factors combined with regional stigmatisation to create popular depictions of Liverpool as a 'basket case', a 'self-pity city': "They should build a fence around [Liverpool] and charge admission. For sadly, it has become a 'showcase' of everything that has gone wrong in Britain's major cities".[29]

The Conservative government was torn between two opposing visions for Liverpool—equally patronising and propagating of the victim mentality stigma that had attached itself to the city and its inhabitants. One was to withdraw public investment entirely and let the city sink or swim, through a policy of 'managed decline'; the other was to inject additional resources through new top-down, post-democratic, property-led urban policies designed to pump-prime the private sector. The latter strategy won out, continuing a trend of government policy experimentation in area-based initiatives for which Liverpool had for a number of decades been at the forefront. By the mid-1980s, however, it was clear that the long line of regeneration experiments conducted on the city had each in turn largely failed to counteract socioeconomic decline, as Liverpool's urban policy guru Michael Parkinson argues in *Liverpool on the Brink*:

> Since the 1960s, the city has been the recipient, or victim, of every urban experiment invented, including Tony Crosland's educational priority areas, Jim Callaghan's traditional urban programme, Roy Jenkins's community development projects, the Home Office's Brunswick neighbourhood project, Peter Walker's inner area studies, Peter Shore's inner city partnerships, Geoffrey Howe's enterprise zones and Michael Heseltine's urban development corporation. Two decades' experience of those policies had not substantially improved the city's problems.[30]

28 Andy Merrifield, "Them and Us: Rebuilding the Ruins in Liverpool", in *Dialectical Urbanism* (Monthly Review Press, 2002), pp. 53–73.

29 Article in *Daily Mirror* (11 Oct. 1982), quoted in Lane, *Liverpool: City of the Sea*.

30 Parkinson, *Liverpool on the Brink: One City's Struggle against Government Cuts*, p. 16.

The real shift in the city's economic fortunes began not from the top down but from the bottom up, with the local election of a left-wing Militant Tendency-led Labour-run Council to pursue a radical policy agenda of municipal socialism. This involved huge public investment in housing, public services and the urban environment, including a massive council house building programme in an era when municipal house building nationally had been slowed to a dribble by hostile neoliberal reforms. The Militant-led Council also came to blows with Thatcher's government, for spending what was seen to be too much on public projects, in setting an 'illegally' high budget. Yet it was precisely this municipal socialist reinvestment in the city's infrastructure and public sector job creation which arguably[31] brought Liverpool, contra the orthodoxy of Michael Parkinson's thesis,[32] 'beyond the brink' of ruin and kick-started its regeneration, which really began to take off in the late 1990s. This was the last gasp of municipal housing in the UK before being plunged beneath a powerful neoliberal tide. It remains a fascinating period for study, not least for its unique local politics, which saw the municipal socialist council turn against its potential ally, the burgeoning co-operative movement. In the council's policy of 'municipalisation', housing co-ops in development were taken into council control and all future projects were foreclosed. The ideological origins of this battle between municipal and cooperative approaches, state-socialist and democratic-socialist conceptions of providing public housing—and how the battle was concluded—are the issues closing Part II. Municipalisation spurred on one co-op campaign group in particular, known as the Eldonians, to go further with their aspirations to become a 'self-regenerating community'. Now characterised as an exemplar of 'social innovation',[33] attracting policy tourists from all over the world, the Eldonians turned around their fortunes through forging alliances with some unlikely bedfellows—the Thatcher government and Minister for Merseyside Michael Heseltine's Task Force—to challenge successfully the Militant-led council. Their struggle against all odds to build the Eldonian Village out of their derelict ex-industrial neighbourhood is the main subject of Part III.

A City Playing the Urban Regeneration Game

Although Militant arguably did more than the Minister for Merseyside to reverse Liverpool's fortunes, it was the approach instated by the Urban Development Corporation and Task Force that gained most traction amongst policymakers and

31 Frost and North, *Militant Liverpool: A City on the Edge*.

32 Michael Parkinson, *Liverpool Beyond the Brink: The Remaking of a Post-Imperial City* (Liverpool University Press, 2019).

33 Peter Roberts, "Social Innovation, Spatial Transformation and Sustainable Communities: Liverpool and the 'Eldonians'", in Paul Drewe, Juan-Luis Klein and Edward Hulsbergen, eds, *The Challenge of Social Innovation in Urban Revitalization* (Techne Press, 2008).

politicians, who have since pursued a succession of regeneration programmes aimed at boosting the city's image, attracting inward investment and resolving the multiple deprivations that remain a drag on economic recovery and growth. Regeneration has become almost a self-generating industry in Liverpool—the first to fill the vacuum created by the collapse of its maritime economy. Some local academics and commentators go so far as to suggest Liverpool's contemporary economy is primarily geared around the so-called 'regeneration game':

> Liverpool's vivid socio-economic and environmental degradation, alongside its rich cultural capital and architectural legacies (often seen as being at risk), has given momentum to intensive processes of "regeneration", latterly drawing upon large sums of national and European Union monies. Ahead of many other urban localities, processes of regeneration have led to the formation of new semi-permanent governance frameworks, involving multi-level "collaborative milieus" of local, regional and national institutions. "Regeneration" has become the city's dominant, if seldom quantified or questioned, objective.[34]

Liverpool went through the post-industrial transition ahead of the curve; it also, rather interestingly, appears to have carved out its own niche in this very space, as a city that specialises in regeneration. The next round of comprehensive redevelopment of the city's ageing housing stock was, therefore, a very different beast from the urban renewal of the 1960s, despite very much embodying the latter's scale and ambition. With the Housing Market Renewal programme of the 2000s, Liverpool once again found itself at the centre of academic and policy debate over the management and renewal of public housing. By the late 1990s, like many of its post-industrial northern counterparts, the city was suffering with what policymakers diagnosed as an oversupply of terraced housing (see Figure 1)—some in public ownership or in the hands of housing associations; much of it privately owned. Their solution was a large-scale housing renewal programme that was to provoke, much like the 'slum clearance programme' of the 1960s, serious opposition amongst some of the communities targeted for 'demolition and rebuild'. A few of these activist groups were galvanised by successful defence of their housing to experiment with the latest collective housing alternative, the CLT model, which had been imported to Britain from the USA where it was first devised as an institutional solution for redistribution of rural property and black empowerment in the Deep South. Thus Liverpool became one of the first places in the UK—alongside London—to witness the emergence of distinctly urban CLTs that challenged the demolition of terraced housing and sought to revitalise urban neighbourhoods. The logic, operation and impacts of Housing

34 Sykes, Brown, Cocks et al., "A City Profile of Liverpool", p. 300.

Figure 1 Dilapidated dwellings and neighbourhood abandonment in Liverpool 8 in 2015.

Market Renewal on Liverpool's inner city, and the development of successful (and failed) campaigns for CLT alternatives is the subject of Part IV.

Structure of the Book

Just as Engels provided a rich description of the terrible housing conditions afflicting Liverpool in the early days of capitalist urbanisation, his seminal work *The Housing Question* provides the perfect point of departure for structuring this book. Those vivid scenes he painted of Liverpool in *The Condition of the Working Class in England* no doubt informed his later work. Although written around a century and a half ago, this still provides a serious challenge for any political project pursuing a housing commons via collective alternatives to public ownership, or, indeed, any intellectual project seeking to understand it. The housing question resurfaced once more in the 1970s in a debate between John F.C. Turner and his Marxist critics over the commodity value of housing.[35] Today, the housing question is yet again being reconsidered by critical geographers eager to highlight how changing capitalist dynamics make much of Engels' thesis moot and put a different, more optimistic spin on the potential of collective alternatives to provide a radical reformist path towards its possible resolution.[36] Most importantly, the housing question has been reinterpreted and expanded beyond the walls of housing into the urban sphere by various neo-Marxist scholars who have sought new ways of reflecting on the evolution of capitalism. The most famous statement in this regard is *The Urban Question* by Manuel Castells, a former student of Lefebvre's, highlighting the new power of 'the urban' in the post-war period as a site of collective consumption, resistance and political change.[37] Engels had seen the housing crisis as a mere secondary contradiction of capitalism, owing to the fact that only at the point of production, in the factory, is surplus value created by workers and in turn extracted by capitalists—the primary contradiction

35 Dennis Conway, "Self-Help Housing, the Commodity Nature of Housing and Amelioration of the Housing Deficit: Continuing the Turner-Burgess Debate", *Antipode* 14.2 (1982): 40–46.

36 Neil Gray, "Spatial Composition and the Urbanization of Capital: The 1915 Glasgow Rent Strikes and the Housing Question Reconsidered", in Neil Gray, ed., *Rent and Its Discontents: A Century of Housing Struggle* (Rowman & Littlefield, 2018), pp. 49–67; Tim Joubert and Stuart Hodkinson, "Beyond the Rent Strike, Towards the Commons: Why the Housing Question Requires Activism That Generates Its Own Alternatives", in Neil Gray, ed., *Rent and Its Discontents: A Century of Housing Struggle* (Rowman & Littlefield, 2018), pp. 185–200; Udi Engelsman, Mike Rowe and Alan Southern, "Community Land Trusts—A Radical or Reformist Response to the Housing Question Today?", *ACME: An International E-Journal for Critical Geographies* 15.3 (2016): 590–615; David Madden and Peter Marcuse, *In Defense of Housing: The Politics of Crisis* (Verso, 2016).

37 Manuel Castells, *The Urban Question: A Marxist Approach* (MIT Press, 1977).

understood as the original alienation of workers from the fruits of their labour. As capitalism advanced, production per se became less important in relation to consumption as a site of value realisation and struggle. Later, as neoliberalism took hold, financialisation intensified, with land and property becoming a spatial fix to capitalist crises in productive sectors. In *The New Urban Question*, Andy Merrifield, building on the work of Lefebvre, Castells as well as his own doctoral supervisor David Harvey,[38] has sought to update the Marxist analysis of the urban to reflect the increasingly central role land and property has to play in capital accumulation.[39] Housing is placed centre-stage in this unfolding drama.

This Marxist history of capitalist urbanisation—and the changing role of housing within it—provides a useful background framing for exploring Liverpool's history of collective housing alternatives. The empirical body of the book is structured into three parts—thc Housing Question, the Neighbourhood Question and the Urban Question. Each deals with a different period in this history and each, respectively, with a different collective housing model: co-operatives (both rehab and new-build movements) in the 1970s; community development trusts (the Eldonians) in the 1980s; and, post-2000, community land trusts. These models can be seen as the most appropriate response to the issues of their time. There is also a progression through geographic scale—from a focus on housing to the neighbourhood and, finally, to the wider scale of the urban. This reflects the way in which the housing question has evolved with new questions thrown up in each era by Marxist urbanists each taking Engels as their departure point. Each part is split into two broad sections: the first introductory chapter of each part addresses more theoretical issues (chapters 3, 7 and 10), acting as a lens through which to explore the empirical history in the more substantial following chapters.

Part II, 'The Housing Question', opens with the original problems posed by Engels and aims to address these through an examination of more recent neo-Marxist theory and anarchist thought on the nature of the state, capitalism, value, housing and social change. I begin my empirical history in the late 1960s, with the re-emergence of anarchist ideas in housing and their influence in Liverpool through the work of John F.C. Turner and Colin Ward, who can be seen as the anarchist descendants of Pierre-Joseph Proudhon, Engels' principal interlocutor in *The Housing Question*. Their ideas—particularly on user autonomy and collective dweller control—had purchase in a budding co-op movement that had grown from a small professional-led project centred on rehabilitating inner-city terraced housing to an increasingly resident-led movement for designing, developing and building new bespoke co-op housing, funded by the state and supported by co-op development agencies. The social, economic and

38 David Harvey, *Limits to Capital* (Verso Books, 2007).
39 Andy Merrifield, *The New Urban Question* (Pluto Press, 2014).

political roots of this movement—and its outcomes—comprise the main subject of chapters 4 and 5. The Engels–Proudhon debate also acts as a precursor to the not-dissimilar antagonism that would later arise between Liverpool's co-operative movement and the Trotskyist Militant council administration's municipal socialist project, explored in chapter 6, which bookends Part II.

Part III primarily explores what I call the 'Neighbourhood Question'. Uneven urban development has become a central preoccupation of Marxist urbanists and critical geographers since the economic restructuring in the 1970s and 1980s, with the crisis of Fordism and ascendance of neoliberal globalisation, impacted heavily upon old industrial cities such as Liverpool. Here, economic decline has not been evenly distributed but spatially concentrated in certain areas, which various state-led urban programmes have sought (in vain) to regenerate. In *The Housing Question*, Engels presciently analysed the way in which 'bourgeois reformist' attempts to revitalise deprived urban neighbourhoods through state intervention would simply displace the problem—deprivation arising from capitalist exploitation—elsewhere in the city and the planet. The Neighbourhood Question thus describes the knot of economic and social problems produced by uneven urban development and coalescing around the scale of the neighbourhood and which cannot easily be resolved through conventional economic development or regeneration policies. Collective housing alternatives, however, might provide an answer. Chapters 8 and 9 explore the efforts of one such alternative, the Eldonian Community Development Trust, to regenerate their blighted, ex-industrial neighbourhood in a local context of political infighting between the municipal socialist council and the housing co-operative movement.

By the late 1990s, Liverpool's neighbourhood question had mutated into the symptomatic spread of empty homes and even neighbourhood abandonment in declining inner-city areas suffering depopulation (see Figure 1)—but was also in some sense produced by regeneration programmes and the perverse incentives written into urban policy funding regimes. Part IV, 'The Urban Question', explores two alternative approaches to tackling this issue. The first, Housing Market Renewal (HMR), originated as a 'grant regime' between public and private partners aiming to revalorise urban space and capitalise on the state funding made available to stimulate new economic growth. This, I argue in chapter 10, is an example of the most recent period in capitalism's evolution towards the commodification and financialisation of urban land as a site of capital accumulation. In its narrow focus on house type and the housing market, without casting its vision any wider to socioeconomic structures, HMR, I argue, commits a kind of housing fetishism that is symptomatic of the way in which policymakers tend to treat housing as a noun rather than a verb. If ever there was an example of an "isolated solution to the housing question", in Engels' terminology, this is it.

The second approach to tackling empty homes arose as a reaction to the demolitions and dispossessions entailed by the first, developing into the CLT movement we see emerging in Liverpool today—the subject of chapters 11 and 12. The CLT campaigns are attempting to produce and protect an urban commons—and not just a housing commons—in their expanded focus on community enterprise, public space, food growing and cultural activities as well as affordable homes. They also hope to act as an arena for democratic encounter between members of the wider community as well as residents and therefore possess something distinctly *urban* about them. Part IV, then, narrates a battle between two opposing visions of the urban question—the question of how to remake urban spaces and cities for people over profit in the context of capitalist restructuring and uneven urban development.

Finally, in the concluding Part V, I attempt to bring all these issues together and consider the prospects for systematically institutionalising collective housing alternatives. Although this book is focused on Liverpool—a city of deep contradictions, where things seem to happen for the first time, both good and bad; a city where the most dystopian and utopian realities appear side by side, often in the very same phenomena, a city providing the (im)perfect testbed for the development and study of collective housing alternatives—this book is also about transcending the particularisms of people and place to find generalisable lessons for the development of collective alternatives to state-socialist and market-capitalist approaches to dwelling. Although this book is focused on the past, it thus looks to the future. The potential of collective housing alternatives is to enact a different way of organising dwelling to the public–private binary with which we currently live. In this sense, much like the utopian-socialist experiments that inspired the early cooperative movement and, so too, like the modernist visions that informed the development of municipal housing, this book is about utopia—but not some utopia out there, some 'non place' in the distant future. Rather, it is concerned with tracing the outlines of what the late Marxist sociologist Erik Olin Wright called 'real utopias'[40]—those already existing housing commons in the here and now which might just, at the turn of unforeseen political events, gain enough traction to create substantive structural transformation. In answer to Engel's bipolarised dilemma between all-out insurrectionary revolution and mere reformism, this book attempts to tread a cautious path between these poles: a 'radical reformism', of the like that post-Marxist Chantal Mouffe envisions[41]—a most transformative reformism working within our political-economic coordinates, slowly and patiently, sometimes through rupture, to transform their shape into something else entirely.

40 Erik Olin Wright, *Envisioning Real Utopias* (Verso, 2010).
41 Chantal Mouffe, *For a Left Populism* (Verso, 2018).

Part II
The Housing Question

CHAPTER 3

Revisiting the Housing Question

> Modernity, it seems, is exemplified not so much by the business park or the airport, but by the dilapidated dwelling. This is especially odd given that dwellings constitute the greater part of the built environment, that they are the spaces where most people spend most of their time, and where what is arguably the 'real' work of society is done.[1]

In his essay and film of the same name, *The Dilapidated Dwelling*, psychogeographer Patrick Keiller asks why housing is so much more visibly run-down and relatively dilapidated than the retail units, corporate offices and business parks that constitute commercial property. He notes that domestic property—what he calls 'old space' in contrast to corporate 'new space'—is in the UK the oldest and most underinvested in Europe, at an average age of 60 years, but that this discrepancy is by no means a uniquely British disease. Capitalism appears to favour investment in spaces of production over spaces of social reproduction despite, as Keiller curiously points out, the latter being "where what is arguably the 'real' work of society is done".

Is this really that surprising? Marxist critics would contend that capital always flows where there is profit to be made, and that some relative underinvestment in our domestic spaces compared with commercial spaces is therefore to be expected. Marx and Engels were amongst the original antagonists in the drama of capitalism but, whilst they may be its staunchest, they are by no means its earliest detractors. As the coordinates of the capitalist mode of production began to reveal themselves amidst the upheavals of enclosure and industrialisation in northern Europe, thinkers of various political stripes set forth their gripes. Not least amongst them were the early utopian-socialists such as Charles Fourier, Pierre-Joseph Proudhon, Henri de Saint-Simon and Robert Owen who imagined and experimented with new ways of living in what we might now call intentional communities or anarchist communes.

1 Patrick Keiller, "The Dilapidated Dwelling", in *The View from the Train: Cities and Other Landscapes* (Verso Books, 2013), pp. 51–63 (p. 54).

These were perhaps the first examples of collective housing alternatives in the modern age. Marx and particularly Engels were quick to denounce them as naïve and utopian—'utopia' was of course a concept coined by Thomas More in his 1516 work of the same name to denote a 'good place' but whose Greek roots also connote 'no place', suggesting *Utopia* was a satire about the impossibility of materialising any utopian vision.[2]

In *The Housing Question*, Engels famously derided the anarchist Proudhon and his followers as mere 'bourgeois reformists' and 'practical socialists' working in vain to improve the lot of the working class through self-help experiments but failing to take account of the structural dynamics of capitalism. Thus the housing question under capitalism was framed by Engels as a debate torn between, on the one hand, a Marxist argument that claims "the solution lies in the abolition of the capitalist mode of production and the appropriation of all the means of life and labour by the working class itself"[3] and, on the other, an anarchist argument ascribed to Proudhon that contends that small-scale collective initiatives in which new forms of social organisation are tested out in the here and now through incremental grassroots experimentation can reform capitalist-state structures from within. Like Marx, Engels saw "the housing shortage from which the workers and part of the petty bourgeoisie suffer in our modern big cities" as just "one of the numerous *smaller*, secondary evils which result from the present-day capitalist mode of production".[4] In other words, the 'evils' suffered by tenants at the hand of profit-maximising landlords is just a symptom—a refracted displacement—of a more fundamental relation of exploitation between workers and capitalists. Proudhon, however, equated the tenant–landlord relation with the labour–capital relation such that, in Engels' caricature, "As the wage worker in relation to the capitalist, so is the tenant in relation to the house owner", which Engels declared "totally untrue".[5] With such assertions the debate commenced between radical-revolutionary and bourgeois-reformist solutions to the housing question and, by extension, the social question of how to transform society as a whole; digging within social theory and political activism a seemingly insurmountable chasm between structural processes and experimental action, between structure and agency.

The housing question has resounded down the decades. A strikingly similar debate emerged in the 1970s between John F.C. Turner[6]—an intellectual heir of Proudhon who will reappear later through his links to the Liverpool

2 Benoît Godin, "Social Innovation: Utopias of Innovation from *c*.1830 to the Present", *Project on the Intellectual History of Innovation* 11 (2012): 1–52.

3 Friedrich Engels, *The Housing Question* (Progress Publishers, 1972), pp. 73–74.

4 Engels, *The Housing Question*, p. 19.

5 Engels, *The Housing Question*, p. 21.

6 John F.C. Turner, "Housing in Three Dimensions: Terms of Reference for the Housing Question Redefined", *World Development* 6.9–10 (1978): 1135–1145.

co-ops—and structuralist Marxists such as Rod Burgess.[7] Engels and co. may be right to deduce that no exploitation as such occurs at the point of rent extraction, for tenants do not produce surplus value to be expropriated in the way that workers do. Logically it then follows that capitalism cannot be transformed by reforming the tenant–landlord relation even if rent extraction is eliminated through collective control of land and housing, for capital would still reign supreme in production, including of housing. In turn, all attempts to do so appear to underestimate the deep penetration of capital into global production processes and therefore commit a kind of technological determinism in believing that small-scale user-led models can flourish independently, let alone challenge, the logic of capital. From such an uncompromisingly structuralist view, the fundamental conflict between capital and labour is the bottom line as to why—in answer to Keiller's conundrum in *The Dilapidated Dwelling*—"one can perhaps discern a general tendency ... that under advanced capitalism it is increasingly difficult to produce and maintain the dwelling".[8]

Despite its apparent internal consistency, the Marxist argument nonetheless begins with some partial basic assumptions about social reality—assumptions which have since divided anarchists and Marxists alike. Here opened schisms—at least four—between opposing perspectives of looking at the same thing: at the primary contradictions of capitalism; at the nature of social change; the nature of value itself; and the role of land in capitalism. These arguments provoked by the housing question about the role and value of housing in capitalism and social change are an illuminating way to frame the historical development of the cooperative housing movement in Liverpool. Before tracing this history and evaluating the impact of collective housing alternatives it is useful, therefore, to understand the import of these arguments.

The fourth issue listed above—the growing importance of land and property in the process of capital accumulation—presents a major challenge to Engels' framing such that housing, and political interventions within it, are increasingly intrinsic to the present functioning and future viability of capitalism, phenomena not yet apparent to Engels when he was writing. This is a historical shift that has occurred over the past half century that sees *The Housing Question* reformulated by neo-Marxist scholars first as *The Urban Question*[9] and more recently as *The New Urban Question*[10]—a history I explore in more depth in Part IV, thus entitled the Urban Question. In the remainder of

7 Rod Burgess, "The Limits of State Self-Help Housing Programmes", *Development and Change* 16.2 (1985): 271–312; Rod Burgess, "Petty Commodity Housing or Dweller Control? A Critique of John Turner's Views on Housing Policy", *World Development* 6.9–10 (1978): 1105–1133.

8 Keiller, "The Dilapidated Dwelling", p. 54.

9 Manuel Castells, *The Urban Question: A Marxist Approach* (MIT Press, 1977).

10 Andy Merrifield, *The New Urban Question* (Pluto Press, 2014).

this chapter I address each of the other three issues in turn as a way to frame the development of co-operative housing in Liverpool.

Nouns and Verbs: On the Nature of Value

Perhaps the most fundamental of issues within this debate is the nature of value. Put simply, this amounts to exchange versus use value—or value versus values. Value in the singular describes exchange value made equivalent as a quantitative measurement to define how something is worth more or less than other things. Values—in the plural—implies multiple use values and principles that are irreducible, not easily reduced to a quantifiable form of equivalence for exchange. Whilst Marx was a rigorously dialectical thinker and showed how any commodity, including housing, contains both use and exchange values simultaneously, there is a sense in which he limits his analysis of value to only that of the commodity form, the social relation of exchange value, in that he admits "use values as such lie outside of the sphere of investigation of political economy".[11] This means that the housing crisis is seen narrowly as a problem of material deprivation within a totalising system of capitalism. Turner, however, draws our attention to the double ontological status of dwelling as both a noun and verb: as an active lived process of doing as well as a static material object in which to invest or to trade.[12] Whilst the market conceives of housing as a material object to be bought and sold, residents see their homes as a means for dwelling.

Whilst this dialectical perspective of seeing value from two opposing vantage points—use and exchange, value and values—is relatively simple to hold in the mind's eye, it gets much trickier to grasp when pondering from where value derives. Marx and Engels arguably subscribed to some rendition of the labour theory of value—the theory that value is produced primarily by acts of human labour to transform nature into useful products that can then be used or traded. Although he acknowledged that ultimately value must derive from the free gifts of nature, Marx held that it is the creative process of applying human labour—imagination, innovation, knowledge, skill, techniques, tools—to natural materials that produces or creates the value that is then (erroneously) deemed to inhere in desirable objects that meet human needs. Their use value to humans makes such objects precious commodities that thereby take on exchange value in being traded for other commodities. In this production process, value is seen to be 'produced' by labourers in the workplace, for this is where the value that workers create through their labour

11 Karl Marx, *A Contribution to the Critique of Political Economy* (International Publishers, 1970), p. 413.

12 John F.C. Turner, "Housing as a Verb", in John F.C. Turner and Robert Fichter, eds, *Freedom to Build* (Collier Macmillan, 1972), pp. 148–175.

is extracted by capitalists as 'surplus value', from which is derived the profit that motivates capitalists and drives the system. Here, the production of value is conflated with the production process itself.

One of the absurd distortions of capitalism, anarchist anthropologist David Graeber is fond of reminding us,[13] is in privileging the production of objects over the (re)production of human beings. He demonstrates how value has come to be conflated with production, even seeping into the way in which we describe the production of human beings as 'going into labour'.[14] Graeber points to a bifurcation in society between 'productive labour' and 'caring labour'—the former associated with factories and manufacturing where surplus value is produced by ever greater efficiencies and technological innovation; the latter with 'unproductive' domestic and civic spaces where education, health, entertainment and the general maintenance of living spaces and communities is performed to enable the so-called 'real' productive labour of society. However, as robots and machines threaten to automate most productive jobs in society, it seems likely that the majority of employment will switch into caring jobs that produce and reproduce human beings rather than commodities. A major component of that task is, of course, housing.

Recall Keiller's consternation at the relative dilapidation of old space vis-à-vis new space despite the fact that this is where the 'real work' of society is performed. Feminist thinkers on the commons such as Silvia Federici and J.K. Gibson-Graham have long argued that domestic labour in the home and community activity in the neighbourhood comprise the hidden and unpaid yet real productive labour of society, in creating and reproducing the conditions for all other production to occur.[15] This is memorably referred to as capitalism's 'hidden abode'.[16] The fundamental though often overlooked importance of daily and generational renewal of human life for capitalist (re)production is the subject of 'social reproduction theory', an influential and recently reinvigorated school of thought in Marxist Feminism.[17] Social reproduction is not just domestic labour for the sake of capital accumulation—the basic daily reproduction of labour power—as important as that is; it also means those familial relationships and social interactions, emotional bonding and cultural creation, caregiving and education, collective joy and festivity that together

13 David Graeber, *Toward an Anthropological Theory of Value: The False Coin of Our Own Dreams* (Palgrave, 2001).

14 David Graeber, *Bullshit Jobs: A Theory* (Allen Lane, 2018).

15 Silvia Federici, *Re-Enchanting the World: Feminism and the Politics of the Commons* (PM Press, 2019); J.K. Gibson-Graham, *The End of Capitalism (As We Knew It): A Feminist Critique of Political Economy* (Blackwell, 1996).

16 Nancy Fraser, "Behind Marx's Hidden Abode", *New Left Review* 86 (2014).

17 See Tithi Bhattacharya, ed., *Social Reproduction Theory: Remapping Class, Recentering Oppression* (Pluto Press, 2017).

constitute and continually reproduce society across households and generations—and imbues life with meaning and (social) value. To the question of where value is really produced in society—in the workplace, at the point of production, or in the home and the street through social reproduction—the answer hinges on what we, so to speak, value as value. If we privilege the value inhering in the labour–capital relation—i.e. valuable products and assets—then we might well subscribe to the traditional Marxist view. If, however, we foreground the social values of being human and dwelling together in societies then it is the production of human beings and cultural practices—rather than commodities—that really count. Marxists, of course, would counter that none of this changes the fact that under capitalism housing is still produced as a commodity however much it is valued in other ways. As I explore below, their interlocutors question whether seeing the world primarily through exchange value—reading the world through the language of capitalism—can ever be the most effective way to transform it.

Exploitation and Alienation: On the Contradictions of Capitalism

Moving onto the second issue, the Engels–Proudhon debate anticipated a break that would re-emerge decades later within Marxism over the relative importance of different 'moments' in the capitalist process of production, distribution and consumption of goods like housing. In broadly subscribing to the labour theory of value Marx and Engels held that the labour–capital relation remains the primary contradiction of capitalism, for this is where surplus value is extracted by capitalists—representing a kind of theft, a discrepancy at the centre of the system, an instance of the central Marxist term 'contradiction'. Marx's genius was in seeing how the "capital-relation presupposes a complete separation between the workers and the ownership of the conditions for the realisation of their labour"[18]—workers who, in being separated from each other and alienated from the fruits of their labour, were "now ruled by *abstractions*, whereas earlier they depended on one another".[19] In short, he identified the distinctively modern condition of alienation that lies at the heart of capitalism and its contradictions.

In reaction to exploitation in the workplace, various social movements arose to resist and find alternative solutions—what collective action scholars refer to as the 'first modern cycle of contention'.[20] This began in 1848, the year Marx and Engels published their revolutionary call to arms, *The Communist*

18 Karl Marx, *Capital: Critique of Political Economy*, vol. 1 (Penguin Classics, 1990), pp. 874–875.

19 Karl Marx, *Grundrisse: Foundations of the Critique of Political Economy*, ed. Martin Nicolaus (Penguin, 1973), p. 164.

20 Sidney Tarrow, *Power in Movement: Social Movements and Contentious Politics* (Cambridge

Manifesto, when the gradual growth of socialist organisation out of localised factory-based associations eventually erupted into self-organised revolt, most famously in the Paris Commune. From there, the movement split into various anarchist, communist and social-democratic strands, eventually absorbed and institutionalised into state-capitalist ensembles through the successful incorporation of worker demands into better working conditions and the formation of formal political parties and trade unions which represented and organised action on behalf of the working class.

It was in this era that radical ideas around mutualism and cooperativism gained traction. Heir to medieval mutualist traditions of guilds, brotherhoods and civic associations, these movements were later enriched by the utopian philosophies of the likes of Proudhon and also socialist ideas emerging in the workers' syndicalist and communist movements to innovate new forms of economic organisation such as worker-owned cooperatives. The thrust of the modern cooperative movement—as originally articulated by the Rochdale Pioneers in northern England—is for economic democracy: from collective ownership of tools and workplaces to democratic management of the production process to equitable distribution of surpluses. These ideas soon spread from the sphere of production into distribution and consumption—creating the consumer co-ops we are most familiar with today—and into the domain of social reproduction more broadly, notably housing. In the following decades, the innovation of various new legal instruments—building societies, credit unions, tenant co-partnerships,[21] co-ownership societies, non-mutual housing co-ops and common ownership co-ops—helped construct the institutional architecture for the (more or less) democratic ownership and organisation of housing. Although they had an enduring political impact, cooperatives were by the early twentieth century overshadowed and marginalised by monopoly capital and the welfare state, through the introduction of mass production techniques and the municipal provision of social necessities.

Although the rise of bureaucratic state management of housing and other basic needs had, by the post-war period, alleviated the worst material deprivation wrought by capitalism, new forms of alienation were becoming apparent. Rather than emerging in the workplace, at the point of production, these forms of alienation were located in cultural and political spheres. Henri Lefebvre, like other leading lights of the New Left, criticised Marx for limiting his analysis to the economic sphere and the commodity form; for not seeing the effects of alienation in the political and cultural spheres of bureaucratic state power and the quantification, calculability and managed spectacle creeping

University Press, 1994); Charles Tilly, *From Mobilisation to Revolution* (Longman Higher Education, 1978).

21 Tenant co-partnerships were incorporated with garden suburbs, including Wavertree in Liverpool; see Johnston Birchall, "Co-Partnership Housing and the Garden City Movement", *Planning Perspectives* 10.4 (1995).

into everyday life.[22] Lefebvre was one of a number of New Left thinkers who provided some theoretical inspiration for the uprisings of 1968, particularly in and around Paris. In the multiplication of 'secondary fronts' of resistance, in the various movements from anti-racism to feminism, environmentalism to anti-colonialism, direct expropriation of surplus value through enforced wage labour—exploitation—was no longer always the prime target. These diverse political movements were all nonetheless responding to some form of exclusion from social life, which neo-Marxists began to re-theorise as secondary contradictions of capital, displaced from the workplace into the sphere of collective consumption and everyday life.[23] In shifting political focus away from the primary contradiction of capitalism in production and towards these secondary fronts in the realm of social reproduction, the organising concept of struggle and critical analysis, exploitation, was displaced by *alienation*, acting as a "'coagulant' making it possible to [consider] the unity of these various struggles".[24]

In post-war attempts to resolve the housing question, Lefebvre identified alienation in the discursive shift from 'residence' to 'housing', replacing a more active, personal process with clinical abstraction:

> It was at this juncture that the idea of *housing* began to take on definition, along with its corollaries: minimal living-space, as quantified in terms of modular units and speed of access; likewise minimal facilities and a programmed environment. What was actually being defined here ... was the lowest possible *threshold of tolerability*. Later, in the present century, slums began to disappear.[25]

As the modernist state began to eliminate the worst conditions brought about by capitalist urbanisation (through 'slum clearances' and the construction of council estates, new towns and the subsidisation of private suburban housing), this was, however, paid for through the imposition of standardised units measured according to the 'bare minimum' of acceptable standards, both in terms of material tolerability and the "lowest possible *threshold of sociability*—the point beyond which survival would be impossible because all social life would have disappeared".[26]

22 Japhy Wilson, "'The Devastating Conquest of the Lived by the Conceived': The Concept of Abstract Space in the Work of Henri Lefebvre", *Space and Culture* 16.3 (2013): 364–380.

23 Henri Lefebvre, *Critique of Everyday Life*, vol. 2 (Verso, 2002); Castells, *The Urban Question: A Marxist Approach*.

24 Razmig Keucheyan, *The Left Hemisphere: Mapping Critical Theory Today*, ed. Gregory Elliott (Verso, 2013), p. 37.

25 Henri Lefebvre, *The Production of Space* (Blackwell, 1991), p. 314.

26 Lefebvre, *The Production of Space*.

Only once the conditions created by technocratic state-capitalism were fully realised, and beginning to be challenged in this 'second modern cycle of contention', did mutualism and cooperativism experience a revival. The original cooperative principles enshrined by the Rochdale Pioneers in 1844 were reinvigorated in 1966 when the International Co-operative Alliance ratified its five principles: (1) open and voluntary membership; (2) democratic control; (3) fair distribution of economic results according to labour or consumption rather than capital ownership; (4) education in cooperation; (5) cooperation between co-ops.[27] This was the era when the housing cooperative movement fledged the nest and really took off. Its two wings were a more bourgeois-bohemian, lifestyle-libertarian movement associated with intentional communities such as squats and communes, and more working-class, place-based and community-led resistance to the alienation of council housing and the displacements of top-down municipal urban renewal. This was supported by an undercurrent of professional interest in an alternative policy solution for managing deteriorating public housing stock via a nascent voluntary housing association sector. It is the combined force of these latter two that are most significant for what would occur in Liverpool amongst other British cities, notably London and Glasgow, through the 1970s.

The co-op movement coincided and collided with several other, related trends in housing. First, self-help housing—defined today as "local people bringing back into use empty properties, and organising whatever repairs are necessary to make them habitable"[28]—drew on a long tradition in Britain of self-build or do-it-yourself techniques by commoners, cotters, squatters, plotlanders, homesteaders and rehabilitators of inner-city terraces.[29] The institutional precursors to community self-help were building societies founded in the nineteenth century as temporary organisations for working-class families collectively to pool resources to build homes. Another influence came from the global South, particularly Latin America, where 'barefoot architect' John F.C. Turner first witnessed user autonomy in practice in the self-organised 'autoconstruction' of informal settlements.[30] The influence of Turner's ideas in British inner cities in the 1970s was palpable—not least in Liverpool. This was the era of 'grassroots professionals' and 'architecture without architects' and became known (in often derisory terms) within the architectural

27 Johnston Birchall, *Building Communities the Co-operative Way* (Routledge, 1988), p. 176.

28 David Mullins, "Self-Help Housing: Could It Play a Greater Role?", *Third Sector Research Centre*, Working Paper 11 (2010), p. 3.

29 Colin Ward, *Cotters and Squatters: The Hidden History of Housing* (Five Leaves Publications, 2002).

30 John F.C. Turner, *Housing by People: Toward Autonomy in Building Environments* (Pantheon Books, 1977).

profession as the 'community architecture' movement.[31] This represented a shift from highly institutionalised, professionalised and technical forms of modernist housing knowledge—attacked as elitist—towards vernacular and quotidian styles designed by users themselves through new participatory design processes.

In this context, a number of writers and activists helped channel and give shape to the grievances with modernist urban planning and municipal housing being voiced by communities. Among them were Jane Jacobs[32] and anarchists such as Robert Goodman[33] and Colin Ward, known rather paradoxically as the 'anarchist planner'. Ward identified a tendency towards bureaucratic paternalism and alienation in public landlordism, which he believed treats tenants like 'inert objects' rather than active subjects. He argued that this 'municipal serfdom' was responsible for the swift physical dilapidation of council housing estates,[34] which in turn contributed to the rationale for their residualisation—the decline from mainstream to an increasingly residual tenure of last resort—and replacement with marketised social housing. Central to this perspective is the idea that housing delivered through impersonal state bureaucracies—and private sector 'absentee landlords'—alienates dwellers from their immediate living environments, thereby failing to instil any real sense of ownership or pride and removing all obvious incentives to care for and maintain the property. Crucially, this severs the psychologically health-giving and spiritually fulfilling direct connection with the home, so important for a sense of personal meaning, empowerment and self-identity. Anarchist philosopher Paul Goodman's ideas on the 'organism–environment field' are influential in all this: he emphasised the importance of direct engagement and interaction between the self and its immediate environment for health and well-being, personal growth and meaningful living.[35]

This holistic view of dwelling is shared by diverse philosophical positions—from those anarchist positions outlined above to more conservative perspectives concerned with the *privacy* of dwelling.[36] For existentialist and phenomenological philosopher (and Nazi sympathiser) Martin Heidegger, dwelling is the very embodiment of what makes us human: "to be a human being means to be on the earth as a mortal. It means to dwell", such that "Man's relation to locales, and through locales to space, inheres in his dwelling. The relationship

31 Nick Wates and Charles Knevitt, *Community Architecture: How People Are Creating Their Own Environment* (Penguin Books, 1987).

32 Jane Jacobs, *The Death and Life of Great American Cities* (Vintage Books, 1961).

33 Robert Goodman, *After the Planners* (Simon & Schuster, 1972).

34 Colin Ward, *When We Build Again: Let's Have Housing That Works!* (Pluto Press, 1985).

35 Carissa Honeywell, "Utopianism and Anarchism", *Journal of Political Ideologies* 12.3 (2007): 239–254.

36 Peter King, *Private Dwelling: Contemplating the Use of Housing* (Routledge, 2004).

between man and space is none other than dwelling".[37] In his exploration of the notion of dwelling, Heidegger asked "what is the state of dwelling in our precarious age?"—highlighting the housing shortage afflicting early twentieth-century Germany—yet rejoinders that "the *proper plight* of *dwelling* does not lie merely in a lack of houses".[38] Heidegger affirmed that dwelling is an essential activity for humans: necessarily including the narrower sense of 'building'—the dual activities of cultivation of the land and construction of dwellings—but also a fuller, more expansive sense of dwelling through the richness of lived experience, in the way in which humans dwell *poetically* in place.[39]

Inverting Heidegger's reactionary romanticism into a revolutionary romanticism,[40] Lefebvre posited dwelling as a fundamentally creative and meaningful activity—*inhabitance*—which he contrasted with the increasingly alienated and abstracted form of *habitat* in late modernity. Thus, for Lefebvre and fellow anarchists[41] Ward and Turner, the housing question was not simply that working-class housing was marked by material deprivation, as a secondary consequence of worker exploitation, but that it also revealed a deeper contradiction in the activity of dwelling, arising from alienation.

Ends and Means: The Point Is to Change It!

Lefebvre's was above all a critique of the disconnection of ends from means and the instrumentality brought about by the abstraction in capitalist rationality. Ward and Turner likewise highlighted the failure of the structuralist Marxists, going back to Engels, to distinguish usefully between ends and means in resolving the housing question. Answering Marx and Engels' critique of utopianism as a naïve faith in some unrealisable future, anarchism foregrounds the real utopian possibility of societal change as immanent within existing social capabilities; refocusing utopianism from idealist future-gazing towards a present pregnant with as yet unrealised possibilities.[42] The intimate relation

37 Martin Heidegger, "Building Dwelling Thinking", in David Farrell Krell, ed., *Basic Writings* (Routledge, 1978), pp. 347–363 (pp. 349 and 362).

38 Heidegger, "Building Dwelling Thinking", p. 363.

39 Martin Heidegger, "'... Poetically Man Dwells...'", in *Poetry, Language, Thought*, ed. Martin Heidegger and Albert Hofstadter (Harper & Row, 1971), pp. 213–229.

40 Japhy Wilson, "'The Devastating Conquest of the Lived by the Conceived': The Concept of Abstract Space in the Work of Henri Lefebvre", *Space and Culture* 16.3 (2013): 364–380.

41 In answer to the question of whether he was an anarchist, Lefebvre is renowned to have replied, "no, I'm a Marxist, of course, so that one day we can all become anarchists!" Quoted in Andy Merrifield, *Henri Lefebvre: A Critical Introduction* (Routledge, 2006), p. xxvi.

42 Stuart White, "Making Anarchism Respectable? The Social Philosophy of Colin Ward", *Journal of Political Ideologies* 12.1 (2007): 11–28; Nathaniel Coleman, "Utopian

between ends and means in political action is expressed in the core principle of 'prefiguration'—the idea of cultivating social relations which prefigure in present practices those aspects aimed for in future. This counterintuitive sense of the performativity of prefiguration is encapsulated by critical geographer Paul Chatterton as 'demanding the urban impossible'.[43] But the idea need not be so paradoxical as initially appears.

For Ward, prefigurative experiments in cooperative living based on quotidian practices of mutual aid are "like a seed beneath the snow, buried under the weight of the state and its bureaucracy, capitalism and its waste".[44] If carefully cultivated and given the space to grow such seeds existing in the "interstices of the dominant power structure"[45] might eventually transform this structure incrementally from within through proactive social change. One of his biggest influences, theological philosopher Martin Buber, was fond of quoting another of Ward's anarchist influences, Gustav Landauer, who viewed the capitalist state not simply as an external apparatus that can be destroyed by revolution but as "a condition, a certain relationship between human beings, a mode of human behaviour; we destroy it by contracting other relationships, by behaving differently".[46] Such a perspective has inspired the autonomist Marxist tradition, which emphasises how capitalism—like any seemingly abstract social structure—is actively created by its participants through embodied everyday action. Interestingly, *Crack Capitalism*, John Holloway's popular book on bringing about revolutionary change through growing alternatives in, and thereby slowly breaking open, the 'cracks in capitalism',[47] was originally to be called—as Graeber has revealed[48]—*Stop Making Capitalism*. Pre- and post-capitalist practices already exist in society, within the very same social spaces as those partially colonised by capitalism, which only survives as an edifice kept alive by the subterranean forces of mutual aid and voluntary association.

From another angle, J.K. Gibson-Graham critique structural Marxism for its 'strong theorising'—a negative, paranoid, conspiratorial perspective reducing all phenomena to expressions of some fundamental threatening thing, notably capitalism or neoliberalism. They describe this reduction of all forms of life to capital as 'capitalocentrism'. In reading for dominance, in being blind to diversity, we ironically reinforce the status quo, dampening and

Prospect of Henri Lefebvre", *Space and Culture* 16.3 (2013): 349–363; Colin Ward, *Anarchy in Action* (Freedom Press, 1973); Honeywell, "Utopianism and Anarchism".

43 Paul Chatterton, "The Urban Impossible: A Eulogy for the Unfinished City", *City* 14.3 (2010): 234–244.

44 Colin Ward, *Anarchy in Action* (Freedom Press, 1973), p. 11.

45 Colin Ward, *Housing: An Anarchist Approach* (Freedom Press, 1983), p. 20.

46 Martin Buber, *Paths in Utopia* (Beacon Press, 1958), p. 46.

47 John Holloway, *Crack Capitalism* (Pluto Press, 2010).

48 Graeber, *Bullshit Jobs: A Theory*, p. 238.

discouraging non-capitalist and post-capitalist possibilities. Gibson-Graham repeat Marx's dictum—'to understand the world in order to change it'—"but with a poststructuralist twist—to change our understanding *is* to change the world, in small and sometimes major ways".[49] Thus they call for *weak theorising* that can *read for difference*, more attuned to the emergence of innovation, possibility and creativity; "to yield something new" rather than simply critique.[50] This enables a clearer view of the diversity, contingency and dynamic nature of the institutions that make up capitalism, which are performed into being through daily practices as much as they appear to be enduring structures. It also brings to light all those diverse economic practices other than class-based wage labour that remain invisible to capitalocentric reasoning: alternative forms of market relations such as cooperatives, self-employment, state enterprise and non-profit social enterprise; and non-market relations, such as the gift economy, mutual aid, neighbourhood association, domestic labour and volunteering. In terms of housing, such alternatives might include squatting, self-build and co-ops. The ultimate solution to the housing question is not to sit back and wait for the Revolution when the conditions are right in some distant future but instead to seek multiple, partial, incremental solutions that prefigure—and thereby potentially bring about—a different society. This might seem merely 'utopian' to old-school Marxists, but it is common sense to feminists, anarchists and 'bourgeois reformists' alike.

Deeply embedded in this common sense, Ward's is characterised as a distinctively pragmatic or 'respectable' brand of anarchy: the modest dignity deriving from personal autonomy and creative self-assertion.[51] He saw such anarchy in the hidden housing history of communes and squats, garden allotments and plotlands.[52] This perspective rejects some totalising abstraction of a post-capitalist society produced in purity as an autonomous zone and affirms a hybrid view that social spaces can be more or less freedom-enhancing, the aim being to make them free-*er*.[53] Ward's radical manifesto for 'collective dweller control'[54]—helping inspire the Liverpool co-op movement—was strongly influenced by Turner's framework for 'user autonomy' in self-help housing. He frequently quotes what he calls Turner's First Law of Housing:

49 J.K. Gibson-Graham, "Diverse Economies: Performative Practices for 'Other Worlds'", *Progress in Human Geography* 32.5 (2008): 613–632 (p. 615).

50 Gibson-Graham, "Diverse Economies", p. 619.

51 Stuart White, "Making Anarchism Respectable? The Social Philosophy of Colin Ward", *Journal of Political Ideologies* 12.1 (2007): 11–28.

52 Ward, *Cotters and Squatters: The Hidden History of Housing*.

53 Stuart White, "Social Anarchism, Lifestyle Anarchism, and the Anarchism of Colin Ward", *Anarchist Studies* 19.2 (2011): 92–104.

54 Colin Ward, *Tenants Take Over* (Architectural Press, 1974).

> When dwellers control the major decisions and are free to make their own contributions in the design, construction, or management of their housing, both this process and the environment produced stimulate individual and social well-being. When people have neither control over nor responsibility for key decisions in the housing process, on the other hand, dwelling environments may instead become a barrier to personal fulfilment and a burden on the economy.[55]

Turner derived his ideas from witnessing self-help housing in urban squatter settlements in Peru, where he worked and researched during the late 1950s and 1960s. He proposed a housing system driven by what he called 'resourcefulness' as an alternative to the logic of 'productivity' driving the large-scale, capital-intensive, efficient yet wasteful, misallocative and unresponsive top-down system of mass housing under state-capitalism.[56] Turner advocated more imaginative, practical, locally attuned and needs-based use of resources for self-housing, through labour-intensive craft-based production, utilising local skills and knowledge. This was to be enabled by state and professional infrastructures, but driven by spontaneous grass-roots energy of people housing themselves through cooperative labour and directly related to the final product. Contrary to Marxist critics, resourcefulness does not entail the abandonment of technologically sophisticated and beneficial systems of capitalist production and organisation—as a kind of romantic fetishism of pre-capitalist rural artisanal culture—but instead promotes the *appropriate* use of tools and technologies to fit the scale and needs of the problem, with a subsidiarity principle favouring localised forms where possible, due to their convivial and fulfilling connection with the user. In this way, Turner's ideas fed off and into a current of radical thought in the 1970s which critiqued the technocratic rationalisation of modern industrial society and foregrounded human-centred technologies and socially useful production, popularised by the likes of Ivan Illich and E.F. Schumacher in their respective works *Tools for Conviviality* and *Small is Beautiful*. Turner's central insight was that the means are just as important as the ends, with direct participation infusing greater satisfaction, personal investment and the will to care into the activity of housing—seen as a verb as well as a noun. These ideas were to find their expression in Liverpool's 1970s housing cooperative movement via Ward.

Ward's radical call for dweller control—strongly influenced by Turner's ideas—found expression in Liverpool's 1970s housing cooperative movement; influencing the development of the country's first new-build co-op to be designed, owned and managed by its working-class residents, the Weller Street

55 Turner and Fichter, *Freedom to Build*, p. 241.

56 Turner, *Housing by People*; Turner, "Housing in Three Dimensions".

Co-op. In a personal interview, Ward explains the impact of his book *Tenants Take Over*:[57]

> The book had a salutary effect in Liverpool during a brief period when the Liberals controlled the city's housing policy. It inspired several instances … of newly-built housing where the tenants of old slum houses were enabled to find a site, and commission an architect to design their own new housing … The proudest moment of my housing advocacy was when the Weller Street Co-op chairman, Billy Floyd, introduced me at a meeting by waving a tattered copy of *Tenants Take Over* and saying: "Here's the man who wrote the Old Testament … But we *built* the New Jerusalem!"[58]

The Weller Street campaign ignited what some have dubbed Liverpool's "Co-op Spring"[59] or "new-build cooperative revolution",[60] fuelling what became the country's largest such movement. This constituted an extraordinary shift from a situation in which most of Liverpool's working-class residents were housed by the 'Corpy', without any control over the type, design or location of their home, to one where for the first time they had genuine decision-making power over these aspects and a real sense of ownership. It incorporated radical new ideas around dweller control, design democracy and participatory techniques, then being experimented with in the community architecture movement; and inspired successive groups of council tenants to develop a new wave of new-build co-ops across Liverpool. This remarkable period in which various fortunate factors came together in mutual combination to produce around 50 resident-led co-ops, of which most still function today, is the subject of the following chapters.

57 Ward, *Tenants Take Over*.

58 Colin Ward and David Goodway, *Talking Anarchy, 2003* (Five Leaves Publications, 2003), pp. 74–75.

59 Ospina, *Housing Ourselves*.

60 CDS, *Building Democracy: Housing Cooperatives on Merseyside. Update '94* (Cooperative Development Services (Liverpool) Ltd, 1994), p. 7.

CHAPTER 4

Liverpool's Co-operative Revolution

From its inception in the late 1970s, the co-operative movement spread rapidly across Liverpool and beyond to Merseyside in the following decade. Its geographical spread suggests the movement was groundbreaking in more than one respect. Catherine Meredith, the chief executive of Co-operative Development Services (CDS), Liverpool's leading co-op support organisation, has claimed that

> The scale and number of co-ops on Merseyside, alongside the very radical approach taken to the control of the design process, represents a major innovation which has no comparable phenomenon in Western Europe.[1]

Paul Lusk, a co-op development worker for CDS, said at the time:

> What's happening now, in Liverpool, is that a new form of public sector housing is being developed … new-build co-ops. Only through new-building do you have the opportunity to shape an environment. And it's going to be … a major, possibly dominant, form of public housing in the twentieth century. And the Weller Streets would have been the model.[2]

More-disinterested commentators have characterised it as the beginning of a new paradigm in public housing—public sector housing 2.0, mark II, or phase 2—as evident in the title of architect Nick Wates' contemporaneous exposition of Liverpool's co-op movement in the *Architects' Journal*.[3] It was seen by many as the birth of the third sector, but one distinct from the large-scale housing association sector we see today, heralding a radical new model,

1 CDS, *Building Democracy: Housing Cooperatives on Merseyside. Update '94* (Cooperative Development Services (Liverpool) Ltd, 1994), p. 10.

2 Interview with Paul Lusk in Alan McDonald, *The Weller Way: The Story of the Weller Street Housing Cooperative* (Faber & Faber, 1986), p. 208.

3 Nick Wates, "The Liverpool Breakthrough: Or Public Sector Housing Phase 2", *Architects' Journal* (8 Sept. 1982).

the Weller Way of doing things. This put residents in the driving seat of a development machine funded, legislated and regulated by the central state but deploying resources through an unprecedentedly decentralised programme of design and construction, using a range of local professional services organisations, all chosen and commissioned by residents themselves. A political figure centrally involved in constructing this new model explained to me the motivation behind the idea:

> There's a possibility here of public housing mark II. Instead of the state or the Corpy being in charge and doing a miserable job, why can't people who don't have educational qualifications, don't have often much of an employment, don't have the money, why can't they nonetheless be in charge of running their own estates?

Clearly, this cuts two ways: hinting at a possible progressive future of democratic control over housing resources yet also of a presently fashionable policy for offloading responsibilities for public services onto communities that lack the capacity to run them. The latter appears to have won out. Why is that the case? Did the Liverpool co-op model ever have a chance of healing the symptoms of the housing question, if only at a local level? And why have we not seen Liverpool's new-build co-op model replicated across the country to become the dominant form of public housing, as a potential solution to the housing question nationally, if not globally? In this chapter I reconstruct the social and political history of how the new-build co-op movement in Liverpool came to be considered by some as the blueprint for Public Housing 2.0—and attempt to provide some explanation as to why such bold predictions ultimately failed to materialise.

To understand why the co-op movement was so successful in Liverpool during the 1970s, we need to grasp the extraordinary historical context from which it sprung. Liverpool was unusual among the northern industrial cities dominated by the working classes for electing Liberal and Tory council administrations when others voted in Labour. This was partly due to the religious sectarianism dividing the city since the Irish Catholic migration in the nineteenth century. Tory paternalism coupled with the desperate need to resolve severe inner-city overcrowding and squalor informed inter-war policies of slum clearance and construction of new estates on the then metropolitan periphery, starting with Norris Green.[4] In the 1950s, the labour movement—boosted locally by national political victories since 1945—began to challenge sectarian influences on party politics. In 1955, the Labour Party was finally

4 John Boughton, "Liverpool's Interwar Multi-Storey Housing: Building an 'A1 Community in a Properly Planned Township of Flats'", Municipal Dreams Blog (10 Feb. 2015): https://municipaldreams.wordpress.com/.

elected, bringing to an end a century of Conservative rule. This inaugurated a period of almost two decades of Labour control of the council, a political machine led by Jack and Bessie Braddock, who represented a distinctively right-wing, traditional, anti-communist 'boss politics'.[5] Under the Braddocks, the council embarked on a more systematic and large-scale plan of comprehensive redevelopment, decanting large numbers of inner-city residents to overspill estates and new towns on the metropolitan periphery. An article published in the *Liverpool Post* in 1957 states that "this exodus would affect close on 125,000 people",[6] revealing the huge scale of the overspill plan:

> 48,000 people would go to Skelmersdale (population at that time 6,216); 18,000 would go to Widnes to increase the population to 66,000; 19,350 would explode the numbers in the Parish of Halewood (population 6,216 at that time); 6,000 would go to Cantril Farm; 3,500 would swell the population of Formby from 10,000 to 13,500; 30,000 would head for Kirkby.

Collective outrage and resistance to these forced relocations expressed itself through various cultural mediums at the time. 'Back Buchanan Street', a popular folk song written by Harry and Gordon Dison in the mid-1960s for a BBC song-writing competition and broadcast on television, was melancholic and nostalgic in its refrain, repeated in each verse, that "We'll miss" various aspects of life in the old terraced streets. The opening and closing stanzas intoned:

> A fella from the Corpy, just out of Planning School
> Has told us that we're being moved right out of Liverpool
> They're sending us to Kirkby, or Skelmersdale or Speke
> Don't want to go from all we know in Back Buchanan Street.
>
> From Walton to the Dingle, you'll hear the same old cry
> Stop messin' round with Liverpool at least until we die
> Don't want to go to Kirkby, or Skelmersdale or Speke
> Don't want to go from all we know in Back Buchanan Street.

The threat of displacement and the breaking up of tight-knit communities was one of the main drivers behind the development of campaigns for cooperative alternatives. But it was not simply resistance to relocation out of Liverpool proper that galvanised the movement from below—it was also

5 Merseyside Socialist Research Group, *Merseyside in Crisis* (Manchester Free Press, 1980).
6 Quoted in chapter 24 of Ken Rogers, *The Lost Tribe of Everton and Scottie Road* (Trinity Mirror Sport Media, 2010).

the terrible conditions of the existing housing within the inner city. The nineteenth-century two-up two-down terraced houses were insanitary by modern standards, often 'back-to-back'—windowless internal back walls built against the houses behind—or else separated by a narrow alley. It was no accident, one of the architects of the new-build co-ops told me, that the Council's redevelopment policy was called the 'Slum Clearance Programme': "You were saying 'slum' is quite a harsh word, but all those houses had outside toilets ... It was pretty primitive, and there were thousands of them like that".

In response, the council replaced thousands of terraces with tenements and high-rise blocks. Part of the slum clearance programme entailed the construction of new tenements on the sites of old terraces. Yet the tenements built in their place soon deteriorated. By far the most notorious of these were the trio of tower blocks colloquially known as 'the Piggeries' or the 'ugly sisters', built in 1965 in Everton to replace slum terraced housing. Conditions deteriorated so rapidly (partly due to a lack of dweller control) that tenants were swiftly moved to rent strike. A council officer at the time recalls how the Piggeries were

> Only about five years old, but so badly built that the tenants had gone on rent strike and therefore the council, in direct retaliation, had gone on a repairs strike ... Within another five or six years the blocks had gone. So there was great hunger for anything that was better.

When residents resisted, in such large numbers, living in these conditions, the council had little choice but to begin emptying flats out in preparation for demolition, which, a resident of the Piggeries remembers, made conditions even worse for those unfortunate enough to remain until the very end:

> The conditions towards the end were appalling. Once something has been declared for demolition everyone stops caring. Some of those flats stood for less than ten years when the previous terraced streets, as bad as the conditions were, had stood for a century.[7]

A leading co-op activist concurs that conditions in the tenements were a principal motivation for co-op campaigning:

> When they actually built them, they were just thrown up, they were laid on top of all the sewerage system, it wasn't replaced, so that started to crack, people had sewage literally coming up into their properties ... I went upstairs, and she had not just black mould in the corner, it was

7 Quoted in chapter 30 in Rogers, *The Lost Tribe*.

> like a black blanket right the way across the ceiling … so they were all living downstairs and the sewage was coming through.

Hidden behind these images is a story of neglect and bureaucratic failure. A council housing manager at the time remembers "one tenement, Melrose Place, where they were actually fitting in new gas fires at one end while they were demolishing the other, because the contract had already been made—it was madness!" Another describes how the Corpy had become "a shockingly poor landlord", exemplified in the working culture of the Scotland Road office, where he "managed fourteen to fifteen thousand properties with a team of about 25 of us, so it was quickly getting out of control; and the culture in there despised the tenants … The poetic name for the tenants was 'deadbeats'". Conditions were so bad in some of the high-rise blocks that repair reports were simply ignored: "At the end of every day they were thrown away, because the council was just refusing to do repairs".

Various rent strikes and marches mark this period, from the 1960s to the 1980s, in which residents of council tenements organised to challenge neglect, mismanagement and rent rises. Collective action came to a head in 1972, in reaction to the Conservative government's 1972 Housing Finance Act, which brought in so-called 'fair rents', representing rent rises for council tenancies of 25 per cent. Many Labour Councils across the country were re-elected on the strength of pledges to resist implementation of the Act.[8] In Liverpool, Labour councillors were unable to prevent Tory and Liberal members forming a majority to vote in the measure. Marches were organised across Merseyside with around three thousand protestors led by tenants' campaign groups marching to the Pier Head.

One particularly prominent example of the 1972 rent strikes occurred in Kirkby, in the Metropolitan Borough of Knowsley, one of the 'overspill' new towns built to the east of Liverpool in the 1950s and 1960s as part of the slum clearance programme but which, by the early 1970s, was, like Liverpool itself, suffering with severe unemployment and social problems as the multinational company branch plants that had located there began to close.[9] Women from one particular estate, Tower Hill—an overspill of an overspill—were particularly vocal in response to the factory closures and the 1972 Housing Finance Act, organising discussion and support groups and forming the Tower Hill Unfair Rents Action Group. The group initiated a fourteen-month-long rent strike involving some three thousand tenants in Kirkby. This is as good an example as any of how the male-dominated domains

8 Merseyside Socialist Research Group, *Merseyside in Crisis*.

9 Richard Meegan, "Merseyside in Crisis and in Conflict", in Michael Harloe, Chris Pickvance and John Urry, eds, *Place, Policy and Politics: Do Localities Matter?* (Routledge, 1990), pp. 67–83.

of docklands militancy outflew their origins into female-led struggles in the sphere of reproduction. A decade later, Kirkby women were once again leading the campaigns for new-build housing co-ops to replace the crumbling tenement blocks—a subject I touch upon towards the end of Part II.

It was these experiences, coupled with growing collective anger over the slum clearance programme, which eventually led to a diminution of support for the local Labour Party. In 1973, the Liberals were elected as controlling party on the council, promising a new kind of 'pavement politics' in place of Labour's boss politics or the Tories' paternalism.[10] The Liberals took advantage of various policy changes at the national level to install a new public housing programme at the local—one which turned its back on council housing and focused on private and cooperative alternatives, in a bid to diversify and decentralise what they and many residents now saw as moribund municipal housing. Before exploring these changes in more detail, we must first turn our attention towards a little-known policy experiment in Liverpool which did a great deal to pave the way for the Liberals' housing policy and the development of the co-op movement.

Rehabilitating Housing in a SNAP

By the 1960s, emerging urban social movements composed of communities and idealistic professionals were beginning to resist top-down comprehensive redevelopment and propose rehabilitation in its place. In response, the government passed the 1969 Housing Act, which put the onus on local authorities to consider rehabilitation through General Improvement Areas, specifically prohibiting combining these with slum clearance in the instances where residents preferred the option of rehabilitation.[11] The development of this new 'rehab' approach to regeneration was profoundly influenced by a policy experiment in Granby, a deprived inner-city neighbourhood to the south of Liverpool city centre in L8, unusual amongst postal districts nationally for standing as a place identity signifier.[12] The Shelter Neighbourhood Action Project (SNAP), an action-research programme rolled out from 1969 to 1972, was one of the first programmes nationwide to deliver rehabilitation rather than demolition of inner-city terraced neighbourhoods.[13] Founded in 1966 as a voluntary charity campaigning for the homeless, Shelter had by 1968

10 Diane Frost and Peter North, *Militant Liverpool: A City on the Edge* (Liverpool University Press, 2013).

11 Michael Hook, "New Homes for Old: A Cold Hard Look at Urban Renewal", *Architects' Journal* (1 July 1970).

12 John Cornelius, *Liverpool 8* (John Murray Publishers, 1982).

13 Des McConaghy, *Another Chance for Cities: SNAP 69–72* (Shelter Neighbourhood Action Project, 1972).

developed its role beyond just housing, seeking to resolve the broader urban issues at the root of homelessness. Shelter's Neighbourhood Action Project aimed to do just that. At the same time, the 1969 Housing Act opened up the space for local authorities to engage with voluntary associations in ameliorating housing problems. Following the 1969 Act, the council set up Granby Planning Action Area and invited Shelter to investigate local demand for rehabilitation of a section of this area.

SNAP paralleled the Community Development Projects (CDPs) then being established on similar principles: understanding the nature and causes of deprivation in twelve deindustrialised inner-city areas across the UK and finding requisite solutions.[14] Shelter lobbied for Granby to be included as a CDP, but lost out to Vauxhall in north Liverpool over council concerns that resources should not be too spatially concentrated. Unlike Vauxhall's largely homogeneous, stable, cohesive working-class Irish-Catholic communities, Granby, like much of L8, was (and still is) seen as the most multicultural and ethnically diverse area of the city.[15] British shipping briefly boomed in the post-war period and many migrants brought to Liverpool through seafaring work settled in and around Granby, including from the Caribbean, West Africa, Somalia and Yemen, Pakistan, India, Malaysia and China, alongside the Irish population.[16] New waves of migration in the 1980s due to civil war and famine brought many more Somali and Yemeni people, who now make up much of the population. Jermyn Street in Granby was home to the Malay Club for many decades—a social club for Liverpool-based seafarers from Malaysia and Singapore.[17] In the 1950s and 1960s, Granby Street was abuzz with shops, cafés, bars and clubs—the home of music culture for much of Liverpool, attracting bohemians and art students from across L8 to dance alongside the predominantly black locals. Some 60 shops lined Granby Street selling things that could not be bought elsewhere in Liverpool. Yet, by the late 1960s and early 1970s, as Liverpool's docks declined, this once prosperous quarter of merchant and artisan houses fronting tree-lined streets and grand boulevards began to fade, accruing a reputation for transience, crime, vandalism and squalor.[18]

SNAP was forward-thinking in conceptualising Granby as a 'twilight area' stuck in a 'twilight trap'—a vicious cycle of poverty compounded by societal

14 Martin Loney, *Community against Government: British Community Development Project, 1968–78* (Heinemann Educational Books, 1983).

15 Cornelius, *Liverpool 8*.

16 Madeline Heneghan and Tony Wailey, "Granby: A History", in Assemble, eds, *Granby Workshop Catalogue 2015*, pp. 5–9.

17 Tim Bunnell, *From World City to the World in One City: Liverpool through Malay Lives* (Wiley-Blackwell, 2016).

18 Michael Hook, "SNAP: Toxteth, Liverpool", *Architects' Journal* (10 June 1970).

discrimination. The acknowledgement of systemic forces by SNAP invited a more holistic approach. Writing in the final report, SNAP Director Des McConaghy (who was a great help in helping me piece together this history) proclaimed that "to deal with such areas in isolation would be to treat local sores without administering any systemic medicine".[19] The report recommendations anticipated those of the final CDP report, provocatively titled *Gilding the Ghetto.*[20] Indeed, SNAP prefigured later ideas in urban theory and the kind of area-based initiatives now de rigueur in urban renewal policy. More immediately, it helped incubate and flesh out in practice the General Improvement Area approach that had been given the bare bones of legal definition in the 1969 Housing Act. SNAP was the "flagship" project for General Improvement Areas and would later influence the development of Housing Action Areas[21]—both important policies for the development of the housing association and co-op movements in Liverpool.

Communications between Granby residents and the council were made difficult by local deprivation, transience, the hostility garnered by the threat of demolition imposed by the post-war slum clearance programme and also by the predominance of small-time investors—absentee landlords for a largely privately renting population. SNAP was to provide the vital link with residents, articulate their needs to the council and offer free advice on health, welfare and housing issues. Its main task was to deliver environmental improvements: reducing housing densities, repairing existing properties, reorganising internal space and installing inside toilets, bathrooms and kitchens. Generally, no such amenities were available in the nineteenth-century slum terraces. This became the blueprint for the General Improvement Area rehab approach. Yet the idea was to go deeper than mere physical upgrading: to work closely with existing residents to understand their complex needs and deliver lasting improvements in health, welfare, environment and employment. A local office for the SNAP team—comprising architects, housing managers and even a sociologist—was opened in Granby, allowing direct contact with residents. Street committees were elected by residents at SNAP meetings and task forces organised on each topic of local concern, such as housing, health and crime. Their findings were incorporated in the SNAP report to the council: an early experiment in community participation in regeneration and the now-ubiquitous 'co-production' of public services.

Yet the SNAP project revealed a complex knot of place-based problems tied into a Byzantine local bureaucracy that presented too many complications to be loosened by a participatory rehab approach alone. The principal

19 McConaghy, *Another Chance for Cities: SNAP 69–72*, p. 11.

20 CDP (Community Development Project), *Gilding the Ghetto: The State and the Poverty Experiments* (CDP Inter-Project Editorial Team, 1977).

21 Christopher Holmes, *A New Vision for Housing* (Routledge, 2005), p. 124.

problem was the scattered distribution of housing ownership and the large number of multi-tenanted private rented dwellings. Absentee landlords were not incentivised to invest voluntarily in rehabilitation, owing to low and unreliable rents. Of the 740 terraced dwellings in the Granby General Improvement Area, only 17 per cent were owner-occupied; almost all the rest owned by private landlords; with 566 in need of improvement.[22] The SNAP final report revealed a convoluted bureaucratic process of 71 separate procedures required to obtain a single council grant. Liverpool's urban governance was marked by too many competing agencies, regulations and contractors resulting in "welfare chaos", as McConaghy put it. Alternatively, SNAP recommended wholesale restructuring into development corporations coordinating local service agencies and strategically directed at the national level through a central urban task force.

The problem of rehabilitating multi-tenanted private rented terraces split between small-time landlords was partly resolved by their consolidation into co-operative and housing association ownership. One flank of the holistic SNAP strategy was to build tenant buy-in and find a common regeneration solution through participatory mechanisms. The other was to persuade absentee landlords to endorse the scheme despite their disinclination, before resorting to Compulsory Purchase Orders (CPO). However, blanket municipal ownership was too expensive in the context of large numbers of individual owners needing to be bought out. Local housing associations were therefore encouraged to buy stock from landlords and owner-occupiers. Shelter had supported the development of two key local associations: Liverpool Housing Trust (LHT), established in 1965 as a church-based initiative; and Merseyside Improved Houses (MIH), established in 1928 as Liverpool Improved Homes, becoming one of the first Shelter-supported associations, and later morphing into Riverside, one of the biggest associations in the UK. Both LHT and MIH were geared towards inner-city neighbourhood improvement using fundraising from Shelter, council improvement grants and mortgages. The SNAP approach innovated by Shelter was a major inspiration for the housing association and co-op movements, as this former LHT officer attests:

> LHT's whole ethos came out of the SNAP project. The SNAP project in Granby had shown, at least for a while, how much good it could do to one small area—not just on the housing but on housing, shops, all of the public services, and work intensively with the community in that area and turn it around. And so that became our idea and that's why we always then had small teams in local offices wherever we then went to work … It's how everybody works now, but at the time it was really quite revolutionary.

22 McConaghy, *Another Chance for Cities: SNAP 69–72.*

SNAP was directly involved in kick-starting the co-op movement. A small group of idealistic architects and housing professionals—living locally and working with SNAP—approached the council to negotiate a mortgage for the acquisition and rehabilitation of terraced houses. Granby Street Housing Co-operative was established in 1972, Liverpool's first rehab co-op.[23] This became the model for a whole series of replications, driven by aspiring and idealistic young professionals seeking to "make a difference". Shortly after Granby Street Co-op's establishment, Liverpool council designated a second General Improvement Area not far away, in the Canning area of Georgian terraces, and invited the co-op to participate directly in the improvement programme.[24] Granby Street Co-op declined this invitation but helped residents set up their own, Canning Co-op, in 1973, to rehabilitate empty council houses. Canning was full of what one co-op member describes as "the arty-farty middle class".[25] These co-ops were 'non-mutual', which meant that not all members were residents or tenants. This allowed outside activists to become members, bringing with them expertise to help establish and manage the co-ops. However, it therefore also dissuaded the full involvement of residents themselves, who were therefore not always given an adequate cooperative education to enable full mutual control.

Granby and Canning Co-ops were run entirely voluntarily, but the acquisition of further houses, totalling 30 between them, meant the workload was taking its strain on volunteers.[26] By pooling resources into a more professionalised secondary co-op, members could service both primaries more effectively. They jointly founded Neighbourhood Housing Services in 1973, as a subsidiary company wholly owned by members of co-ops using its services. This was Britain's first secondary housing cooperative—what many in the movement refer to as the 'mother' of multiple 'daughter' co-ops. Once in place to promote their development, the co-op movement grew rapidly: Neighbourhood Housing Services began with just two employees but by 1977 it had twenty staff serving eight rehab co-ops completing over a hundred housing improvements a year.[27]

A secondary co-op is a necessary but not sufficient condition for such rapid growth. How did prospective co-ops establish themselves and acquire land? And where did the funding come from? To understand the swift genesis of the

23 Graham Towers, *Building Democracy: Community Architecture in the Inner Cities* (Routledge, 1995).

24 Tom Clay, "The Liverpool Co-ops", *Architects' Journal* (5 July 1978).

25 Quoted in Paul Lusk, "Citizenship and Consumption in the Development of Social Rights: The Liverpool New-Build Housing Co-operative Movement", unpublished thesis, Salford University, 1998.

26 Lusk, "Citizenship and Consumption in the Development of Social Rights".

27 Towers, *Building Democracy: Community Architecture in the Inner Cities*, p. 91.

new-build movement that followed the rehab co-ops in Liverpool, we must first rescale our attention to the national level, to build a picture of the critical changes to the legislative landscape occurring in the 1960s. Co-op growth at the local level was preceded by the development of a supportive legislative, regulatory and funding regime at the national scale.[28] The establishment of the Housing Corporation as a government agency dedicated to funding and regulating a new collective form of tenure, co-ownership societies, was the result of colliding political impulses. From one direction came the promotion by key figures in the cooperative movement of housing co-ops as an alternative form of public provision. From another came largely Conservative calls for an enlarged private rented sector to assume responsibility for state provision and fill in the growing supply gap between owner-occupation and council housing. In the early 1960s, the Conservative government identified unmet housing needs in good-quality, low-cost private rented housing and homeownership, and sought to expand the cost-rental sector with £25 million made available in the 1961 Housing Act.

Inserting themselves into this policy context were two especially significant individuals: Harold Campbell, then serving as Secretary of the Co-operative Party, and, later, Reg Freeson, Housing Minister in the 1974–79 Labour government, also a Co-op Party member, and key supporter of the very first post-war cooperative housing experiments in London. Campbell was an influential promoter of cooperative ownership in the early 1960s. He persuaded Conservative government ministers to support co-operative housing alongside cost-rental in the 1961 Act, but dubbed 'co-ownership' societies as a political tactic to assuage Conservative suspicions of cooperative—and, by association, socialist—values. Campbell's lobbying of the Conservative government led to the establishment of the Housing Corporation—and his appointment as its Deputy Chairman—in the 1964 Housing Act as a body to fund co-ownership societies, a collective model originally imported from Scandinavia, alongside other forms of cost-rental housing. In 1965, Campbell helped found the Co-ownership Development Society, a secondary service organisation borrowing from the Scandinavian system, in which a 'mother' or secondary society helps establish many independent 'daughter' or primary co-ownership societies.

Co-ownership societies, however, had several failings. They were developed by professionals with financial stakes in the projects with too little participation

28 Birchall, "The Hidden History of Co-operative Housing in Britain"; Johnston Birchall, "Co-Partnership Housing and the Garden City Movement", *Planning Perspectives* 10.4 (1995): 329–358; Lusk, "Citizenship and Consumption in the Development of Social Rights"; David Clapham and Keith Kintrea, *Housing Co-operatives in Britain* (Longman, 1992); David Clapham and Keith Kintrea, "Importing Housing Policy: Housing Co-operatives in Britain and Scandinavia", *Housing Studies* 2.3 (1987): 157–169.

or input from residents, who were often unaware they were even living in a co-op. Moreover, spiralling house price inflation in the 1970s revealed a fatal flaw in the co-ownership financial model—trapping individual equity stakes in inflationary bubbles, enabling individuals to profit from their sale, and making capital loans too expensive to fund, eventually leading to its demise as a viable model. Yet the co-ownership model nonetheless helped pave the way for the next phase of collective housing experimentation: the 'common ownership co-op'. SNAP Director, Des McConaghy, paints the background context:

> The major 1972 "sea change" occurred when governments began to panic about a threatened collapse of the lower end of the private housing rental market. They feared the threat of US style "abandonment" of property and in particular the bi-partisan fear of any further "municipalisation" of our older housing areas. This triggered a Ministerial bid for direct control over public-sector housing—and that called for a new super national quango. Hence the Conservative's 1973 Housing Bill became Labour's 1974 Housing Act—and a tiny and moribund Housing Corporation was resurrected to promote and oversee a whole multitude of new local quangos ... a truly massive expansion of our "voluntary" housing movement. However, the bottom drawer plan was to eventually replace all our UK public sector housing in this way; and almost immediately, ambitious civil servants—and many charities and voluntary movement leaders themselves—saw this as an opportunity to pioneer the wider concept of the "privatised and voluntary state"—albeit one initially and indeed still mainly reliant on central government funding.[29]

This provocative account suggests this period of housing policy innovation inaugurated the now-familiar 'shadow state'[30]—the quasi-public 'third sector' to which our public services are increasingly outsourced. The Housing Corporation was resurrected to oversee the outsourcing of public housing to (previously independent) non-profit voluntary associations—like MIH and LHT in Liverpool. The 'great breakthrough' for common ownership co-ops came after Labour won the 1974 national election, appointing Reg Freeson as Housing Minister and turning the Conservative Bill into the 1974 Housing Act. This empowered the Housing Corporation to become the funder and regulator of housing associations, administering an extraordinarily generous funding regime of 100 per cent capital and revenue Housing Association Grants (HAGs) for land acquisition, development costs and ongoing management and

29 Personal correspondence with Des McConaghy, 2013.

30 Jennifer Wolch, *The Shadow State: Government and Voluntary Sector in Transition* (Foundation Centre, 1990).

maintenance. Labour's influence on the Conservative bill led to inclusion of 'fair rents', to be fixed by a rents officer, and tenancy allocations according to 'need', which guaranteed affordability for low-income tenants. Cooperatives, however, were not initially eligible for funding, as they were not officially housing associations. It was only with Freeson's appointing his political ally Harold Campbell as his advisor that co-ops were to be given this vital statutory status. Campbell set up a working party on co-ops to report findings just in time to amend the 1975 Housing Rents and Subsidies Act, which was to make amendments to the 1974 Act. What became known as the Campbell Report recommended that co-ops be allowed to register as housing associations with the Housing Corporation and therefore gain access to HAGs. Due to their inclusion in this regime of 'fair rents', co-ops became uniformly affordable to those on low incomes for the first time.[31]

The Campbell Report also recommended the establishment of a national representative body for housing co-ops, resulting in the formation within the Housing Corporation of the Cooperative Housing Agency—described as the "official launch" of the housing cooperative movement "after nearly 150 years of private experiment".[32] With 10 per cent of the Housing Corporation budget, the Cooperative Housing Agency was to fund the development of local secondary co-ops and crucially provide education and training for primary co-op members. This resulted in the rapid growth of co-ops nationwide, a quarter of which were in Liverpool, including a further eight rehab co-ops. The Co-ownership Development Society went into voluntary liquidation around 1975, following the demise of the co-ownership movement. It was nonetheless quickly reincarnated under a different guise, Co-operative Housing Services, maintaining its original staff and Campbell as its chair. Just as the Co-ownership Development Society had been set up by Campbell to support the development of co-ownership societies, Co-operative Housing Services was to be the secondary organisation providing services for local primary co-ops. And so the institutional architecture of one prevailing collective housing model was transferred to the next.

The 1974 Housing Act enabled MIH and LHT, as well as Neighbourhood Housing Services, to reposition themselves as leading players just as Liverpool Council policy turned increasingly towards rehabilitation. With the 1969 Act supporting the establishment of General Improvement Areas and the 1974 Act providing the financial and institutional infrastructure for housing associations and co-ops to deliver improvements, all the building blocks were in place for a large-scale rehabilitation policy. But the impetus was to come from a fortuitous change in local politics. In 1973, the Liberals broke the nearly

31 Birchall, "The Hidden History of Co-operative Housing in Britain".

32 Michael Hook, "Housing Co-operatives", *Architects' Journal* (29 June 1977), p. 1215.

two-decade Labour hold.[33] In minority control in coalition with the Tories, the Liberals pursued an alternative policy of neighbourhood improvement, expanding the voluntary rental housing sector and owner-occupation, whilst halting demolition and council house building. The result, a former Housing Corporation official told me, was that

> Liverpool declared the biggest number of Housing Action Areas in the country. Probably *the* most successful and prolific take up of the housing association movement was in this city—so major portfolios of private stock transferred from the private sector to housing associations in the older housing.

By the mid-1970s, Liverpool Council had the largest Housing Action Area policy in the UK, covering 23 inner-city nineteenth-century neighbourhoods. At this time, around three thousand terraced houses in south inner-city Liverpool suddenly became available for improvement, following the bankruptcy and liquidation of a big property investment company, known as the 'Hibernian' or 'Realmdeal' Portfolio. This was divided between the housing associations operating in each area, with the council zoning whole neighbourhoods over to preferred partner organisations for rehab. These council-demarcated zones created natural monopolies for the housing associations, thereby ensuring they were the only actors capable of delivering improvements under the 1974 legislation. The 'fair rents' regime proved too stringent for private landlords to cover relatively high costs of rehab, whilst the Housing Corporation's generous HAG funding and tight eligibility requirements guaranteed the economic viability of only housing associations. With the 1975 amendment these powers were extended to co-ops too.

Looking for secondary support to develop its rehabilitation programme, Liverpool Council and the Housing Corporation invited Harold Campbell's new London-based body for developing co-ops, Co-operative Housing Services, to work with them in Liverpool. But Neighbourhood Housing Services also decided to pursue rehabilitation as a means of expanding the co-op sector, and lobbied the council to be considered in the zoning policy. As a result, large parts of Toxteth and Granby in L8 were zoned for 'cooperatives' as part of council General Improvement Area strategy, with Neighbourhood Housing Services owning and managing the stock. Out of this competition, a Liverpool branch of Co-operative Housing Services was established, detaching itself from London as an independent organisation in 1977. Specialising specifically in the development of Liverpool co-ops, it was named Co-operative Development Services—commonly known in Merseyside as CDS. Rather confusingly (and ironically, for a movement promoting cooperation and coordination),

33 Peter Taafe and Tony Mulhearn, *Liverpool. A City That Dared to Fight* (Fortress, 1988).

Co-operative Housing Services in London went on to reconstitute itself as the Co-operative Development Society, still operating today as CDS Co-operatives, one of the largest co-operative support organisations in the UK. The Liverpool CDS (from here on, I will refer to CDS only in its Liverpool incarnation) was to spawn dozens of new-build common-ownership co-ops across Merseyside as the mother of the movement.[34]

CDS was now well-placed to capitalise on the Liberals' rehab policy regime, having inherited swathes of land in areas zoned for co-operative development originally bought by Co-operative Housing Services in the wake of the Realmdeal/Hibernian Portfolio. The majority of CDS's work initially involved improvement—with 823 families helped in total—building on the pioneering participatory techniques of SNAP to identify local needs through resident committees, meetings and surveys, conducted from a local office. A big change was to occur, however, through contact with a particular group of residents in an area of Toxteth around Weller Street. Having lived with deteriorating housing conditions for several decades, with no inside toilets, baths or gardens, and growing draught and damp problems, those residents who had not already moved away into more modern accommodation formed an action group in the 1970s to pressure the council to be rehoused. Despite the Liberals' preference for rehabilitation, by 1976 the council had nonetheless earmarked 57 additional neighbourhoods for 'slum clearance', "the fifty-seven varieties, somebody called them—and the Weller Streets was at the bottom".[35] But being at the bottom of the list crucially gave the Weller Street community time to campaign against demolition and explore alternatives. Initial action was direct and pointed, as community planner Tony Gibson details in his comparative account of neighbourhood alternatives: "They went in procession with most of their neighbours balancing tin baths on their heads and carrying leaky umbrellas to make their point"[36]—an early sign of the creativity and resolve the Weller Street community would show in their struggle to be rehoused together.

The council's was not a careful approach to regeneration: knocking down whole streets and blocks and rehousing residents wherever they had available properties scattered across the city. This meant communities were rehoused without being moved together—dispersed as well as displaced—as the council simply did not have the empty stock. However, it was generally agreed across the 57 clearance areas that the tiny insanitary houses were beyond repair, lacking most basic amenities. Indeed, despite nostalgic tendencies among some

34 Much of this background historical account of the Liverpool co-operative sector I owe to one of CDS's very first employees, Paul Lusk, whom I interviewed and whose excellent thesis on the topic I draw upon here. Lusk, "Citizenship and Consumption in the Development of Social Rights".

35 McDonald, *The Weller Way*, p. 30.

36 Tony Gibson, *Counterweight: The Neighbourhood Option* (Russell Press, 1984), pp. 20–21.

residents and populist commentators[37] to romanticise life in the old terraces there was a real need for state intervention to upgrade such housing, as this interviewee recounts:

> People's memories are with tinted glasses, some of those properties that they demolished needed demolishing ... People remember playing ball in the street and they don't remember playing with the rats in the street.

Weller Street residents were thus not against demolition per se but, says a CDS worker, "didn't want to be rehoused by the council, partly because of the quality of the housing on offer, but mainly because they would lose their community ties". They wanted to be kept together as a community and so approached CDS who, unsurprisingly, suggested they establish a co-op: one aiming to develop new-build housing rather than rehabilitate an old terrace. Starting with a committee of just eight—mostly young housewives—the Weller Street action group researched cooperatives and the local housing market, self-funded the creation of informative leaflets, held a public meeting in a local church hall and did some door-knocking, and by Autumn 1977 they had secured a membership of 61 households who elected a committee of fifteen who met monthly and reported back to the community.[38] In December that year, they registered legally as a co-op—a Friendly Society—and appointed CDS as their secondary agency, who helped them negotiate with the council for a site and the Housing Corporation for grant funding. Weller Street, like many communities across inner-city Liverpool, had a deeply antagonistic relationship with the 'Corpy' and sought greater autonomy from council control. When they finally acquired from the council their new site for the co-op in 1979, two years after the first community co-op meeting, a new slogan was scrawled across a wall: THIS LAND NOW BELONGS TO THE PEOPLE.[39]

Unlike the early rehab co-ops, the Weller model was fully mutual, with all and only residents represented as members, as joint collective owners—the most fully realised form of cooperative. Non-mutual rehab co-ops were led by local professionals who had indirect personal interests in the rehabilitation projects, as a CDS development manager attests:

> The early housing associations formed in the early '70s were actually formed by architects and surveyors and lawyers who saw it as being a

37 Ken Rogers, *Lost Tribe: The People's Memories: 2* (Trinity Mirror North West and North Wales, 2012); Rogers, *The Lost Tribe of Everton and Scottie Road*.

38 Gibson, *Counterweight: The Neighbourhood Option*, p. 21.

39 McDonald, *The Weller Way*, p. 137.

> pretty good way of getting a load of business, and at that time there wasn't a rule that said that they couldn't earn money out of it.

This interest often included protecting their own homes from demolition, if situated in nearby clearance zones, and furthering their professional careers in the housing sector. Tenants were given more choice over the design of architectural improvements for their homes, and Neighbourhood Housing Services was more open and responsive to tenant preferences than their private landlord predecessors or housing association competitors. But the secondary organisation effectively maintained a monopoly in architectural and housing services. Whilst residents had some say over cosmetic design issues, there was no real choice between agencies, nor was education in cooperative principles sufficiently realised. Real power over the process remained with Neighbourhood Housing Services and its managing team of professionals rather than with residents themselves, treated more like powerless tenants than the collective landlords they were meant to be.

During their bid for preferred partner status in rehab zones, Neighbourhood Housing Services committee members talked of "buying property over the heads of tenants and then pretending that you are a co-op".[40] This top-down strategy led to rehab co-ops being scattered or 'pepper-potted' throughout an area rather than clustered together as a tight-knit community at street scale. This resembled the structure developed by housing associations or speculative landlords more than by co-ops, which rely on spatial proximity for cooperative relations. Corn and Yates Streets Co-op, however, was the exception that proved the rule. Residents here were tightly clustered within the two titular parallel terraced streets, which they successfully campaigned to save from demolition. But the power to exert collective control was to truly assert itself with the innovation of the new-build model—co-produced by CDS professionals and Weller Street residents through a mutual learning process instilling dweller control in almost every aspect of housing: from planning and design to ownership and management.

You Hold the Pen, We'll Tell You What to Draw!

'The Weller Way' of doing new-build co-ops relocated control from external professionals to users themselves in a process first innovated by CDS with Weller Street but later adopted by other secondary organisations and groups:

(1) Residents of slum clearance areas self-organise into cooperatives as a means of being rehoused without being displaced.

40 Lusk, "Citizenship and Consumption in the Development of Social Rights", p. 127.

(2) A secondary organisation (e.g., CDS) helps the co-op identify a site, acquire land and apply for funding from the council or Housing Corporation.

(3) The secondary organisation works closely with co-op residents on education and training in a range of essential skills and knowledge, such as the planning process, interviewing, chairing meetings, accounting.

(4) The secondary organisation advises the co-op on suitable local firms and contractors, and co-op residents select a shortlist of competing agencies and then personally interviews them.

(5) Co-op residents are given the chance to select their preferred secondary organisation, aside from CDS, as their development agency to build, manage and advise on the project, as well as choosing their preferred architect.

(6) Residents work closely with their chosen architect to design a scheme according to community preferences through tenant participation.

(7) The final design reflects local needs but must meet Housing Corporation regulations to be eligible for funding, with tenants paying 'fair rents'.

Whilst this might seem relatively straightforward on paper, in reality it involved jumping through multiple hoops in a complex bureaucratic process:

(1) Registering as a friendly society (the legal form of a co-op) under Industrial and Provident Societies legislation.

(2) Registering with the Housing Corporation as a housing association capable of providing social housing, and receiving state funding.

(3) Making a formal application to the Housing Corporation for HAG funding for land acquisition and development.

(4) Negotiating contracts with architects, developers, building suppliers, accountants and other professionals.

(5) Negotiating with the council the number of council nominees for allocations, which was often set at 50 per cent if the council had part-funded development.

(6) Working with architects and developers to design and build the scheme according to planning regulations.

(7) Managing the co-op according to regulations pertaining to public grant obligations, such as developing a formal allocations policy which houses people according to need and on 'fair rents', and dealing with rent arrears and other legal complications.

For the Weller Street Co-op, hoop number five proved particularly tricky: the sites available were already almost too small to fit enough new homes for the entire community to live together, let alone additional council nominees. CDS chief executive, Catherine Meredith, ardently supported the co-op in council meetings, persuading them to give Weller Street full control over their own allocations. This is just one example of how secondaries like CDS were vitally important for helping co-op groups navigate the many pitfalls in this bureaucratic journey. Much of the political brokering, technical expertise and administrative oversight came from CDS. They became an indispensable source of professional prowess and cooperative idealism for helping Weller Street residents—and, subsequently, dozens of other communities—achieve their goal of collective dweller control.

Notwithstanding the crucial administrative, educational and support role played by CDS in the successful development of new-build co-ops, the energy for the Weller Street campaign grew from the grassroots. The community was determined to be rehoused locally, together, rather than displaced to an outer estate by the council slum clearance programme. Developing a co-op in your neighbourhood required extraordinary energy, time and dedication throughout a long and arduous process, which could often take four years to complete. This was an all-consuming and exhausting process for many involved, but one which produced some amazing unforeseen benefits. In *The Weller Way*,[41] Alan McDonald, a CDS worker who worked with Weller Street residents (and whose first-hand account I draw on as my main secondary source), renders a rich description of the campaign process: attending countless seemingly endless meetings after work; piling into cars in search of suitable empty sites across the locality; presenting site surveys to the council; petitioning local Labour councillors to back bids to acquire public land. Then there were the more formal committee meetings with CDS, interviewing architects and builders, and working with them on a weekly basis thereafter. According to the Weller Street Co-op's architect, Bill Halsall, this involved "late night debates in the pub … like three nights a week in the pub, getting it going in the early phases". Halsall goes on to reveal how the

> Intensity of what people were going through was at one level very exciting for all of us, but it was also kind of very destructive, you know, destructive of marriages … It was a high pressure cooker. At the time

41 McDonald, *The Weller Way*.

obviously people were living in a slum, so you can imagine a lot of domestic tensions and uncertainties.

Maintaining a high level of input over a long period, keeping the whole community faithful to the project, whilst also sustaining personal domestic life, was all the more stressful what with constant doubt and the niggling feeling that it was an experiment, that it might not even work. Tony Gibson concurs: "They told me that among the management committee membership there was not a single marriage which had not been at risk as a result of the tensions that the work imposed".[42] Whilst campaigning placed great strain on people's lives—the threat of burnout or domestic division a lingering presence—it also brought people together in solidarity, strengthening the community in common cause. It garnered trust between members, forged new friendships and deepened old ties—helping the co-op survive and flourish long after the more exciting development period was over. It also created mutually beneficial relationships between residents and professionals—each exposed to different perspectives and ways of working. This was helped by the fact that Weller Street, and the following first few new-build co-ops, were established exclusively in cohesive working-class communities with strong familial, kinship, cultural and religious ties, of overwhelmingly English, Welsh and Irish ethnic origin. There are sharp divisions between Granby—renowned for being the most multicultural area of the city, with the oldest black community in the UK—and the Dingle part of Toxteth, nearer the Mersey and the docks, where Weller Street and many of the new builds are located. No new-build co-op ever developed in Granby—perhaps because the early work of SNAP helped save and rehabilitate the artisanal housing stock, of higher quality than the smaller, denser terraces in the Dingle. More multicultural and diverse campaigns for mutual housing were to emerge several decades later, with Granby CLT.

Central to the success of Weller Street Co-op was strong leadership. A traditionally gendered image of a strong male leader silhouetted a common military metaphor used to describe new-build co-op campaigning. Many participants I spoke to likened the campaign process to a "battle" with the authorities; their male activists to "dictators" or "war leaders". McDonald cites similar examples in his study: the transition from campaign to management characterised as that "from the 'military' administration to the 'civil' one".[43] Once the war was over, the skills of leadership required would be very different, calling for peacetime leaders to take over day-to-day management: "Like Churchill, he [Billy Floyd, Weller Street's Chairman] was a warmonger; he was all right while the battle was going on; in peacetime maybe somebody else should lead".[44]

42 Gibson, *Counterweight: The Neighbourhood Option*, p. 23.

43 McDonald, *The Weller Way*, p. 203.

44 Weller Street resident, quoted in McDonald, *The Weller Way*, p. 177.

Such wartime leaders were crucial to the success of co-ops, using their authority to persuade powerful political figures to support their respective campaigns as well as convincing key gatekeepers to open doors to land, funding and planning permission. These 'warmongers' were strong-willed men with untapped skills in organisation and leadership, often employed on the docks—or whose fathers had been—and infused in local traditions of worker organisation and trade unionism, proving transferable talents for community organising. A fascinating possibility—implied by Liverpool scholars such as John Belchem,[45] Mark O'Brien,[46] Tony Lane[47] and Alan Southern[48] but requiring deeper historical investigation—is that Liverpool's encounter with anarcho-syndicalism, brought here in the early twentieth century through maritime contact with Spain's anarchist movement and the Industrial Workers of the World in the USA, had influenced local culture and traditions of political revolt and trade unionism (in the sphere of production) and, in turn, community organising and housing activism (in the sphere of social reproduction). What else could account for the radical edge of Liverpool's distinctive working-class culture, versed in spontaneous direct action and anti-authoritarian contrariness?

If such an influence can be seen to animate the co-op campaigns, it is less direct than indirect. Weller Street leader Billy Floyd was not a docker but a milkman, who, Bill Halsall told me, was "up at four in the morning delivering milk, and then finishing eleven or twelve at night, after the end of meetings: long, alcohol-fuelled meetings". Men like Billy were suddenly given the chance to flex their dormant skills and capabilities, wasted in their previous life. As one professional working closely with Weller Street remarks, co-op campaigners had been "lost in their day jobs until they found a vehicle. So the co-op process was a kind of a university for some people. In the same way that the trade union movement was a university for other people".

This process of empowerment and political awakening is evident throughout the rank-and-file members and remains one of the most remarkable and lasting contributions co-ops made to life in Liverpool. However, many of the benefits, and certainly the power, accrued to those in leadership positions: sitting

45 John Belchem and Bryan Biggs, eds, *Liverpool: City of Radicals* (Liverpool University Press, 2011).

46 Mark O'Brien, "Liverpool 1911 and Its Era: Foundational Myth or Authentic Tradition", in John Belchem and Bryan Biggs, eds, *Liverpool: City of Radicals* (Liverpool University Press, 2011), pp. 140–158.

47 Tony Lane, *Liverpool: City of the Sea*, 2nd ed. (Liverpool University Press, 1997).

48 Alan Southern, "Enterprise, Wealth Creation and Place: A Case Study of the Liverpool City-Region", in Lee Pugalis and Joyce Liddle, eds, *Enterprising Places: Leadership and Governance Networks*, Contemporary Issues in Entrepreneurship Research, 3 (Emerald Group Publishing Limited, 2014), pp. 227–257.

awkwardly, incompatibly even, with cooperative principles of participation, democracy and equity. Weller Street was marked by a problematic division between general membership and leadership, the self-appointed representatives speaking and acting on behalf of the rest: "The co-op, in its development period, was clearly more a 'collective' than a broadly-based democratic organisation. Members put their trust in a leadership, an inner cabinet that they believed represented them".[49]

This 'inner cabinet'—or 'war cabinet'—was composed of a management committee led by Billy Floyd, with three main specialist sub-committees, each deciding on different design and development issues. Despite efforts, largely on the part of women, to encourage other residents to get involved, the committee failed to inspire much interest from the general membership, resulting in Weller Street "operating on two levels: the committee involved in the 'co-op idea' [and] the general membership in it for a house".[50] But it was the female members who played a fundamentally important role in holding the co-op together despite this bifurcation. They tended to run the committees, rally the community, communicate information, gather opinion and sustain the tight-knit communitarianism "connected with the women's network on the streets"[51] that would nourish the lifeblood of cooperative governance. True of most co-ops across Liverpool, "generally speaking the men were the figureheads ... the women were the people who made it work".[52] A Liberal councillor at the time concurs, in interview, that Liverpool in the 1970s, particularly neighbourhoods in the south end, was a "matriarchal society".

Whilst the community, spearheaded by strong leadership, was the driving force of co-op campaigns, it was their interaction with key professionals committed to cooperative ideals that would prove so fertile a ground for social innovation. CDS was central to the development of an intensive participatory design process unprecedented in public housing. Its small team of architects, housing officers and community workers were, according to an outside observer from a housing association, "sparky individuals with enquiring minds", passionate about cooperative housing, carefully selected by Catherine Meredith, who had become director of the Liverpool branch before its independence. Meredith's management philosophy was to bring a diverse group of creative people together for a uniquely inventive and resourceful working culture in finding solutions to tough housing problems. One of those recruited was Paul Lusk, who "took on most of the 'educational' work with the [Weller Street] co-op".[53] Such an inquisitive and experimental problem-solving

49 McDonald, *The Weller Way*, p. 201.
50 McDonald, *The Weller Way*, p. 104.
51 McDonald, *The Weller Way*, p. 175.
52 McDonald, *The Weller Way*, p. 104.
53 McDonald, *The Weller Way*, p. 73.

style was critically important in the task of developing new-build co-ops from a blank page.

The learning process was ad hoc, auto-didactical, driven through mutual exchange between CDS workers and co-op residents. Lusk admits that "none of us knew anything about new-build. We were sitting there desperately trying to find books about new-build".[54] Whilst the initial co-op idea came from CDS, the design of the housing development process was the result of a creative collision with resident needs and desires. Residents demanded they appoint their own architect. This not only put working-class people in a newly powerful position as clients, but also radically redrew the coordinates of the traditional architect–client professional relationship. CDS's role, says a contemporaneous housing association officer, was "not to provide residents all the assistance they wanted, it was actually to provide them with mentoring guidance, so that they were able to organise themselves as entities". Thus CDS was more 'enabler' than 'adviser'.

The agency had a seminal role to play in educating and training residents with the requisite skills and confidence to 'do-it-themselves'. A CDS development manager explains how they "developed a set of training packages for doing architect interviews; because how does someone without any background in that sort of stuff interview an architect?" Four local architectural practices were involved in bidding for and delivering co-op schemes, including Brock Carmichael Associates, Innes Wilkin Ainsley Gommon, McDonnell Hughes and Wilkinson, Hindle and Partners. The last were chosen by Weller Street, and one young recruit in particular, Bill Halsall, was to be their architect and go on to design many of Liverpool's new-build co-ops, including the Eldonians. Bill was brought up in Liverpool with a loyal sense of place, not long out of Liverpool University, influenced by radical ideas associated with the emerging 'community architecture' movement. This was a loose coalition of minority interests within the architecture profession but with strong links into wider community resistance and alternative experiments in cooperative and self-help housing of the early 1970s, including SNAP and Neighbourhood Housing Services in Granby.[55] Probably the leading figure in Liverpool's new-build co-op participatory design methods, Halsall's thinking was shaped early on by SNAP. He describes how his "former partner Dave Wilkinson was the architect with SNAP, and as a young idealistic student I got involved with SNAP, on a voluntary basis". Indeed, SNAP was a fecund seedbed for co-op activists and professionals, as a co-op officer explains: "A lot of the architects, landscape architects—the 'urban discontents'—all worked for SNAP; and the

54 McDonald, *The Weller Way*, p. 73.

55 Towers, *Building Democracy: Community Architecture in the Inner Cities*; Nick Wates and Charles Knevitt, *Community Architecture: How People Are Creating Their Own Environment* (Penguin Books, 1987).

early generation of all those people who worked then with the co-ops were around and were graduates of the SNAP programme".

With the election of self-build pioneer Rod Hackney as Royal Institute of British Architects (RIBA) President in 1987, coupled with (or perhaps in spite of) Prince Charles' endorsement, the community architecture movement gained considerable influence.[56] Prince Charles, surprisingly enough, was a key ally of Liverpool's co-ops, writing the foreword to McDonald's *The Weller Way*, for instance. However, the label was not something consciously identified with at the time, as Halsall explains: "Community architecture was not a phrase that we used, because we wanted to be architects, real architects ... I always felt community architecture was a way to say, 'well you do that bit, we'll get on with the main act'".

Participatory design was about architecture being self-designed, self-built and self-defined—by users themselves—not labelled condescendingly as a 'community' offshoot of an elite profession. Nonetheless, the community architecture movement was to gain much of its shape from cooperative experiments in Liverpool. Halsall's work with Weller Street Co-op pioneered the radical participatory design process with which community architecture sought to associate itself. This involved participatory techniques and 'planning for real' exercises aiming to traverse the wall—for so long maintained by the architecture profession, not least RIBA—between technical architectural knowledge and lived experience of residents.

Just as the CDS–co-op relationship involved an intensive mutual learning process, so too was the architectural education more a dialogical interaction than didactical lecture. The architect was to learn as much about residents' needs and desires as the latter were to understand design possibilities and constraints. This enabled particular obstacles in understanding to be easily surmounted. A common confusion was the location of the 'kitchen' in two-up two-down terraces, which in working-class Liverpool could refer to either the living room, the 'front kitchen', where the cooking was traditionally done, or the 'back kitchen', which was more of a scullery. By simply engaging residents in modelling exercises such misunderstandings were easily overcome. The resulting design (see Figure 2) reflected residents' desires and aspirations, and better responded to their need for more durable and manageable dwellings.

Skills learnt in the co-op campaigns could be life-changing. Working-class people otherwise denied access to the professional discourses and mores of architects and planners were suddenly immersed in these alien worlds, picking up new knowledge and skills which would help them in their own lives. What might have initially seemed alienating and intimidating jargon—'cost yardsticks' and the like—was absorbed and put to good use in negotiations with professionals. Turning power relations on their head, individual members

56 Wates and Knevitt, *Community Architecture*.

Figure 2 "Utalitarian" community architecture of the Weller Street Co-op.

grasped the tools to expand their aptitudes and open opportunities to new areas of employment. The secretary of Mill Street Co-op, for instance, explains how a CDS development manager

> Got a secretarial job in an architect's office, not the architect who had done the work, but a different architect, because of what she learned: she'd minuted meetings, she'd explored the options for bricks and joist and roof tiles and goodness knows what.

Empowerment was not simply a matter of education and skills, but also of power, confidence, self-belief, identity and personal growth. Co-op development was like a "kind of political school" for many members who, inspired by co-op campaigning to enter politics full-time, stood for local election to represent the interests of their communities as councillors. One of the significant examples was Phil Hughes, the Treasurer of Weller Street, who was elected as a Labour councillor and eventually Chair of Housing following the fall of the Militant-led administration, helping later co-op campaigns to acquire public land.[57] I explore this remarkable turn of events in the final chapter of this part.

57 Tim Mars, "Mersey Tunnel Vision?", *ROOF* 12.6 (1987).

Competition: The Counterintuitive Component of Cooperativism

Another key innovation of the new-build model was the level of choice residents enjoyed in selecting their own agents and architects from competing firms. "A really big factor in the new-build co-ops was", Paul Lusk claims, "the competitive market". He continues:

> If we had been reliant on the architectural services that were provided by the CDS in London, and then by Neighbourhood Housing Services, the new-build co-ops would never have got off the ground. Those guys would never have gone out to evening meetings and listen to a bunch of residents ... The competitive market has got to be intrinsic to empowerment. It was because those private architects were competing with each other for the work, that they were prepared to go so far out of their way.

Lusk's seemingly contradictory assessment—that competitive markets played a central role in achieving greater user control in cooperative development—does not necessarily imply a capitalist model of competition based on the profit motive alone. The motivations of firms involved appeared to be a strange mix of political idealism and seeking status and prestige. Architects in particular placed themselves under great pressure to deliver participatory design, which involved countless extra hours and voluntary work from staff, generally working for nothing until the site was purchased. Some firms worked for two years without fees returned.[58] Most did not receive any payment until at least ten meetings into the process, with 15 per cent greater costs than their average housing projects.[59] New-build co-ops required great personal dedication and time commitments from their architects and co-op development workers alike. Yet local architects nonetheless competed for the work, believing the process to be worthwhile and enjoyable, for releasing the architectural imagination from the straitjacket of council housing and placing it in the service of the user.

Moreover, CDS's introduction of a market in architectural services was not only important for user choice but for the financial viability of secondary agencies themselves. Neighbourhood Housing Services, which used a monopoly model for secondary services, employing in-house architects and surveyors, was left dependent on its original rehab co-ops. In failing to expand and diversify its customer base, develop its own assets or compete for new contracts with the new-build co-ops, Neighbourhood Housing Services eventually went under.[60] Closing in 1987, its clients were shared out amongst Merseyside

58 Wates, "The Liverpool Breakthrough: Or Public Sector Housing Phase 2".

59 Hugh Anderson, "Co-op Dividends", *Architects' Journal* (18 July 1984).

60 Lusk, "Citizenship and Consumption in the Development of Social Rights".

Improved Houses (MIH) and Liverpool Housing Trust (LHT), as well as CDS. These housing associations were, however, keen to compete for the new business CDS had initially opened up, despite the commonly held belief, according to a former LHT officer, that "CDS were quite territorial about the idea". CDS's main rival was MIH, whose chief executive, Barry Natton, was locked into a competitive rivalry for prestige with CDS's Catherine Meredith. Tom Clay, who had started his career as in-house architect for Neighbourhood Housing Services, left the organisation for its lack of interest in competing for new business, and joined MIH, becoming Development Director, and bringing with him experience and commitment in co-op development. Another key figure was Jack McBane, a Canadian community development worker who told me he had his first glimpse of how co-ops could revolutionise public housing whilst working in London borough councils before being hired by MIH. He went on to help develop the Eldonian Village, writing the principal historical account of their achievements.[61] I explore their co-op campaign and successful development of a Community Development Trust in Part III. Jack explains that

> one of the critical things about MIH—and they weren't alone—was they were willing to use some of their surplus money (there was a lot of surplus money around in those days for housing associations to do innovative stuff) and they were really quite courageous in allowing that to happen. So they had for example a special projects team that I was put in, I was hired as co-op project manager.

After visiting the Weller Street Co-op and south end co-ops for inspiration, McBane realised that "the deal here is new-build, and it was pretty much agreed [with Natton] that the MIH co-ops would be in north Liverpool". Unlike the first new-build co-ops, who approached CDS for help, McBane claims how, at least for MIH co-ops, the "very initial push came from me", knocking on doors of council tenants in clearance areas and asking, "Would you like to be involved in what your house looks like?" These residents were already organising against the threat of displacement, but it was Jack's enthusiasm for, coupled with MIH's commitment to, the co-op idea that opened this up as a realistic possibility. Thirlmere Co-op was established in 1980, and this helped persuade from their initial scepticism residents of another clearance zone, in Leta and Claudia Streets. Leta-Claudia Co-op was established in the same year—both based on the Weller Way model and likewise designed by Bill Halsall.

The new-build co-op model was so successful that within a few years of Weller Street's completion a further ten co-ops were replicating the model.

61 Jack McBane, *The Rebirth of Liverpool: The Eldonian Way* (Liverpool University Press, 2008).

Hot on their heels was Hesketh Street, another CDS-supported co-op built on land that the council had initially offered to Weller Street residents, who turned it down due to size constraints. Hesketh Street residents had likewise come from slum terraces assigned for demolition and were funded directly by the Housing Corporation, relying on support from the Director of its northwest regional division, Max Steinberg. Together, Weller and Hesketh represented the vanguard of new-build co-ops, with a strong communal identity and collective will, headed by an ideologically motivated leadership, to stay together as a community and become politically self-governing.

The later new-build co-ops, however, tended to emerge from different housing contexts from the nineteenth-century terraced streets of Hesketh, Weller, Thirlmere and Leta-Claudia. This second wave of new-build co-op campaigning arose in the municipal tenements built in roughly four phases.[62] The first phase were pre-war perimeter block tenements, including one of the world's first examples of prefabricated concrete housing, at Eldon Street in 1905. The second, inter-war period, during the 1930s, saw the construction of monumental art deco tenement blocks, inspired by site visits made by Liverpool's city architect and housing director to Vienna. Third, the post-war phase consisted of three-storey 'walk-up' tenements built in the 1940s and 1950s on infill sites left over by war damage or pre-war clearance. The fourth and final phase comprised the four- and five-storey flats and notorious tower blocks, such as the Piggeries, built to replace terraced housing in the comprehensive redevelopment of the 1960s. Although much of the terraced housing was in good enough condition to rehabilitate, tenement blocks were by the 1970s in need of a drastic overhaul, and so the 'slum clearance programme' was rearticulated as the Liberals' 'tenement rehousing programme'.[63] Out of this came the second wave of new-build co-ops. Unlike the earlier and more recent collective housing activism, such as the rehab co-ops and contemporary CLTs, these co-op initiatives were almost unanimously pro-demolition. The first was Prince Albert Gardens in the south end, formed in 1979 and completed in 1983; shortly followed by other tenement-based co-ops, such as Dingle and Mill Street and Shorefields. Bill Taylor, a CDS manager in the 1980s, explains:

> The people on these two [Mill Street and Shorefields co-ops] were living in really appalling conditions—mostly four or five storey walk up deck access flats. I'm from a northern steel town and I'd previously worked in St Ann's in Nottingham and in Brixton, but these flats really

62 Tim Mars, "Housing in Liverpool 8", *ROOF* 6.5 (1981); Mars, "Mersey Tunnel Vision?"; Anne Grosskurth, "Bringing Back the Braddocks", *ROOF* 10.1 (1985): 19–23; McBane, *The Rebirth of Liverpool*.

63 McBane, *The Rebirth of Liverpool*.

> shocked me. To be frank, they were inhuman, and the council had not invested in them through lack of resources or whatever. Although the brick structures were probably sound, though in disrepair, their facilities, like kitchens, and heating systems, were really poor—probably not much better than the Victorian slums that people had left to move into them originally.

In part, the cooperative movement was a pragmatic popular response to these conditions. An ex-council officer believes that, during this new-build second-wave period, "The co-operative movement grew because our housing offer was just awful: the waiting lists were huge, we had squatters coming out of our ears and we couldn't manage voids". Her colleague agrees, indicating the scale of unmet housing needs and remembering how would-be tenants turned to desperate measures:

> Well, people on the waiting list used to just open up voids and just let themselves in. At one stage we had three or four hundred squatters … it was madness! So you can see why the co-operative movement was ripe really: "these won't do it for us, let's do it ourselves!"

Two relatively distinct phases therefore mark the new-build co-op movement: the first arising from 'slum' terraces among tightly knit communities who wanted above all to be rehoused together; the second emanating from dissatisfaction with housing conditions in the tenements built only a few decades earlier. Why had the municipal tenements deteriorated so rapidly? A large part of the problem was insufficient public funding for maintenance. This was not a flaw in the architecture itself or the design per se, but the result of careless treatment and deficient investment following construction. Depending on your political perspective, you can lay the blame at either too much public intervention in housing or too little. Owing to unique circumstances in Liverpool in the 1970s, in which neither perspective was able to hold sway over public policy, this debate was never truly resolved. Thus the housing crisis was left unabated.

CHAPTER 5

Liberal Compromises

Diluting the Cooperative Revolution?

Through the 1970s, Liverpool suffered political inertia—lacking majority party control or clear leadership in the 'hung' council administrations of 1973–83. In what has been dubbed Liverpool's 'lost decade', too little was done to rectify the city's worsening economic and housing problems.[1] The Liberals exercised some overall control over this decade, but did little to abate deteriorating council-housing conditions, pursuing a policy of municipal retrenchment. By 1979, all new council house building was completely halted by the Liberals—despite 12,000 people on council waiting lists and 10,000 awaiting transfer;[2] and around 25,000 increasingly dilapidated dwellings, a third of the stock, classified as 'hard to let'.[3] Given such worsening conditions, there is an obvious question to ask: why did the Liberals let this happen?

After nearly two decades of Labour control, the Liberals came out of nowhere in 1973 to beat both main parties as the controlling force on Liverpool City Council. This extraordinary electoral success was largely founded on Labour's failures, yet it was also down to clever tactics of capturing votes where the main parties were weakest, thereby making housing the main political battleground, as Michael Parkinson suggests: "The in-joke went that the Liberals had only one housing strategy—to build houses for sale in Labour wards and houses for rent in Tory wards".[4]

Resources were consequently concentrated into a private sector renewal strategy complemented by housing co-ops in potential Liberal wards, diverting limited funds away from existing public sector housing to do so. Yet there is no evidence that co-operative membership itself secured the Liberals any more votes. Most co-op members were traditional Labour voters and remained so after establishing a co-op; a few even went on to become Labour councillors,

1 Michael Parkinson, *Liverpool on the Brink: One City's Struggle Against Government Cuts* (Policy Journals Ltd, 1985).

2 Anne Grosskurth, "Bringing Back the Braddocks", *ROOF* 10.1 (1985): 19–23.

3 Nick Wates, "Co-op Consolidation", *Architectural Review* (Apr. 1985).

4 Parkinson, *Liverpool on the Brink: One City's Struggle Against Government Cuts*, p. 21.

notably Weller Street's Phil Hughes and Peter Tyrell and the Eldonians' Margaret Clark and John Livingstone.[5]

A more convincing explanation—than policy distorted by the Liberal's electoral ambitions—is the *lack* of policy altogether. Council housing strategy was paralysed by the peculiar political settlement—or unsettlement—produced by electoral stalemate. The 'lost decade', in which no one party had an absolute majority, resulted in minority administrations having to forge precarious coalitions. For the Liberals this meant the Conservatives. For four of these years, Labour was the largest party but refused to take control of a minority administration, leaving a fragile Liberal–Tory alliance to rule, but without sufficiently shared politics or coherent an agenda to push through necessary reforms. Conflict between parties over budgets meant that plans could not be made. Particularly controversial was the Liberal's 1975/76 budget, which used some of the additional £21 million central government funds allocated to Liverpool to top up revenue from local 'rates' actually to cut council taxes instead of supporting services like council housing.[6] The anger this instilled on the Left helped sow the seeds for the backlash within the Labour Party, ushering in a Militant Tendency-led Labour Council which pursued a high-spending municipal socialist programme[7]—including the municipalisation of co-ops—a subject I explore in the next chapter.

The reasons for this curious turn of events are revealed as we dig deeper into the party politics of the era. The Liberals were opposed to the notion of a unitary bureaucratic authority meeting housing needs for all. They opposed council control over tenant choices and monopolisation of maintenance services—believing this to be costly, inefficient and paternalistic and damaging to citizen capabilities to manage their own lives. Liberals such as Richard Kemp, who was Chair of the Housing Committee from 1979 to 1981, and Chris Davies, Kemp's Deputy who succeeded him as Chair, laid the housing crisis at the door of a bloated bureaucracy. This was held to be too unwieldy and distant to manage properly the ninety thousand or so properties owned by the council, which, according to Parkinson, "had virtually become a 'slumlord'".[8] Specifically, they located the problem in the heavily unionised and politically powerful Works Department—"the inefficient and poorly-managed direct labour organisation which maintains council houses"[9]—which

5 Paul Lusk, "Citizenship and Consumption in the Development of Social Rights: The Liverpool New-Build Housing Co-operative Movement", unpublished thesis, Salford University, 1998.

6 Parkinson, *Liverpool on the Brink: One City's Struggle Against Government Cuts*, p. 28.

7 Diane Frost and Peter North, *Militant Liverpool: A City on the Edge* (Liverpool University Press, 2013).

8 Parkinson, *Liverpool on the Brink: One City's Struggle Against Government Cuts*, p. 19.

9 Parkinson, *Liverpool on the Brink: One City's Struggle Against Government Cuts*, p. 23.

was leaving a backlog of repairs and failing to deliver decent services for tenants. Richard Kemp admits to me that "repairs cost us a fortune, we didn't manage our stock properly", and that such a state of affairs contributed to the Liberals' refusal to build more council housing:

> I used to go to public meetings and say, "We're such a bad landlord I'm not going to build anymore except special needs and specific ones", and that's what we did for three years ... Everything that we then put in new was housing cooperatives.

For a city substantially housed by the council and relying on in-house services for the upkeep of their homes, the Works Department enjoyed a surprisingly powerful position in city politics—threatening strike if its budget was cut, which in turn might inspire mass protest, or at the least incite the city's other trade unions to strike. This was at a time when public sector employment had become a crucial counterweight to Liverpool's evaporating port economy. Over a third of the city's working population was employed by the public sector; a third of these in turn employed directly by the council.[10] "Every 100th person in Liverpool", Kemp exclaims, "was employed in the Works Department!"

Whilst the housing revenue budget for maintenance went mostly to the Works Department, the capital budget for new building was controlled by council committees. This apportionment of political control over public resources created an interesting dynamic for co-op housing. The Works Department was understandably opposed to working on rehabilitating council-owned terraced housing for co-ops, funded out of the revenue budget. This diversion of funds out of council housing and into the third sector translated into a loss of future work. Tenants of the rehab co-ops would no longer be tied into maintenance jobs with the Works Department—they could choose their own contractors. The Liverpool Labour Party—alongside the labour movement—opposed co-ops precisely for this reason: their potential power to weaken the trade unions and liberate what was once guaranteed work for the public sector into open competition with the private and voluntary sectors. Thus the Works Department, according to Chris Davies, "threatened to go on strike immediately if we did this [diverted council budgets towards rehab co-op housing] because it would be a chink in their armour". This made rehabilitation politically difficult—and may account for the policy shift away from rehab co-ops towards new build, funded out of the Liberal-controlled capital budget rather than union-controlled revenue budget. So long as the Liberals could win a vote in the housing committee through their loose alliance with the Conservatives, Davies concludes, the capital budget could nonetheless be diverted to co-operative and housing association schemes.

10 Parkinson, *Liverpool on the Brink: One City's Struggle Against Government Cuts*, p. 13.

You Can Have Any House You Like So Long as It's a New-Build Co-op

Thus Liberal policy came to be geared around circumventing problems associated with council management of housing by expanding alternative forms. Moreover, they had come to power on the back of Labour losing working-class voters opposed to the slum clearance programme and frustrated with the poor service of council house maintenance. Liberal housing policy was a three-pronged approach. First, they promoted the development of private houses for sale on council-owned land around the city centre, for the first time since the 1920s, in a bid to end the council's century-long obsession with tenement-building. Aiming to instil a new social mix, this was augmented by a policy of selling off council homes to tenants, presaging Thatcher's Right to Buy and New Labour's Mixed Communities agenda. Second, they shifted from demolition to rehabilitation. Building on the work of SNAP and utilising the 1969 and 1974 Housing Acts, the Liberals rehabilitated over thirty thousand terraced homes though the country's largest Housing Action Area programme and housing association sector outside London. Third, as part of this strategy, housing co-operatives were to be, says Chris Davies, the "icing on the cake, they were the Public Sector 2.0—a Liberal approach to public sector housing in the inner city".

However, the Liberals' policy approach was by no means a coherent or systematic programme: described by Parkinson as "one-legged only"[11] for its overemphasis on developing the private sector at the expense—neglect even—of municipal ownership. On the other hand, it was passionately informed by liberal ideals for dweller control, choice and self-government—and this translated into one of the most favourable co-op housing regimes in the UK. But such a lucid ideology was strangely distorted by a lopsided housing strategy. Richard Kemp acknowledges their motivations were an incongruous mix of "a high blown Liberal viewpoint that people can and should be able to run their own lives", and a "response to the practicalities". He continues: "We didn't want to throw good money after bad; we knew that if we provided more council housing it would be useful, but it wouldn't be as cost effective or as good as finding other ways of doing it".

In this way, the Liberals gradually abandoned council house building, switching the 'tenement rehousing programme' towards new-build co-ops. Their inability to reform the Works Department for better maintenance services further fuelled the physical deterioration of the tenements. An increased demand for rehousing coincided with a diminution of options to just one, with perverse consequences. By presenting co-ops as the only route for Corpy tenants to be rehoused, the Liberals inadvertently created a surge

11 Parkinson, *Liverpool on the Brink: One City's Struggle Against Government Cuts*, p. 21.

in demand that slammed up against tight fiscal limits. Chris Davies reveals the impact:

> It started to snowball ... more and more groups started to come to us in the course of this period, saying "We'd like a new house please, we know that if we form a co-op, we can get one". OK that goes so far, but there's also a limited amount of money.

Money was limited for a number of reasons.[12] First, new-build co-ops were much more expensive than rehab, owing to greater costs incurred in demolition, design, land assembly, construction and development. Second, the Housing Corporation's budget was cut and the Cooperative Housing Agency—the subsidiary agency Harold Campbell set up to support co-op growth—was closed down in 1979. Third, this meant funding for the co-ops had to come increasingly from the council, with only Weller and Hesketh Street getting through the Housing Corporation funding process before an expenditure moratorium was imposed in 1980 by the new Conservative government. Hesketh Street found itself caught up in the uncertainty, with development put on hold whilst replacement funding streams were secured from the council. From then on, all co-ops were funded predominantly by Liverpool City Council, but whose housing budget was tightly constricted by the Liberals, responding to these strange and complicated political circumstances unique to Liverpool in the 1970s.

Despite the principle of choice underpinning the Liberal overhaul of public housing, their policies had the paradoxical effect of reducing choice to just one underfunded alternative. This undermined the foundations of the entire co-op movement—built on the ethos of co-operability and the active cooperation among members. This is formulated in the Campbell Report—the seminal document written by Harold Campbell that ensured co-ops were included as housing associations in the 1975 amendments to the 1974 Housing Act—which recommended that co-ops be developed only where "it can be clearly established that the tenants really want to take part in a cooperative venture and are not simply anxious to be rehoused".[13] Yet due to the failure of Liberal policies to overcome the distortions of coalition politics, co-op housing was now almost the only way council tenants of crumbling tenements could get rehoused.

What had started out as a radical—and marginal—movement for cooperative dweller control was watered down as the new mainstream. Ironically, the success of the new-build model had a 'bandwagon effect' that created a

12 Anderson, "Co-op Dividends"; Birchall, *Building Communities the Co-operative Way*.

13 Quotation from Campbell Report, cited in Hook, "Housing Co-operatives", *Architects' Journal* (29 June 1977).

groundswell for undiscerning co-op development. In response, CDS made sure that potential co-operators were sufficiently motivated. A CDS development manager recalls that

> People used to ring CDS quite a lot and say—especially if they'd seen their friend move into one—"I want to form one of these co-op things", and the standard line was "No you can't, it's too hard, go away", put the phone down virtually; and if they rang back like three times then you thought they were quite serious ... But you would actually challenge them in the early days just to see if they had the nous to go away and do this stuff, because the resilience it takes to see it through was incredible!

Popularity diluted the original principles of dweller control, reducing co-ops to little more than glorified housing associations, and splintering the movement into factions. On the one side you had Weller Street, who were vehemently political and thought of themselves as the pioneers. In his first-hand account of the co-op, McDonald notes that "to the likes of Billy, Steve, Rory and Kevin the co-op seemed to be a socialist idea: bringing 'power and control' that unions wielded in the workplace to bear on people's housing".[14] They were a "group that was 'high on an idea', the idea of a fight, a mission, a mini-revolution, not merely a way of getting decent housing for themselves".[15] Such ambitions were not limited to internal debate but often publicly stated:

> The intention of the Cooperative is that we should eventually become a completely autonomous organisation, responsible for running our own affairs. ... With the services of a grant-aided worker, we can work towards our goal of establishing a self-sufficient community[16]

Their aspirations for radical self-government distinguished Weller Street from most that followed, inflating their sense of ideological righteousness and collective confidence to go it alone. They eventually severed ties with CDS and set up their own independent secondary co-op as "an anti-professional alternative to the likes of CDS", which aimed:

1. To encourage co-operative housing

14 Alan McDonald, *The Weller Way: The Story of the Weller Street Housing Cooperative* (Faber & Faber, 1986), p. 49.
15 McDonald, *The Weller Way*, p. 69.
16 Billy Floyd, letter to Minister for Housing of new Conservative government, quoted in McDonald, *The Weller Way*, pp. 162–163.

2. To offer mutual support between co-ops and strengthen the movement.

By:

(a) Offering Weller Streets' experience to other co-operatives.

(b) Teaching co-operatives how to become self-sufficient.

(c) Providing an alternative style of education with co-op members teaching one another.[17]

Without the professional expertise of CDS, however, the Weller Street's secondary experiment failed within a matter of months—partly attributable to their fiercely independent, sometimes violent approach to getting what they wanted. This brought them into repeated conflict with their professional partners, culminating in a bitter feud with CDS—an organisation marked by an "odd mixture of business and idealism" and run by "middle-class student types" and "trendy left-wingers" with whom Weller Street residents had always harboured a sceptical mistrust.[18]

CDS did indeed have financial interests in the scheme, asking for 90 per cent of the co-op's administrative allowances provided as part of Housing Corporation funding. Yet the organisation relied on such income for survival as a business—and they certainly earned their fees. Almost all the administrative work was done by CDS, albeit increasingly entrusted to the co-op committee themselves, but who were initially trained by CDS. It is highly likely that without CDS neither the co-op nor the movement would have developed. They supported progress from conception through gestation, birth and early life: overseeing the full arc of growth and development. This was important, for the residents "never understood the problem as a whole. They only ever saw it in stages".[19] Despite these debts to their 'mother' agency—and the close relationship cultivated—Weller Street was quick to sever the umbilical cord. The split culminated in residents storming CDS offices to recover all 'their' files, provoking a prolonged legal battle. Weller Street promoted their new secondary to other co-ops at the Liverpool Federation of Housing Co-ops in 1980—a city-wide member organisation recently established on the suggestion of CDS—but were regarded as "oddballs, the socialists, the sometimes rather arrogant pioneers".[20] What set Weller Street apart from the rest were their belligerently political

17 McDonald, *The Weller Way*, p. 186.

18 Weller Street resident members, quoted in McDonald, *The Weller Way*, pp. 70–78.

19 McDonald, *The Weller Way*, p. 65.

20 McDonald, *The Weller Way*, p. 209.

motivations, expressed by a committee member as being about "Mainly the fight, mainly the idea: let's take *them* on, let's see who *they* are—'cause your life had been fucking dominated by people you never knew ... Let's have a go at them".[21]

Such a fighting spirit earned them a reputation. Weller Street got drunk on their own story of success, reflected in the common belief that they were the "only real co-op".[22] Their aggressive and uncompromising style of campaigning and political lobbying unsurprisingly alienated potential allies. In November 1980, McDonald recounts, they invaded a private dinner party hosted by Hugh Cubitt, then chairman of the Housing Corporation, to protest at possible cuts to housing co-operative schemes; climaxing in one of the members sticking their finger into Cubitt's soup and saying, "You won't eat that will you? It's contaminated. That's what our places are: contaminated".[23]

Ironically, Weller Street's single-minded defence of cooperative principles undermined cooperation with outsiders. Such an obstinate stance explains their dramatic fall out with CDS. This escalated from their specific opposition to CDS offering advice to the council on how to set up local authority co-ops. Weller Street's gripe was not with new co-ops per se—they were all for expanding the movement through their own secondary. Indeed, members were happy to be held up as the demonstration project for the likes of Paul Lusk to show the (Weller) way to budding co-op groups. Says Lusk: "Once they got big ... I was very keen we should use the Weller as a demonstration project, the model, the teacher for others".[24] What Weller Street opposed, rather, was CDS's idea of forming co-ops among council tenants, which, according to a leading member, was "assisting the Corpy to manage their fucking shite".[25] They saw council tenants as less deserving, having not earned their right to form a co-op, and whose "'housing need' was less urgent than the need of the Weller Streets members living in clearance".[26] Thus a division was cut between, on the one hand, the politically principled Weller Street—joined by close cousins, Hesketh, Thirlmere and Leta-Claudia—and, on the other, those that followed in their wake, forming co-ops with council support and funding as a means to get better housing.

21 McDonald, *The Weller Way*, p. 207.
22 McDonald, *The Weller Way*, p. 184.
23 McDonald, *The Weller Way*, p. 182.
24 Quoted in McDonald, *The Weller Way*, p. 181.
25 Quoted in McDonald, *The Weller Way*, p. 208.
26 McDonald, *The Weller Way*, p. 181.

Utalitarianism (Utilitarian plus Totalitarian): On Form Following Function

Co-op design outcomes reflected distinctions between factions. Weller Street's design was for ten identical courts of six houses each wrapped around a communal landscaped area. Rob MacDonald, now an architecture academic at Liverpool John Moores University who once worked with the community as a student, explained to me the layout:

> A series of L-shaped courtyards, very different from all the other co-ops … I actually thought almost Japanese really in its logic. Each northwest-facing courtyard, in terms of landscaping and management, each cluster was supposed to be responsible for their own courtyard, and then at the back you had the private gardens, individual gardens.

These courtyards were conceived as the replicable cell structure for cooperative self-governance, with management devolved down to what was thought the optimal spatial unit for everyone to get involved in organising collective life:

> Self-management will mostly be organised around the activities of individual courts, with each group of people co-operating amongst themselves. The overseeing and overall control of management and maintenance will remain with our management committee.[27]

The cell-like layout of identical courtyard units was the material expression of a uniquely egalitarian political philosophy. One of the leading members explains how "the idea of the design was to make the courts, to make them more intimate, packed away, everyone the same, no one having more'".[28] Bill Halsall remembers the internal debates between residents arguing for individual design choices set against the more puritanical committee:

> One of the co-op members dared to say, "Could people have different coloured baths?" which was debated round and round and round, and stamped on firmly, on the basis that this was like a bourgeois tendency coming out—to have an avocado bath. So the answer to him at the end was "You can have white with a grey ring around it like everybody else!"

Such an ideological commitment to egalitarianism produced what some observers describe as 'Stalinist' tendencies. Citing the Scouse propensity to "invent words on the hoof out of other words", Halsall fondly recounts

27 Letter to rent officer July 1981, quoted in McDonald, *The Weller Way*, p. 191.
28 Quoted in McDonald, *The Weller Way*, p. 98.

how members dreamt up a neologism for the Weller Street's distinctive blend of totalitarianism and utilitarianism: "our 'utalitarian' style—a sort of Mersey-propism".

The co-op leadership were acutely aware of the political sensitivity surrounding co-ops, anticipating the controversy they would help kick up during the Militant period, accused of being elitist and exclusive. Seeing as "half the co-op was related to somebody else in the co-op" and "two-thirds of committee members had a relative among the general membership", there was a concerted effort to "look to be fair. It couldn't be houses for the boys or the girls".[29] The 'utalitarian' design was intended to ensure that everybody had exactly the same housing—allocated according to need regardless of who they knew or how much effort they put in. This principle was taken to its extreme, with uniformity across almost all aspects, from bricks to letterboxes to internal fittings. Says Halsall: "Everybody had to have the same share of sunlight … no frills. It's like what socialist housing might have looked like".

Weller Street was an anomaly, an imposter, a mutation of the cooperative model into something more akin to state socialism, albeit at the neighbourhood scale. The principle of equality was taken so far as to contradict other key components of cooperativism: individual autonomy and choice. Weller Street was unusual for its persistent insistence on the principles of uniformity and utility. Responding to the opportunity to have different colour bricks for different courts, and different internal fittings for each household, questionnaire surveys revealed "an amazing degree of unanimity" among residents, despite individual choice not costing any more or causing any delay.[30] Uniformity was the answer because "uniformity would avoid arguments"[31]—an important rationale for 'utalitarianism'. But some members were understandably concerned that "some degree of 'choice' ought to be possible, otherwise how would the co-op be different from the Corpy?"[32] A significant strand in the motivational matrix was indeed choice. This not only included collective choice as a community—to stay together and not be displaced—but also as an individual, over the design of personal living space. Colin Ward's conception of dweller control is as much about individual as it is collective self-governance. What are presented in anarchist thought as complementary notions came into conflict in the Weller Street Co-op. The inner cabinet did not tolerate much individual expression, leading some members eventually to choose to leave the co-op, which they characterised as a clique.

29 McDonald, *The Weller Way*.
30 McDonald, *The Weller Way*, p. 175.
31 McDonald, *The Weller Way*, p. 160.
32 McDonald, *The Weller Way*, p. 104.

Contradictions of Choice: Defensive Urbanism or (Extra)Ordinary Sub-urbanism?

Hesketh Street was different. Residents chose a variety of individualised designs, with a resulting 25 or so different porch choices in a scheme of some 40 houses. It was derided by architectural critics for being "cluttered" and "not particularly outstanding", incorporating

> Many of the vernacular themes popular at the end of the '70s ... Like other "landscaped" schemes of this sort, it blends awkwardly with its urban surroundings and its design is somewhat inappropriate to an urban infill site.[33]

This reflected the striking incongruity—of the Liverpool co-ops in general—between their political radicalism and the ordinary, conservative, suburban design outcomes (see Figure 3 for an indicative example). The same critics, however, also acknowledge that "to be revolutionary doesn't mean that you have to lose sight of common sense".[34] The common sense of co-op members was for warm, dry, clean, spacious houses, arranged to promote social interaction among neighbours, where their children could play safely in secluded streets sheltered from encroaching dereliction. Having lived for so long in a state of neglect, amidst decay, dereliction, vandalism and crime, communities were adamant to enclose themselves off from the city. One of the leading Weller Street activists explains how they "all wanted to leave them streets; get down here; surround ourselves with a fucking wall and gun-turrets. We'd lived in that shite, we wanted to protect ourselves.[35] But such extreme fantasies were partly counterbalanced by their architect:

> Bill pointed out that "as soon as you have a wall, you get people wanting to get over it". They began to look at ways of making the scheme uninviting to outsiders without a wall: screening with trees, houses not looking directly out on to Miles Street.[36]

This defensive instinct arose from a strong desire to escape harsh inner-city conditions, combined with aspirations for something better than council housing, something more akin to a wealthy suburban housing estate: "They didn't want to live in terraced blocks put it that way, 'cause they associated that with slums. They wanted something detached or semi-detached and that

33 Anderson, "Co-op Dividends", p. 45.
34 Anderson, "Co-op Dividends".
35 McDonald, *The Weller Way*, p. 96.
36 McDonald, *The Weller Way*.

Figure 3 Typical Eldonian Village streetscape, overshadowed by the world's largest brick warehouse at Stanley Dock.

was the nearest we could give 'em".[37] Having lived in poorly managed council houses all their lives, the first thing co-op residents would tell their architect was that they wanted homes as different from 'Corpy housing' as possible.[38] Weller Street initially toyed with the idea of creating a village green as the focal point; their fantasy was the rural idyll of English village life. "Our intention", said Billy Floyd, "is to build a rural village in the heart of a dilapidated inner city area and rehabilitate a community".[39] This anti-urbanism was taken to its extreme by some of community architecture's highest-profile supporters, notably Prince Charles, who advocated turning the derelict sites of "crushed tower blocks" in inner-city Liverpool "back into countryside".[40] However, due to the physical constraints of their site, requiring a dense design in which to fit the entire community, Weller Street took on a more urban quality, of courtyard squares. Most of the other co-ops, by contrast, were typically

37 Billy Floyd, quoted in McDonald, *The Weller Way*, p. 92.

38 Nick Wates, "The Liverpool Breakthrough: Or Public Sector Housing Phase 2", *Architects' Journal* (8 Sept. 1982).

39 Quoted in McDonald, *The Weller Way*, p. 133.

40 Quoted in Patrick Wright, *A Journey Through Ruins: The Last Days of London* (Radius, 1991), p. 246.

cul-de-sacs, which Bill Taylor likens to "a sort of wagon train when they're stopped for the night", arranged in a tight, inward-facing circle. For instance, Leta-Claudia's curved terraced layout is, according to architect-academic Rob MacDonald, "like a very organic snake"—created by residents asking for more curves when their architect Bill Halsall presented right-angled layouts. At the end of the snake, in the middle of the co-op, MacDonald continues, is "a circle of bungalows for the elderly people and in the middle of the circle there's a little pyramid, like a community facility" with flexible communal space and toilet and kitchen amenities for shared use by all co-op residents. But without a masterplan connecting these wagon trains at a higher scale they are "like oases in a desert of dereliction".[41] Indeed, a Weller Street annual report describes the co-op as an "oasis in the desert".[42] The overall pattern is, for Rob MacDonald, "mini clusters of garden cities that are disconnected". What appear internally connected schemes are externally cut off from the wider city—a dialectic of simultaneous inward inclusion and outward exclusion.

This is not for want of city planners trying to assert their professional expertise. Residents' desires came into conflict with the professional mores of planners, who feared the creation of isolated, exclusionary ghettos disconnected from the urban fabric, lacking connectivity and permeability. A participant recited to me a showdown between planners and Thirlmere co-op, whose chairman, Reg Cummings, a generally "quiet, peaceful man", spoke up against professional aversions to their cul-de-sac design of inward-facing houses:

> "I tell you what mate, you either change your fucking mind right now or I'll get on that phone ... There's a bus load of people down on the dock road, they're going to fucking come in here and sit in this fucking office until you fucking change your mind all right?!" And the planner said, "Well, what do you mean? Mine is a professional decision". He said, "Stick your profession, I have to live here, and I come from here, and I'm telling you, we're going to sit in this office until you change your mind and see it from our perspective!"

Ironically, it was planning decisions that first created the urban conditions against which residents turned. Understandably not wanting to "look out onto an empty derelict site", with "no faith in the council ever rebuilding here", co-ops literally turned their backs on the city, preferring, explains an MIH co-op development worker, the "security of looking inwards so we can keep an eye on each other". In being given a voice for the first time, residents

41 Graham Towers, *Building Democracy: Community Architecture in the Inner Cities* (Routledge, 1995), p. 230.
42 McDonald, *The Weller Way*, p. 108.

were empowered to challenge professional decision-makers and contest their knowledge claims.

Not only did large-scale municipal urban renewal incite cooperative desires for defensible space: religious sectarianism played its part, too. The historical conflict between Protestants and Catholics produced divisive forms of urban design. Owing to council housing policy allocating on the basis of need alone, many tenements were, according to a co-op development manager, "mixed Catholic and Protestant, so there were disputes all the time, religious disputes". Two particular co-ops in the south end, Shorefields and Mill Street, had formed out of a group of residents occupying four- and five-storey walk-up tenements, but split into two along religious lines: Protestant Shorefields; Catholic Mill Street. This produced some interesting results: two separate cul-de-sac developments by two different architects, sharing the same entrance road, but spatially distinct and divided by back garden fences fixing firmly in space sectarian divisions (Shorefields opting for semi-detached layout; Mill Street for denser terraces). Yet even in the more celebrated examples of co-op design, problems still persist. Orienting co-op housing around an inward focal point—a community anchor or communal area—is great for internal community cohesion, but has the simultaneous effect of enclosing co-ops, cutting them off from the city, discouraging through-flow, and imposing spatial barriers between surrounding neighbourhoods.

In summing up this chapter, whilst the new-build co-op model produced so many benefits for those residents lucky enough to be a part of it, it also required painstaking efforts and considerable investment of time and resources—demands which made it difficult for the minority Liberal council, constrained by problematic political circumstances during the 'lost decade', to support new co-ops to a significant degree such that even a majority could benefit. Without this political and financial support, the co-op movement failed to grow beyond a marginal sector for a privileged minority. But what gave those fortunate few residents the right to reap the rewards of new co-op housing when most other council tenants had to put up with deteriorating conditions? Was it their ability and opportunity to organise proactively as a community and vocally express demands for better housing to the right organisation at the right time, coupled with the willingness and capacity to carry a campaign through to the bitter end? Should adequate shelter not be a social right granted to everyone regardless of their inclination to be entrepreneurial, to 'do it themselves'? These were precisely the questions the Labour Party, led by certain key figures associated with the radical left Militant Tendency, were asking when elected to the council in 1983, largely on the back of campaign promises to fix the housing crisis, left to spiral out of control through the 1970s. The following chapter explores this battle of ideas, and its concrete consequences for the co-op movement.

CHAPTER 6

Municipalisation

A Militant Response to the Housing Question

By the end of the 1970s, towards the end of the lost decade in which the Liberals did too little to address the housing question, council housing in Liverpool was in a dire condition. It also still housed a large proportion of the city's population and therefore remained a hot topic in local elections. Popular concern with housing helped secure the election victory of the Militant Tendency-controlled Labour administration in May 1983.[1] The Militant Tendency was a far-left entryist group within the national Labour Party, embodying a peculiar strain of hard-line socialism, shaped locally by Liverpool's history of radical politics.[2] Militant were able to inspire and mobilise large sections of the Left, many of whom had become disillusioned with the local Labour Party's historical connections with the Labour Right, carved by traditional sectarian loyalties. For some Labour councillors, such as Peter Kilfoyle, the Militant Tendency offered a "clear and simple analysis of the political condition, together with soundbite solutions, which struck a chord with the young, the idealistic and the naïve".[3] For others, they simply captured the mood of the city at a time, particularly among the young Left, when the Labour Party had forgotten its roots as the party of working people and needed to be reformed from the inside.[4] Through this initial appeal, Militant built support in the District Labour Party, which in turn exercised its power in selecting council candidates and developing the policies that would then be implemented by councillors once in office. By using the District Labour Party as a conduit to power, Militant intended to short-circuit the infamous 'boss politics' of personal favours that secured power for many ward-elected councillors. This meant Militant put forward District Labour Party delegates

1 Peter Taafe and Tony Mulhearn, *Liverpool. A City That Dared to Fight* (Fortress, 1988).

2 Jonny Ball, "'Militant Liverpool' as Liverpool Exceptionalism: The Rise, Fall and Character of the City Council, 1983–1987", *Transactions of the Historic Society of Lancashire and Cheshire* 166 (2017): 145–186.

3 Peter Kilfoyle, *Left Behind: Winning Back a Labour Heartland and the Defeat of Militant* (Politico's Publishing, 2000), p. 39.

4 Diane Frost and Peter North, *Militant Liverpool: A City on the Edge* (Liverpool University Press, 2013), p. 44.

rather than elected representatives as council candidates, which critics saw as bypassing the democratic process. The strategy worked: by 1978, there were seven Militant-supporting councillors on the council, and by the early 1980s, the Liberals were campaigning against what they saw as a poisonous infiltration of Marxists into the Labour Party.

Militant were excellent at mobilising the trade union movement and the broader Left into a Labour group which shared political priorities—anti-cuts, anti-rent rises, pro-public spending on schools, housing and public services. Labour went into the local election of 1983 with a manifesto that promised no job losses or council tax rises—proving very popular among voters. The promise of investment in housing, jobs and services was appealing after a decade of underinvestment in public services and a decline in employment by a third.[5] By 1983, unemployment was 24 per cent, double the national average.[6] Liberal Councillor Chris Davies, Chair of Housing at the time, recalls how "we'd lost sixty thousand jobs in Liverpool, across Merseyside, in those first Thatcher years ... Labour had this massive surge—it was a bit of a revolution really". Labour's famous political strapline—'no cuts in jobs and services'—was a straightforward vote catcher. A leading co-op activist, who fought against Militant policies before becoming a Labour councillor herself, explains the powerful process galvanised by Militant's political message: "People can gather around very quickly ... You get people on the streets, you get people energised, you get people politicised, you get people out there, you control that agenda, you move it forward". When Labour won the council election in May 1983, they secured an unprecedented 46 per cent of the vote.[7] Only nine of the 51 Labour councillors elected that year supported Militant, yet they exercised extraordinary power over the council's policies for the five years they remained in effective control.

Following election, the council announced a budget with a £30 million deficit to pay for their ambitious municipal socialist programme of rebuilding the economy and built environment. A large component of the budget was additional government funding for the appalling housing situation. The council argued this was a unique problem, under-recognised by government, which had cut spending on housing from £61 million to £38 million since 1979.[8] Central government contributions to Liverpool Council's budget had fallen from 62 per cent in 1980 to just 44 per cent in 1983 due to a recalculation of the block grant based upon previous expenditure, which had been lower than in other comparable major urban authorities.[9] Labour accused the Liberals

5 Frost and North, *Militant Liverpool.*

6 Parkinson, *Liverpool on the Brink: One City's Struggle Against Government Cuts.*

7 Hilary Wainwright, *Labour: A Tale of Two Parties* (Hogarth Press, 1987).

8 Frost and North, *Militant Liverpool*, p. 62.

9 Wainwright, *Labour: A Tale of Two Parties*, p. 127.

of running down the budget and setting (council tax) rates intentionally low in order to appease potential Liberal voters.[10] To implement their ambitious programme of municipal socialism, the council would either have to raise rates by 170 per cent—and by 60 per cent just to maintain existing services—or run a deficit, which would bring them into confrontation with the government. The Militant-led council not only pursued the latter but argued that this was owed anyway—that £270 million had been "stolen" from Liverpool by the government in response to Liberal under-spending. This created an enemy in the Thatcher government, which then sought to bypass local authority control to fund Liverpool's regeneration via centrally directed measures, such as the Merseyside Development Corporation, and support alternative schemes (such as the Eldonian Community Trust) that were either sidelined or outright opposed by Militant.

A central policy of the new Militant-led council was a radical programme of urban renewal—the Urban Regeneration Strategy (URS)—which, according to prominent Militants Peter Taafe and Tony Mulhearn, in their appropriately titled account, *The City that Dared to Fight*, "represented a complete rupture with all previous housing schemes in Liverpool".[11] The URS was a bold and ambitious £350 million programme of council housebuilding, centred on 17 Priority Areas, with a target of a thousand new homes built per year up to 1988—a remarkable figure for a time when, nationally, municipal housebuilding had all but come to a standstill.[12] The new homes—replacing over five thousand dwellings in dilapidated tenements and tower blocks—were to be simple suburban semi-detached two-storey houses with gardens; whilst fifteen thousand remaining council houses were to be upgraded through conversion, improvement and repair.[13] Housing was only one, albeit central, component of the URS, which adopted a 'Total Approach' to regeneration, including provision of new leisure centres, schools, parks and other public infrastructures and environmental improvements.

Despite highly critical commentary in the voluntary housing press,[14] the URS was undeniably popular among residents, especially Liverpool's large council tenant population. Workers too—including some fifteen thousand unemployed construction workers—were generally very supportive of the Urban Regeneration Strategy, which promised new homes as well as jobs for

10 Kilfoyle, *Left Behind: Winning Back a Labour Heartland and the Defeat of Militant*.

11 Taafe and Mulhearn, *Liverpool. A City That Dared to Fight*, p. 158.

12 Robert Cowan, P. Hannay and R. Owens, "The Light on Top of the Tunnel, in Vauxhall Victors: Eldonians Special Issue", *Architects' Journal* (23 Mar. 1988): 37–66.

13 Anne Grosskurth, "Bringing Back the Braddocks", *ROOF* 10.1 (1985): 19–23.

14 Tim Mars, "Mersey Tunnel Vision?", *ROOF* 12.6 (1987); Robert Cowan, "Co-op or Cop-Out?", *ROOF* 11.4 (1986); Cowan, Hannay and Owens, "The Light on Top of the Tunnel"; Grosskurth, "Bringing Back the Braddocks".

those who would build, maintain and manage them. But the URS was bad news for the growing co-op housing movement in Liverpool—for its apparent ideological incompatibility.

Rightly or wrongly, Militant associated co-ops with the privatisation of public housing. They accused the Liberals of diverting public funds into a privatised sector of housing provision incapable of addressing the structural issues facing the city. In contrast to the huge scale of the problem—with over ten thousand people on waiting lists needing to be housed—the tiny capacity of the marginal co-op movement was inadequate to meet the challenge: estimates ranged from just eight hundred families housed by co-ops[15] to around two thousand homes built in the six years up to 1985.[16] Even staunch supporters, such as Bill Halsall, the pioneering architect of the Weller Street Co-op and Eldonian Village, nonetheless recognises that

> The Liberals' housing policy was "if you want a new house, form a co-op". So they kind of forced it ... and when it all blew up in 1983 one of the things that the Militants were saying was "your housing policy is elitist", because the people who formed a co-op get the new houses, the people who aren't in co-ops don't get a new house—and that was actually true, they had a point.

Indeed, Militant's more deeply held ideological opposition to co-ops—as an elitist, exclusionary and nepotistic form of housing—was grounded in experience. Co-ops were not open to new members on the basis of need alone and so in this respect fell far short of the socialist ideal of universality. The pre-allocations process, requiring that residents be selected before design or construction commenced, was a fundamental part of co-op development, ensuring that residents were centrally involved in the process of creating their own homes—an intrinsic part of dweller control. Yet this also gave legitimacy to the lever by which close-knit communities ensured only their own kind—those sharing similar ethnic, religious and cultural identities, if not literally friends and families—would be included within the resulting co-ops. Self-selection is visible in the sharply divided yet adjoining Mill Street and Shorefields Co-ops, each exclusively catering for Catholic and Protestant residents respectively. There was also a co-op actually called 'Friends and Neighbours' and, adds a CDS development manager, "they *were* friends and neighbours". Even those supportive of co-ops nonetheless acknowledge that, for instance, "the reasons Militant—and this is actually quite justifiable I think—had a problem with it was you formed it from your mates". Max Steinberg at the Housing Corporation, a life-long supporter of co-ops, admits

15 Nick Wates, "Co-op Consolidation", *Architectural Review* (Apr. 1985).

16 Grosskurth, "Bringing Back the Braddocks".

that "we began to wonder as years went by, was this causing allocation policies to be controlled in a paternalistic way—was it creating little enclaves?" Despite the fact that all co-op members were sourced from poor working-class communities, with many in severe housing need, the co-ops were, if not elitist, then certainly exclusionary.

A Tory–Liberal Plot: The Gravedigger of Municipal Housing?

Whilst Militant had a point about the shortcomings of co-op housing, their reaction against the movement was not commensurate with the threat posed to socialist values. First, they assumed co-ops were a threat rather than an ally. They assumed that co-ops were incompatible with other forms of public housing and conflated the model with the Liberals' 'bourgeois' approach to housing policy. Militant animosity to co-ops as a form of nepotistic, even elitist, public housing, diverting resources away from universal municipal provision, is made explicit in a District Labour Party policy statement from 1984, entitled "The Co-op Issue".[17] I cite it here in full as a stark and candid insight into their thinking:

> The co-op issue has been the most controversial one as far as housing is concerned. The question to be asked is:
>
> (a) Did co-ops in Liverpool start as a spontaneous desire by people for an alternative form of tenure which is compatible with municipal housing, or,
>
> (b) Were co-ops part of a deliberate and calculated attack on municipal housing by the Tory Party nationally, aided and abetted by the local Liberal/Tory alliance?
>
> The Housing Sub Committee holds the view that the latter is the answer to the question. That is not to say that individual families were of that mind but that was clearly government's, both local and national, intention. There is also little doubt that the Housing Associations and leading advocates involved in the issue knew full well the consequences on public housing of the policies being pursued. The co-ops which have been part of the controversy were all formed since 1979.

This policy statement discloses Militant's deeply held suspicion of cooperatives as a Tory conspiracy rather than the pragmatic form of democratic socialism

17 Quoted in Paul Lusk, "Citizenship and Consumption in the Development of Social Rights: The Liverpool New-Build Housing Co-operative Movement", unpublished thesis, Salford University, 1998, p. 161.

as they are conventionally perceived. Writing in his account of the period, co-op advocate and former CDS worker Paul Lusk makes the strong claim that the District Labour Party's "opposition to co-ops could only be justified by a paranoid conspiracy theory of Stalinist intensity".[18] Rather than see co-ops as the natural ally of socialism—or simply a compatible and complementary sector of public housing, catering to a minority desiring more dweller control and choice—Militant associated the movement with the failings of the Liberal administration, as an integral part of a Tory plot; holding it accountable as the "gravedigger of municipal housing".[19]

The Liberals, of course, saw things differently. There is no evidence that co-op membership persuaded people to vote for the Liberals, who "gained nothing politically by building co-ops in inner-city wards for loyal socialists".[20] If anything, co-ops strengthened the socialist leanings of what were largely traditional working-class Labour voters. The co-op campaign process politicised members into more active involvement in the Labour Party—evident by the surprising number of co-op members who went on to become Labour councillors and leading lights in a later reformed District Labour Party. Some were radicalised further to the left. Frank Carroll from Prince Albert Gardens Co-op, for instance, was a regular councillor candidate for the Communist Party. Those professionals promoting co-ops were also affiliated with socialist politics. George Howarth, former Labour councillor and now Labour MP for Knowsley, was responsible for seeding the idea of co-ops into Kirkby while he worked for CDS in the early 1980s. Several CDS staff were members of the Communist Party. The Liverpool co-operators saw co-ops as the cell form of a socialist society in the tradition of mutualism and libertarian socialism—celebrating the collective self-sufficiency, dignity and autonomy of working-class culture. The Militant view, a more extreme variant of the traditional Labour perspective, saw co-ops as an alternative middle-class lifestyle choice, less about need than want, and therefore incompatible with their socialist agenda of ensuring needs are met through universal provision of all public services.

Despite Militant conspiracy claims, no explicit link was made between the cooperative movement and the Liberal Party, other than a vague ideological belief in choice and autonomy. The principal supporters were driven more by disinterested political principles than by electoral interests. Chris Davies, Chair of Housing during the new-build co-op revolution before becoming an MEP for Northwest England, explains how

> There was an upsurge of hatred for Liberals ... Labour had very cleverly portrayed us as the Liberal–Tory alliance, and it was quite true that

18 Lusk, "Citizenship and Consumption in the Development of Social Rights", p. 162.
19 Cowan, "Co-op or Cop-Out?".
20 Lusk, "Citizenship and Consumption in the Development of Social Rights", p. 177.

> we were dependent on Tory votes because we couldn't get any votes at all, even for sort of socialist measures … So it was the Lib–Con Alliance, only there was no alliance … every vote was see which way the cookie crumbles.

When Labour councillors from Glasgow—the other notable city council of the era pioneering cooperative housing development—came to Liverpool on a study tour of the co-ops, they were, according to Davies, "horrified at their Liverpool counterparts' attitude". He continues: "They were saying 'but co-operatives are a good thing, you know it's socialism, it's proper socialism, it's people in charge—it doesn't have to be all this top down stuff'. But the Militants were having none of it".

Not all in the Labour-led Council—far from it—bought into the hard line on co-ops as a conspiracy against municipal housing. Conspiracy theories cut both ways. There is certainly a sense in which co-op advocates and activists exaggerated—perhaps understandably, in feeling the full force of municipalisation—the hostility from Militant. Some observers, such as Bill Halsall here, saw the decision to municipalise as much as a pragmatic strategy to deliver the URS as it was an ideological project: "The deal was: the council wanted numbers. Militants wanted to be able to say that 'we built five thousand houses over three years', and the co-ops would just be added onto that total; they became part of building council houses".

Leading Militant activists Peter Taafe and Tony Mulhearn explain the practical financial reasons behind municipalisation: that "to have given housing co-ops the £6.5 million being demanded would have meant severely cutting the council's housebuilding programme".[21] The council was under great pressure to deliver its promised URS plans with diminishing budgetary allocations from hard-won funds, and so diverting scarce resources away from the main priority areas and towards what some of its socialist leaders saw as petit bourgeois housing was politically untenable.

The most powerful players in the Militant-led council had diverse motivations for their stance against co-ops: split between socialist convictions, loyalty to their constituencies and shrewd political self-interest. Towards the latter end of the spectrum was Derek Hatton, the prominent public face of the Militant Tendency and Deputy Leader of the council—whose Leader, John Hamilton, was Labour but not Militant. At the other extreme was Tony Byrne, the principal architect of URS but avowedly 'non-Militant', whose policy ideas gained support in the District Labour Party and who later became Chair of the council's powerful Housing and Finance Committees. The differences between Byrne and Hatton are neatly captured by a co-op activist who would become a Labour councillor through her experience of campaigning:

21 Taafe and Mulhearn, *Liverpool. A City That Dared to Fight*, p. 161.

> Tony Byrne particularly—very, very bright guy, very sharp, took no prisoners, just went for it, Exocet missiles kind of stuff. Apparently, he was going to be a Jesuit priest at one stage and then stepped back from that—very, very principled. He was the one guy that I would say didn't change, so you know, he'd always turn up in a trackie and his plassie bag to carry his papers in; he wouldn't go a Hatton route of getting smart and booted, and using the money and kudos and status and all of that. So Byrne was quite scary; he had this vision and the council had this vision of municipal housing, getting that back on the agenda, they would provide for the people, you know, false consciousness of the working class and all of that stuff.

Byrne famously stated his position in a local newspaper interview:

> I am a Socialist. I believe in public ownership, control and accountability for housing through the elected council. It is the local authority who must satisfy the needs of the working class. Working-class organisation in this city lies in the Labour Party and the unions, and not in housing associations.[22]

This fundamentalist view of socialism, in which power is to be firmly invested in the centralised state—a representative 'dictatorship of the proletariat', elected by the people, working for the people, making decisions in the interests of the people (but all too often without their further input or participation)—is, as Byrne makes clear above, strictly opposed to all forms of decentralised public provision through housing associations, however popular, democratic and free from capitalist relations they may prove to be. Byrne's belief in the universalist socialist state—that people have a right to a decent home regardless of political participation or social engagement—rested on a concomitant suspicion of community control as just another form of petit bourgeois privatism.

Defensible Principles and (Policy) Design Disadvantagement

Not least due to his ideological opposition to capitalism, Tony Byrne believed the council's ability to influence the private sector was limited. Municipal power lay in harnessing the public sector for socioeconomic recovery: "I can't do anything to locate a new factory in Speke or anywhere else, but what we can do is to deal with unemployment, and the environment and living

22 Quoted in Alan McDonald, *The Weller Way: The Story of the Weller Street Housing Cooperative* (Faber & Faber, 1986), p. 211.

conditions within the limits of our capabilities".[23] For Byrne, the answer was large-scale municipal housebuilding, which would provide jobs and decent homes for all and improve the urban environment in the process. But in promoting municipal housing as a panacea to urban ills Byrne became seduced by a form of design determinism that sat awkwardly next to socialist beliefs in controlling the material means of production. The URS rationale was to target 17 (later extended to 22) "Priority Areas" of modernist 'hard-to-let' flats and tenements built between the 1930s and 1970s, which had become unpopular sites marked by crime, vandalism, squalor and dereliction.[24] Byrne's assessment of council house designs revealed one promising inter-war period of problem-free semi-detached housing and concluded that this was the pinnacle of British council housing design. This insight, according to commentator Tim Mars, "was the germ of the URS housing programme".[25]

At around the same time, the geographer Alice Coleman was popularising her ideas on the 'design disadvantagement' of modernist council housing estates, which she had adapted from Oscar Newman's theory of defensible space developed in North America.[26] In her provocatively named book *Utopia on Trial*, Coleman recommended that 'corrective measures' should modify the worst features of existing council blocks; that no further council flats should be built; and that in their place should be semi-detached houses with front and back gardens, bounded territorially by walls or fences.[27] These ideas were taken up by Thatcher's government, informing the Right to Buy policy and the general trend towards the privatisation of council estates and the 'responsibilisation' of tenants. This made Coleman perhaps *the* most politically influential academic geographer of her and subsequent generations. The Prince of Wales was also very impressed and met Coleman, incorporating some of her ideas into his advocacy of community architecture. In this way, Coleman became, ironically enough, one of the ideological bedfellows of the new co-op movement and participatory design process.[28] The Liverpool co-ops have indeed adopted some defensible space principles in their design, especially

23 Tony Byrne, quoted in Richard Meegan, "Merseyside in Crisis and in Conflict", in Michael Harloe, Chris Pickvance and John Urry, eds, *Place, Policy and Politics: Do Localities Matter?* (Routledge, 1990), pp. 67–83 (p. 94).

24 Taafe and Mulhearn, *Liverpool. A City That Dared to Fight*.

25 Mars, "Mersey Tunnel Vision?", p. 26.

26 Jane M. Jacobs and Loretta Lees, "Defensible Space on the Move: Revisiting the Urban Geography of Alice Coleman", *International Journal of Urban and Regional Research* 37.5 (2013): 1559–1583.

27 Alice Coleman, *Utopia on Trial: Vision and Reality in Planned Housing* (Hilary Shipman Ltd, 1985).

28 Nick Wates and Charles Knevitt, *Community Architecture: How People Are Creating Their Own Environment* (Penguin Books, 1987).

in the wagon circle enclosures, overlooked gardens and external boundary fencing. In a counterintuitive convergence with Militant council housing design, the co-ops also embodied, wittingly or not, Alice Coleman's defensible space principles. A CDS development manager describes how:

> So you've got loads of overlooking, you've got shared surfaces, you've got good strong boundaries at the back, you've got very little permeability through the site—they've got all those aspects of defensible space, so from Alice's point of view that's good.

Despite the surprising connections between Alice Coleman and Militant's most despised ideological opponents—Thatcherism and cooperativism, each also opposing the other—Byrne was adamant that Coleman was on to something and invited her up to Liverpool for a site visit.[29] In a strange twist, Coleman gave her seal of approval to Militant housing policy, proclaiming that, in an interview with the *Liverpool Daily Post* in 1985, "Liverpool has got it right".[30] Leading Militant members were proud to report that "she completely concurred with the main thrust of the URS and of the council's conviction that the majority of people preferred to live in traditional houses".[31] The URS development principles that Coleman praised had been published in 1984 as new development guidelines, ensuring only houses and bungalows, semi-detached where possible, were to be built. Amongst the many prescriptions, certain phrases stand out—"no shared surfaces"; "generally conventional with through routes rather than cul-de-sacs"; "no clusters"; "short streets"; "dwellings to face roads"; "solely private gardens and pavements"; "no common areas; no play spaces"[32]—conditions which would have devastating effects on the co-ops.

Militant believed they were giving people what they truly wanted; and in many respects they had accurately captured the mood of many tenants, alienated by dysfunctional and decaying council flats. Owing to fiscal constraints on the URS imposed by the ongoing budget battle, however, the new housing—nicknamed 'Hatton houses', quite simply because, a former LHT officer tells me, "they were directly controlled by Derek Hatton"—was often of a lower design quality than the council housing it replaced. The HAG-funded co-ops were in fact the last form of public sector housing to benefit from generous Parker Morris standards, and so remained more spacious and fit to live in than Hatton houses—often not big enough for new tenants to fit in the furniture

29 Mars, "Mersey Tunnel Vision?"

30 Taafe and Mulhearn, *Liverpool. A City That Dared to Fight*, p. 159.

31 Taafe and Mulhearn, *Liverpool. A City That Dared to Fight*.

32 Quoted in Lusk, "Citizenship and Consumption in the Development of Social Rights", p. 157.

from their old houses. Little wonder, then, that local Labour politician Peter Kilfoyle—albeit a vociferous critic of Militant—described them as "stupid little doll's houses".[33] More recent critiques have been no less scathing. In his architectural dérive of Liverpool, Owen Hatherley points to "bizarre" effects on Liverpool's impressive urban landscape:

> They [the council] built the sort of story book look of what a house was supposed to look like, in a way entirely wrong for a hundred yards from here. ... It's not dignified for the city centre to mimic the 'burbs. It leads to depressing juxtapositions ... the scale is preposterous, with the houses seeming to desperately want to be somewhere less dramatic ... It becomes a tragicomedy.[34]

From construction process to final design the comedy continued. Despite definite gains made by the URS in creating an extra ten thousand jobs in the construction industry, the council's rather contradictory political partnership with private building companies had adverse consequences. Here's a common view amongst observers:

> They did deals with Wimpey's where the quality was just crap. They had very high voids because they had real maintenance problems in those properties that they'd built that were supposed to be better ... Terribly designed housing is no better than terribly designed flats—you have to manage and maintain them in the right way.

Byrne's critics found him guilty of a 'monomania' for housing—an obsession not just with housing policy per se but with a very specific architectural model, reflected in the stringent URS prescriptions, which bordered on a kind of design determinism not dissimilar to Coleman's design disadvantagement theory. CDS chief executive Catherine Meredith accused Byrne of a "megalomaniac belief in housing type" and of failing to recognise the importance of dweller control in the management and maintenance of housing.[35] The Coleman/Byrne design modification approach worked on the assumption that people wanted semi-detached houses arranged along streets with through-flow, overlooking the fact that in the co-op participatory design process residents had opted for terraces, enclosed courtyards, cul-de-sacs and communal features. In many ways, the URS made the same mistake as the post-war modernist council designs it critiqued: a top-down focus on form

33 Kilfoyle, *Left Behind*, p. 91.

34 Owen Hatherley, *A Guide to the New Ruins of Great Britain* (Verso Books, 2011), pp. 335–338.

35 Quoted in Mars, "Mersey Tunnel Vision?", p. 27.

over function, on housing type over any consideration of tenant participation in its design, management or ownership. The URS replaced many alienating high-rise flats and council estates with more-popular, human-scale traditional houses, but the rigid, distant paternalistic management structure remained unmoved.

Keeping the Cooperative Spirit Alive: The Movement Migrates to Knowsley

Militant came to power with a manifesto promise to permit co-ops so long as they did not divert resources from the URS. In practice, however, Militant pursued an aggressive campaign against co-ops, going so far as actively to move URS Priority Area boundaries to include a block of flats they had initially agreed to transfer to local residents to renovate as a co-op, so as to build new council houses instead. Quickly after the election, the council decided to place a moratorium on all further funding of co-ops and to take into municipal control those already started. What did this mean for the co-ops? If a co-op had already signed a contractual commitment with the council to acquire land, then it was left to complete the scheme under cooperative ownership. Six HAG-funded co-ops—including the MIH co-ops in the north end, Leta-Claudia and Thirlmere—were safe, building 170 homes in total.[36] However, for those already started on design work but yet to exchange contracts, this meant municipalisation. At least eight co-ops were affected: six small CDS co-ops in the south end, totalling 220 dwellings; a new LHT co-op at Gerrard Gardens in Vauxhall, with over a hundred homes; and the Eldonians' project at Portland Gardens, also over a hundred. A few co-ops were shielded by being built on land not owned by the council—notably by the Merseyside Development Corporation—but the standard development model utilised council land. Part of the problem was that the co-ops could not exchange contracts until formal approval of the outline design proposals had been granted by the government Department of Environment. However, there were other reasons why so many had yet to sign contracts, which, with hindsight, as this community housing trust director and ex-council officer reflects, was

> Probably a mistake. The idea was that the land was owned by the city, the finance was coming through the city to do the development, and the co-op would buy the units back at the end, when they were completed … And the reason why that was done was to save everyone the VAT. Because the co-ops weren't VAT registered (they were too small to be VAT registered) and the local authority didn't charge VAT

36 Lusk, *Citizenship and Consumption in the Development of Social Rights.*

> on development of houses, so it was getting done the most economical way. But it still meant that the council owned the land and they were paying for the development initially, which is why in '83 the initial co-ops that we'd started were able to be municipalised because the council owned the land, were putting the money in. The Militants who took over were not interested in selling them back to the communities.

What had seemed an ingenious idea—exploiting a loophole in the tax system to improve economic viability—was exposed as a fatal flaw, rendering new-build co-ops vulnerable to the whims of electoral politics. Through its legal powers, the council was able to take full control of the eight co-ops lacking contracts. Their chosen architects would be kept on by the council but CDS and MIH would receive no compensation for their work, and it was unclear whether co-ops would be allowed to proceed on the designs co-produced by residents. The URS design guidelines meant that all new developments had to accord with standardised through-road semi-detached housing layouts, foreclosing all possibility of cooperative designs that incorporated communal spaces or courtyards. The loss of central communal play spaces, gardens and community centres—the heart of cooperative housing—was particularly problematic for the successful functioning of co-ops unlucky enough to be caught up in municipalisation.

Except in rare cases of resistance—which I explore below—the Militants brought the cooperative movement to a standstill in Liverpool at a time when they received unprecedented policy support nationally. In local jurisdictions outside Militant influence, however, prospects were different. Knowsley, a neighbouring Metropolitan Borough Council within Merseyside (now one of six local authorities comprising the Liverpool City Region) is constituted mainly of overspill outer estates and new towns such as Kirkby, built during post-war urban renewal to house many of those Liverpudlians displaced by the slum clearances. Knowsley residents still had familial connections to the neighbourhoods in which the co-ops were springing up, and so just as residents were exported out to Kirkby so too was the co-op idea: seeding the second generation of new-build co-ops. Knowsley Metropolitan Borough Council was a non-Militant Labour administration with links into the co-op movement, perhaps the most pivotal of which being George Howarth—now a Labour MP for Knowsley, then a Labour councillor and Chair of Knowsley's Housing Committee as well as a CDS co-op development officer. Howarth talks of the unusual political partnership between Liverpool's Liberal councillors and Knowsley's Labour councillors against the Militants of their own party. In the early 1980s, Knowsley was likewise dealing with an oversupply of unpopular hard-to-let flats, and had a strategy to clear some of the three-storey walk-up flats and 'top down' some of the maisonettes, essentially knocking storeys off to create two-storey houses. CDS had begun working with some of the tenants being rehoused, and Howarth saw similar opportunities here as in Liverpool's tenements. Alongside other CDS workers he began a more proactive approach of dropping leaflets through front doors, headlined 'design your own homes', in an attempt to rally co-op groups.

Much of the initial interest in Kirkby was drummed up through neighbourly pressure, despite less entrenched community ties or defined neighbourhood identities than in inner-city Liverpool due to the relative newness and rationalised nature of the urban environment, lacking the convivial density of the terraces or the 1930s tenements. For the first Kirkby co-op, Southdene, it was more a case of proactively recruiting co-op members from across Kirkby, scattered in isolated blocks, than reacting as a pre-existing community wanting to stay together. The remaining members were hand-picked from high-rise flats (families and elderly residents who wanted a garden) to eventually form a total of seventeen—much smaller than the Liverpool new-builds reflecting a general trend across Kirkby.

This mobilisation was facilitated by CDS armed with pictures of the first new-build co-ops such as Weller Street. The principal proponents of the Kirkby movement, however, were young single mothers, who often felt isolated in the flats and wanted something better for their children. Max Steinberg, Northwest Regional Director of the Housing Corporation at the time, described to me how

> So many of the housing cooperatives I dealt with in Kirkby were being promoted, negotiated through the requirements of the Housing Corporation, by women, who were often their leaders. They became very powerful figures who wanted to see improvements in their neighbourhood ... very much the sort of dominant household figure regarding the future of the households in the area.

Kirkby co-ops shared with the south end Liverpool co-ops this characteristic—of being dominated by women in their everyday practices—but, unlike Weller Street, were also led by women who took the role of outward leader and figurehead. Female empowerment was a major feature of the Kirkby co-ops. Women like Jackie Harris, a founding member of Southdene, threw themselves into running campaigns, mobilising their communities, and lobbying authorities for support—a stepping stone into successful political careers. Harris is now a Labour councillor for Knowsley, leading on Crime and Disorder for the council, and involved in numerous community initiatives. Her experience as arguably the leading co-op proponent in Kirkby took her around the country as a consultant and lobbyist, speaking at political party events and housing conferences. Jackie often travelled to London to lobby the Housing Corporation for funding further co-ops, including others in Kirkby.

The empowering effect of co-ops was not limited to formal politics.

When Southdene was formally registered in 1983, all seventeen members were unemployed, but by the time the houses were built and occupied—with additional tenants moving in by 1987—around 90 per cent were employed. This is seen by many of those involved as the product of training and skills learnt in co-op campaigning and development. Many of the single mothers were very young when they first started, around 21–22 years old, and the co-op development process proved invaluable for their own personal development as well as an inadvertent educational experience for their children, who were often involved in the design and decoration of campaign materials and later the houses themselves.

By this point, co-ops had begun to take over from CDS the role of organising the process of education, training and knowledge transfer. First, the Kirkby co-ops would go on site visits to the more established Liverpool new-builds to learn from the 'pioneers': "to speak to them", as Jackie explains, "about the early stages, how they got where they were, designing the co-ops, campaigning—they did give you a lot of guidance". Second, the Liverpool Federation of Housing Cooperatives, established by CDS several years earlier, was in 1984 reincorporated into the Merseyside Federation by its membership to include the Kirkby co-ops. Each co-op would send representatives to monthly meetings to share experiences, trade knowledge, develop best practice, build solidarity in a difficult economic period and socialise with fellow co-operators. For Harris, it became

> The meeting place where you got your better ideas … As a group of co-ops, our Federation, that was where we discussed the political side: of how we get funding, where we go, if we had to go to London, if we were putting Federation stuff into the co-ops to adopt, you know, strategic planning on co-ops all being a part of the same one constitution.

Co-op members would pay £1 'subs' at weekly co-op meetings, which would go towards helping fund bus fares for representatives to travel to Merseyside Federation meetings, as well as small fees to CDS for their administrative work and advice and capital reserves for useful items like a typewriter to type up minutes and publish newsletters and leaflets. The Federation was the beginning of a more outward-facing, self-organised and collaborative process of movement-building through cooperative education, support and knowledge transfer. It could have become a successful self-governing membership organisation—a kind of democratically governed secondary development agency to Weller Street's unilaterally oriented failed experiment. However, Militant's opposition to co-ops in Liverpool hindered this by shifting the focus from creative institution-building to defensive protection of existing assets. Co-ops, at least in Liverpool, became more combative—forced to focus on protecting immediate interests from the Militant threat rather than building bridges with others.

Whilst the Kirkby co-ops were strengthening institutional ties, the Liverpool co-ops were galvanised into contentious political action. The Merseyside Federation organised public demonstrations in 1984, with over a thousand co-operators marching from the heartland of south-end co-ops in the Dingle to the town hall in the city centre, alongside various prominent political allies, such as the then Liberal Chair of Housing, Richard Kemp. The public campaign drew on media sympathy, and supportive commentary in the *Architects' Journal* and Shelter's *ROOF* magazine.[37] An open letter to Tony Byrne pleaded for concessions towards "principles of tenant control", and was signed by four of the municipalised co-ops.[38] Others pursued successful legal appeals and managed to stay in the homes they had helped design but only under the condition of remaining council tenants without taking collective action for a co-op any further. Some co-ops were able to use arm's-length planning instruments controlled by central government to bypass council opposition. CDS negotiated a site for two co-ops in the south end, Mill Street and Shorefields from the Merseyside Development Corporation just before municipalisation hit. CDS also managed to secure payment of remediation costs from the Merseyside Development Corporation for what was contaminated land near the docks. Located on land owned by the Merseyside Development Corporation, these and several smaller co-ops were safe. Using this tactic, the Eldonians were also able to bypass council opposition: a unique struggle against adversity which will be examined in the following chapter.

One example of direct action contesting Militant municipalisation was the Langrove Community Housing Co-op. Langrove Street was situated in the West Everton community straddling the ridge that forms a bowl around Liverpool city centre broadly marking the historical urban division between the Catholic neighbourhoods nearer the docks and the Protestants who moved up the hill. The community faced demolition threats from Tony Byrne's vision for Everton Park: a "magnificent park on traditional Victorian lines" by way of clearing "unsatisfactory post-war housing".[39] Some of this housing was deeply unpopular—decaying high-rise flats pockmarked the area—but a collection of two-storey four-bed parlour houses built in the 1950s were in high demand. Resistance mounted to their planned demolition. The community had a strong identity unusually united by the involvement of both Anglican Protestants

37 Cowan, "Co-op or Cop-Out?"; Mars, "Mersey Tunnel Vision?"; Cowan, Hannay and Owens, "The Light on Top of the Tunnel"; Grosskurth, "Bringing Back the Braddocks"; Wates, "Co-op Consolidation".

38 Quoted in Lusk, "Citizenship and Consumption in the Development of Social Rights", p. 156.

39 URS document, quoted in Mars, "Mersey Tunnel Vision?"

and Catholics in churches that spanned sectarian divides, garnering a strong culture of working together, evident in the active influence of the West Everton Community Council since 1965. As the city council began decanting tenants and demolishing houses, the community resorted to desperate measures—deciding to squat in the last house left standing on Arkwright Street and establishing the Langrove Street Action Group in 1986.[40] A 24-hour occupation commenced; protesting residents barricaded in against demolition. Langrove Street Action Group made sure, as one activist put it, to "learn the rules" of the game, and got Shelter and CDS involved to advise on campaign strategy. Representatives from the two organisations ran a crash course on non-violent direct action, inspired by Martin Luther King and adapting Paulo Freire's emancipatory ideas on critical pedagogy and community development.[41] The resulting fusion of radical secular politics and deep Christian faith was reflected in the banners displayed on the occupied house, which juxtaposed familiar activist slogans ('Occupation Not Demolition'; 'Council Vandalism'; 'Save These Houses') with verses from the Bible—"Love does not delight in evil but rejoices with the truth. It always protects, always trusts, always hopes, always perseveres. Love never fails".[42]

While occupying the houses, Langrove Street Action Group set in motion a court case against the Militant decision, with pro bono support from a sympathetic local barrister. The political situation in Liverpool was about to change dramatically. The battle between Militant and Thatcher came to a head and 47 Labour councillors were disqualified from office, with surcharges against them, leaving the council run by a 'caretaker' Liberal administration for just six weeks until the forthcoming elections in 1987. In May that year, Labour was re-elected. Despite opposition from countless community groups and cooperatives, the URS had been broadly popular with voters for attempting to tackle the deep socioeconomic and environmental challenges facing Liverpool. Interestingly, Weller Street's Treasurer, Phil Hughes—politicised by the co-op campaign into becoming a Labour councillor—was elected as the new Chair of Housing to replace Tony Byrne. Hughes was upfront about his only qualification for the job being membership of the Weller Street Co-op, and Tony Byrne asserted that "Labour fought and won the local election on the Urban Regeneration Strategy, so it seems strange to choose Phil Hughes as a chair of housing".[43] His tenure was indeed odd. Although there was no outward change of policy—Hughes admitting "it can't be stopped"—he nonetheless vowed to

40 For a first-person account of the campaign, see Henry Corbett, "Langrove Action Story: A Community and a Council at Odds", *Together for the Common Good*, 2012: http://togetherforthecommongood.co.uk/case-studies/articles/the-langrove-action-story.html.

41 Paulo Freire, *Pedagogy of the Oppressed* (Continuum, 1970).

42 Corinthians 13:6–8.

43 Quoted in Mars, "Mersey Tunnel Vision?", p. 25.

'humanise' the URS and make it compatible with co-ops.[44] Hughes agreed to sell the remaining thirty Langrove houses to the community co-op and, in fact, amended the URS plan so that the park would be developed around the community, as a green urban village. In a twist of fate, the early pioneers of Liverpool's co-op movement were enabled to exercise direct positive influence on the future of several cooperative schemes, such as Langrove, through their empowerment to powerful positions on the council coinciding and colliding with an extraordinary turn of political events. Indeed, the leading Langrove activist, Jane Corbett—herself politicised by the campaign to become a Labour councillor—now exerts influence in her present position (at the time of writing) as Assistant Mayor of Liverpool and Mayoral Lead for Fairness and Tackling Poverty.

Langrove members have since capitalised on their experience with community development to pursue a more ambitious vision for neighbourhood regeneration—with aspirations for eco-homes, a park café, new shops, allotments and self-sufficiency in energy and food—and are now working in partnership with public agencies on the latest regeneration plans for Everton Park. Since their initial success in saving the four-bed parlour houses, they have developed further phases of co-op housing, attracting CDS to develop their own scheme locally as well as developers of private housing. They have sought partnerships with other housing associations, most recently with Riverside—previously MIH—on the first new housing co-op development in the city in over a decade. Riverside are converting a block of flats into five homes for rent, having negotiated with Langrove to transfer at a pre-agreed below-market price rather than sell on the open market. These homes have been pre-allocated to new Langrove co-op members, who are involved in some of the design work. Coming full circle from their MIH roots in co-op development, Riverside are transferring the properties to Langrove at cost, driven forward by staff who were often involved personally in the cooperative movement, through either CDS or MIH as part of a strategy of giving something back to the local area and potentially rejuvenating the co-op movement after decades of dormancy. In the meantime, a different model of collective housing and community-led regeneration was being developed by the Eldonians. Like Langrove, they pushed for a more holistic and comprehensive form of local economic redevelopment than just housing alone, going much further in pursuing collective ownership over an entire neighbourhood. The next Part, the Neighbourhood Question, tells their story.

44 Mars, "Mersey Tunnel Vision?", p. 25.

Part III
The Neighbourhood Question

CHAPTER 7

Locating the Neighbourhood Question

> In reality the bourgeoisie has only one method of solving the housing question after its fashion—that is to say, of solving it in such a way that the solution continually reproduces the question anew. This method is called "Haussmann" …
>
> By "Haussmann" I mean the practice which has now become general of making breaches in the working class quarters of our big towns, and particularly in those which are centrally situated, quite apart from whether this is done from considerations of public health and for beautifying the town, or owing to the demand for big centrally situated business premises, or owing to traffic requirements, such as the laying down of railways, streets, etc. No matter how different the reasons may be, the result is everywhere the same: the scandalous alleys and lanes disappear to the accompaniment of lavish self-praise from the bourgeoisie on account of this tremendous success, but they appear again immediately somewhere else and often in the immediate neighbourhood.[1]

Since Engels first identified the method of urban renewal he names after Baron Haussmann, who remade Paris at the dawn of industrial modernity, these structural processes of creating, destroying and recreating urban spaces through successive bouts of state intervention punctuating but never fully arresting capital flow and flight have become all too familiar. Although prescient in his prognosis of uneven urban development, Engels was writing at the peak of British industrialisation—at the forefront of a nascent and expanding colonial-capitalism—and so his critique of capitalist urban development was focused on the ill-effects of full-throttled growth, capital's unbridled thirst for revalorising investments through creative destruction. He therefore failed to consider the impacts of economic decline, capital flight and blight. We can see this in his characterisation of the 'Haussmannisation' of working-class housing:

1 Friedrich Engels, *The Housing Question* (Progress Publishers, 1972), p. 71.

> But the spirit of Haussmann has also been abroad in London, Manchester and Liverpool ... The result is that the workers are forced out of the centre of the towns towards the outskirts; that workers' dwellings, and small dwellings in general, become rare and expensive and often altogether unobtainable, for under these circumstances the building industry, which is offered a much better field for speculation by more expensive houses, builds workers' dwellings only by way of exception.[2]

Here, Engels appears to anticipate several forces that have come to bear on urban life in late modernity, not least gentrification. He identifies the essential shortcoming of Haussmannisation: that it simply displaces the problem (capitalism's production of scarcity) rather than resolves it *in situ*. These processes of displacement and dispossession—whether driven by capital flows and gentrification or else augmented by the capitalist state through Haussmannisation—are the levers through which capital accumulation revalorises land for growth, pushing workers into socio-spatial peripheries in a seemingly endless process resulting in an uneven development within and between cities. Since Engels wrote these passages, capitalism has gone global and the process that he describes as operating within cities has been scaled up to planetary proportions, flooding some global urban regions with capital and leaving others in drought. Something that Engels could not anticipate at the time he was writing, perhaps, was the eventuality that some cities, neighbourhoods and their inhabitants were not simply left behind by uneven urban development, still awaiting investment, but came to suffer from disinvestment, devalorisation and decline—*after* a period of capitalist growth. What if Patrick Keiller's conundrum of capitalism's production of the *dilapidated dwelling* were reconstituted as the *dilapidated neighbourhood* or even the *dilapidated city*? What would Engels make of the economic conditions that motivated the spirit of Haussmann all but evacuating Liverpool (if not London)?

Liverpool's Second Blitz

Perhaps nowhere better exemplifies the neighbourhood question than the city of Liverpool. Foreshadowing a general trend across the old heartlands of global industrial production—from Detroit to Leipzig—Liverpool suffered brutal deindustrialisation and economic decline, as globalisation enabled the smoother flow of capital elsewhere. The rapid rise of Liverpool as a world-leading seaport—at the apex of the British Empire—is matched only by the rate and depth of its fall from grace. By the late 1970s, political commentators were reporting, in astonishment, that

2 Engels, *The Housing Question*, pp. 20–21.

> Liverpool, at the heart of the region, has been ravaged. From a thriving merchant city, with more millionaires than any other provincial city, it has become an "unwanted mausoleum". People are leaving Liverpool at an alarming rate—12,000 a year. Many see no hope for the future.[3]

The seeds of decline were sown in the early twentieth century as the British Empire began to dissolve and Britain's trading partners shifted from Atlantic-facing colonies to Europe and Asia, thereby leaving Liverpool, in historian Tony Lane's oft-quoted maritime metaphor, "marooned on the wrong side of the country".[4] This long-term structural shift slowly devastated the maritime economy upon which Liverpool's wealth and purpose were built: from the 1960s to the 1980s, Liverpool's port activity all but collapsed; the seven-and-a-half-mile-long southern dock system closing entirely in 1971. Within Liverpool, economic decline was dramatically unevenly distributed: felt far more keenly in the inner-city dockside communities, being so dependent on the largely unskilled casualised jobs associated with the docks. Liverpool's experience puts a new spin on Keiller's formulation: placing the dilapidated neighbourhood or the dilapidated city within a narrative of uneven urban development in which deindustrialised rustbelt 'old space' is increasingly peripheralised by the 'new space' of growth regions.

This, however, was by no means a structural process alone. Haussmannisation in the post-war era played its part too. A "traumatic combination" of brute economic decline combined with "major self-inflicted public policy mistakes"—the removal of much of the city's workforce to peripheral new towns and outer estates in the 1960s slum clearances—resulted in a dramatic population loss from a peak of some 870,000 in the 1930s to around 400,000 today.[5] Some estimates put the number of residents removed from the inner city to the new towns and outer estates through comprehensive redevelopment as high as 160,000.[6] As a result, Liverpool has attracted much academic and policy attention as a 'shrinking city' with an especially acute housing vacancy problem—part of a global trend of urban shrinkage in deindustrialising regions.[7]

3 Merseyside Socialist Research Group, *Merseyside in Crisis* (Manchester Free Press, 1980), p. 7.

4 Tony Lane, *Liverpool: City of the Sea*, 2nd ed. (Liverpool University Press, 1997), p. 46.

5 Olivier Sykes, Jonathan Brown, Matthew Cocks et al., "A City Profile of Liverpool", *Cities* 35 (2013): 299–318 (p. 307).

6 Sykes, Brown, Cocks et al., "A City Profile of Liverpool".

7 Matthew Cocks and Chris Couch, "The Governance of a Shrinking City: Housing Renewal in the Liverpool Conurbation, UK", *International Planning Studies* 17.3 (2012): 277–301; Chris Couch and Matthew Cocks, "Housing Vacancy and the Shrinking City:

The dual effect of economic restructuring and state-led urban renewal has been described by Tony Lane as "a sort of latter-day urban equivalent of the Highland clearances of several hundred years ago".[8] Such impassioned language is echoed by the Merseyside Socialist Research Group in *Merseyside in Crisis*:

> Between 1966 and 1977 the heart was torn out of Liverpool ... 15% of land is either vacant or derelict. The largest amount of open space in any city in Britain. A testimony to the folly of politicians and planners ... Clear the slums, build a motorway system to the docks, rehouse people on the estates ... The population of the inner city was cut by half in these 'boom' years—800,000 to 500,000 ... The people of Liverpool have to live with the devastation that remains.[9]

It is important to stress that such figures should be read in light of the limited power of the local state vis-à-vis the brute economic reality—even with this internal metropolitan migration taken into account, the population of the overall Merseyside conurbation still fell as a consequence of more structural processes of capital flight and unemployment from a peak of 1.8 million to around 1.3 million today.[10] Nonetheless, the specific effects of Haussmannisation were devastating for the city as a whole as much as for the directly impacted dockside neighbourhoods. Although the council had attempted to extend the city of Liverpool's boundaries several times during the post-war years, they had been unsuccessful, so the effect of shipping thousands of the active, if then underemployed, workforce out of the city beyond the tax base was to remove a large proportion of the council's income stream from rates, or council tax, to pay for the services for those left behind.[11] The consequent "reduction in population", Tony Lane explains, "was not accompanied by a pro rata reduction in the cost of services and so the gap between costs and rate revenue grew steadily wider".[12] This left Liverpool with a black hole in its finances for decades to come.

Such a Gordian knot helped carve the ensuing economic blight deeper into the city's fabric, tipping some particularly hard-hit neighbourhoods

Trends and Policies in the UK and the City of Liverpool", *Housing Studies* 28.3 (2013): 499–519; Justin B. Hollander and Jeremy Németh, "The Bounds of Smart Decline: A Foundational Theory for Planning Shrinking Cities", *Housing Policy Debate* 21.3 (2011): 349–367.

8 Lane, *Liverpool: City of the Sea*, p. 140.

9 Merseyside Socialist Research Group, *Merseyside in Crisis*, p. 57.

10 Cocks and Couch, "The Governance of a Shrinking City".

11 Tony Lane, "We Are The Champions: Liverpool vs the 1980s", *Marxism Today* (Jan. 1986): 8–11.

12 Lane, "We Are The Champions, p. 11.

into a spiral of decline. The weakening of collective consumption capacity and spending power on local goods and services by this loss of working-age population left large parts of the city without the critical mass to keep local shops, businesses and communities alive. This precipitated a vicious spiral in which population loss and unemployment conspired to create a self-reinforcing cycle resulting in poverty, housing vacancies, environmental neglect, dereliction, crime, social unrest and eventually neighbourhood abandonment. "Parts of this city, it is no exaggeration to say", said Lane in 1981, "are the European equivalents of the shanty towns of Rio de Janeiro, Lima and Santiago".[13] How to deal with these consequences is the subject of the neighbourhood question. Building on Engels, this can be seen as a more spatialised version of the housing question—a question for which Liverpool has long been trying to answer.

One of the earliest (and most radical) attempts to answer the neighbourhood question, the Community Development Project (CDP) programme of the late 1960s, provides a lesson in how state-led regeneration is not enough to transform the capitalist structures at its root. Like its close cousin SNAP in Granby, the CDP in the Vauxhall neighbourhood of north Liverpool was launched with the intention of understanding more about the causes of poverty whilst at the same time helping resolve it through social action.[14] However, as community workers and academic researchers began working with local people and became embedded in communities, they developed a critical analysis of the complex systemic problems productive of place-based poverty. They criticised the programme, and others like it, for doing little to combat entrenched structural problems, for merely *Gilding the Ghetto*, as the title of the 1977 final report for the CDP programme put it:

> The poverty initiatives then have clearly not made any great inroads on inner-Liverpool's real material problems. All they have done is to restate, usually in academic terms, what the people who live there have known for a long time. If you live on Merseyside you have a better than average chance of being made redundant, being on the dole for a long time, living in slum conditions, being evicted, and forced to wait over six months for hospital treatment. Your children are more likely to die in infancy, or when, after getting no nursery schooling, they finally get to school, of being in larger classes in worse buildings, only to emerge finally onto the dole. Over 10,000 people leave Liverpool each year as a way of avoiding these problems. Those who are left can debate them

13 Tony Lane, "Merseyside under the Hammer", *Marxism Today* (Feb. 1981): 18–21 (p. 18).

14 Diane Frost and Peter North, *Militant Liverpool: A City on the Edge* (Liverpool University Press, 2013).

in the neighbourhood councils and area management experiments left behind by the "poverty projects".[15]

Their suggestions to government—of radical restructuring of industrial policy, public housing management, education, health and welfare—fell on deaf ears; and it soon became apparent that central government departments were less interested in necessary structural reforms than in communities' capabilities to pull themselves up (by their bootstraps, as the saying goes) out of poverty through localised self-help. But without redistribution of economic assets, the participatory approaches embodied in programmes like SNAP and the CDPs were not enough alone to combat socio-economic problems rooted in structural inequalities. Interestingly, as a measure of their radicalisation and rejection of the government's agenda, those professionals involved in the Vauxhall CDP helped tenants organise various resistances to welfare cuts and council housing rent rises, leading up to Liverpool's 1972 Rent Strike.

An enduring legacy of the Vauxhall CDP is the development of community development trusts in north Liverpool. The Eldonian Community Trust in Vauxhall, the same neighbourhood as the CDP, has proven a successful example of how a community development trust can regenerate declining inner-city areas suffering from mass unemployment and extreme dereliction.[16] The key difference with the initiatives emanating from the CDP is that the Eldonians gained collective ownership of assets, including but not limited to housing, maintaining community control of local services to this day. The Eldonians have radically transformed a large area of north Liverpool from a state of decay into a thriving community with a promising future—despite prevailing economic headwinds pushing against them. The extent to which the community development trust model as mobilised by the Eldonians can resolve the neighbourhood question is one of the issues that I try to answer below.

How to Make Water Flow Uphill

In 1981, the neighbourhood question made its indelible mark on the city and the nation in the violent social unrest that became known as the Toxteth Riots. Partly reacting to skyrocketing unemployment levels, the black community

15 CDP (Community Development Project), *Gilding the Ghetto: The State and the Poverty Experiments* (CDP Inter-Project Editorial Team, 1977).

16 Peter Roberts, "Social Innovation, Spatial Transformation and Sustainable Communities: Liverpool and the 'Eldonians'", in Paul Drewe, Juan-Luis Klein and Edward Hulsbergen, eds, *The Challenge of Social Innovation in Urban Revitalization* (Techne Press, 2008); Jack McBane, *The Rebirth of Liverpool: The Eldonian Way* (Liverpool University Press, 2008).

in and around Granby protested for nine consecutive nights against racial discrimination in public jobs and against police brutality—actions resulting in 70 buildings burnt to the ground, 500 arrests, 470 police officers injured, and a disabled man killed by a police vehicle.[17] The government was forced to respond. The nature of that response seemed to hinge upon the imputed causes of the unrest—whether it was a moral issue or one related to the terrible social and economic conditions endured in Liverpool for so many years. It also pivoted upon how that decline in Granby was perceived—was it one of political and economic decisions taken at multiple levels that could therefore be reversed or one of inexorable deterioration in the economy of Liverpool and character of its people? The Chancellor of the Exchequer, Geoffrey Howe, wrote to the Prime Minister Margaret Thatcher arguing the "need to be careful not to over-commit scare resources to Liverpool". The letter concludes with the astounding lines:

> It would be even more regrettable if some of the brighter ideas for renewing economic activity were to be sown only on relatively stony ground on the banks of the Mersey. I cannot help feeling that the option of managed decline, which the CPRS rejected in its study of Merseyside, is one which we should not forget altogether. We must not expend all our resources in trying to make water flow uphill.[18]

Howe was not alone amongst his Cabinet colleagues for such extreme views. The arch-neoliberal, Sir Keith Joseph, has likewise been revealed as favouring the "managed rundown" of Merseyside.[19] Howe and Joseph were effectively arguing for what some critics have recently described as urban 'autotomy'—"the conscious abandonment of a damaged or diseased part of the body politic in order to preserve the healthy remainder"[20]—a practice first emerging in Northern Ireland in the early 1970s as a strategy of containment of Irish Republican communities.[21] Such views appear to express a very traditional notion of urban-economic change as natural—just

17 Diane Frost and Richard Phillips, *Liverpool '81: Remembering the Riots* (Liverpool University Press, 2011).

18 Geoffrey Howe, letter dated 11 Aug. 1981, quoted in Simon Parker and Rowland Atkinson, "Disorderly Cities and the Policy-Making Field: The 1981 English Riots and the Management of Urban Decline", *British Politics* 15 (2020): 160–177.

19 Parker and Atkinson, "Disorderly Cities".

20 Simon Parker, "The Leaving of Liverpool: Managed Decline and the Enduring Legacy of Thatcherism's Urban Policy", LSE Blog, 17 Jan. 2019: https://blogs.lse.ac.uk/politicsandpolicy/the-leaving-of-liverpool/.

21 Rowland Atkinson, Simon Parker and Emma Regina Morales, "Non-State Space: The Strategic Ejection of Dangerous and High Maintenance Urban Space", *Territory, Politics, Governance* 5.4 (2017): 443–458.

a feature of a neighbourhood's or city's natural progression from birth to death. Trying to counter water flowing downhill, as Howe put it, by intervening in the 'natural' course of things by, say, building a dam or planting trees downstream to encourage the hydrological cycle to replenish water upstream, at its source, was simply unthinkable for the likes of Howe and Joseph. Whether we are persuaded by this metaphor or not, it is clear that this policy position of 'managed decline' or 'managed rundown' has proven very influential in Liverpool's recent history. As late as the 1990s, according to a council officer I interviewed, Managed Decline was the name of a council budget tasked with (dis)investments in certain declining inner-city neighbourhoods, such as Granby. I explore the damage done to Granby by this policy discourse in Part IV.

Fatalistic belief in the natural decline of certain cities or neighbourhoods reflects the 'urban lifecycle' theory that has proven popular among policymakers on both sides of the Atlantic. This emphasises the transitions commonly experienced by urban agglomerations as a combination of various interacting structural processes—economic shifts from industrialisation through deindustrialisation; changing demographic structures, such as ageing populations, placing different demands on housing types and locations; the introduction of new technologies (e.g., cars) and changing cultural preferences for different lifestyles—with inner-city decline partly attributed to these factors. We see a similar account operating at the more micro-scale in the 'neighbourhood life-cycle' theory. This view holds that neighbourhoods have a natural lifecycle, much as human beings do, whereby as the housing stock gets older—just as biological cells age—the neighbourhood goes through a series of succession stages, ultimately leading to death. Lifecycle theory—which various critics have shown to be highly influential in American urban development policy[22]—goes so far as to claim that this decline is an inevitable end state of the natural process of ageing building stock. On this reading, the causal factors and spatial symptoms of neighbourhood decline—such as rising poverty, low demand, housing vacancy, dereliction, neglect, stigma, crime, social disorder and eventual abandonment—are simply natural consequences to which all urban neighbourhoods eventually succumb. It thereby underplays if not completely overlooks the effects on urban space of the actions and interactions of various economic agents and the political decisions made by policymakers and, indeed, the entire discipline of urban regeneration as a concerted attempt made by urban policy to resuscitate or give new life to places.

22 John T. Metzger, "Planned Abandonment: The Neighborhood Life-Cycle Theory and National Urban Policy", *Housing Policy Debate* 11.1 (2000): 7–40; Manuel B. Aalbers, "Do Maps Make Geography? Part 1: Redlining, Planned Shrinkage, and the Places of Decline", *ACME: An International E-Journal for Critical Geographies* 13.4 (2014): 525–556.

We might see such a lifecycle view as misapprehending the nature of the neighbourhood or the city as a noun rather than a verb—as a given abstract container of distinct territorial content and identity rather than, following Lefebvre,[23] as a socially performed and materially mediated space of flows produced and reproduced through the actions and interactions of various actors. A dialectical approach to urban change acknowledges both the more structural processes—demographic, technological, architectural, economic shifts—but, importantly, foregrounds other factors of change emanating from human agency, collective action, political decisions and cultural practices. Such a perspectival refocus allows us to see neighbourhood decline not simply as the result of inevitable processes beyond our capacity to modify (for example, buildings of a certain age coming to the end of their life) but as the cumulative consequence of willed political decisions and socioeconomic activities that enact particular perceptions of space, inscribing a vision of place into its material fabric.

Thus politicians, policymakers, academics and commentators are torn between two opposing views on the nature of the neighbourhood question. On one side are those who believe the neighbourhood question is posed purely by the 'natural' forces of urban-economic change and that the best we can hope for is to encourage growth or minimise the pain of inevitable decline—embodied in Howe's and Joseph's managed decline. On the other are those who contend that, through collective decision-making over resources, we can have a performative impact on the direction of urban change and that the fate of place is the product of political choices as much as structural forces.

At its most extreme, a belief in the natural lifecycle of neighbourhoods and cities may even evolve, rather ironically, into a more proactive policy of 'planned shrinkage', in which decisions are made to rationalise and redirect scarce public resources away from declining areas to those supposed to be *on the up*, in ways which may actually precipitate and perform that decline. American urbanist Roberta Brandes Gratz describes planned shrinkage as a policy of

> selectively abandoning old neighborhoods in unpopular areas of a city, while continuing to build new ones in popular sections; selectively allowing old parks and other public amenities to continue to deteriorate, while building new ones elsewhere; selectively allowing mass transit, old streets, sewer lines and other elements of a city's infrastructure to continue to decay, while building highways to encourage more of the cars that choke cities and creating new neighborhoods or

23 Lefebvre, *The Production of Space*. See also David Madden, "Neighborhood as Spatial Project: Making the Urban Order on the Downtown Brooklyn Waterfront", *International Journal of Urban and Regional Research* 38.2 (2014): 471–497.

> "new towns" that require new infrastructures and the disruption of existing networks.[24]

Critical health scholars have demonstrated the devastating effects for marginalised black communities in particular when planned shrinkage combines with racist urban policies in a process Mindy Thompson Fullilove describes as 'root shock'.[25] Here, a biological metaphor evokes collective trauma. Root shock is also perceptible in Granby, the neighbourhood of SNAP where collective alternatives have grown in spite of state-administered violence—an experience I dissect below, in Part IV.

There is certainly a sense in which Tory Cabinet Ministers in the early 1980s were toying with the idea of selectively abandoning to brute economic forces not just specific neighbourhoods in Liverpool but the entire city itself. The Labour Council administration directing resources into the slum clearance programme of the 1960s, in moving tenants and resources from inner-city areas to new towns on the periphery, might also be seen in this light. Although this was not a conscious policy of selectively abandoning inner-city areas, its effects suggest otherwise. The most damning critics of Liverpool's post-war planning policies go so far as to draw analogies with the Blitz rained down upon the city during the Second World War:

> Liverpool ... has suffered two blitzes in the last 30 years. The first left the whole city ruined but defiant. The second has picked off areas with equally devastating results. The new enemy is faceless.
>
> The peace-time blitz of Liverpool does not simply consist of waste-land where buildings once stood: it consists also of publicly-owned dwellings, none of them more than 50 years old and most a good deal newer, in an advanced state of decay.[26]

> Liverpool was left with the largest amount of "open-space" of any city in Britain. The decline of Liverpool is not simply statistical—it is visible. "It looks as if it's been bombed" is a favourite local expression that does not exaggerate.[27]

Planned shrinkage may be the proactive American equivalent of a seemingly more passive British tradition of managed decline, founded on an apparent inability to do anything other than manage an 'inevitable' regression. Yet

24 Roberta Brandes Gratz, *The Living City* (Simon & Schuster, 1989), p. 156.

25 Mindy Thompson Fullilove, *Root Shock: How Tearing up City Neighborhoods Hurts America, and What We Can Do about It* (One World/Ballantine Books, 2004).

26 Merseyside Socialist Research Group, *Merseyside in Crisis*, pp. 67 and 338.

27 Lane, "Liverpool—City of Harder Times to Come", p. 337.

both inflections connote a belief in decline as natural and outside the power of people to change. All such ideas can be incredibly destructive once entered into policy discourse. This is acknowledged in Howe's subsequent correspondence with Thatcher, stating that, in reference to managed decline, "This is not a term for use, even privately".[28]

As it rather fortuitously turned out, Howe's extremist position did not win out in Cabinet discussions and Thatcher eventually endorsed the alternative, more moderate perspective of (now Lord) Michael Heseltine, who argued for renewed government intervention and public investment in Liverpool, albeit through the imposition of anti-democratic, pro-market, property-led mechanisms of central state control over local development. In the self-styled Minister for Merseyside's personal crusade to turn the city around, Liverpool found itself at the centre of experimentation with a neoliberal urban policy regime in which the state took an interventionist role in stimulating private demand, attracting inward investment and boosting property-led development. In 1981, in the aftermath of the Toxteth Riots, Merseyside became the site of one of the country's first Enterprise Zones, in the southern outer estate of Speke, as well as, alongside London Docklands, one of the pioneering Urban Development Corporations, tasked with regenerating Liverpool's derelict docks and overseen by a specialist quango, the Merseyside Task Force. These top-down planning prescriptions were amongst the first of their kind to be tried and tested in the UK but ultimately failed to do much more than successfully restore or redevelop specific sites, such as the historic Albert Dock, due to their narrow, noun-like focus on property-led redevelopment as opposed to a more holistic approach (such as SNAP and the CDPs) considering deeper socioeconomic structures and processes, such as skills, health, housing, resource redistribution and economic ownership.

The failure of regeneration projects funded by the central state to resolve the neighbourhood question was perhaps one reason why the people of Liverpool turned their attention to the local state. In electing a Labour Council in the mid-1980s strongly influenced by the Trotskyist faction of the Militant Tendency, Liverpool experimented with a radical agenda of municipal socialism promising massive public investment in new council housing, infrastructure, parks, leisure facilities and associated new jobs. Along with only a handful of other Labour-led localities around the country pursing municipal socialist experiments,[29] Liverpool City Council clashed fiercely with central government under Thatcher but, unlike the others, also came into conflict with its potential

28 Letter, Geoffrey Howe, 4 Sept. 1981, quoted in Parker and Atkinson, "Disorderly Cities and the Policy-Making Field: The 1981 English Riots and the Management of Urban Decline".

29 Wainwright, *Labour: A Tale of Two Parties*.

local ally, Liverpool's growing housing cooperative movement. Unfortunately, the renewed municipal socialism of the 1980s proved ultimately incapable of challenging the capitalist consensus: local governments struggled to fund ambitious social programmes amidst tightening fiscal constraints. Militant councillors, as we have seen in the previous chapter, were eventually disbarred from office for setting an illegal budget.[30] Moreover, municipal socialist programmes were not just politically unsustainable. The very same concerns motivating resistance to state bureaucracy shared by urban communities and the intellectual New Left, in such actions as urban renewal protests and anti-demolition campaigns, likewise alienated residents, especially those involved in smaller-scale grassroots innovations like the co-ops. The flirtation with municipal socialism in the 1980s may have revealed the flaws in top-down state solutions to uneven urban development but also showed that localities could act against wider structural and political forces—actions which brought Liverpool back from the brink of devastation and, arguably, did far more to propel the city 'beyond the brink' than any of the neoliberal urban-entrepreneurial policies following in its wake and celebrated in conventionally boosterist fashion.[31]

Militant's municipal socialism, the Eldonians' 'self-regenerating community' and Heseltine's Task Force were three creative solutions to the neighbourhood question—three distinct strands spun from the vortex of economic restructuring in which Liverpool was so tightly caught in the 1980s. In this context of urban experimentation, Liverpool found itself at the centre of a heated academic debate in geography in the 1980s, known as the locality debate. Critical geographer Doreen Massey's classic text *Spatial Division of Labour* helped shape the debate, which hinged on the relative power of localities to respond positively to the effects of structural economic shifts.[32] Merseyside was one of seven key case studies in the localities studies research conducted in the late 1980s and which sought to show how localities could proactively shape their fates in the face of intense global forces.[33] Richard Meegan's study of Merseyside emphasised the resistance and policy innovations made in response to the swift destruction of the city's raison d'être.[34] Despite being criticised by

30 Frost and North, *Militant Liverpool: A City on the Edge.*

31 Michael Parkinson, *Liverpool Beyond the Brink: The Remaking of a Post-Imperial City* (Liverpool University Press, 2019).

32 Doreen Massey, *Spatial Division of Labour: Social Structures and the Geography of Production* (Palgrave Macmillan, 1984).

33 Philip Cooke, ed., *Localities: Changing Face of Urban Britain* (Routledge, 1989); Michael Harloe, Chris Pickvance and John Urry, eds, *Place, Policy and Politics: Do Localities Matter?* (Routledge, 1990).

34 Richard Meegan, "Merseyside in Crisis and in Conflict", in Michael Harloe, Chris Pickvance and John Urry, eds, *Place, Policy and Politics: Do Localities Matter?* (Routledge, 1990).

Marxist geographers[35] for their spatial fetishism and dense empiricism, these studies showed how structural processes had to be grounded *somewhere*, to manifest their effects in one spatial setting or another, and that the converse held true: global forces could in turn be countered and potentially altered—if only minutely—by changes occurring at the local level, initiated by political resistance or proactive experimentation with different policies and projects. In many ways this was yet another rehash of the classic debate between Marxists and anarchists around the nature of social change and the most effective scale of resistance.

What the Eldonians, Militant and the Minister for Merseyside all had in common—notwithstanding deep ideological differences—was their unflinching belief that they could positively impact the fate of neighbourhoods and, indeed, an entire city despite popular influential political narratives to the contrary. But their approaches to delivering their respective visions for Liverpool were highly divergent. Except, that is, for a striking similarity between the otherwise diametrically opposed Militant URS and the Minister for Merseyside's Task Force. Each cared more about *what* was delivered than *how* it was delivered. They cared more about ends than means. These policy agendas were done more *for* or *to* people than *with* them. The Eldonian model, on the other hand, represents an alternative, community-led approach more grounded in democratic self-governance. Although some of their aspirations were in reality never more than that and their governing structures were deeply flawed and riven by internal contradictions, as will be explored in the following chapter, it nonetheless prefigures something qualitatively different from the state–market, public–private dichotomy represented by the Militant-led Council and Thatcher's government—something inhering more in the social economy than the public or private sector; in the commons rather than the socialist state or the capitalist market.

Can Collective Housing Save the City?

So how can a more social economy begin to resolve the neighbourhood question? This is the subject of a growing field of research around 'territorial social innovation' that poses its own question: can neighbourhoods save the city?[36] One of its leading theorists Frank Moulaert provides some answers as to why the neighbourhood scale has become important for both urban policy and social action over recent decades. Partly because economic restructuring and

35 David Harvey, "Three myths in search of a reality in urban studies", *Environment and Planning D: Society and Space* 5 (1987): 367–376; Neil Smith, "Dangers of the Empirical Turn: Some Comments on the CURS Initiative", *Antipode* 19.1 (1987): 59–68.

36 Frank Moulaert, Flavia Martinelli, Erik Swyngedouw and Sara González, *Can Neighbourhoods Save the City?: Community Development and Social Innovation* (Routledge, 2010).

urban decline are most *tangible* in neighbourhoods: "social relations, governance dynamics and agents 'responsible for' the decline are more easily identifiable in urban neighbourhoods than in lower density areas or at higher spatial scales".[37] Partly because the *spatial concentration* of exclusion factors in these places simultaneously creates a downward spiral of neglect and hopelessness: "proximity feeds depression, fatalism, localised *déjà-vus*" and state agencies and investors gradually withdraw, as a kind of self-fulfilling prophecy, but which simultaneously acts as a catalyst and opportunity for alternatives to develop.

But what exactly creates this catalyst for change? Human needs being left unmet by the state and the market leaves a vacuum to be filled by other actors, who reach towards alternative solutions through a process of social innovation. In terms of Liverpool, market failure can be discerned in the collapse of its maritime economy; state failure in the way in which post-war urban renewal efforts only exacerbated the problem, by removing much of the workforce to outer estates, where jobs also failed to materialise. But human needs are not only economic or 'material'—they amount to more than having a job and a house in which to live. For social innovation scholars, needs also include at least two other dimensions: cultural or 'existential' needs of self-expression and creativity; and 'political' needs of participatory citizenship and self-government.[38] In this way, social innovation moves beyond any supposed one-dimensional solution to the housing question critiqued by Engels, where deprivation is too narrowly conceived as simply material exploitation. These various forms—alienation from existential deprivation, social exclusion from political deprivation, as well as exploitation from material deprivation—can be seen to spark reactions amongst affected citizens who, under the right conditions, may self-organise and mobilise for change.

Social innovation builds on traditions of self-organisation in civil society stretching back centuries to practices of commoning and guild socialism through mutualism and cooperativism. Since capitalist institutions were constructed to commodify land, labour, capital and knowledge, these movements have sought to innovate new institutional forms that de-commodify, decentralise and democratise these domains. In the domain of knowledge we see the recent innovation of cooperative, peer-to-peer and open source digital platforms; in capital, we see credit unions and building societies; in labour, we see worker-owned cooperatives; and, most importantly for our purposes, in land, we see the innovation of housing cooperatives, mutual ownership societies and community land trusts. Innovations in the

37 Frank Moulaert, "Social Innovation: Institutionally Embedded, Territorially (Re) Produced", in Diana MacCullum, Frank Moulaert, Jean Hillier and Serena Vicari Haddock (eds), *Social Innovation and Territorial Development* (Ashgate, 2009), pp. 11–24 (p. 16).
38 Frank Moulaert, Flavia Martinelli, Erik Swyngedouw and Sara González, "Towards Alternative Model(s) of Local Innovation", *Urban Studies* 42.11 (2005): 1969–1990.

institutions that govern social and economic life for the creation of greater social value and community benefit have thus been conceptualised as 'social innovations'.[39] Taken together, social innovations help bring about a distinct kind of economy, known variously as the social economy, the community economy or the solidarity economy.[40] This describes a different form of economic relationship to either capitalist market exchange or state redistribution—one founded on voluntary association, cooperation, gift exchange, mutual aid and solidarity. It is a 'social' rather than public (state) or private (market) logic. The social economy organises economic functions primarily according to democratic, co-operative and reciprocal principles; aims for high levels of equality, redistribution and empowerment of marginalised citizens; and works towards the satisfaction of unmet human needs.

Social innovation is defined as social change that achieves conditions of empowerment in three domains: the satisfaction of human needs previously left unmet; changes in the social relations of governance that enable full participation in society; and increased socio-political capabilities to access the resources required to satisfy needs and enable participation. In terms of housing, we can see how collective housing alternatives such as co-ops can—in theory at least—achieve these three conditions of empowerment. In these alternative models, the ownership of economic assets (e.g., land and buildings) is radically redistributed so that previously deprived groups gain access to shelter but also to the economic benefits that accrue from having a stake in common property. Democratised development and management processes restructure power relations both between residents and with other stakeholders, as we have seen in the radical equalisation of power with architects and developers in the Liverpool new-build co-ops. Cooperative governance structures enable the participation of members in decision-making and, as we have seen in the generation of councillors from the new-build co-ops in Liverpool, empower people to become more involved in the politics of wider society.

However, achieving social innovation in the realm of housing alone is not enough to revitalise neighbourhoods, let alone stem the tide of decline. What about enterprise? What about jobs? What about access to finance? The relative success or impact of social innovations such as cooperatives depends on their ability to construct relatively autonomous local 'circuits of value' in which

39 Moulaert, Martinelli, Swyngedouw and González, *Can Neighbourhoods Save the City?*

40 Frank Moulaert and Oana Ailenei, "Social Economy, Third Sector and Solidarity Relations: A Conceptual Synthesis from History to Present", *Urban Studies* 42.11 (2005): 2037–2054; Ethan Miller, "Community Economy: Ontology, Ethics, and Politics for Radically Democratic Economic Organizing", *Rethinking Marxism* 25.4 (2013): 518–533; Peter North and Molly Scott Cato, eds, *Towards Just and Sustainable Economies: The Social and Solidarity Economy North and South* (Policy Press, 2017).

resources flow between domains within communities rather than siphoned off into global circuits of capital.[41] The idea is to develop local democratic institutional structures "organised around the goal of 'reclaiming' that capital by limiting its potential mobility by anchoring it within localities".[42] Community development scholar James DeFilippis[43] categorises the different types of autonomous local development corresponding to three spheres in circuits of value: community control over the means of production (labour), such as worker cooperatives; the means of exchange (capital), such as credit unions and community-owned shops; and the means of social reproduction (land), the domestic spaces of the home and neighbourhood, through mutual ownership of housing such as cooperatives and community land trusts. The aim is not only to build wealth but to fix it in place and lock it within democratic ownership models that plug the gaps in leaking local economies and enable the recycling and reinvestment of wealth locally.

Viewing the neighbourhood or city as a holistic 'circuit of value' plugged into wider regional, national and global circuits allows us to see that reappropriating just one sphere of the economy—housing—is not enough to build a sustainable alternative. This is where a particular collective model comes in—the 'community development trust'—a model distinct from housing co-ops in a number of ways but fundamentally because it develops more than just housing. Community development trusts originated in 1960s campaigns against inner urban renewal—paralleling the housing cooperative movement.[44] They share a great deal with the more established 'community development *corporations*' in the USA, which grew up as 'coordinating agents' for a whole range of community-owned activities, not just housing.[45] Community development trusts aim to acquire land and assets as means of protection from demolition, speculation or public disinvestment, for more sustainable and participatory community-led property development and, crucially, as incubating hubs for the development of other community businesses and social enterprises—i.e., the

41 Roger Lee, Andrew Leyshon, Theresa Aldridge et al., "Making Geographies and Histories? Constructing Local Circuits of Value", *Environment and Planning D: Society and Space* 22.4 (2004): 595–617.

42 James DeFilippis, "Alternatives to the 'New Urban Politics': Finding Locality and Autonomy in Local Economic Development", *Political Geography* 18 (1999): 973–990 (p. 983).

43 DeFilippis, "Alternatives to the 'New Urban Politics'"; James DeFilippis, *Unmaking Goliath: Community Control in the Face of Global Capital* (Routledge, 2004).

44 Nick Bailey, "The Role, Organisation and Contribution of Community Enterprise to Urban Regeneration Policy in the UK", *Progress in Planning* 77.1 (2012): 1–35.

45 David Imbroscio, *Reconstructing City Politics: Alternative Economic Development and Urban Regimes* (SAGE, 1997); Severyn Bruyn and James Meehan, *Beyond the Market and the State: New Directions in Community Development* (Temple University Press, 1987).

social economy. They have been characterised as 'community anchors' for their *anchoring* role in communities—as hubs of social and economic activity, growing wealth from the grassroots and anchoring it in place.[46] Early exemplars of local struggles that successfully campaigned for the transfer of public land and assets into community ownership include Coin Street Community Builders, established in 1984 to manage land for cooperative housing and community facilities on London's South Bank.[47] Coin Street was one of the founding members of the national umbrella group (or secondary organisation) for community development trusts, the Development Trust Association, now named Locality. And in Liverpool we have the Eldonian Community Trust, still the country's largest community-owned housing trust and enterprise and seen as a pioneering example of social innovation.[48] Whereas Coin Street was supported by the local state—in fact, one of the final acts of the Greater London Council before its abolition by Thatcher's government was the gifting of prime real estate to the Community Builders—in the case of the Eldonians, Liverpool City Council was dead set against them. The story of how they got to where they are today, despite such challenges, is the subject of the next chapter.

46 James Henderson and Christopher McWilliams, "The UK Community Anchor Model and Its Challenges for Community Sector Theory and Practice", *Urban Studies* 54.16 (2017): 3826–3842.

47 Guy Baeten, "From Community Planning to Partnership Planning: Urban Regeneration and Shifting Power Geometries on the South Bank, London", *GeoJournal* 51 (2000): 293–300; Guy Baeten, "Urban Regeneration, Social Exclusion and Shifting Power Geometries on the South Bank, London", *Geographische Zeitschrift* 89.2/3 (2001): 104–113.

48 Roberts, "Social Innovation, Spatial Transformation and Sustainable Communities: Liverpool and the 'Eldonians'".

CHAPTER 8

The Eldonians

From Parish Politics to Global Exemplar

The story of the Eldonians is an epic struggle against adversity. This is a story that has been told comprehensively elsewhere, notably by Jack McBane, the MIH co-op development officer who worked very closely with the Eldonians and whose historical account, *The Rebirth of Liverpool: The Eldonian Way*, I draw on extensively in what follows, triangulating with my own research, comprising observation and interviews with residents, activists, politicians, housing professionals and community leaders, as well as with other commentaries.[1] Like most other co-op communities in Liverpool, the Eldonians are a homogeneous white working-class community, but unlike many of the co-ops in the south end, rooted in Protestantism, the Eldonians are staunchly Catholic, descendants of Irish migrants, many of whom came to Liverpool to escape the Potato Famine of 1845–47. Of the hundreds of thousands of migrants that fled the famine for Liverpool—over half of whom were designated by the authorities as 'paupers'—tens of thousands stayed, many settling in slums built behind the docks in the inner north end. Most of these back-to-back tenements were concentrated around the north docks in areas like Vauxhall, close to the employment opportunities, far away from much of the wealthy merchant and artisan housing further inland and in the south end, in areas like Granby. Vauxhall became increasingly overcrowded and housing conditions worsened as 'Jerry-built' terraces were thrown up.

Amidst these terrible conditions, people turned to each other and to the church for solace and support. The Catholic Church was a central component of people's lives and a powerful presence in the somewhat parochial politics of Vauxhall, which alone had around fourteen parish churches. Irish Catholic

1 Tim Mars, "Mersey Tunnel Vision?", *ROOF* 12.6 (1987); Peter Roberts, "Social Innovation, Spatial Transformation and Sustainable Communities: Liverpool and the 'Eldonians'", in Paul Drewe, Juan-Luis Klein and Edward Hulsbergen, eds, *The Challenge of Social Innovation in Urban Revitalization* (Techne Press, 2008); Ken Rogers, *The Lost Tribe of Everton and Scottie Road* (Trinity Mirror Sport Media, 2010); Ken Rogers, *Lost Tribe: The People's Memories: 2* (Trinity Mirror North West and North Wales, 2012); David Sheppard and Derek Worlock, *Better Together: Christian Partnership in a Hurt City* (Hodder & Stoughton, 1988).

migrants displaced existing Protestant communities, who moved further up the ridge that frames Liverpool, away from the docks, heightening sectarian resentments. A former council housing officer describes them as "really old, well-established communities" with strong communal identities, in which "families know each other". She explains that "you didn't cross parishes really, you didn't go to St Marys, 'cause although you could spit that far it felt like you needed a passport to go there". But this was not a sectarian issue, for all these parishes were Catholic, with fiercely loyal, "parochial" internal attachments. Liverpool has often been described to me as a "city of a thousand villages", each looking no further across so many imagined boundaries. The depth of such attachments can be seen in the very name of the Eldonians, derived from Eldon Street, where the local parish church, Our Lady of Reconciliation, was located, defining the centre of the community, as well as the church social club, in which community meetings were held. An alternative explanation is the name of the football team that Paul Orr, the local Labour councillor and Eldonian ally, played for as a youngster.[2] Football and religion: defining features of Liverpudlian identity.

Despite the obvious challenges for building broader civic cohesion and 'bridging' social capital,[3] these parish-based communities had the advantage of strong 'bonding' capital—internal solidarity, networks of mutual aid, communality and togetherness—which would prove invaluable in keeping the Eldonians unified in their campaign for better housing. In a recent populist history of the north end, an edited collection of "the people's memories" prior to slum clearance, journalist and historian Ken Rogers, addresses his audience directly: "You speak with one voice. It's as if you all come from the same group, the same family, dare I say it, the same TRIBE".[4] Written to express the feelings of residents, the book laments the 1960s slum clearance policies for displacing and breaking up communities, even if supportive of the need to improve the terrible conditions besetting the tenements. One such episode in this tragic history was particularly disruptive and became an important lesson in the formation of the Eldonians. Constructed from 1968 to 1971 and described by Rogers as the "biggest hole in the ground ever dug in Liverpool",[5] the Kingsway Mersey Tunnel required the demolition of most housing in the immediate area, including five hundred dwellings built just five years earlier by the council to rehouse people from the slums. Local resident Tony McGann, who would later become the leader of the Eldonians, describes to me how

2 Peter Kilfoyle, *Left Behind: Winning Back a Labour Heartland and the Defeat of Militant* (Politico's Publishing, 2000).

3 Robert Putnam, *Bowling Alone: The Collapse and Revival of American Community* (Simon & Schuster, 2000).

4 Rogers, *Lost Tribe: The People's Memories: 2*, p. 174; original emphasis.

5 Rogers, *Lost Tribe: The People's Memories: 2*, p. 177.

"we lived in really bad conditions, ten of us in two rooms … and we had no running water". Urban renewal of some sort was therefore welcome, but in the event

> Thousands of people were put out their homes and sent all over the place … People had no say. And what went down that hole was my home, my home and thousands of others and all the small firms went down that hole in the ground, and people were scattered to the four winds.

Not only did countless small family-run businesses and local jobs 'go down the hole' of the Mersey Tunnel but the community as a whole—characterised by Tony as "heartbroken"—was fragmented. This was the principal motivation behind the Eldonians' campaign for a co-op. In 1978, the council decided to demolish the tenement blocks around Eldon and Burlington Streets, affecting 1,500 people in the heart of the parish, as part of the Liberals' Tenement Rehousing Programme. McGann, who had managed to secure a new tenancy in the Eldon Street area, quickly became the community contact for housing issues—a 'go to man' or an 'unpaid councillor'[6]—and, inspired by his personal experience of displacement, used his new leadership role to rally tenants around opposing the plans. An infamous meeting called by the council planners was attended by local councillors, the priesthood and 250 local residents. Parish priest Father O'Reilly questioned for the first time the authority of the planners to dictate tenement demolition. This sparked dissent from the community, and local councillor, Paul Orr, suggested a survey of residents' views should be conducted. Implemented by McGann, the survey discovered that some 90 per cent did not want to move away but nonetheless wanted demolition or improvement. This was the first time the people of Vauxhall had ever been asked what they actually wanted. It provided a community mandate for an alternative to council rehousing which led to the formation of the Eldonian Community Association in the early 1980s, with McGann elected as chair. The Eldonians then began negotiating with city councillors and housing officers, leading to contact with Chris Davies, the council's Chair of Housing, who explained to me the proactive attitude of the Eldonians compared with other groups fighting displacement he encountered:

> The thing about the Eldonians was they were always so positive! Other people would come in and whinge and say, "This should be done for us" … and Tony would come along with his people and say, "Look, we know you're doing your best, and you're facing difficulties; now what if

6 Jack McBane, *The Rebirth of Liverpool: The Eldonian Way* (Liverpool University Press, 2008).

> we were to do this; could you do that?" Just positive and good feedback, and you wanted to work with them—I did anyway.

The Eldonians had heard about other groups facing similar challenges establishing themselves as co-ops as a means to contest displacement, and it was during these negotiations with Davies that the Eldonians first learned how to run a co-op campaign. Between the five hundred or so families living in the various 1930s-built tenements around Eldon Street who were involved in the Eldonian Community Association, it was agreed in 1982 that Portland Gardens was the priority. Of the Portland Gardens tenants, 140 opted to stay with the council, in a conversion scheme around the old blocks, whilst 326 voted for a co-op.[7] The council agreed to a 'top-downing' improvement scheme, reducing Portland Gardens from four to two storeys. At this point, the Eldonians sought the advice of the leading co-op development agencies and Chris Davies put them in touch with Jack McBane at MIH. McBane describes how, upon first meeting the Eldonians, he fell "instantly in love" with the people and, in particular, Tony's "mix of aggression with humour and charm". He explains to me how he was asked to interview along with CDS and Neighbourhood Housing Services:

> So the interview panel was like 30 people and I'll never forget it. They had a big social hall, they had an organisation, and they were used to running things, and I said, "I don't think you're thinking big enough. This place is a shithole, you know that, why don't you take on the whole neighbourhood?" And at this McGann's eyes began to light up … I said, "Nobody else cares for this place. It's been abandoned by the council, the businesses have already left town, housing associations aren't even active here. The only thing that's alive and well here is you. What's the point in doing a housing co-op surrounded by this? Because you're going to waste a huge amount of resources and my time and the architect's time doing a co-op—why don't we just change the whole thing and gear it up?"

McBane got the job on the back of a personal 'click' with the Eldonians and for his ambitious ideas for local economic development beyond just housing. This was the genesis of a grander vision for a self-regenerating community which would transform the project into a community development trust aimed at wholesale neighbourhood regeneration and community ownership of multiple assets. These aspirations for self-government were reflected in the tagline for the first exhibition and brochures presenting the Portland

7 Robert Cowan, P. Hannay and R. Owens, "The Light on Top of the Tunnel, in Vauxhall Victors: Eldonians Special Issue", *Architects' Journal* (23 Mar. 1988).

Gardens Co-op: 'We'll do a better job ourselves!'[8] With the help of McBane and MIH, the co-op appointed two architects for four smaller and one larger site—Bill Halsall for the former; for the latter Vernon Gracie, who had worked on Byker Wall in Newcastle, an exemplar of participatory design and community architecture.[9] Divvying up the project between different architects was intended to inspire, says Halsall, some "creative competition". For his four sites, Halsall employed the principles of the Weller Way. From January 1983, there proceeded four months of intensive weekly participatory design meetings between the architects, MIH and resident representatives.

Militant Tactics, Boss Politics, Tribal Loyalties, Friends in High Places

The Eldonians' participatory planning process was suddenly cut short, however, by the election of the Militant-controlled council in May. Whatever Militant's justification for opposing the co-ops—fiscal, political, ethical—their decision to municipalise was disastrous for Portland Gardens. The co-op was registered with the Housing Corporation, but the land had yet to be transferred from the council, who were also the main funders. Portland Gardens Co-op rejected the offer made to them that would mean the council receiving full nomination rights and the Works Department being guaranteed all maintenance work. Eventually, the council agreed that co-op members would be able to move into their new homes—co-designed to suit their needs—only later to withdraw this offer and demand that houses go onto the council waiting list. The original design, too, had to be changed, with the communal elements removed in favour of a more traditional layout as dictated by the new URS guidelines. MIH was dismissed without compensation for the work already completed, amounting to tens of thousands of pounds in losses—no small sum for a secondary agency in the 1970s. MIH chief executive Barry Natton nonetheless continued to support McBane's involvement despite the uncertainty and with no payment forthcoming. McBane describes Natton as "willing to stick his neck out in a very big way" for the prestige of supporting what was at the time the biggest housing cooperative development project in Western Europe, and for the satisfaction of getting "one up on Catherine", his counterpart at CDS.

During this process, residents hoping to move into the first eleven completed homes were forcibly prevented by council officers. An ex-council officer explains how in "being an officer, stuck in the middle of that, you had to make sure you didn't get caught in the crossfire. It was a deliberate intention of my own to get to know Tony McGann and to work with the local

8 McBane, *The Rebirth of Liverpool: The Eldonian Way.*

9 Graham Towers, *Building Democracy: Community Architecture in the Inner Cities* (Routledge, 1995).

councillors there, in the north Vauxhall area". Sympathy from the officers was not enough to secure tenants their houses and so the Eldonians took more radical measures. McGann describes how

> The next day the tenant turned up with the council but, in the meantime, we'd moved our one in, put all her furniture in and we had a big Alsatian there and we had all the neighbours around, and I said, "Go on then get passed us, this is her house" ... So he said, "Oh you're just squatting! You've got 28 days' notice" ... The following week they were ready, the council, they put security in and everything now and the lad who was the vice chairman [Billy Little], great fella, he went round with a camera and said, "I'm from a magazine", went on the site and he started taking photos, looking at all the locks, and we got keys to some of the houses and then we moved some more in ... We were running rings round them!

The Eldonians successfully occupied 37 of the 55 dwellings on the larger site and 45 out of 51 on the smaller sites. This enabled those residents who had co-designed them to move into their new homes, and bought time—extra-legally—until the judicial review eventually ruled in their favour. Their successful legal challenge against Militant mirrors other campaigns in similar tenements, as a former council officer explains: "We had to take possession proceedings against those people, because they wouldn't move ... A number of the groups took action against not allocating the properties on other sites, and the judge effectively supported those groups".

Setting the Eldonians apart was their use of direct action, squatting and legal challenges as stepping stones to more ambitious political ends. The local ward Labour Party was dominated by Militant, who held meetings in an old school down a back alley to discourage attendance. McGann realised that the best way to challenge municipalisation was to join the Labour Party, fight them from the inside and take control of the ward. The Eldonians mobilised their members in large numbers—some 150—to attend local party meetings but it quickly transpired that it would be difficult to sustain those numbers. The next tactic was to move the meetings onto "home territory". The Eldonians have effectively controlled the local Labour Party ever since.

The scale of this achievement can only be understood in context. Local politics in the late 1970s was marked by a rift between the "two Labour parties of Liverpool at the time", explains a Liberal councillor: one of which was the "old Catholic mafia"; the other, Militant. Each saw the other as not truly representative of Labour politics. These internal differences reflected the sectarianism that divided Liverpool more broadly.[10] The Tories were

10 Sheppard and Worlock, *Better Together: Christian Partnership in a Hurt City*.

traditionally the party of the Protestants; Labour of Catholic. The incursion of Militant, as a broadly secular socialist faction, was a break with this tradition, upsetting the established working order of the so-called 'Catholic mafia' associated with the Liverpudlian tradition of 'boss politics'.[11] This traditionalist right-wing Catholic wing of the local Labour Party was rooted socially in Vauxhall. When Militant were eventually removed in 1987—47 Labour councillors disbarred from public office for voting for an illegal budget—six Labour councillors escaped disqualification in voting against their party, known as the 'scabby' or 'sensible six'. Three of the six were councillors for Vauxhall, including Paul Orr and an Eldonian resident John Livingstone, whose traditional views, including anti-abortion, placed them in almost polar opposition to Militant. Embedded in his tight-knit Catholic community as the principal community organiser, Tony McGann had in many respects also become a boss. Indeed, many I spoke with see Tony as a "tribal leader". This is reflected in the main office building for the Eldonian Community Trust named after him, the Tony McGann Centre. Such a tribal loyalty and reverence for leaders may seem incongruous next to the egalitarianism of cooperative principles. Nonetheless, it has enabled the Eldonians to establish a successful community housing scheme against political opposition through trust in strong leadership, an established hierarchy, internal cohesion and commitment to a common cause. Critics acknowledge that the Eldonians could not have achieved what they did without the "pragmatic alliances, their politics, their chauvinism or their macho style".[12]

McGann played a pivotal role in driving forward the Eldonian campaign, attracting loyal partners and building crucial alliances with powerful elites who would support their cause against Militant—much like Billy Floyd for Weller Street. Two agents of change were recruited from MIH: Jack McBane to work on co-op development and George Evans as housing manager. An outsider like McBane, Evans likewise describes to me how he "just got an affinity for the people, and then they asked me if I'd be their first housing manager, and I agreed, and I've been here ever since". One co-op development worker distinguishes the difference between CDS's work in the south end from MIH's for the Eldonians:

> Jack McBane was more a vanguardist if that makes sense, and I don't think Jack necessarily distinguishes his own role from that of the Eldonians, who were—I use this word in a very loose way—more Stalinist: "We'll decide, and the rest will follow". The leadership were very effective, though it was very kind of centrally directed, and I think Jack was more a part of that than a servant.

11 Tony Lane, *Liverpool: City of the Sea*, 2nd ed. (Liverpool University Press, 1997).

12 Cowan, Hannay and Owens, "The Light on Top of the Tunnel", p. 43.

Jack and George supported Tony to comprise the unofficial Eldonians leadership. But it was Tony's exceptional capability to attract people to the cause that was so crucial in the eventual success of the campaign. Bill Halsall puts it plainly:

> Tony McGann is a very persuasive man; you can't take the individual factor out of it ... He has an ability—a unique ability in my experience—he can go in all guns blazing to have a big argument with somebody and come out with a lifelong friend. Max [Steinberg] is his best mate, and the number of times he's stormed into Max's office ... I'm sure Max will say he's a very hard man to say no to.

Tony used these skills to make friends in high places, not just locally—notably Max Steinberg (at the Housing Corporation) and the two bishops of Liverpool (Catholic Archbishop Worlock and Anglican Bishop Sheppard)—but also nationally. This included a diverse, and rather incongruous, panoply of powerful individuals. Prince Charles—"a good friend of ours", says McGann—visited the Eldonians and later officially opened the village. Then Prime Minister Margaret Thatcher, with whom McGann had dinner at Downing Street, succumbed to Tony's charm and agreed to fund the Eldonian Village against the advice of her aides. And also Neil Kinnock, then Leader of the Labour Party, who personally advised McGann, in Tony's recollection, to "stay in the trenches son", around the time of Kinnock's infamous Labour Party Conference speech in October 1985 in which he railed against Militant and ushered in the ensuing age of New Labour.

We Do It Better Together: Towards a Self-Regenerating Community

With strong leadership and alliances in place, the Eldonians were able to capitalise on the tumultuous events of the early 1980s. Deep structural shifts in the British economy left Liverpool's maritime industries in a state of terminal decline, with severe impacts for Vauxhall. Here, unemployment reached 36 per cent by the end of the 1970s, twice the Liverpool average.[13] Then, in 1981, Tate & Lyle, the biggest local employer, closed its sugar refinery, causing a further 1,700 job losses, leaving many of the Eldonians without work. Exacerbating this was the closure of the British American Tobacco factory in 1984, with knock-on bankruptcies of local feeder firms. The site was just outside Merseyside Development Corporation boundaries, but Heseltine's Task Force secured the transfer of the Tate & Lyle site to English Estates (a quasi-governmental agency for industrial property development) and opened an ideas competition

13 Chris Couch, *City of Change and Challenge: Urban Planning and Regeneration in Liverpool* (Ashgate, 2003), p. 75.

for the site in 1982. The Eldonians' bid for a *Self-Regenerating Community* built on the previous work of Bill Halsall and MIH with a vision of self-sustaining economic development and plans for new housing, jobs, training, social enterprises, community facilities and heritage conservation—the revitalisation of the Leeds–Liverpool canal—all managed by a community-owned development trust. The main aim was to house the 145 remaining families who were not part of the Portland Gardens scheme. Although the bid was disqualified from the ideas competition, for being leaked to the press by Tony, English Estates were impressed and sought to explore it further.

Over a period of eighteen months, the Eldonian campaign leadership—McGann, Orr, McBane and Halsall—met with the Task Force, English Estates, the Department of Environment and the Housing Corporation to negotiate an option on the site. Through their lobbying, with the political support of Thatcher, the Eldonians managed to secure the site and the funding required for remediation. McGann was critical in this process in personally persuading British Waterways—who owned the 'ransom strip' of the canal part of the site—to sell their land at a price reasonable enough to make it viable. Due to centuries of heavy industrial use the land was highly contaminated, requiring £2.1 million of Derelict Land Grant, signed off by Heseltine's Task Force.[14] Max Steinberg secured the rest of the funding through the Housing Corporation in 1984. Site acquisition and remediation alone took over five years and £2.2 million of public investment. The total cost of just the first phase of the village was £6.6 million. In being wholly reliant on government subsidy, the scheme would fail the conventional viability test of leveraging at least match funding from private sector investment. This was an incredibly high price to pay for just 145 households in a city in which thousands were in need of better housing. It suggests that the project was first and foremost of *political* value to its funders, which were all arms of central government.

The true worth of the project is revealed by the wider political context. Whilst Militant were in negotiations with the Tory government to secure a greater budget allocation for URS expenditure, the Eldonians were likewise visiting key politicians to secure their own ends. In July 1984, Tony McGann visited Patrick Jenkin, then Secretary of State for Environment, to lobby for government funding. Just the day before McGann's visit was the "infamous confrontation" between Militant and Jenkin, in which the 'gentlemen's agreement' of government funding for the £130 million shortfall to complete the URS was used by Militant as political ammunition—made public to embarrass and effectively blackmail central government into acquiescence.[15]

14 The following figures in this section have been sourced from McBane, *The Rebirth of Liverpool: The Eldonian Way*; Cowan, Hannay and Owens, "The Light on Top of the Tunnel"; Mars, "Mersey Tunnel Vision?"

15 Cowan, Hannay and Owens, "The Light on Top of the Tunnel".

Jenkin then visited Liverpool to witness the work of the URS in tackling the housing situation, stating his shock at "families living in conditions the like I have never seen before … They are very grim indeed [and] beggar description".[16] Angered by Militant's manoeuvring, however, Jenkin cut his tour short to visit the Eldonians instead, on Tony's offer. Jenkin was impressed and pledged his support for the scheme, signing off in October 1984 the £6.5 million of Housing Corporation funding Steinberg had earmarked. The Eldonian Housing Cooperative was established in the same year, with McGann as chairman. A representative committee drawn from the 145 families appointed Bill Halsall as architect, who convened a participatory design process with a core design committee of fifteen.

It seemed the hand was won for the Eldonians to begin development on site, but the Militants had one last card to play. Despite the Eldonians' bypassing council control, via central government ownership and funding of the land, the council still retained power over the planning process. An application for 'change of use' from industrial to residential was required before development could commence, but the submission in early 1985 was refused by planning officers, under effective command of Militant, on grounds of health risk from noxious smells from nearby factories. The Eldonians appealed and requested a planning inquiry. English Estates advised the hiring of the best planning QC in the country and paid the £35,000 fee. In court, the council's defence collapsed into farce upon the Eldonians' barrister pointing out that the map—purportedly showing the transmission of noxious factory fumes into the planned site according to prevailing winds—was actually upside down. The depth of support and common feeling felt for the Eldonians by the public and high profile allies alike is captured by Archbishop Derek Worlock's words in the inquiry: "If you move these people on against their will, I'm going to stand shoulder to shoulder with them in the street".[17]

Upon winning the public inquiry, the Eldonians celebrated in the traditional manner: a huge street party and brass band procession to the Eldonian village site emblazoned with the banner 'we did it better together'.[18] This would later morph into the new Eldonian motto, 'we do it better together'—softening the message of their earlier slogan 'we'll do a better job ourselves'. This discursive shift signals a subtle but deep-felt change in the Eldonian mindset from a more independent and embattled stance against the council towards a realisation that collaborative partnerships are the only way to make things happen. 'We do it better together' not only captures the collective nature of the campaign and internally tight togetherness of the community

16 Diane Frost and Peter North, *Militant Liverpool: A City on the Edge* (Liverpool University Press, 2013), p. 81.

17 Quoted in Rogers, *Lost Tribe: The People's Memories: 2*, p. 185.

18 McBane, *The Rebirth of Liverpool: The Eldonian Way.*

but also expresses appropriately their new partnership style of working, their forging of pragmatic alliances and, perhaps, their promiscuous seeking of support from whoever would offer it, even those they would normally count as ideological enemies. Catholic Archbishop Worlock and Anglican Bishop Sheppard—very active at the time in bridging denominational divides across Liverpool—celebrated and adopted the Eldonians' motto in titling their joint-authored book on healing sectarianism *Better Together*.[19] In return, the Eldonians memorialised their two biggest local supporters by naming two roads in the Eldonian village after them—Bishop Sheppard Court and Archbishop Worlock Court. In fact, they have honoured all their significant partners, allies and supporters in this way. Many of the cul-de-sac 'Courts' adjoining Eldonian Way are prefixed with 'Jack McBane', 'Paul Orr', 'O'Reilly', 'Steinberg'. Such cultic veneration does not, however, extend so far as Jenkin Drive or Thatcher Close.

This is not to say that the Eldonians are unaware of the debt they owe to Thatcher—or, indeed, in a roundabout way, Militant, for provoking the Tories into uncharacteristic policy moves. George Evans is certainly not fooled:

> Right, £6.4 million, £2.1 million derelict land grants for a piece of land which was highly contaminated and had been valued at just over a quarter of a million—you're not telling me that there wasn't some politics in that! We then get within a couple of weeks an appeal set up, a top barrister from London representing us, and we get a finding within a month! Well, there's got to be some political pressure hasn't there otherwise you got to be so naïve … I mean if Margaret Thatcher wanted it done it was going to get done.

In the context of an intensifying battle between the Tory government and Militant-controlled Liverpool Council over the city's budget, Thatcher was looking to undermine their authority and reassert central control. The Eldonian scheme was the perfect pawn to play. By using arm's-length instruments and experimental regeneration programmes, such as the Merseyside Development Corporation and Task Force, central government was able effectively to bypass the city council, who not only stood in opposition to the scheme but also presented a very real risk to the government's credibility and the stability of central–local state relations. In 1988, Merseyside Development Corporation boundaries were extended to include the Tate & Lyle site within its remit—the crucial move that circumvented council control and guaranteed planning permission for housing. By 1990, the site had been cleared and remediated, 145 houses built, and the first tenants moving in. This was the first time any substantial community-led or residential development had been

19 Sheppard and Worlock, *Better Together: Christian Partnership in a Hurt City*.

incorporated within an urban development corporation zone, which were fundamentally for commercial redevelopment.[20] The counterintuitive support offered by the Conservative government to a Labour-voting, socialist-leaning community housing cooperative can be explained as a political tactic to "drive a wedge between a municipal housing authority and the people who would normally have been its natural constituency".[21] In Bill Halsall's final analysis, the "Eldonians became a bit of a political football—but they got what they wanted".

The Eldonians are adamant, however, that they would have succeeded in redeveloping their neighbourhood with or without Thatcher's support, just on a more incremental and piecemeal scale. They had originally envisioned Portland Gardens as the first of many smaller federated co-ops, had it not been so suddenly municipalised. What the political battle with Militant enabled was far greater levels of political support for the (too) costly redevelopment of the Tate & Lyle site and the wholesale transformation of an area that would most likely have otherwise remained derelict and contaminated ex-industrial land for decades to come. This unique set of circumstances casts doubt on whether such a process of local economic development and regeneration of declining industrial areas is a sustainable or replicable model—at least within conventional parameters of politically acceptable costs. Most importantly, it highlights the necessity of state funding where private investment is non-existent. The Eldonians' 'self-regenerating' achievements—contradictions notwithstanding—have been recognised internationally. In 2004, the Eldonian Village was awarded the UN World Habitat Award for Sustainable Development, and in 2017 the Eldonian community-based housing association was awarded the Freedom of Liverpool, alongside Tony McGann, who has also been honoured with an OBE for his community leadership.

Eldonia: An Independent Micro-State?

The Eldonians have since built on initial successes to pursue a more holistic neighbourhood planning approach, proactively forging new partnerships to develop further the Eldonian Village and the surrounding urban area. Phase Two was completed in 1994, involving 150 more homes and the decontamination and landscaping of the Leeds–Liverpool canal that flows through the site, later extended into the city centre docks. This was financed by another Housing Corporation grant of £5.5 million and a £1.5 million loan from the Co-operative

20 Richard Meegan, "Urban Development Corporations, Urban Entrepreneurialism, and Locality: The Merseyside Development Corporation", in Rob Imrie and Huw Thomas, eds, *British Urban Policy: An Evaluation of the Urban Development Corporations* (SAGE, 1999), pp. 64–105.

21 Robert Cowan, "Co-op or Cop-Out?", *ROOF* 11.4 (1986), p. 22.

Bank. The village now has over 2,500 residents and over a hundred staff are employed by associated community-owned organisations. In the early 1990s, shortly after the completion of Phase One, the Eldonian Housing Cooperative was reconstituted as the Eldonian Community Based Housing Association. The Association was registered with the Housing Corporation as a social landlord, but remained under the direct control of the community through an overarching charitable body, the Eldonian Community Trust, whose board directors are democratically elected by members. The trust is described by George Evans as the "charitable arm, a registered charity that looks after the social aspects within the area—looking after the elderly, arranging activities, summer activities for the children, community transport"—as well as overseeing, as an umbrella body, the two operational organisations, the housing association and the development trust. The Eldonian Development Trust was established in 1987 by the Eldonian Community Trust as a community-based social enterprise and business arm of the Eldonians and since renamed the Eldonian Group Ltd. EGL's remit is socioeconomic development broadly defined and the provision and management of various services and on-site facilities, including the Tony McGann Centre, village hall, sports centre, day nursery, extra-care facility, residential elderly care home and several community enterprises. It remains directly accountable to the Eldonian Community Trust, governed by a board originally comprising four selected local businessmen and seven Eldonian residents—a ratio later weakened to 5 : 6, such that the residents need to vote together, in consensus, in order to retain overall control over board decisions.

Indeed, residents hold EGL to account more through informal networks. EGL is located in an old school next to the Eldonian Village, and EGL staff are often met after work, or confronted in the street, an EGL employee tells me, by Eldonian residents asking about future plans and particular programmes. The Community Trust board regularly provides feedback in formal meetings with the EGL board—to "inform us what is happening on the street, what're the needs on the street". George Evans explains how "there's a common denominator in that some board members are on both; and they [the two organisations] have the same name. Other than that we're totally separate structures, but we try to help each other". Through EGL's economic development work, the Eldonians are fast becoming self-sufficient in most public services and basic needs. Housing has always been the lynchpin of the project but, as Tony McGann remarks, "you can't just look at housing in isolation!" What separates the Eldonians from the Liverpool co-ops is their ambition to look at more than just housing—at training, jobs, enterprise, energy, transport, social care and community activities—as a means to create a truly self-regenerating community.

The Eldonians have become powerful economic players on Merseyside. EGL are in negotiation with various local and multinational companies to forge new partnerships for ambitious development schemes. They now have a partnership agreement with Peel Holdings for various redevelopment projects connected to Peel's 'Atlantic Gateway' vision for the Merseyside–Manchester conurbation corridor—Europe's first private-led regional spatial strategy.[22] EGL's decision to explore the prospects for local energy production in a combined heat and power (CHP) system led them to consider retrofitting the Eldonian Community Based Housing Association's stock, because, an EGL officer explains, "if we're going to produce our own energy, we can't put it into houses that are sieves". They set up a non-profit energy service company, the Eldonian Energy Partnership (with E.ON, the massive multinational European energy provider, and Peel Holdings as junior partner) and developed a CHP energy centre and district heating network (DHN)—the first of its kind to be delivered by a social enterprise. This could create 180 local jobs, with apprenticeship opportunities for young people, as well as "generating heating and power that can then be sold on to the community at an advantageous rate". The Eldonians were partners in developing the Strategic Regeneration Framework for north Liverpool with the council. The CHP-DHN centre is the flagship project of a larger strategic plan to transform north Liverpool into a leading centre for green industry through the creation of an eco-park and an environmental technologies zone, which Liverpool Mayor Joe Anderson has stated as a Mayoral pledge. To this end, EGL have been exploring ways to consolidate the city's recycling industry in the area, as well as possibilities of developing broadband infrastructure. EGL have also been very active in developing spin-off social enterprises as well as supporting other local start-ups through local enterprise programmes. An EGL representative is proud that "we have used seed grants to start companies up; we've got 23 businesses under this Group".

In housing, too, the Eldonians are involved in several development projects locally, working with big companies such as Barratt and Wimpey to deliver new homes. Whilst losing 'Eldonian' in the organisation's name purportedly helped EGL gain professional credibility in their dealings with larger commercial companies, the opposite is true for attracting homeowners. Private developers have piggybacked on the success and reputation of the Eldonians by naming after them nearby streets with new homes for sale. "It's got 'Eldon' on it, it's called 'Eldon Way' or 'Eldon Grove' or something like that", explains George Evans, "but they've used the name Eldon as a selling point—as did the people who built the houses for sale just in the corner of the

22 Sebastian Dembski, "Structure and Imagination of Changing Cities: Manchester, Liverpool and the Spatial in-Between", *Urban Studies* 52.9 (2015): 1647–1664; Iain Deas, Graham Haughton and Stephen Hincks, "'A Good Geography Is Whatever It Needs to Be': Evolving Spatial Imaginaries in North West England", in Phil Allmendinger, Graham Haughton, Jörg Knieling and Frank Othengrafen, eds, *Soft Spaces in Europe: Re-Negotiating Governance, Boundaries and Borders* (Routledge, 2014), pp. 25–44.

village". Shrewd branding is a big part of the success. George continues: "the cleverest thing we ever did was to call this a 'village'. It's a dead simple word but it gives you a picture—as opposed to the 'Eldonian Estate', of burnt out cars and kids running all over the place—of a village green, trees all over the place, and a nice place to live".

Through their community-based housing association, the Eldonians have increasingly adopted the role of facilitator, or expert development agent, opening up possibilities for private profit as ways to spur economic development and redevelop some of the local residential sites. They are keen to point out that their role is to ensure the local community benefits from any such deals with private investors. A plot of land owned by the Eldonians has been sold to an American investor planning to redevelop the site into 22 apartments and four shops, including a post office, cash machine and grocery store, which the local community—previously located in a 'food desert'—desperately needed. In such deals the Eldonians' method is to take only a down payment for the land and retain the right to withdraw the offer unless the development is built within two years so as to insure against land banking in the interests of delivering community benefit. Most recently, the housing association is planning a sheltered scheme for elderly residents consisting of 40 apartments and is working with the council on creating a gateway development to the Ten Streets cultural and creative quarter on the docks.

Embodying the logic of a self-regenerating community, EGL orient their activities, lock their assets and recycle their surpluses for community benefit. An EGL manager is upfront about their making profit from contracts with big business and consultancy work delivered elsewhere around the country:

> Profit's not a dirty word to us, but we make profit, we bring it back here and we then use that money to subsidise services we want to provide here, so "dads' and lads' clubs"—costing us fifty grand each a year—"after school clubs", things like that where the local authority will fund to a level, but we want it to be a decent level.

Such a high degree of self-provision suggests that the Eldonians have, if not fully seceded from local authority control, at least partly replaced the council as primary provider of basic services. Amongst EGL staff, a manager reveals there is an

> In-joke in here … and we do laugh because I've done it for God knows how many presentations, and people go "How would you describe the Eldonians?", and I go: "Listen, you go down through the wardrobe, down to the back of Narnia and there's another wardrobe, you go through that wardrobe, and you end up in Eldonia".

Asked whether 'Eldonia' is an alternative model to local government, this EGL manager replied:

> It probably would be. We would always work with the powers that be, we've not got a problem with that ... We're not going to declare UDI [unilateral declaration of independence], we're not an independent state. I think some of them would love to be but we're not.

The mere suggestion of UDI, however comically intended, demonstrates the Eldonians' separation from their urban surroundings—in both self-presentation and public perception. Although they work very closely with the council now—especially since Labour's Joe Anderson took office as Liverpool's first Mayor—partnership arrangements, as with economic contracts, are sought primarily to serve the needs of the village. This sometimes provokes local hostility, despite claims of positive spillover effects and benefits for neighbouring areas. One such partnership is with the police, to which the Eldonians pay an annual fee for extra services, including a direct private phone line to the local station for residents to call in case of crime or nuisance, as well as police officer patrols around the village—daily and nightly—signing in to the Tony McGann Centre as if it were a police station. Tony assures me this is neither creating a "shortfall anywhere else" in the city nor "depriving anyone else"—as they do their Eldonian rounds on overtime—and in fact it increases safety for the surrounding areas, often added into the extra patrols. Tony is adamant that "you can't live on an island". Yet the perception nonetheless exists that the Eldonians receive special treatment and isolate themselves from their neighbours' problems. An ex-council housing manager recalls a common (mis)perception that

> If you moved into the Eldonians you were fine: there's no anti-social behaviour 'cause they won't tolerate it; but there's a perception from the people who lived the other side of the road that the kids from the Eldonians used to do their anti-social behaviour elsewhere ... because they couldn't do anything on their own doorstep, so they'd go and—for want of a better phrase—shit on someone else's.

A large part of this perception may be a reaction to the fortress-like design of the village, whose defensive urbanism is intentional. An interview with the police community liaison officer published by the Eldonians explains the deliberate logic of protecting against crime "in the context of a 'Them and Us' situation, with incidents of petty burglary, car theft, and vandalism being amongst the highest in Liverpool".[23] The design chosen by residents, therefore,

23 Eldonians, *The Eldonians ... An Insight* (Eldonian Community Trust, 1996), pp. 6–7.

explains the police officer, aimed purposefully to minimise crime by deterring outsiders from coming in:

> Cul-de-sacs were created with only one entry/exit leading onto the main road through the village. Houses overlook one another offering natural surveillance. Further features include symbolic barriers, such as change of road surfaces, promoting safety and close territory.

In sum, this went much further than the URS in incorporating defensible space principles promulgated by the likes of Alice Coleman. In many ways, as Bill Halsall has professed in a recent retrospective,[24] the Eldonians anticipated and influenced emerging trends in 'sustainable' urbanism towards secured-by-design, home zones and other neighbourhood safety initiatives. Take secured-by-design, for instance: it is now a legal requirement that planning documents for all new social housing are submitted to the police, who make sure they accord with defensible space principles to reduce the potential for crime.

Threat of crime was one motivation for the Eldonians' defensive design inclinations. These were also a spatial manifestation of conflict with the council as well as tribal hostilities towards neighbouring parishes. Despite working closely with counterpart community development trusts, social enterprises and co-ops—among them Vauxhall Neighbourhood Council, Athol Village Co-op and Everton Development Trust—EGL has been careful not to publicise to Eldonian residents that they are helping or even visiting any one of them, or vice versa. Rivalries between these organisations are rooted in parish politics, deeply divided by clan. One EGL manager believes "they're jealous" of the Eldonians for their comparative success in securing long-term contracts with companies over mere grants from government—generating stable and growing income with greater long-term security and economic self-sufficiency than one-off grants provide. Vauxhall Neighbourhood Council, in particular, has a rivalry as old as the organisations themselves. Having emerged out of the Vauxhall CDP of 1967–72, Vauxhall Neighbourhood Council precedes the Eldonians yet has imitated many of their practices by, for example, establishing their own nearby housing cooperative, Athol Village, completed in 1994 also by MIH. An ex-housing manager remembers "when the first member of the Eldonian staff went—ever went—into Vauxhall Neighbourhood Council premises, it was like the end of the Cold War!" With this historical tribalism in place it is understandable why the Eldonians have prioritised supporting their own even if this means guarding against their neighbours. By the same

24 Bill Halsall, *Alternative Third Wave Housing Futures*, presented at "Housing—A Critical Perspective", Conference 8–9 Apr. 2015, Liverpool (Architecture Media Politics Society, 2015).

token, it is extraordinary just how proactive and collaborative they have been in developing partnerships with other organisations to deliver socioeconomic change not just in their neighbourhood but across the city.

CHAPTER 9

Cooperative by Name If Not by Nature

In assessing the achievements of the Eldonians today it is clear there is a relative lack of resident participation or internal democracy, at least compared with some of the new-build co-ops. The sheer size of thc village alone—160 families—is enough to make direct participation near impossible, with representative democracy favoured over more participatory forms. The Eldonians are upfront about not being a co-op; they are rather a community-based housing association and community development trust, having changed their legal structure as soon as the first houses were built. It is questionable whether the Eldonians were ever really seriously interested in cooperative principles or, rather, simply saw the co-op model as a useful tool with funding opportunities and political support attached to get them where they wanted to go. During the 1970s, there was a broad consensus in the wider cooperative movement that the upper functional limit to co-op membership size was around 40 families or 40 houses. Most co-ops in Liverpool were indeed around this size. Weller Street breached that theory with 60 households yet seemed to work relatively successfully as an integrated, cohesive, participatory co-operative—albeit one with a central committee. Beyond this it was doubtful whether a co-op could sustain or even manage in a practical sense the active involvement of all members.

Originally at 150 families, the Eldonians received much criticism from the movement for being far too big to constitute a co-op. Initially, they were looking at splitting the tenements into three smaller, 50-person co-ops, which could then be federated into an overarching housing management group to take advantage of pooling resources through economies of scale, with representatives elected by members from each co-op. "When it came down to it", recalls George Evans, "our thinking was that naturally by demolishing a tenement, which sometimes had three hundred units in, you couldn't split an estate in half just because of numbers". Jack McBane was one of the renegade voices who questioned this "magical figure" of 50—daring the community to think bigger still, bigger than even the resulting figure of 112. Their quibbling appears to have been a factor of the Eldonians' lack of genuine enthusiasm—beyond pragmatic opportunism—for the co-operative ideal. Bill Halsall imparts a little-known fact:

> They started off not as a co-op at all, and the original scheme was part home ownership and part housing association, but that collapsed because unemployment was astronomical ... So then there weren't enough people in employment to get mortgages to do the for-sale element of the scheme, so it was suggested, "why not be a co-op?"

Although Portland Gardens had originally been planned as a co-op, after its municipalisation the Eldonian leadership were not necessarily out to form another one but find the best way to regenerate their neighbourhood and provide decent housing for all their people. Once built, the inclusion of democratic decision-making in the management process was not so important so long as it effectively met needs. This approach raises questions over the democratic legitimacy of the Eldonians as a community trust. Members of the Community Based Housing Association have a nominal £1 share and get a vote in the general meetings; they elect tenant representatives annually to the trust board; but there has been a relatively "static board for over ten years", admits Evans. It remains unclear whether this is more attributable to a democratic deficit or to their success at meeting needs. McGann and his 'lieutenants', notably Evans—who together have exercised a tight grip on the Eldonians long after the campaign required it—have been instrumental in delivering effective housing management and neighbourhood services for residents. However, fears are growing that if the unofficial central committee does not relinquish some control then there will be no one coming through to take their place. The Eldonian Village is perhaps more akin, as one observer likens it, to a "community dictatorship" than a community-based cooperative.

Nonetheless, many efforts have been made over the years to ensure parity and transparency between the leadership and community. In the bingo ballot impartially adjudicated by the parish priest that decided the order of choice in the original housing allocations, Tony's ball came up last—perhaps not by accident—and he was the very final resident to move out of his decaying flat into his new home in the village. At great personal pain, he ruthlessly ensured fair treatment when his own son was found dealing drugs on the village and was consequently thrown out of his home. Moreover, the centrally directed structure seems to work very effectively for most residents—so responsive to local needs that EGL staff warn of Eldonia becoming a "nanny state". They complain they sometimes have to act like the "nasty stepfather" with some residents, who expect help with all sorts of civic and everyday issues, like schooling for their children. One manager felt the need to say to a resident "I'm not your dad!" Such a paternalistic dependency culture is the other side of the coin to the Eldonians' renowned strength, pride and extraordinary self-belief, as a community that fought a successful campaign against all odds. Whilst a testament to the success of the Eldonian structure in delivering local services, this might also stem from a peculiar sense of entitlement that has arisen on the back of 'winning the war'. Many Eldonians are still very proud of their achievements in fighting Militant, as this EGL employee testifies:

> We had a presentation once of how "we won the war" ... I was looking at this person and was thinking, "You weren't around in the war!" What they actually meant was the war for the Eldonians—guerrilla tactics and all this sort of thing, quite revolutionary ... And they see themselves like guerrilla fighters. There's a lot of them there that think because they've done that they deserve everything, somebody should be doing it for them, even though you still got to live your own life ... And you say to them: "Do revolutionaries ever retire?"

Singing the Post-Development Blues: On Revolutionaries Retiring

Taking a step back from the Eldonians to take in the wider historical landscape of Liverpool's co-op movement, of which they were arguably the last significant example, we can see that this shift in energy—revolutionaries retiring after the battle is won—is not unique to the Eldonians. It cannot be easily attributed to their effective if rather authoritarian leadership style making free-riding possible. A common phenomenon, experienced by co-op activists and professionals alike, was for what was known as the 'post-development blues'—a kind of anti-climactic melancholy and exhaustion—to take hold once the excitement of the campaign victory had finally dissipated. Bill Taylor, formerly of CDS, puts it like this:

> There was always a bit called the "post-development blues" when you'd been working for four years towards this thing and, finally, "bloody hell, practical completion, move in!" And then the people who have really led the co-op through that gestation period and the delivery period go "*phhhhheeeewwww*, right I just want a break now, I'm going to resign ..." It's almost like post-natal depression. You've been looking forward to this thing for so long, it comes along and actually then you've got a whole set of different challenges because you've got something that's alive and squawking—things like collecting rent, and tackling people who've been your friends and neighbours and who live next door about their rent arrears ...

Unlike in the case of Tony McGann, most of the co-op 'war leaders' did indeed retire to let peacetime managers take over the very different tasks of day-to-day management—described by McDonald as the "transition from development to management; from the 'military' administration to the 'civil' one".[1] This, however, created difficulties for both parties. The old guard would often become bitter and overly critical of their successors, whom they saw as untested or unaware of the challenges of campaigning, whilst the new committee members would struggle with the thankless, unending tasks of long-term financial planning and regulatory assessments as well as the tricky job of allocations. It is little surprise, then, to find that many co-ops contracted out most of their administration and housing management tasks to a secondary co-op, principally CDS, which later became North West Housing Services (NWHS). Today the majority of the remaining 50 or so Liverpool co-ops are managed by NWHS, in ways which make it difficult for tenants to feel part of the project of housing themselves. Unusually, the Eldonians have retained their housing management services in-house—their much larger membership base enabling economies of scale. This has no doubt contributed to their goal of becoming a self-regenerating community through job creation for local residents. Whether it has enabled residents to feel part of the project is another question.

Motivations tend to weaken with each transition from one generation to the next. As new members necessarily replace old, they come with very different perceptions, attitudes and expectations. Not having lived through or personally experienced the intense political campaigning, as did the founders, new generations are often more dismissive of the value of cooperative governance and do not share the same commitments in keeping the enterprise alive. There is perhaps an inevitable trade-off between, on the one hand, the kind of radical political energy, risk-taking and collective commitment to the cooperative cause that first animates resistance and, on the other, the patience, perseverance and technical expertise required collectively to manage housing over time. As maintenance costs rise, new technologies are introduced and regulatory and policy environments are renewed, and as generations come and go, with varying personal commitments, professional outsourcing and managerial procedures look more and more attractive as measures to put in place to maintain a consistent housing service. And so, over time, co-ops come to resemble just that—a housing service. Revolutionary hopes and dreams are well and truly retired.

Third Sector Empire-Building

Following the largest movement of new-build housing cooperative development in the country, Liverpool experienced several decades of relative inactivity in collective housing activism. Some of this can be explained by post-development blues but the primary constraint was legislative reforms enacted in the 1988 Housing Act, making it almost impossible for housing co-ops

1 Alan McDonald, *The Weller Way: The Story of the Weller Street Housing Cooperative* (Faber & Faber, 1986), p. 203.

to develop anew.[2] First, the generous funding system of grants paid directly from the Housing Corporation to co-ops to finance development and ongoing revenue deficits was replaced by one increasingly geared towards private finance, requiring housing associations (including co-ops) to borrow capital on private markets to finance development. Second, the 1988 Act introduced new requirements for new housing providers to demonstrate a successful track record of management before being registered with the Housing Corporation as a registered provider of social housing. Together, these changes forced small community-led co-ops, reliant on state support but otherwise relatively autonomous, to seek formal development and management agreements with larger housing associations in order to demonstrate competency and make it at all economically viable to develop expensive new housing. This threatened the independence and credibility of the co-op movement—at least in Liverpool's incarnation—as a collective housing alternative.

Another effect of the 1988 Housing Act was to strengthen the role of housing associations in public provision, which in many ways helped Liverpool Council meet its housing challenges. Conditions have improved since the days when the council was the single largest landlord and struggled physically to maintain—or manage in a socially responsive way—its 55,000 stock. Partly these improvements can be attributed to Militant Labour. Despite criticism of 'Hatton houses' and the damage to future fiscal viability of the local state, the URS had done a great deal to address the severe problems of the 1970s, by demolishing tower blocks, building relatively decent semi-detached houses amenable to upkeep, and investing in parks and leisure centres. Militant's URS was a housing-led strategy that has been in many ways continued with successive policies. Liverpool Housing Action Trust—one of six rolled out across the country, running from 1993 to 2008—seemed to blend lessons from the new-build co-op participatory design approach with the scale and ambition of the URS. Working closely with residents to refurbish 13 tower blocks and demolish 54 across the city, replacing these with 1,536 low-rise dwellings according to tenant preferences, the Liverpool Housing Action Trust has been described by housing academic Chris Couch as "not so much bottom-up community activism but a more altruistic state machine choosing to work with the community".[3] Relatively effective interventions such as this help explain why Liverpool saw a diminution in housing activism for collective alternatives through the 1990s.

More instrumental, perhaps, was the transfer and decentralisation of public stock to a multitudinous group of housing associations, empowered by the

2 Peter Malpass, "The Discontinuous History of Housing Associations in England", *Housing Studies* 15.2 (2000): 195–212; Peter Malpass and Ceri Victory, "The Modernisation of Social Housing in England", *International Journal of Housing Policy* 10.1 (2010): 3–18.

3 Chris Couch, "Housing Renewal and the Community in a Shrinking City", *Town Planning Review* 79.6 (2008): 695–703 (p. 701).

1988 Act to access private capital markets, cross-subsidise expensive rehabilitation work and invest in new social housing and maintenance of old stock in ways of which the council was made increasingly incapable. The pressure on local authorities—from both government legislation and tenant demands—to transfer their remaining stock into the hands of the growing third sector can be seen in Liverpool Council's last and largest stock transfer of its 15,000 remaining properties, in 2008, to newly created Liverpool Mutual Homes—the youngest of the largest Liverpool-born housing associations in the city today. Council tenants voted overwhelmingly in favour of transfer into Liverpool Mutual Homes' management, which is now a tenant-led organisation priding itself on tenant participation and a generally high level of tenant satisfaction, at least compared with the 'bad old days' of the Corpy. One of the officers managing the transfer process remembers that amongst all the tenant groups consulted

> There was an application for them to do something cooperative that was already on the books, but anyway it didn't come off, so all those people voted to go into Liverpool Mutual Homes housing association … So there was no drive really for independence.

The fact that conditions have improved through professionalised services is perhaps explanation enough for the lack of collective housing activism: there was simply no longer the need. This perspective is supported by the housing managers I interviewed—some of whom had worked in Liverpool through the cooperative movement; others for the council to implement the URS; most now working for some of the city's leading housing associations. They believe the lack of interest in, or emergence of, collective alternatives to public housing is explicable by placation with better housing conditions delivered by more responsive and accountable housing associations, which tend to have resident representation on their boards and certainly have more effective mechanisms for responding to tenant demands than did the council during the darkest days of the late 1970s.

Today, organisations like MIH and LHT—starting out as small place-based organisations—now rival Liverpool Council at its peak in the scale of their operations and, arguably, in the distance from and lack of accountability to the tenants they are meant to serve. By the turn of the millennium, the city's leading housing associations were engaged in a process of growth and expansion through mergers, acquisitions and stock transfer. LHT, for instance, has witnessed many mergers over the last few decades and is now part of the recently amalgamated Onward Homes, with 35,000 homes across the north-west. Few have escaped this fate—certainly not CDS, which merged with another small association, Hornby Homes, to become Plus, and then later with Cheshire-based Dane to become Plus Dane Group, which now owns and manages 18,000 homes not just in Merseyside but also across Cheshire. This logic of expansion and commercialisation increasingly marginalised the co-op side of the business within Plus Dane and led to what was formerly CDS splitting and seeking independence as North West Housing Services (NWHS), which today still manages the maintenance and finance services for the majority of co-ops across Merseyside. A leading figure within NWHS explains:

> When I joined [in 1987] they had 300 properties that belonged to CDS and 600 properties that belonged to co-ops; then they got tempted and put down a transfer and they got 900 units out of that so it suddenly became a 1,400 unit organisation. Then there was a transfer of local authority stock, so they became 6,000 units, and then they wanted to build an empire …

Empire building started for CDS when it registered with the Housing Corporation as a Registered Provider, which enabled the organisation to utilise the new housing association powers, granted in the 1988 Act, to borrow capital, build houses and administer social housing—moving away from its more modest, bespoke role as a cooperative development agency. Commercialisation has certainly separated the Liverpool housing associations from their original ideological purpose of helping people house themselves. The founder of NWHS sees this as the root of the problem:

> I didn't register North West [Housing Services] with the HCA [Homes and Communities Agency, formerly the Housing Corporation, now Homes England] because I didn't want the temptation of saying "Oh we'll buy two houses in our own name …" and then we become a straightforward housing association.

This process of expansion is accompanied by a geographical decoupling from place, reflected in the change of organisational identity: from names identified with a specific place to increasingly abstracted and placeless regional brands. MIH is an interesting example of this trend: starting out in 1928 as a small charitable trust called Liverpool Improved Homes, it later expanded its remit to become Merseyside Improved Houses, and now operates as Riverside, having dropped all reference to the Mersey but for the generic signifier of River. Today, Riverside manages over fifty thousand properties across the country. A Housing Corporation manager reasons that 'dis-placing' the brand is "also a better way of attracting partners, and moving into other areas". She continues: "Riverside stopped being Merseyside Improved Houses because it wanted to go beyond Merseyside and when you go into partnership with people, they don't want the Merseyside tag".

There are now fears in the smaller community-based housing and co-op sector that these housing associations have mutated into the same monolithic behemoths as the municipal bureaucracies they replaced, repeating many of the same mistakes. Says a housing manager:

> If you take Riverside, it had fifty thousand houses. If you go and ask any officer how many voids they have they don't even sometimes know, because it's so big and it's become so impersonal ... The board manages properties from London to Newcastle to Wales ... They've become so big that very few agenda items cover what is actually needed for the tenants. It's become like a local authority.

This phenomenon is not restricted to housing associations. The Eldonian Development Trust, which grew out of a grassroots campaign, has shed much of its community connection, in first becoming Eldonian Group Ltd and then just EGL. According to one EGL employee, this makes it more amenable to work with large multinationals without the "weight of history around your shoulders" or the "baggage" of the Eldonian affiliation:

> It's good for us to use the Eldonians when we need it, but when we don't, we're EGL ... But occasionally you think they'll appreciate the Eldonian brand, and we'll turn around and we'll say, "Well, as the Eldonians", and you're not lying 'cause we are still the bloody Eldonians ... and you can see the seismic change in their attitude to us.

The new name, bleached of place identity and history, reflects EGL's increasingly independent, detached, inter-regional business culture. The only thing apparently preventing EGL from flying the nest altogether is the unique trust structure, which ties to place the Eldonian organisations—including the community-based housing association—and makes them directly accountable to the democratically elected community trust. Or so it seemed, until events proved otherwise.

Recent signs suggest that EGL has overreached itself; that its business model is unsustainable. Following an application for a consumer credit licence, EGL have been issued several warning notices by the Financial Conduct Authority (FCA). Upon reviewing EGL's application, the FCA had concerns over the viability of EGL business practices and after no responses were received to repeated requests for further information the FCA conducted an audit, issuing a Final Notice, stating its "concerns over whether Eldonian Group Ltd can be effectively supervised, has appropriate resources, is suitable and has a suitable business model having regard to all the circumstances".[4] Since the FCA audit began, the chief executive and most of the staff, including at least one of those

4 FCA, "Final Notice 2015: Eldonian Group Ltd" (Financial Conduct Authority, 2015): www.fca.org.uk/your-fca/documents/final-notices/2015/eldonian-group-ltd, p. 2.

interviewed for this study, have all resigned from EGL. Many of its project partners, including those from the University of Liverpool, have not heard from them since. EGL has all but dissolved. Yet nothing has been reported in the local press—strange considering the Eldonians' prominent role in Liverpool's politics and economy. From what little detail those willing to talk disclosed to me, it seems that the organisation fell prey to a takeover following financial difficulties. It came to the attention of the Eldonian leadership that EGL had debts mounting up—over a million pounds, one source claimed—with higher staff overheads than revenue coming in. Others have argued that these 'debts' were time-limited and showed up on the spreadsheet due to the kind of contracts EGL was winning with big companies, often paying only in quarters, and would show as surpluses in the long run. Either way, the Eldonian leadership invited a group of local property speculators to take on EGL's debts in the hope of retaining staff. This group was linked to the Eldonians through their business connections—partners in various property redevelopment schemes in the area and also through Tony McGann's son, evicted from the village for drug dealing.

Soon after brokering this arrangement, it became apparent that the new owners were not all that interested in fulfilling EGL's original ethos of community enterprise and reinvestment for social value. Instead, EGL was stripped of its assets—siphoned off through a number of shell companies. Staff numbers fell from over two hundred to around 50. The sports centre in the Eldonian Village was closed down and demolished. The site awaits profitable redevelopment as residential flats, outside of Eldonian management. The disused primary school in which EGL was once headquartered caught fire and burnt down. One of the new directors committed suicide. Prominent board members of EGL, such as former Labour Councillor and Lord Mayor of Liverpool Sharon Sullivan, duly resigned. All of the projects and activities funded by EGL have since been suspended. Many of the community enterprises and local firms supported by EGL have suffered the same fate although some have continued to survive under new management, often former EGL staff, such as with six of the eight children's nurseries. The various EGL offices located around the city—thirteen venues at its peak—have all shut down. EGL has been all but dissolved: a victim of predatory asset-stripping by countervailing interests.

This raises grave doubts over just how viable and sustainable the self-assertively 'dynamic' and 'entrepreneurial' approach of EGL really was. It also raises questions over the relationship with the Eldonians: the extent to which the Eldonian Community Trust is implicated. Is failure attributable to the distinct business culture of EGL, which had become increasingly detached from the ethos of not-for-profit social enterprise and its roots in a place-based community? Was EGL allowed to stray too far from its mother organisation? Some fellow travellers suggest it could have happened to anyone—a misfortune and a hard lesson to learn. Others suggest that it was the Eldonians' prominent position within local politics and in the property industry that made it attractive for predatory investment and money laundering—activities for which Liverpool, an anarchic port city, has long been renowned. If indeed this is true, why was EGL so vulnerable to corruption? Asset stripping is precisely the kind of problem which the community development trust model is designed to preclude. In the mid-2000s, around the time Eldonian Group Ltd was renamed EGL, released from its place-based identity, its chief executive loosened many of the checks and balances of the trust structure, including the asset lock, and reoriented the organisation in a more commercial direction. This enabled EGL to shed its obligations to the Eldonian community, expand across the country and make large surpluses (and debts), but which also left the organisation without collective accountability and vulnerable to hostile takeover and asset-stripping. EGL's demise can be read as a product of mission drift and local corruption more than any fundamental flaw in the community development trust model. It shows that governance structures and legal rules are never completely impervious to being bent out of shape; that these are necessary but not sufficient conditions for sustaining a strong community business ethic.

The Story So Far: How Self-Regenerating, Really?

Despite recent events, the Eldonian Village remains an excellent example of what a community development trust can do to reverse the fortunes of a blighted place. This model seemed to work so well in Vauxhall due largely to the will of the people involved in envisioning and campaigning for a localist collective alternative to post-industrial decline. Yet it owes just as much to circumstance. The 1980s was a tumultuous time for Liverpool, struggling to deal with the housing crisis hanging over from the 'lost decade' of the 1970s and reeling from growing social unrest, exploding in the Toxteth Riots in 1981. Militant came to power on the back of promises to reinvest in council housing and other public services—funded by an 'illegal' budget—which resulted in direct conflict with central government. Fearing a Tory/Liberal plot to privatise and undermine municipal housing, Militant opposed the development of co-ops, actively municipalising those still in development phase, and created enemies of many. Not least of their enemies were the Eldonians, who were fortunate enough to be in "the right place at the right time",[5] but also clever enough to be able to exploit the political battle going on around them—to attract unprecedented levels of government funding and support from the 'great and the good' for what was a relatively insignificant community housing project like many others across the country at that time. Unlike others, however, the

5 Meegan, "Urban Development Corporations, Urban Entrepreneurialism, and Locality: The Merseyside Development Corporation", p. 79.

Eldonians were funded by central government to the tune of some £6 million, an unprecedented amount of money for a small community-based organisation to regenerate derelict land in an era when local authority budgets were being slashed. The Eldonians' vision for a 'self-regenerating community' has in some respects come to light. But how self-regenerating is the model, really, when set in this context of such an unusual local political climate precipitating huge financial flows from central government?

What does the Eldonian story say about the possibility of replicating their success? In being the product of a unique local history and set of political circumstances, it suggests historical 'place effects' greatly determine the ability of collective housing alternatives to embed themselves in place or to inspire urban change. Structural forces do not operate everywhere the same; general processes have very distinctive effects based on the way they coalesce with other place-based factors with different results according to local conditions and historical path-dependencies. With the requisite will and resources, huge progress can be made by relatively small-scale localist interventions to challenge and partly reverse the economic fortunes of places confronted by economic restructuring. The Eldonians have been the most successful of all the Liverpool co-op campaigns in achieving radical urban transformation. However, this poses problems for the possibility of replicating the Eldonian model, which remains financially unsustainable at least in terms of conventional regeneration costs; a product of politics unlikely to be repeated.

One argument of this book is that such conventions are a question of political priorities as opposed to material constraints and are therefore amenable to change. The real question here, then, is what lessons can be learned from the story of the Eldonians and the co-op movement if and when political winds do change? In this concluding section of Part III, I review the story so far—drawing out the continuities and differences between the Eldonians and the co-op movement and earlier housing history from which they sprang. In summarising Parts II and III, I sketch out some answers to the questions posed at their outset, evaluating the success of both the co-op and community development trust models in resolving the housing and neighbourhood questions.

To recap, bottom-up motivations for cooperative housing in Liverpool had two fundamental sources born out of reaction to some negative threat: the need for better housing in the face of dire conditions and the fight against displacement and community dissolution. Engels' housing question is perhaps most pertinently addressed to Liverpool of all cities—having witnessed dire overcrowding and insanitary slum conditions due to rapid urban growth and inflows of economic migrants from its maritime connections as well as refugees from the Irish Potato Famine. Co-op campaigns were initiated in reaction to such appalling conditions as well as the heavy-handed response enacted through the slum clearance programme. But so too were the co-ops inspired by more positive and proactive desires for individual autonomy and collective control. Weller Street and the Eldonians were pioneering among the co-ops for placing great value on radical self-governance—an explicit aim for both but most fully realised by the Eldonians. Colin Ward's manifesto for 'collective dweller control' was highly influential in the gestation of Weller Street's political philosophy. The Eldonians expanded this concept into domains beyond housing to take collective control of various public services, community enterprise and parts of the foundational economy.

Both communities were more collectivist than individualist in their orientation to autonomy: driven by a desire to assert community self-determination over individual self-actualisation. This is reflected in claims that the Eldonians were 'Stalinist' in their egalitarianism and also in Weller Street's 'utalitarian' (utilitarian-cum-totalitarian) ethos. In others, such as Hesketh Street (derided by some as "flower-powery"), individual dweller control was given more room to grow, with greater self-expression and creative choice granted over the design, decoration and management of housing. Yet, on the whole, Liverpool co-ops were distinct from the kind of lifestyle anarchism of more middle-class co-op movements—they were more pragmatic than ideological. Indeed, rooted as they were in a deeply traditional working-class culture, closely associated with the docks, trade unionism, organised religion and the old Labour Party, the Liverpool co-operators dissociated themselves from what they saw, so one fellow traveller characterised it, as the "brown rice and sandals brigade". Communal principles of shared living have not been so fully realised, perhaps, as in co-housing or commune-type arrangements. In the original participatory design sessions, popular preferences were for traditional family homes—although shared spaces for community gatherings, celebrations, children's play and meetings for the collective governance of housing were also highly prized. Socialist and communitarian aspects of cooperativism—managing common assets as self-governing communities—were major motivations and not only for the vanguard co-ops.

Nonetheless, a large proportion of co-operators simply wanted a better house. Through viral replication, the co-op movement was in some sense co-opted by the Liberal council's political project of pluralising, decentralising and privatising municipal housing. This explains the gradual dilution of cooperative principles and radical autonomy in the growth of the cooperative model into a more mainstream tenure of choice, driven by the 'bandwagon effect' of people seeking to secure better housing rather than by any cooperative ideal or practice. Such a tension has severe implications for the integrity of cooperative housing. The foundational 1975 Campbell Report recommended that co-ops be developed only where "it can be clearly established that the tenants really want to take part in a cooperative venture and are not simply anxious to be rehoused". If we do not wish to accept such a social limit on the outward expansion of co-ops and their potential to become Public Sector Housing 2.0, more work needs to be done on developing the requisite institutional infrastructure that can provide incentives for people to participate whilst also protecting collective alternatives from the vagaries of local politics and tendencies towards the dilution of cooperative values as they scale up or go viral.

In evaluating the co-op and community development trust models, it is important to bear in mind that they were designed as long-term solutions, with thirty- to forty-year maturation cycles in the minds of their initiators. Says one: "We always said with the Eldonians, we wouldn't know their success probably until 2010". So how successful are these collective housing alternatives in terms of resolving Liverpool's housing and neighbourhood questions? First, the co-ops have achieved a great deal in personal and collective empowerment: attuned to incorporating into the process of development the skills, labour, education and imaginative desires of their resident-members. The new-build co-ops, following the Weller Way, were talented at carving out the space for residents to develop their capacities and personalities through campaigning and community organising and to learn such new skills as architectural drawing, accountancy and business planning. This was achieved through close working relationships with architects and development managers; participatory 'planning for real' techniques; and democratic input into the design process itself. Many of the outcomes are intangibles: gains made in self-confidence, self-respect and collective purpose. Others are more empirically observable: countless residents gained new employment, particularly in architectural and planning practices, utilising new-found fluency in professional discourses. Many others were politically empowered and radicalised by the campaign process, inspired to stand for election as Labour councillors, some becoming powerful figures on the council, shaping local politics in pro-mutual directions, reflecting their earlier experience with the co-op movement.

These benefits for individual empowerment combine with material environmental and housing improvements in mutually reinforcing virtuous circles to make neighbourhood regeneration more effective, durable and self-sustaining. Original community aspirations have in large part been realised: co-op residents secured better homes and were protected from the dissolution of their communities; the Eldonians achieved the regeneration of their neighbourhood and their vision to become a self-regenerating community. In the long run, democratically designed co-op housing has proven better able to respond to residents' needs, express desires and be collectively manageable than their pre-fabricated, mass-produced counterparts built by profit-making developers and even those planned in technocratic-utopian fashion by local state bureaucracies. Many of the co-ops came to resemble—or, rather, influence—ordinary suburban estates of the 1970s with their defensive secured-by-designs, yet received scathing criticism from the architectural press. But this is what people wanted: spacious semi-detached housing with a garden set in a clean, green, safe environment for children to play and neighbours to meet in the street, arranged in cul-de-sacs around a communal area or community centre, as the anchor for co-op activities. Unlike their mass-produced imitations, they have stood the test of time. Almost all the co-ops, as well as the Eldonian Village, are still here today, in better condition than surrounding housing built before or after. One local politician contrasts the co-ops favourably with comparable public or private housing:

> Not only did they provide much better housing at much better cost, but actually because they had this communal ethos, they weathered the recession of the early '80s and the '90s far better than other parts of Liverpool ...

Other commentators liken the co-ops to "beacons of hope"—exhibiting higher quality housing, cheaper to manage, with higher occupancy rates, greater resident involvement, less unemployment and fewer social problems than their surrounds.[6] Yet such success comes at a price. Many co-ops and especially the Eldonians are commonly perceived to be exclusive, inward-facing tight-knit communities closed-off to surrounding neighbourhoods and other potential residents unless they have personal connections.

Of all the experiments in the 1970s and 1980s, the Eldonians are most far-reaching in achieving radical self-governance and delivering urban-economic transformation. They have transformed a large area of contaminated ex-industrial land into a sustainable community—albeit with high levels of public subsidy difficult to justify again. In many respects they have replaced the council as the dominant arm of the local state—increasingly involved in creating jobs, incubating community enterprise and delivering a number of localised public services, such as energy, heating, policing, environmental management as well as housing. Setting them apart from the rest of the co-op movement from which they sprang, as a co-op development worker remarked to me, is the fact that they "took over the whole neighbourhood; so they aren't just a housing landlord, not just a social club, not just a social enterprise creator, they're not just a partner—they are the driving force".

In many ways, the Eldonians anticipated and benefited from the emerging era of 'urban entrepreneurialism' documented by Harvey.[7] Despite socialist aspirations for collective self-government through community ownership of land and housing, the Eldonian model resonated with the enterprising and entrepreneurial culture of self-help and resilience then being promoted by the Conservatives and which has since become a hallmark of neoliberal ideology and urban governance. This was a period in which the concepts of innovation, enterprise and entrepreneurialism entered the lexicon of the political Left as

6 Christopher Holmes, *A New Vision for Housing* (Routledge, 2005).

7 David Harvey, "From Managerialism to Entrepreneurialism: The Transformation in Urban Governance in Late Capitalism", *Geografiska Annaler* 71.1 (1989): 3–17.

much as they did the Right—if not the Militant Tendency then certainly their enemies in the Labour Party, those 'modernisers' who would create New Labour. Urban entrepreneurialism, social enterprise and sustainable communities became the new leitmotif of urban regeneration and local economic development policy discourses—the final death knell for the modernist dream of municipal socialism that was once embodied in the Militant-led Liverpool Council.

What set the Eldonians apart from neoliberal urban policy—and that which counterintuitively united, despite deep ideological differences, Militant's municipal socialism with Conservative urban policy—was the way in which they approached the housing and neighbourhood questions. Both Militant's URS and the emerging neoliberal regime were property-led—that is, fixated on the physical, material condition of the housing itself rather than the structures, flows and processes which go into producing it as an active, lived space. Tony Byrne's URS was predicated on a kind of design determinism, which resonated strangely with Thatcher's policies through the shared reference point of Alice Coleman's work on design disadvantagement. Inverting John F.C. Turner's dictum,[8] this amounts to treating dwelling as a noun rather than a verb. Taken together, such property-led approaches to the housing question are best understood as a form of housing fetishism, which therefore fails to get at the root of the problem. The Eldonians, like the new-build co-op movement in general, understood the benefits of engaging in the *process* of designing housing as much as the overall design itself. But, unlike the other co-ops, they aimed at more than just housing, incorporating other key elements of economic development into their vision for a self-regenerating community. To get there, the Eldonians had to secure partnerships with a whole range of local, regional and national agencies—revealing how a partnership-based approach to regeneration can take different guises.

At the same time, the Eldonians—and Langrove Street Co-op too—employed political tactics of direct action, insurgency and illegal occupation, and fought fierce battles with the council. This suggests that successful campaigns for collective housing alternatives—whose success depends on actively engaging with the state and other professional partners further down the line—must first be forcefully claimed through insurgent methods which challenge, subvert and circumvent as much as utilise the law. Whereas earlier new-build co-op campaigns were pro-demolition and in favour of better housing conditions, these later campaigns—particularly Langrove—set off a trend for anti-demolition activism that defended communities' right to place, culminating in the CLT movement several decades later. By this point, in the twenty-first century, housing conditions were much improved or were at least

8 John F.C. Turner, "Housing as a Verb", in John F.C. Turner and Robert Fichter, eds, *Freedom to Build* (Collier Macmillan, 1972), pp. 148–175.

beginning to be managed more effectively by the growing housing association sector, having taken over most municipal management. As a result, community motivations turned increasingly towards gaining autonomy and choice in the design and location of housing rather than its quality per se.

In order to grow during the period of Militant municipalisation, the co-op movement effectively fled the city of Liverpool proper into the neighbouring borough of Knowsley. The successful transmission of the co-op model into a new jurisdiction allowed it to continue its growth just as political conditions prevented further expansion locally in Liverpool. The transfer agent in this process was CDS, illustrating the importance of secondary professional networks for the replication of social innovation. Through this process of policy mobility, we can see the importance of 'place effects' in the development of social innovation. Kirkby was in many ways ripe for co-op experimentation owing to the residual cultural practices of community organising embedded in place by such relatively recent collective action as the 1972 Kirkby Rent Strike, which mobilised some three thousand tenants in the area. Just as the Rent Strike was organised predominantly by women, so too were the co-ops a principally women-led initiative, mostly driven by single mothers who wanted better housing conditions for their children than the deteriorating and alienating tenements and tower blocks thrown up to house the 'overspill' from Liverpool. The co-op model developed here in a different way, shaped by the particular urban and social context: smaller in size than the Liverpool co-ops and less defined by existing place-based communities.

In contrast to the Kirkby co-ops, the Eldonians show how far collective housing models can be stretched. Unlike other co-ops, which were small enough—no more than 60 households—to maintain a meaningful level of participation among members, fitting their needs around the co-op model offered by CDS and MIH as a solution to their problems, the Eldonians did it the other way around. They twisted the shape of the model to fit their needs, for a much larger structure of community ownership. Ultimately, the Eldonians needed a vehicle for regeneration of an entire inner-city area and not just for housing, and so the community development trust model suggested itself over a co-operative. Although democratic involvement in the Eldonians appears to have waned over the years, the mutual ownership of land and assets under a community trust umbrella structure has enabled recycling of surpluses for community benefit. This distinguishes the Eldonians from the co-ops and other housing associations, which—despite delivering better housing conditions than the Corpy—have stopped short of the challenge of ongoing community-led urban renewal.

The seeming strength—and revealed weakness—of the Eldonian trust structure was to allow the separation of functions into a housing arm and a business development arm. Each was able to pursue real economic empowerment for local residents above and beyond those modest gains made by the new-build co-ops towards collective property ownership and circuitous routes to employment: helping provide employment directly for a hundred or so local residents and supporting the development of countless other social enterprises and community businesses. However, a fatal flaw in the model has led to the asset-stripping and dissolution of EGL, explicable through mission drift towards commercial over social ends and institutional changes removing it from democratic scrutiny and community accountability.

Moreover, such scaled-up operations and specialisation comes at a social cost. The Eldonians' hard-won sense of ownership over the village has mutated down the generations into a more passive sense of entitlement, shored up by a bureaucratic paternalism: the hated 'Corpy' has been partially replaced by another, albeit more effective, landlord at a smaller scale, a "nanny state" in community trust clothing. A large part of these problems derives from the cultural origins and sheer scale of the scheme. The original community of 150 families—way bigger than the supposed functional upper limit for co-ops of 40 households—were not interested in forming a co-op per se so much as an ownership model which could accommodate them all, keep the community together, and provide greater collective control over their living conditions. After their co-op scheme was thwarted by Militant, their plans evolved into a community development trust model, which proved most useful as a means to achieve their long-term aims for socioeconomic self-sufficiency. To a great extent, it worked; but in handing so much power over to the leadership, and becoming more 'state-like', there has been an inevitable price to pay in the domain of democracy.

This story is not unique to the Eldonians, however, and the majority of cooperative development agencies and housing associations on Merseyside starting out as small charitable trusts have, following the effects of the 1988 Housing Act, since morphed into huge commercial organisations, losing their ties to people and place. This reflects the privatisation and commercialisation of the social housing sector in general.[9] The full implications of this transition are considered in the next part, Part IV, where I explore how the very same housing associations that started the co-op movement in the 1970s became centrally involved in the latest round of state-led demolition-and-rebuild, known as Housing Market Renewal. This placed these organisations in conflict with Liverpool's next generation of collective housing activism, growing out of grassroots campaigns for CLTs that sought to defend housing from redevelopment and take it into community control.

9 Peter Malpass, "The Discontinuous History of Housing Associations in England", *Housing Studies* 15.2 (2000): 195–212.

Part IV
The Urban Question

CHAPTER 10

Grappling with the Urban Question

> Housing is the battlefield of our time and the house is its monument.
>
> Slogan of Homebaked Community Land Trust.[1]

Housing is in many respects the political battlefield of our time—a field in which the contradictions and injustices of capitalism are once again socially and materially manifest. Ours is an age of neoliberal financialisation, in which capitalism has exhausted primary avenues for productive investment and is now turning towards the 'secondary' circuit of capital—fixed assets such as the built environment—to make a profit. Indeed, financialisation has been nowhere more acute than in land and property: the 2008 global financial crash was bound up with sub-prime mortgages, precipitating foreclosure crises across Europe and the USA.[2] Some believe it is only a matter of time before the UK housing mortgage market—for decades state-subsidised through tax concessions and record low interest rates—likewise collapses.[3] As housing becomes increasingly central to global capitalism, liberal-democratic citizenship gets ever more entangled with homeownership and national politics ever more embroiled by widespread financial interests in inflating housing markets.[4] Unsustainable property price growth leads to increasingly volatile boom–bust cycles. The costs of fuelling this bubble of illusory wealth creation are manifold and the social impacts pernicious.[5] In the UK, in particular,

1 Jeanne van Heeswijk and Britt Jurgensen, "Introduction", *Stages: Liverpool Biennial #2*, Homebaked: A Perfect Recipe (2014).

2 Michael Edwards, *Prospects for Land, Rent and Housing in UK Cities*, Foresight Future of Cities: Working Paper (Government Office for Science, 2015).

3 Stuart Hodkinson, Paul Watt and Gerry Mooney, "Introduction: Neoliberal Housing Policy—Time for a Critical Re-Appraisal", *Critical Social Policy* 33.1 (2013): 3–16.

4 Raquel Rolnik, "Late Neoliberalism: The Financialization of Homeownership and Housing Rights", *International Journal of Urban and Regional Research* 37.3 (2013): 1058–1066.

5 Edwards, *Prospects for Land, Rent and Housing in UK Cities*; Danny Dorling, *All That Is Solid: How the Great Housing Disaster Defines Our Times, and What We Can Do About It* (Allen

housing deprivation and socioeconomic exclusion collude with the privatisation and retrenchment of public housing provision to create a homelessness crisis—despite thousands of empty homes across the country. Public assets are transferred from taxpayers to privileged homeowners as a growing rentier class of speculative landlords exploit Generation Rent, who face a future far less secure or prosperous than that to which their parents—even grandparents—looked forward.

In Britain, residential property constitutes the largest component of wealth yet this is deeply unevenly distributed, both socially and spatially.[6] Combined with uneven spatial development, such financialisation leads to gross contradictions: 'housing market failure' in economically depressed regions—where state-funded renewal programmes demolish 'obsolete' houses—only a few hundred miles away from areas where demand, inflation and speculation are so intense that local authorities engage in creative destruction of ex-council estates: stripping public assets to plug the gap in squeezed budgets. In stark language harking back centuries ago to the original enclosures of the commons, this is what critical geographer Stuart Hodkinson has labelled the 'new urban enclosures'.[7]

If in this new battle over the soul of housing, the commons are increasingly threatened by intensifying enclosures and financialisation of land and assets, then the CLT model is gaining traction as a weapon wielded in the counteroffensive. In this opening chapter to Part IV, I explore the power of CLTs to contest forces of enclosure and how they might constitute an alternative model of providing public housing and managing our neighbourhoods and cities before, in chapter 11, delving into the historical detail of how CLTs emerged in Liverpool as a tool employed by communities whose homes were threatened in the latest round of state-led comprehensive urban redevelopment.

Weapons Wielded against Enclosure of the Commons

Community land trusts can be seen as tools of defence against the new urban enclosures—heir to an ancient battle fought out over centuries. Acts of enclosure date back to the Roman Empire's introduction of the juridical concept of ownership to Britain to support conquest and slavery, forming the basis for feudalism, after which the commons were eradicated in three

Lane, 2014); Herman Schwartz and Leonard Seabrooke, eds, *The Politics of Housing Booms and Busts* (Palgrave Macmillan, 2009).

6 Manuel B. Aalbers and Brett Christophers, "Centring Housing in Political Economy", *Housing, Theory and Society* 31.4 (2014): 373–394.

7 Stuart Hodkinson, "The New Urban Enclosures", *City: Analysis of Urban Trends, Culture, Theory, Policy, Action* 16.5 (2012): 500–518. See also Brett Christophers, *The New Enclosure: The Appropriation of Public Land in Neoliberal Britain* (Verso, 2018).

waves: by the Normans, the Tudors, and the Enclosure Acts during the rise of industrial capitalism. These initial acts of enclosure—forcing commoners from the land and into industrialising cities—constitute what Marx called primitive accumulation, which signalled the beginning of capitalist history.[8] Enclosure, dispossession and commodification of common land created the capitalist preconditions of mass wage labour—as the 'midwife' of the capitalist city.[9] This has been extended and deepened through capitalist history to the present: what Harvey terms 'accumulation by dispossession', the ongoing, state-led process of enclosing social value for private capital and divorcing people from the means of sustaining themselves.[10] In neo-Marxist thought, the commons is the original condition of humanity—the soil in which capitalism then took root.[11] It is antithetical to the concepts of property and ownership, commodities and capital.

Countless forms of resistance to the enclosure of the commons have sprung up to (re)claim common land rights for the poor and dispossessed. Cooperatives are an obvious—albeit historically recent—form of resistance, but which have proven vulnerable to co-optation and incapable of protecting against subsequent enclosures through common ownership alone. A more direct form of defence is through the institutionalisation of trusts, which seek to remove land from the market entirely and protect it through a distinctive legal framework. The first, prototypical trusts emerged out of the anti-enclosure revolts of the early modern period, most famously the Levellers and the Diggers, whose great advocate Gerrard Winstanley made the powerful declaration to the 'Lords of the Land' that

> The earth was not made purposely for you, to be Lords of it, and we to be your Slaves, Servants, and Beggars; but it was made to be a common Livelihood to all, without respect of persons.[12]

The Diggers' occupation of St George's Hill in Surrey in 1649—settling as an experimental agrarian commons—suffered violent attacks by the landlord and proved short-lived, but their ideas lived on, influencing critical figures in the later development of land trusts, such as Henry George, John Ruskin,

8 Massimo De Angelis, *The Beginning of History: Value Struggles and Global Capital* (Pluto Press, 2006).

9 Hodkinson, "The New Urban Enclosures".

10 David Harvey, *The New Imperialism* (Oxford University Press, 2003).

11 Peter Linebaugh, *The Magna Carta Manifesto: Liberties and Commons for All* (University of California Press, 2009); De Angelis, *The Beginning of History: Value Struggles and Global Capital*; Michael Hardt and Antonio Negri, *Commonwealth* (Harvard University Press, 2009).

12 Gerrard Winstanley, *A Common Treasury* (Verso, 2011).

William Morris and Ebenezer Howard. In 1871, Ruskin founded the Guild of St George as a non-profit association holding land in trust—pioneering the concept of a 'trusteeship company', securing 'enduring community benefit' rather than profit. In the UK, the most ambitious articulation of this idea was Howard's Garden Cities,[13] whilst in the USA it influenced the development of the contemporary community land trust movement, later imported (back) to Britain, where CLT advocates see early experiments by Winstanley, Ruskin and Howard as embryonic forms of modern CLTs.[14]

One of the greatest advocates for common ownership, and the first American influence on the contemporary CLT movement, was Henry George, who claimed—contra Engels' position in *The Housing Question*—that land, not capital, was the source of the deepest antagonism in modern society. For George, the appropriation of land by economic elites was the primary cause of urban injustice, inequality and poverty, by diverting land away from the production of benefits for the common good into the unproductive generation of profits from rents. George argued that

> To extirpate poverty, to make wages what justice commands they should be, the full earnings of the laborer, we must therefore substitute for the individual ownership of land a common ownership. … The unequal ownership of land necessitates the unequal distribution of wealth.[15]

What has since been called the 'tyranny of property'[16] operates to produce a cumulative concentration of wealth and power in the hands of elites, who exercise their advantage in political and economic power to accumulate ever-greater swathes of property for its financial benefits, thereby further excluding the poor from land and asset ownership and their associated social benefits. Unproductive ownership of land not only excludes the poor from its productive use, but also creates the motivation for financial speculation, contributing to inflationary bubbles—and their inevitable deflationary collapse—with severe impacts on tenants, rendered precariously vulnerable to such instability by their neo-feudal status of dependence on landlords. As a

13 Ebenezer Howard, *To-Morrow: A Peaceful Path to Real Reform*, *Town And Country Planning* (Cambridge University Press, 1898).

14 Such as Pat Conaty and Martin Large, eds, *Commons Sense: Co-operative Place Making and the Capturing of Land Value for 21st Century Garden Cities* (Hawthorn Press, 2014).

15 Henry George, *Progress and Poverty: An Inquiry into the Cause of Industrial Depressions and of Increase of Want with Increase of Wealth. The Remedy* (Doubleday, Page & Co., 1879), p. 194.

16 Emmanuel Midheme and Frank Moulaert, "Pushing Back the Frontiers of Property: Community Land Trusts and Low-Income Housing in Urban Kenya", *Land Use Policy* 35 (2013): 73–84.

solution to the tyranny of property, George advocated for the long-term goal of common ownership of land and interim policy measures such as a single tax on all increases in land value to remove the motive for speculation.[17]

George portrayed land as existing independently of labour in nature, as the original source of wealth and autonomy, as opposed to the ownership of the means of production, for these must be located on land anyway. This departed from the Marxian labour theory of value, which holds that the actions of human labour on nature—as opposed to nature (or land) in and of itself—is the source of value. Regardless of which is deemed a more accurate reflection of reality, this idea was picked up by Ralph Borsodi, one of the founders of the American CLT movement, in his distinction between property commonly understood, as deriving from human labour, and what he calls 'trusterty', things existing by other means, i.e., nature.[18] Land, existing independently of labour, should therefore not be owned but only 'entrusted', as in a parent's relationship to their child, thereby bringing to fruition the concept of trusteeship, or stewardship. The latter is a concept distinct from 'ownership' in whatever form it may take—be it public, private or common—in that civil title to land is never absolute but held in 'trust' for other and future users, with duties of care and social responsibility at its core.[19] This is the ethical principle underpinning the rejection of the individual's 'right to transfer' and the 'right to speculate' in the contemporary CLT model. Although part of the property owner's full stake in the equity is 'earned' through their own sweat, labour and personal investment, the larger part is actually 'unearned', being a product of the community and wider social relations. On the intuitive understanding of 'just deserts' based on proportionality, the leading American CLT advocate, John Emmeus Davis, calls for a reallocation of equity so that "to the individual goes the fruits of individual labour; to the community goes the social increment".[20]

Borsodi attempted to implement the trusterty concept in experiments with prototypical land trusts, notably the 'homestead model', which separated the ownership of land from buildings, and effectively put a floor under tenants as a micro-scale welfare state—thereby defining the first two pillars of CLTs: cooperative ownership and individual leaseholds.[21] But it was only through the involvement of Robert Swann—a conscientious Second World War

17 John Emmeus Davis, ed., *The Community Land Trust Reader* (Lincoln Institute of Land Policy, 2010).

18 James Meehan, "Reinventing Real Estate: The Community Land Trust and the Social Market in Land", *Journal of Applied Social Science* 8.2 (2014): 113–133.

19 Charles Geisler and Gail Daneker, *Property and Values: Alternatives to Public and Private Ownership* (Island Press, 2000).

20 Davis, *Community Land Trust Reader*, p. 363.

21 Meehan, "Reinventing Real Estate: The Community Land Trust and the Social Market in Land".

objector influenced by Gandhi and the Civil Rights movement—that the CLT model gained its distinctive third pillar. Swann observed some of Borsodi's cooperative homestead communities and critiqued their inward-looking closure as 'enclaves', with no means to reach out beyond the membership to society. He therefore introduced a governance mechanism that would ensure openness to the locality and wider publics and provide the basis for mobilising a social movement. The CLT tripartite governance structure—with equal parts resident-members, wider community representatives and expert stakeholders—is the result of this innovation.[22] Thus CLTs are unique among collective forms of ownership for engaging with and recycling surpluses for the wider community, and not just for member-residents, as in the case of co-ops.

A further elaboration in the CLT model developed through the practical application of Swann's introduction of stewardship.[23] These early rural CLTs in the late 1970s were influenced by the Catholic theology of their founders, established as vehicles to empower politically and economically excluded, low-income people, with an in-built 'preferential option for the poor'—not simply building houses protected from the market, but "building a community of the dispossessed".[24] Thus the CLT movement moved from Borsodi's concept of trusterty towards Gandhi's trusteeship. The first urban CLT, Community Land Cooperative of Cincinnati, built on this heritage, developing out of grassroots organising by church-based community organisations, helped by key activists and infrastructures of the national American CLT movement, to adapt the CLT model as a vehicle for community empowerment and urban regeneration in an impoverished inner-city neighbourhood.[25] Earlier experiments following Borsodi had not imposed long-term contractual controls over the resale of buildings on leased land, but the Community Land Cooperative of Cincinnati had to contend with unstable urban property markets and the threat of gentrification, thus introducing resale limits into the CLT constitution—institutionalising the principle of permanent affordability. These innovations opened up opportunities to use CLTs to address post-industrial urban issues of decline, disinvestment, gentrification and speculation. The next wave in the late 1980s included the world's largest CLT today, the city-wide municipal housing programme in Burlington, Vermont—supported

22 Davis, *Community Land Trust Reader.*

23 John Emmeus Davis, "Origins and Evolution of the Community Land Trust in the United States", in Davis, *Community Land Trust Reader*, pp. 3–47.

24 Davis, "Origins and Evolution of the Community Land Trust in the United States", p. 20.

25 John Emmeus Davis, *Contested Ground: Collective Action and the Urban Neighborhood* (Cornell University Press, 1990).

by the then socialist Mayor of Burlington Bernie Sanders[26]—and in the 1990s notable grassroots inner-city community campaigns, Cooper Square in New York City[27] and Dudley Street in Boston.[28]

Through this combination of institutional covenants, CLTs have the practical potential to address pernicious effects of markets both too 'hot' (affordability crises, absentee landlordism, speculative development and gentrification) and those too 'cold' (capital flight, spirals of decline, poverty, inequality, deprivation, dereliction, abandonment).[29] They also have the potential to resolve problems of state management of these issues: the alienation of public landlordism and the displacement pressures from municipal urban renewal schemes. However, CLTs have mostly been developed for the provision and local collective control of affordable housing, with growing international application in, amongst others, the UK, Canada, Australia, France, Belgium and Kenya.[30] The CLT model was first imported to the UK from the USA in the 1990s by British land reform advocates seeking to resolve issues of rural housing affordability. The government-funded National CLT Demonstration Programme from 2006 to 2008 piloted fourteen CLT projects leading to the formation in 2010 of the National CLT Network, an umbrella organisation that connects and supports member CLTs. The model was first adapted to help resolve rural affordability crises, especially in the south-west of England, but has since been mobilised by advocates across diverse domains, from rural to urban contexts, from core to periphery, from land markets too hot to markets too cold. Two cities in particular—two sides of the same coin: London and Liverpool—now lead the way in British CLT experimentation, applying the model as an innovative solution to respective divergent problems: to provide access to affordable housing arising from gentrification and financial speculation in the overheated capital; to resist urban blight and heavy-handed state redevelopment programmes and as a vehicle for environmental improvement, urban regeneration, socioeconomic empowerment and political participation in Liverpool.

26 James DeFilippis, *Unmaking Goliath: Community Control in the Face of Global Capital* (Routledge, 2004); Steven D. Soifer, "The Burlington Community Land Trust: A Socialist Approach to Affordable Housing?", *Journal of Urban Affairs* 12.3 (1990): 237–252.

27 Tom Angotti, *New York for Sale: Community Planning Confronts Global Real Estate* (MIT Press, 2007).

28 Peter Medoff and Holly Sklar, *Streets of Hope: The Fall and Rise of an Urban Neighborhood* (South End Press, 1994).

29 DeFilippis, *Unmaking Goliath*; Davis, *Community Land Trust Reader*; Udi Engelsman, Mike Rowe and Alan Southern, "Community Land Trusts—A Radical or Reformist Response to the Housing Question Today?", *ACME: An International E-Journal for Critical Geographies* 15.3 (2016): 590–615.

30 Tom Moore and Kim McKee, "Empowering Local Communities? An International Review of Community Land Trusts", *Housing Studies* 27.2 (2012): 280–290.

On the one hand, CLTs have found support right across the political spectrum, not least in Conservative policy: Boris Johnson's 2008 manifesto for his successful Mayor of London campaign included the promise of "creating a network of CLTs across London".[31] Yet on the other hand, CLTs are being mobilised by activists—and critically evaluated by researchers—as radical campaigns for the reappropriation of our 'housing commons',[32] especially in the UK's first urban CLT, in East London,[33] and in the Granby Four Streets and Homebaked CLTs in Liverpool, which I discuss in detail in chapters 11 and 12. London's urban CLT movement in particular is fast expanding and at a critical stage in its early development and consolidation as a social movement, including a growing number of embryonic projects in East London, West Kensington, Brixton and Lewisham. The first forays into its urban application, having been a rural movement in Britain for many years, were by public–private regeneration partnerships, particularly ex-New Deal for Communities organisations like the Shoreditch Trust, as 'legacy vehicles' to take on and manage assets for enduring community control and benefit long after these programmes have ended.[34] There were also early experiments by tenants' associations to challenge the large-scale stock transfer, privatisation and state-led redevelopment of social housing estates: unsuccessfully at the Heygate Estate in Elephant and Castle,[35] and most recently by West Kensington and Gibbs Green Community Homes, pioneering the application of the Right to Transfer to 'buy back' two estates being compulsorily purchased for redevelopment as luxury flats by an international conglomerate. This latter struggle against enclosure and displacement turns on its head government legislation published in 2013 for the 'Right to Transfer from a Local Authority Landlord'—using it not simply to galvanise stock transfer from the council to a private registered landlord but to establish a CLT as a community-controlled landlord for local democratic protection of the estate. Likewise in the case of the successfully institutionalised East London CLT, the rights of residents appear to form the

31 Boris Johnson, "Building a Better London: Manifesto for Mayor of London" (2008), p. 13.

32 Stuart Hodkinson, "Housing in Common: In Search of Strategy for Housing Alterity in England in the 21st Century", in Duncan Fuller, Andrew Jonas and Roger Lee, eds, *Interrogating Alterity* (Ashgate, 2010), pp. 241–258.

33 Susannah Bunce, "Pursuing Urban Commons: Politics and Alliances in Community Land Trust Activism in East London", *Antipode* 478.1 (2016): 134–150.

34 Stephanie Saulter, Alison Masterman and Anna Eagar, *The Community Equity Trust: A Report on a Community-Based Self-Funding Urban Regeneration Model Developed by the Shoreditch Trust* (The Shoreditch Trust, 2008).

35 James DeFilippis and Peter North, "The Emancipatory Community? Place, Politics and Collective Action in Cities", in Loretta Lees, ed., *The Emancipatory City? Paradoxes and Possibilities* (SAGE, 2004), pp. 72–88.

main motivation for campaigning for the model led by London Citizens.[36] Both mobilise the CLT model as a potential institutional vehicle for the realisation of common rights to centrally located affordable housing currently left unmet or unprotected by the state. In this way, they tentatively assert a Right to Stay Put,[37] as part of the Right to Place,[38] or, indeed, more expansively, the Right to the City.[39]

There are thus real prospects for using the CLT model for neighbourhood regeneration in the UK. In contrast to London, the Liverpool campaigns are motivated by the threat of disinvestment and demolition in a shrinking city, rather than the pressures of speculative investment, offering a potentially powerful antidote to problems of capital flight, public disinvestment and neighbourhood decline. They are among the first attempts successfully to utilise the CLT model as an institutional vehicle for neighbourhood rehabilitation, with an emphasis on collective control of assets that contrasts with the narrower focus on housing affordability of the more established rural CLT movement.[40] It is their focus on the stewardship of land rather than ownership of assets that sets the CLT model apart as especially capable of responding to the new urban enclosures that would sweep through post-industrial cities, including Liverpool, as the state became increasingly involved in redeveloping urban land.

Grounding Capitalism in the Land Question

Henry George's contention, in the 1870s, that land—and not capital per se—is primary to deprivation dynamics has proven remarkably insightful as urbanisation has intensified. Turning back once again to *The Housing Question* we can see how changing conditions in the way capitalism operates have not only moved the goalposts but perhaps even overturned the very rules of the game. For Marx and Engels, production and reproduction—the factory/office and the home/neighbourhood—were sharply delineated such that the housing question was merely a *secondary* contradiction to the primary conflict

36 Bunce, "Pursuing Urban Commons: Politics and Alliances in Community Land Trust Activism in East London"; Conaty and Large, *Commons Sense*.
37 Chester Hartman, "The Right to Stay Put", in Chester Hartman, ed., *Between Eminence and Notoriety: Four Decades of Radical Urban Planning* (CUPR Press, 1984), pp. 304–318.
38 David Imbroscio, "Can We Grant a Right to Place?", *Politics & Society* 32.4 (2004): 575–609.
39 Kafui Attoh, "What Kind of Right Is the Right to the City?", *Progress in Human Geography* 35.5 (2011): 669–685; Mark Purcell, "Excavating Lefebvre: The Right to the City and Its Urban Politics of the Inhabitant", *GeoJournal* 58.2–3 (2002): 99–108.
40 Tom Moore and Kim McKee, "Empowering Local Communities? An International Review of Community Land Trusts", *Housing Studies* 27.2 (2012): 280–290.

of exploitation in the labour–capital relation or, as Harvey puts it, a 'displaced' form of class struggle.[41] It was only through the sphere of production, through syndicalism, trade unionism and direct action in the workplace, that labour could challenge the power of capital and, in turn, ever hope to resolve the housing question. However, writing when they did, Marx and Engels simply could not see that the urban would become an increasingly central site for capitalist development and resistance over the coming century or so. This trend can be understood as the deterritorialisation and fragmentation of production away from tangible, localised factory-based sites where labour could once organise and directly challenge capital—towards more mobile and flexibilised operations at a regional and increasingly global scale through the rise of multinational corporations, communications technologies and global financial trade agreements, with decreasing control at a local level. When coupled with the growing importance of the urban scale as a site for not only social reproduction and consumption but so too for accumulation of capital—through speculative property investment, for instance—we can see how Engels' original formulation of the housing question is too simplistic and reductive.

Observing the rising frequency of urban struggles over collective consumption issues, such as housing, Manuel Castells sought to reformulate the housing question as *The Urban Question*, arguing that the 'secondary' nature of social reproduction was fast becoming primary:

> But this does not mean that urban struggles are necessarily relegated to the world of administrative reformism. Quite the reverse; their decisive importance in certain political conjunctures has been determined, for a structurally secondary issue can be a conjuncturally principal one.[42]

Castells pointed out that public goods, services and collective consumption activities—together supporting social reproduction—were governed and accessed at the urban scale. The urban was the key site of intervention in everyday life: first by the state, through public service provision, urban planning, redevelopment and political organisation; second by citizens in the form of community groups and civil society organisations aiming to challenge or lobby for greater state interventions, or campaign for alternatives. This was the era of the second cycle of contention of which Liverpool's housing co-op movement was a quintessential example.

Writing during the 1970s crisis of Fordism—the waning of the post-war golden age of prosperity—Castells had identified the importance of 'the urban' as a site for collective consumption and resistance, but, like Engels, could not

41 Quoted in Andy Merrifield, *The New Urban Question* (Pluto Press, 2014), p. 104.
42 Manuel Castells, *The Urban Question: A Marxist Approach* (MIT Press, 1977), p. 377.

predict its increasing importance in the Post-Fordist era as a site of accumulation itself. As capital gradually began to exhaust opportunities for productive investment in the primary circuit (manufacturing) through the latter half of the twentieth century it turned to new potential sources in the secondary circuit—that is, the asset base of buildings, fixed infrastructure and land. Harvey has more recently identified the built environment as a 'spatial fix' for the 'over-accumulation' of capital—oversupply, devaluation, falling profits and exhaustion of new opportunities for profitable investment in the primary circuit of productive industries—in which the switching of capital into the secondary circuit of the built environment provides new opportunities for investment to absorb over-accumulation elsewhere.[43] Harvey's theory is based on Lefebvre's insight that

> "Real property" (along with "construction") is no longer a secondary form of circulation, no longer the auxiliary and backward branch of industrial and financial capitalism that it once was. Instead it has a leading role, albeit in an uneven way ... Capitalism has taken possession of the land, and mobilized it to the point where this sector is fast becoming *central*. Why? Because it is a new sector—and hence less beset by the obstacles, surfeits, and miscellaneous problems that slow down old industries. Capital has thus rushed into the production of space in preference to the classical forms of production—in preference to the production of the means of production (machinery) and that of consumer goods. This process accelerates whenever "classical" sectors show the slightest sign of flagging.[44]

'Spatial fix' has multiple meanings: providing a temporary solution to the crisis tendencies of capitalism; 'fixing' capital in space as a means to realise profits and as a sponge to soak up excess mobile capital sloshing around the global markets; and as the next injection—a narcotic 'fix'—for the rapacious, insatiable cravings of profit addiction built into the logic of capitalism.[45] The contradictions of capital are displaced into the secondary circuit: the long 'amortisation' time in fixing capital in space through the expensive and time-consuming construction of new buildings and infrastructure—and their relative resilience and longevity as physical structures—creates sturdy new barriers to further accumulation, leading to pressures for intensified processes of creative destruction and the demolition of old structures that have

43 Harvey, *The New Imperialism*.

44 Henri Lefebvre, *The Production of Space* (Blackwell, 1991), p. 335.

45 John Lovering, "The Relationship between Urban Regeneration and Neoliberalism: Two Presumptuous Theories and a Research Agenda", *International Journal of Urban and Regional Research* 12.4 (2007): 343–366.

exhausted their profitability to make way for shiny new profit opportunities.[46] When devalorisation of urban assets makes returns on existing uses lower than possible future uses, capital will seek the support of the state either to raze former investments to the ground or to upgrade them for a new population of more affluent consumers, who in turn may consume the goods produced in the primary circuit at a fast enough rate to resolve over-accumulation.[47] The resulting pattern of capital investment and disinvestment as it restlessly roves the planet in search of profit differentials is described by Neil Smith as the 'locational see-saw':

> the successive development, underdevelopment, and redevelopment of given areas as capital jumps from one place to another, then back again, both creating and destroying its own opportunities for development.[48]

The 'locational see-saw' between capital fixity and flight creates a pattern of uneven urban development, leaving some areas derelict and vacant until the economic conditions are right for reinvestment, and others in a continual process of redevelopment due to localised overheated speculative property markets. This turns urban land from a simple site of productive industries, housing, retail and civic spaces into the locus of struggle and conflict, as residents resist attempts by speculative investors either to redevelop and displace them or to disinvest and undermine the conditions for their survival.[49] The stakes are raised further still when the state gets involved in this process of 'spatially fixing' capital, under ostensible public policy auspices variously described as 'urban redevelopment', 'urban regeneration', 'urban renewal', 'urban revitalisation' and, in Britain, New Labour's 'urban renaissance' agenda.[50]

As all this was beginning to emerge in the 1990s, particularly in post-industrial cities of the global North, local politics likewise took a turn towards the territorial. Two forms of a 'politics of turf' emerged in this period, catalysed by the locational see-saw.[51] The first was a class- or community-based struggle *within* localities where local homeowners or ex-council tenants, for

46 David Harvey, *Limits to Capital* (Verso Books, 2007).

47 Davis, *Contested Ground: Collective Action and the Urban Neighborhood*.

48 Neil Smith, "Gentrification and Uneven Development", *Economic Geography* 58.2 (1982): 139–155 (p. 151).

49 Davis, *Contested Ground: Collective Action and the Urban Neighborhood*.

50 Mike Raco and Robert Imrie, *Urban Renaissance?: New Labour, Community and Urban Policy* (Policy Press, 2003); Loretta Lees, "Policy (Re)Turns: Gentrification Research and Urban Policy—Urban Policy and Gentrification Research", *Environment and Planning A* 35.4 (2003): 571–574.

51 Kevin R. Cox, "The Local and the Global in the New Urban Politics: A Critical View", *Environment and Planning D: Society and Space* 11.4 (1993): 433–448.

instance, mobilised against developers to protect their neighbourhoods against state-led renewal. The second fed off parallel trends in globalisation—cities set against each other in an intensified inter-urban competition for mobile capital—to create a struggle *between* localities in which cross-class coalitions, or 'growth coalitions', attempted to kick-start urban regeneration and drive forward economic growth.

At the other end of the locational see-saw, in cities suffering from deindustrialisation and capital flight, 'grant coalitions' or 'grant regimes' have emerged in post-industrial cities to compete and lobby for state funding of large-scale renewal programmes to tackle inner-city deprivation. Put simply, where growth coalitions compete for private capital investment, grant regimes compete for state subsidies. Grant regimes are public–private partnerships formed to protect their territories and constituencies from further decline, safeguard their assets from depreciation, transform dilapidated neighbourhoods into spaces that would attract creative professionals, kick-start economic regeneration and potentially make surpluses from new funding streams for redevelopment. It is through this lens that we can understand the recent history of housing redevelopment in Liverpool.

Housing Market Renewal, Neo-Haussmannisation and the New Urban Enclosures

For the governing elite of a city like Liverpool in the late 1990s—scarred, as it was, from decades of economic decline and population loss—forming a grant regime to attract government funding to address its worst housing problems seemed like an obvious solution. Local planners and policymakers had identified a pattern of what they called 'housing market failure' emerging across parts of inner-city Liverpool—mirroring trends towards empty homes and neighbourhood abandonment in post-industrial cities across the country, particularly in the north, catalogued by sociologists and geographers such as Anne Power.[52] Liverpool City Council—controlled by the Liberal Democrats from 1998 until 2010—became centrally involved in designing and securing government backing for a new regeneration scheme called the Housing Market Renewal Pathfinder programme. Council officers commissioned the original research[53] into housing market failure that would become the evidence base for the HMR national policy intervention—a £2.3 billion programme rolled

52 Anne Power and Katharine Mumford, *The Slow Death of Great Cities? Urban Abandonment or Urban Renaissance* (Joseph Rowntree Foundation, 1999).

53 Brendan Nevin, Peter Lee, Jenny Phillimore, Alex Burfitt and Lisa Goodson, *Measuring the Sustainability of Neighbourhoods in Liverpool* (Centre for Urban and Regional Studies, University of Birmingham, 1999).

out across deindustrialised inner-city areas in nine northern cities from 2003 to 2011.[54]

HMR Pathfinders are exemplars of grant regimes, initiated by councils and their 'natural allies'—housing associations, and also mass house-builders—in shrinking cities. In seeking to renew the *market* for housing—not just the houses themselves—HMR represents a rupture with previous modes of regeneration that sought to make improvements to the urban environment, housing and its management and offer skills training and other routes of empowerment for residents. The main research report justifying HMR—the so-called M62 Study, for identifying housing market failure along the M62 motorway corridor—identified the problem facing 'difficult-to-let' neighbourhoods with "voids" of boarded-up houses as one of "failing" markets.[55] HMR was designed to intervene in failing local housing markets to reverse neighbourhood decline and attract new residents by replacing 'obsolete' and largely vacant terraced housing with new desirable housing products.[56] This was a major shift from a focus on improving either the physical condition of homes or the life chances of their inhabitants—an 'inward-looking' approach—towards an 'outward-looking' approach that sought to reconnect those buildings and people with others elsewhere, but which sometimes meant replacing them entirely.

Whilst inward-looking approaches to the urban renewal of housing estates, in planning theorist Peter Hall's typology,[57] focus on compositional characteristics of the targeted neighbourhoods and their populations, outward-looking approaches account for spatial and socioeconomic relations with wider society. The former is easy to critique for drawing an artificial line around a neighbourhood and treating it as a container of which supposed negative features—such as urban design or poor environmental quality—are all too often held responsible for determining psychological and socioeconomic outcomes. Outward-looking approaches, by contrast, seek to connect neighbourhoods with their wider socioeconomic context, and which Hall saw as replacing inward-looking approaches from the late 1990s, which we see in the emergence of market restructuring policies like HMR. In many ways this is a progressive move: understanding blight as a relational, market-driven outcome

54 Philip Leather and Brendan Nevin, "The Housing Market Renewal Programme: Origins, Outcomes and the Effectiveness of Public Policy Interventions in a Volatile Market", *Urban Studies* 50.5 (2013): 856–875.

55 David Webb, "Rethinking the Role of Markets in Urban Renewal: The Housing Market Renewal Initiative in England", *Housing, Theory and Society* 27.4 (2010): 313–331.

56 Ian Cole, "Housing Market Renewal and Demolition in England in the 2000s: The Governance of 'Wicked Problems'", *International Journal of Housing Policy* 12.3 (2012): 347–366.

57 Peter Hall, "Regeneration Policies for Peripheral Housing Estates: Inward- and Outward-Looking Approaches", *Urban Studies* 34.5 (1997): 873–890.

of uneven development—as a 'space of flows', reflecting advances in urban geography towards a relational perspective[58]—rather than an internal failure of the neighbourhood or residents themselves.[59] Thus HMR sought to regenerate failing local housing markets by restructuring and reconnecting sub-regional markets with more functional regional and national markets. Like much of the New Labour government's regeneration policy agenda, HMR was an ambitious attempt to rejuvenate the state's role in urban renewal, mimicking the comprehensive redevelopment of the 1960s but with market-oriented objectives.[60]

However, this entailed new problems. Despite flexible strategies, multi-layered partnership-working, and a sophisticated understanding of scale, HMR was limited in problematic ways: for its economistic and abstract conceptualisation of neighbourhoods as housing markets; for its narrow focus on the single issue of housing alone; and for its one-size-fits-all monolithic approach to restructuring, centring on comprehensive redevelopment.[61] This has provoked a number of critiques. First, as a policy programme that attempts to regenerate neighbourhoods by attracting a new mix of residential tenures (and thus residents of different social classes), HMR is seen as an archetype of the 'mixed communities' agenda, with all that this entails. This is a distinctly New Labour discourse but with parallels around the world, particularly in Anglophone and Northern European neo-liberalising contexts,[62] and with historical antecedents in early town and country planning.[63] In its explicit aim, through demolition and displacement, to inject deprived areas with a more sustainable mix of residential tenures—a crude proxy for social classes[64]—

58 Joseph Pierce, Deborah Martin and James Murphy, "Relational Place-Making: The Networked Politics of Place", *Transactions of the Institute of British Geographers* 36.1 (2011): 54–70.
59 Simon Pinnegar, "The Question of Scale in Housing-Led Regeneration: Tied to the Neighbourhood?", *Environment and Planning A* 41.12 (2009): 2911–2928.
60 John Flint, "Housing Policy, the Right to the City and the Construction of Knowledge", *International Journal of Housing Policy* 12.3 (2012): 253–261.
61 Pinnegar, "The Question of Scale in Housing-Led Regeneration: Tied to the Neighbourhood?"; Cole, "Housing Market Renewal and Demolition in England in the 2000s: The Governance of 'Wicked Problems'".
62 For Dutch, American and Australian examples see: Gideon Bolt and Ronald Van Kempen, "Successful Mixing? Effects of Urban Restructuring Policies in Dutch Neighbourhoods", *Tijdschrift Voor Economische En Sociale Geografie* 102.3 (2011): 361–368; Katherine T. Jones and Jeff Popke, "Re-Envisioning the City: Lefebvre, HOPE VI, and the Neoliberalization of Urban Space", *Urban Geography* 31.1 (2010): 114–133; Michael Darcy, "De-Concentration of Disadvantage and Mixed Income Housing: A Critical Discourse Approach", *Housing, Theory and Society* 27.1 (2010): 1–22.
63 Wendy Sarkissian, "The Idea of Social Mix in Town Planning: An Historical Review", *Urban Studies* 13.3 (1976): 231–246.
64 Rebecca Tunstall, "'Mixed Tenure' Policy in the UK: Privatisation, Pluralism or Euphemism?", *Housing, Theory and Society* 20.3 (2003): 153–159.

the mixed communities agenda has been criticised for enacting a state-led form of gentrification—or 'gentrification by stealth'.[65] By this, critics imply the hidden, indirect way in which gentrification is brought about through a government policy ostensibly intended to revitalise dilapidated housing and thereby help the urban poor—as opposed to classical gentrification, which involves the gradual replacement of poorer populations by richer through the colonisation of urban space and residential sorting over time. In the USA, this approach has been critiqued as the 'Dispersal Consensus', part of a new 'mobility paradigm' in neoliberal urban policy, which has a "heavy reliance on moving people through metropolitan space as a means of addressing urban social problems" rather than improving the lives of the poor directly.[66]

Whilst this all appears detached when viewed from a bird's-eye policy perspective, it has serious implications for those affected on the ground. HMR's most vehement critics see it as a form of symbolic violence—violently erasing working-class lived space and radically transforming place in the image of a target middle-class population attracted through an improved 'residential offer'.[67] According to these critics, HMR logic represents a narrowly aspirational, market-based perspective on housing as a 'space of positions' in which middle-class consumers vie for position on the housing ladder—disregarding use values for exchange value. In aiming to reposition whole neighbourhoods within a 'space of positions' in the wider metropolitan housing market, HMR Pathfinders marginalise alternative ways of valuing housing—as an end in itself, for shelter, collective use, emotional attachment and belonging—which urban sociologist Chris Allen has shown are bound up in the lives of Liverpool's existing working-class residents, who, by virtue of proximity to necessity, live largely outside the positional market for housing consumption.[68] In extensive interviews in Liverpool HMR areas, Allen established that existing residents were 'unable to see the point' of demolishing 'perfectly good houses', which are simply 'bricks and mortar' as opposed to an investment opportunity, and 'just there' for living in.

Second, HMR stands accused of failing to account for the human scale of everyday life, as a policy that instrumentalises homes and neighbourhoods

65 Gary Bridge, Tim Butler and Loretta Lees, eds, *Mixed Communities: Gentrification by Stealth?* (Policy Press, 2012).

66 David Imbroscio, "Beyond Mobility: The Limits of Liberal Urban Policy", *Journal of Urban Affairs* 34.1 (2012): 1–20 (p. 2).

67 Chris Allen, *Housing Market Renewal and Social Class* (Routledge, 2008); Anna Minton, *Ground Control: Fear and Happiness in the Twenty-First-Century City* (Penguin, 2012); Chris Allen and Lee Crookes, "Fables of the Reconstruction: A Phenomenology of 'Place Shaping' in the North of England", *Town Planning Review* 80.4 (2009): 455–480.

68 Allen, *Housing Market Renewal and Social Class.*

for abstract ends: one which conceives of the 'city-as-property' rather than the 'city-as-inhabited'.[69] Merseyside's HMR Pathfinder area, named New Heartlands, covered inner urban areas of Sefton and Wirral boroughs as well as Liverpool and was divided into four 'Zones of Opportunity'. Presumably by accident, this created the unfortunate acronym ZOO—the perfect ammunition for activists and critics (myself included) to deride the policy for its mistreatment of residents, framed by policymakers as if animals cruelly held in captivity.[70] Each ZOO was appointed a single preferred developer to work in partnership with existing housing associations, made accountable to a governing board of stakeholders, which, unlike previous regeneration programmes, included no representation from local residents. Perhaps the lack of diversity and democratic deficit created the conditions for the monolithic approach of earmarking for demolition entire street blocks rather than individual piecemeal plots.

In turn, ZOOs were cut up into individual renewal areas. These 'regeneration zones' are marked by signs welcoming visitors to the '[Insert neighbourhood here] Regeneration Zone', repeated across the city in the same generic format, font and pictorial style, with the tagline: 'creating neighbourhoods for the future'—as if to emphasise the idea that these neighbourhoods are not for present (working-class) residents but for future (middle-class) occupants. Regeneration zones encompassed large residential blocks, including houses worth saving, in order to create large enough 'land banks' and economies of scale for profitable redevelopment by the grant regime partners. The centralised systematic and large-scale approach of the British housing development industry means that developers will only take on land for redevelopment above a certain spatial scale, which leads to a questionable approach akin, as planning researcher Andreas Schulze Bäing attested in a public inquiry into HMR, to "pulling out all teeth and replacing them with dentures even if only a few teeth show signs of caries, rather than keeping and repairing all teeth as long as possible by fillings or root canal treatments".[71] Indeed, assets of architectural and social value remaining in these cordoned off areas have been described as "collateral damage" by a politically prominent proponent of HMR whom I interviewed in 2014. According to another interviewee, a regeneration consultant, these zones were treated not as lived spaces but as abstract sites in a "chessboard" of strategic land parcels, to be stripped bare of

69 Simon Pinnegar, "For the City? The Difficult Spaces of Market Restructuring Policy for the City?", *International Journal of Housing Policy* 12.3 (2012): 281–297.

70 Matthew Thompson, "LIFE in a ZOO: Henri Lefebvre and the (Social) Production of (Abstract) Space in Liverpool", *City: Analysis of Urban Trends, Culture, Theory, Policy, Action* 21.2 (2017): 104–126.

71 Andreas Schulze Bäing, *The Welsh Streets: A Written Statement to the Welsh Streets Inquiry* (University of Liverpool, 2014).

residents and packaged up for redevelopment, so the HMR partnership may "shift pieces around" to be activated at different stages according to changing dynamics of market profitability and resident opposition. This was the start of the abstract monolithic one-size-fits-all approach that characterised HMR.

Third, building on these two critiques, HMR is framed as a process of accumulation by dispossession[72]—by virtue of spending public funds to dispossess public tenants and homeowners from their homes for redevelopment and produce profits for private developers and quasi-privatised housing associations. Harvey defines 'accumulation by dispossession' as

> The continuation and proliferation of accumulation practices that Marx had treated of as "primitive" or "original" during the rise of capitalism. These include the commodification and privatization of land and the forceful expulsion of peasant populations ... [and] colonial, neo-colonial and imperial processes of appropriation of assets ... particularly of land ... The state, with its monopoly of violence and definitions of legality, plays a crucial role in both backing and promoting these processes and in many instances has resorted to violence.[73]

From this perspective, the HMR grant coalition dispossessed poor residents of their homes—through compulsory purchase orders and compensation or rehousing by the state—and then revalorised the land so that the grant coalition partners could pocket the difference in value from what Neil Smith terms the 'rent gap'.[74] Indeed, an unconscious recognition of the violence played out in the accumulative asset-stripping in Liverpool is expressed in the aggressive standardised signs put up on CPO'd property in HMR zones to dissuade thieves and squatters—"ALL ITEMS OF VALUE HAVE BEEN REMOVED FROM THIS PROPERTY". Might this unwittingly signify the violent removal of human beings? Or is it a reflection of an abstract perspective that only sees value in items or objects—physical commodities—that can be exchanged?

Based on these three critiques, we can characterise HMR alternatively as part of what Hodkinson calls the 'new urban enclosures'[75] and what Merrifield—rather pertinently—dubs Neo-Haussmannisation. This,

72 Gordon MacLeod and Craig Johnstone, "Stretching Urban Renaissance: Privatizing Space, Civilizing Place, Summoning 'Community'", *International Journal of Urban and Regional Research* 36.1 (2012): 1–28.

73 David Harvey, "Neo-Liberalism as Creative Destruction", *Geografiska Annaler, Series B: Human Geography* 88.2 (2006): 145–158 (p. 153).

74 Neil Smith, "Gentrification, the Frontier, and Restructuring of Urban Space", in Neil Smith and Peter Williams, eds, *Gentrification of the City* (Allen & Unwin, 1989).

75 Hodkinson, "The New Urban Enclosures".

Merrifield argues, is the contemporary incarnation and intensification of that classic urban strategy first identified by Engels (in the opening quote to chapter 7) and embodied in Baron Haussmann's restructuring of Paris in the eighteenth century:

> A process that likewise integrates financial, corporate and state interests, yet tears into the globe and seizes land through forcible slum clearance and a handy vehicle for dispossession known as "eminent domain". Once, seemingly long ago, this latter act of public sequestration was done, albeit disruptively, in the name of some greater common good ... Now, it expresses the public sector expropriating land and then giving it away for upscale private re-appropriation, letting private economic interests cash in on legalized looting.[76]

These are strong words from Marxist critics with which we would be hard-pressed to describe the full story of HMR in Liverpool. However, whilst the reality is, as always, rather more granular and complicated, they certainly contain more than a grain of truth. This brings us to the fourth critique—one which locates the violence and abstraction of HMR not so much in a deliberate strategy of state-led gentrification as in a more subtle perversion of a seemingly impersonally abstract programme for the financial interests of key grant coalition partners. The story is long and complex but leads inexorably to a final conclusion: that HMR enacted a kind of accumulation by dispossession on Merseyside for the financial benefit of the grant coalition. HMR adopted an 'objective' research approach to identify neighbourhoods ripe for intervention through pseudo-scientific methods based on quantification and statistical comparison.[77] An economistic perspective was built into the very objectives of the original research commissioned by Liverpool Council. In his critical comparison of HMR as it developed in Whitefield, Lancashire and in Liverpool, critical planner David Webb reveals how the approach was seen to be 'objective'. The most undervalued, least-occupied housing with the lowest market demand became the highest priority for demolition, so the logic goes, because market price—"an imperfect proxy for democratic approval"—was assumed to reflect popularity and therefore viability.[78] Indicators of decline were then abstracted from international academic data and used to 'rate'

76 Merrifield, *The New Urban Question*, pp. 72–73.

77 David Webb, "Conceptualising the Bounded Agency of Housing Researchers: The Case of Housing Market Renewal in England", *International Journal of Housing Policy* 12.3 (2012): 315–330.

78 David Webb, "'Problem Neighbourhoods' in a Part-Linear, Part-Network Regime: Problems with, and Possible Responses to, the Housing Market Renewal Leviathan" (unpublished PhD thesis, Newcastle University, 2011), p. 5.

different neighbourhoods based on their relative popularity and projected sustainability, so as to identify 'problem areas' for intervention. However, affected communities themselves were not invited to contribute to this process of problem definition, and so the evidence reflected only the biases of researchers and broader cultural trends in the wider policy environment. Moreover, once these 'problem areas' were identified through statistical measurement, policymakers were able to delineate distinct zones earmarked for demolition or refurbishment. This was the basis by which the four Zones of Opportunity (ZOOs) of the New Heartlands Pathfinder were delineated.

Most in need of intervention in Liverpool—according to the indicators of decline concocted to identify 'problem areas'—were the mono-tenure concentrations of social housing in the peripheral estates built in the post-war years on the southern and eastern metropolitan fringe. This reflected national trends towards the stigmatisation and residualisation of mono-tenure council estates and was therefore relatively uncontroversial in recommending intervention. However, at this point the researchers liaised with the key property players in these problem areas—the principal partners in the HMR grant coalition, the council and housing associations, which now owned most of the city's social housing stock—to incorporate their views and interests into this problematisation process and to negotiate a shared vision for what would replace cleared housing.[79] At the same time that these organisations were brought more centrally into decision-making, those residents and communities targeted by the programme were sidelined. Their exclusion resulted in a definition of the 'problem' that narrowly reflected the views and interests of the council commissioners and researchers and the housing association and developer partners.

This move towards incorporating the views of grant coalition partners—notably housing associations—was radically to alter the design and outcomes of the HMR programme. Fundamentally, this meant a socio-spatial shift in problematisation of target areas—away from outer estates of mono-tenure social housing and towards mixed tenure inner-city terraced neighbourhoods, like Anfield, Granby, Kensington and Little Klondyke (whose experiences with HMR I explore in chapter 11). This inner-city focus is reflected in the name of the Merseyside Pathfinder Partnership, New Heartlands—a label, incidentally, that was soon mockingly redubbed by locals as the 'New Heartbreak' or 'New Wastelands'.[80] Traditionally, these were areas with high levels of private rented housing and some owner-occupation—remaining difficult, therefore, due to multiple diverse stakeholders, for the state to manage or regenerate. Increasingly, however, this housing stock has been taken over by housing

79 Webb, "'Problem Neighbourhoods'".

80 Jonathan Brown, "Why Were the Four Streets Emptied out Anyway? A Granby Back Story", in Assemble, eds, *Granby Workshop Catalogue 2015*, p. 11.

associations as properties have become unpopular and owners have moved on to escape the blight caused by local economic decline. Housing associations were by the 1990s the largest managers of social housing in Liverpool, following the transfer and decentralisation of public stock to a multitudinous group of organisations, which had been empowered by the 1988 Housing Act to access private capital markets, cross-subsidise expensive rehabilitation work and invest in new social housing and maintenance of old in ways which local authorities were—for various reasons: political, economic and organisational—made incapable. Coupled to this were legislative reforms following the 1988 Housing Act that placed increased commercial pressures on housing associations to procure the funds needed for managing and rehabilitating stock from private loans and market lenders, thereby making them increasingly reliant on the value of their stock in order to borrow capital. It was therefore in the housing associations' direct financial interests to see Merseyside's inner-city terraced housing—which they now had responsibility for managing—either dramatically improved or demolished and replaced entirely with higher-value housing. This would turn what were low-value assets, often liabilities, on their spreadsheets into high-value assets and enable greater borrowing capacities for further housing development, asset growth and organisational expansion—in other words, empire building. There were also strong motivations among city councillors and planners to build an evidence base for a policy of well-funded large-scale intervention that could enable newly empowered housing associations finally to resolve the longstanding problem of inner-city dilapidation. It was the job of HMR, therefore, to provide the means—both the financial resources and the political legitimacy through central government support—for the public and third sectors to wrest control of these fragmented areas by way of compulsory purchase orders, tenancy evictions, site preparation and land assembly for large-scale redevelopment.

The strength of these motivations is illuminated by the lengths HMR's researchers had to go to in order to justify this shift in objectives, warping the rationale for intervention. The third commissioned research report in 2001, as Webb has demonstrated,[81] identified the student accommodation construction boom in the city centre as a causal factor in the supply and demand imbalance in low-demand inner-city areas, whereby a speculative rash of new flats were being successfully marketed to students, key workers and economic migrants, who otherwise would have settled in the inner-city terraced neighbourhoods. If HMR was to stay true to its original objective of rationalising the structure of housing markets—to rebalance supply and demand so as to reconnect failing markets with sustainable regional markets—then surely a key recommendation of the report would be to stop the building of flats that were directly creating an oversupply of accommodation in central areas adjacent to the low-demand

81 Webb, "'Problem Neighbourhoods'".

neighbourhoods, which were themselves often located within walking distance of the city centre and these new student flats. Such a holistic, integrated strategy would most likely have worked well to correct this supply/demand imbalance and recreate demand for inner-city terraced houses, but, against all common sense, an integrated approach was not adopted. The city council refused to retract their policy of city centre repopulation through student flat construction and instead sought a synthesis with the incompatible policy of inner-city redevelopment. For the HMR rationale to be at all consistent, it required a new narrative to explain away the contradictions between flat construction in the centre and housing demolition around it.

That new narrative is the object of the fifth and final critique of HMR—a narrative that marked a transition in the problematisation of vacant unpopular housing from a structural issue of equalising supply and demand towards a simplified focus on the age, type and tenure of the housing stock itself, thereby reducing the complexities of the problem to one of the housing 'product'. In other words, the issue was reproblematised from one of failing markets to one of failed product. The terraced house was blamed, in the language of HMR researchers, as 'obsolete' and incapable of attracting the right residents who would revalorise declining neighbourhoods and who preferred the modern flats down the road. This internalised the problem into the terraced house itself, which fitted in neatly with the increasingly marketised and abstract logic of HMR—subjectifying residents as 'consumers' looking for quality and choice, and the terraced house as a 'product' unfit for modern consumption preferences. Thus the M62 Study assumed a linear model of urban history: statistically linking rising prosperity with suburbanisation as a means to denounce inner-city terraced housing as defunct and obsolete for the ambitions of a post-industrial city. Old 'back-to-back' terraced housing was framed as unsuitable for contemporary flexibilities; framed as creating the 'wrong' image through association with the old industrial working class—something which must be overcome through reimaging the city to attract the likes of the so-called 'creative class' championed by self-styled urban guru Richard Florida.[82] In elevating housing type, design and image over more complex socioeconomic and spatial explanations, HMR can be critiqued for committing a kind of 'housing fetishism' or 'spatial determinism'—not unlike the design determinism of Militant's URS or Alice Coleman's defensive urbanism.[83]

82 Jamie Peck, "Struggling with the Creative Class", *International Journal of Urban and Regional Research* 29.4 (2005): 740–770.

83 I explore these ideas in relation to commodity fetishism in Thompson, "Contesting Dilapidated Dwelling", in Graham Cairns, Georgios Artopoulos and Kirsten Day, eds, *From Conflict to Inclusion in Housing: Interaction of Communities, Residents and Activists* (UCL Press, 2017), pp. 199–226.

Five critiques—some quite simplistic; others more complex; all interrelated; all, fairly or unfairly, damning of HMR. These five charges set against it—state-led gentrification; monolithic development logic; accumulation by dispossession; distorted incentive structures; housing type fetishism—may well be overstated in some cases, simplified in others and, in almost every instance, hotly contested. But what cannot be disputed is the huge controversy provoked in the media and in public opinion—both locally, in the *Liverpool Echo*,[84] and nationally[85]—and the huge hostility felt towards HMR, despite broad-based popularity, in so many of the neighbourhoods it targeted. Whilst for the majority of residents HMR was welcomed for redeveloping deteriorating, poorly insulated terraced housing long in need of renewal, for others it was fiercely contested for mistakenly targeting good-quality houses of great architectural merit, historical interest and social value. Much of this resistance to HMR grew in tandem with, or evolved slowly into, more proactive forms of collective housing activism. In what follows I explore case studies of where residents attempted, to greater or lesser effect, not only to challenge the logic of HMR but also to experiment with regeneration alternatives, which most often took shape as community land trusts. Where some CLT campaigns failed, in Little Klondyke and Kensington, for example, others succeeded elsewhere, in Homebaked and Granby Four Streets CLTs.

The story of one particular neighbourhood in south Liverpool, Granby, provides the best example of how urban decline, public policy, social unrest and community activism all came together to produce a unique reaction to HMR demolition. This reaction began as anti-demolition campaigning and evolved into more proactive demonstrations of how the neighbourhood's houses and streets could be managed differently, more collectively and imaginatively. As documented in Part II, Granby was the site of the original experiment—SNAP, led by Shelter—that paved the way for the Council's policy switch from demolition to rehabilitation of terraced housing and the transfer of dilapidated council stock into housing association and co-op ownership. Today it is also

84 Gary Stewart, "Anger as Toxteth Granby Triangle House 'Damaged' by Contractors", *Liverpool Echo* (29 Sept. 2011); Tom Duffy, "Peaceful Protest on Toxteth Street Forces Demolition Men to Down Tools", *Liverpool Echo* (12 July 2011); David Bartlett, "Council Leader Warren Bradley: We Ripped Heart out of Liverpool Communities", *Liverpool Echo* (26 Apr. 2010); Marc Waddington, "88-Year-Old Bootle Woman Evicted from Her Home to Make Way for the Bulldozers", *Liverpool Echo* (9 Mar. 2012).

85 Charles Clover, "Nightmare on Lime Street", *Daily Telegraph* (21 May 2005); Rowan Moore, "Liverpool Biennial—Review", *The Guardian* (23 Sept. 2012); Lynsey Hanley, "This Is How We Can Solve the Housing Crisis—One Home at a Time", *The Guardian* (13 Aug. 2012); Owen Hatherley, "Liverpool's Rotting, Shocking 'Housing Renewal': How Did It Come to This?", *The Guardian* (27 Mar. 2013).

the site of the city's first CLT on the very same four streets—hence the name Granby Four Streets—that SNAP first saved from demolition and which CLT activists would likewise later save from HMR. But before delving into these developments, I first explore Granby's history of redevelopment efforts in the interim period between SNAP and the CLT to reveal other more-contextual and place-based explanatory factors for understanding the particular direction taken by HMR in Liverpool.

CHAPTER 11

Growing Granby from the Grassroots

A (Plant) Potted History

Despite the work of SNAP in rehabilitating Granby's terraced housing stock and providing new routes through to socioeconomic regeneration, the neighbourhood eventually succumbed to the fate befalling Liverpool as a whole. Through the 1970s and 1980s, as Liverpool lost its economic *raison d'être*, Granby once again fell on hard times. By the 1990s, concludes Andy Merrifield, Granby was a "battleground for a whole gamut of urban ills".[1] The once bustling central shopping avenue, Granby Street, was almost entirely vacant and derelict, its Post Office closing in 1994 owing to successive hold-ups. According to the 1981 census, 39.6 per cent of men in Granby ward were jobless, a figure reaching as high as 90 per cent for black teenagers.[2] By the early 1980s, Granby had effectively become, in the words of historian Andy Beckett, "Liverpool's ghetto".[3] The coincidence of unemployment and poverty with certain ethnic and demographic groups, notably young black men, compounded by racial discrimination against the local black community, the most established in the UK, had severe repercussions in 1981 when rioting erupted in reaction to police brutality.[4] The so-called Toxteth Riots—or what locals prefer to call the 1981 Uprising—resulted in street combat with police, cars set alight, the burning down of the Rialto Theatre (an imposing early twentieth-century cinema on Upper Parliament Street) and violent repression from the state—the unprecedented use of CS gas upon citizens on mainland Britain.

Not only did the Uprising create a cycle of mutual mistrust between locals and city authorities, which still haunts Granby today, it also imprinted the area with a social stigma, thereby reinforcing the spiral of decline. Informal economic activity, minor criminality, street gangs and drug dealing became common responses to the sheer lack of formal economic opportunities. In

1 Andy Merrifield, "Social Justice and Communities of Difference: A Snapshot from Liverpool", in *The Urbanization of Injustice*, ed. Andy Merrifield and Erik Swyngedouw (New York University Press, 1996), pp. 256–285 (p. 206).

2 Merrifield, "Them and Us: Rebuilding the Ruins in Liverpool", p. 59.

3 Andy Beckett, *Promised You a Miracle: UK 80–82* (Penguin Books, 2015).

4 Frost and Phillips, *Liverpool '81: Remembering the Riots.*

his mid-1990s study of Granby's politics,[5] Merrifield notes the prevalence of conspiracy theories among locals of police intentionally allowing stolen cars into Granby Street as an excuse to move in with force; of the council's abject neglect; of their repeated attempts to demolish streets and force people to leave as a kind of punishment for the riots. Resentment lingers two decades on, when I spoke with a number of locals. A former housing association officer turned community enterprise developer characterises the problem as one of reputational damage:

> I think the decline really had begun after the 1981 Riots. There was a general feeling in Liverpool that Granby itself ended up getting blamed for the riots and that the best thing to do was to clear it; so most of the streets were gone by the end of the 1980s and replaced by new neighbourhoods, the typical low-level, low-density, low-quality housing.

Another interviewee, a leading activist in the CLT campaign, suggests some sort of institutional racism is at the root of the neighbourhood's problems:

> In Granby it's the general Corpy thing, but there is also definitely a race element as well, as that was always the most mixed area of the city, and especially after the riots in the early '80s ... "They want us to just fuck off and die", was what people felt was the council attitude; "You're just too much trouble, we're not going to give you any services ..." Things like bins not being cleaned for a couple of years, that kind of general neglect, street lights not being kept on.

Basic public services such as street lighting, cleaning and rubbish collection were on all accounts much neglected by the council. Local residents have long believed that the actions—or *inaction*—of the city council in response to the riots has been an intentional policy of wilful neglect or managed decline, as this longstanding resident muses:

> So after the riots you'd have thought that a huge investment would be made to kind of patch things over wouldn't you? But nobody gave a shit actually. You'd have thought that a lot of effort—government, council—would have gone into putting an Elastoplast over, cleaning it up, making it at least look okay, and the exact opposite was done. Absolutely nothing happened except twenty years of boarded up housing and filthy, really incredibly degraded environment ... You can see why people would deduce punishment, because what happened—or didn't happen—was quite extraordinary.

5 Merrifield, "Social Justice and Communities of Difference".

Whether Granby's terminal decline is best explained by institutional racism or structural economic processes—or a combination of both—the result is a kind of 'root shock',[6] damaging for residents and built environment alike. As people left the neighbourhood, 'hard-to-let' properties fell into disrepair, made worse once improvement grants disappeared, leaving housing associations struggling to maintain their stock. A general shift in tenure composition from one dominated by private renters and owner-occupiers to social renters had implications. Liverpool's rising unemployment coupled with the national trend towards residualisation of social housing translated into increased poverty for housing association tenants, leaving less disposable income to be circulated through local shops and services. The council's response was to change approach from the rehabilitation model pioneered by SNAP—successful for some time, especially with co-ops, but constrained under more austere funding regimes—towards a more interventionist policy of wholesale demolition and rebuild. It was hoped that replacement of dilapidated 'hard-to-let' terraces—too expensive to repair and too numerous to repopulate—with lower density modern housing with lower maintenance costs would at least help kick-start the physical regeneration of the area and resolve the immediate issues of vacancy and decay. However, this logic was challenged by many housing association staff and owner-occupiers, who felt it only sped up the downward spiral as a policy of managed decline. One former LHT officer divulges his qualms:

> I left Liverpool Housing Trust in 1996, and I remember in those late days there, there was the beginning of talk that Granby was getting "hard to let", and once housing associations start labelling the place "hard to let" it stops really trying, and so what had happened from those days onwards—so well before Housing Market Renewal—was that the housing associations were tinning the properties up. That began to atrophy the area, and the city council then started buying up all the empty properties so they would eventually have the power to decide what to do … And then when Housing Market Renewal came in, that accelerated it, but they accelerated something that had already started.

Owing to the complexity of urban change it is difficult to identify causal mechanisms or, indeed, impute blame. The council cannot be criticised for want of trying nor accused of underinvestment. One ex-council officer claims that she "once did a kind of reckoning up of how much money had gone into Granby from the 1980s, early 1980s onwards, and it was huge, it was like £25 to £30 million, and people keep saying managed decline, but if you look there's

6 Fullilove, *Root Shock: How Tearing up City Neighborhoods Hurts America, and What We Can Do about It*.

been quite a lot of new stuff built there". But this still leaves unexplained the council budget earmarked specifically for 'managed decline'.

Since the late 1970s, the council had been fighting a losing battle. The initial private sector grants recommended by SNAP were written into Housing Action Areas in the 1970s, in which the council offered generous funding to private landlords and owner-occupiers to refurbish their properties. As a secondary move, the council would use its compulsory purchase order (CPO) powers to buy up any under-maintained property and transfer to the growing housing association sector, a dual approach described by an ex-council officer as "Offering the carrot—which was a grant to the landlord—and the stick was CPO if they didn't take that up; and the ultimate sanction was that the properties were CPO'd and transferred to co-ops or housing associations".

Despite worsening local socioeconomic conditions and accusations of neglect from local residents, the housing stock was effectively sustained by this dual system: council grants to private landlords and owner-occupiers alongside government grants via the Housing Corporation to co-ops and housing associations. In this way, housing associations would become the largest landlords in the area through a process of council CPO and stock transfer of those properties failing to be maintained by private owners. However, the 1988 Housing Act radically restructured public housing provision, virtually removing the grant system, thereby leaving associations without these additional state funding streams to deal with worsening housing conditions and having to fund any improvements out of rent revenues alone. This came at a time when the original private rehab work completed in the 1970s was coming to the end of its proposed lifespan, long after pre-1919 speculative 'Jerry-built' houses were ever intended to last.[7] A former council officer explains that the rehab grant system was never intended to be "a forever solution; it was a sticking plaster, and it was twenty year life standards we talked about, and that was going back to the '70s".

Several decades on, terraces saved from clearance through the private sector grant rehab programme were unsurprisingly in poor condition; made worse by a context of rising unemployment and falling population leading to housing vacancies, dereliction and abandonment. Housing associations were faced with severe structural maintenance problems and tenants with dwindling employment prospects who, for instance, wanted smaller modern flats with lower heating bills. As a result, many of Granby's grander Georgian and Victorian properties became vacant and housing associations began boarding up the area. This only contributed to the general perception of decline, dissuading any prospective tenants or buyers from investing their lives in the area. A housing condition survey conducted in 1992 by the council found that 25 per cent of the wards' properties were vacant, 5 per cent derelict and

7 Cowan, Hannay and Owens, "The Light on Top of the Tunnel".

boarded up, and another 50 per cent 'unfit' or 'seriously unfit' for human habitation.[8]

Without the necessary state funding to finance refurbishment, the council took action by declaring Granby a Renewal Area in 1992 and successfully lobbied for £9.4 million funding, mostly as government subsidy from the Merseyside Special Allocation set up by Heseltine alongside the Merseyside Development Corporation.[9] Following initial consultation exercises with local housing associations and residents the latter formed Granby Residents Association. The council planned to demolish and rebuild and began strategically buying up private properties and requesting that housing associations transfer their properties back into council ownership, emptying the area of residents to prepare for redevelopment. A council officer working on the project explained to me that

> The council decided the best way of dealing with that area—I'm not saying they were right—was to try and get control of the properties, so that at least then they would have the ability to make a decision about the long term future, whether it be improving them all or demolishing them all. But it was doing it on a voluntary basis, and you can't ever get control like that on a voluntary basis: you need some kind of CPO action if you're going to be successful.

Meanwhile, Granby Residents Association—increasingly composed of stalwart homeowners as public tenants were being evicted from their homes—began to resist council plans, and started the Granby Residents Against Demolition campaign. With house prices bottoming out at £20,000 to as low as £8,000,[10] homeowners were forced either to sell up fast, absorbing a loss, or, trapped in negative equity, to stick it out until the market regained strength. Initial resistance to council-led demolition was driven by a minority of remaining homeowners seeking to protect their investments. And not just financial investments—they had invested their lives in the area, developed attachments to community and place, only to see it get run down. Place attachment grew all the stronger as the decline deepened; an embattled, belligerent, stubborn loyalty in response to what many perceived as "punishment" dished out by the council. Anger simmered on from the 1981 Uprising, from police and council treatment of the local black community, many of whom had been evicted out of the area. Other residents, however, in surrounding streets not immediately earmarked for demolition, were more supportive of council plans, relieved something was finally happening to arrest decline.

8 Merrifield, "Them and Us: Rebuilding the Ruins in Liverpool", p. 61.
9 Merrifield, "Them and Us: Rebuilding the Ruins in Liverpool".
10 Merrifield, "Social Justice and Communities of Difference".

The anti-demolition campaign was successful in preventing demolition and bringing the council to public inquiry in 1997, yet this ruled in favour of a CPO for all units along Granby Street. Owner-occupied housing was bought up by the council at an average price of £17,000, not enough to buy a similar property elsewhere in Liverpool.[11] Having replaced most of the terraces with lower density estates, this left intact only four original streets—the 'Granby Triangle'—in which the council had to contend with fierce resistance from a small minority of remaining homeowners organised as the Granby Residents Association. In 2013, there were 128 vacant boarded-up houses and shops, leaving only around 60 households still occupied. These four streets map precisely onto SNAP's original boundaries, suggesting that early rehabilitation efforts had secured a longer life for the buildings and empowered the community to fight for their neighbourhood several decades later. Described by an ex-council officer as the "final battleground", these four streets became centre-stage to a bitter process of fraught negotiations, direct action, occupations, street demos, and creative community activism that helped pave the way for the successful CLT campaign. The resistance attracted the support of national lobby organisations, Empty Homes Agency and SAVE Britain's Heritage, helping raise the media profile of efforts to rehabilitate rather than demolish empty terraces.

The deadlock in decision-making over the area was a testament to the collective power and successful community organising of a small group of passionate homeowners who wanted to see something different from demolition; but it also reflected the lack of overall control, coordination or direction offered by any one competing agency and the messy disorganisation of a range of stakeholders, housing associations and council departments. A council report from the mid-1990s stated that "If no clear programme is put in place for the whole area this resource will be lost … It is felt that the loss of the MSA [Merseyside Special Allocation] funding would be disastrous for the area without which any solution would be impossible".[12] It was the council's difficult experience of working in neighbourhoods like Granby that led to a game-changing policy for bringing clearer leadership and greater coordination to addressing such complicated regeneration dilemmas. The Liberal Democrats took council control in 1998 and initiated a new Housing Strategy and the Liverpool Strategic Housing Partnership to bring about more coordinated collaboration between council, housing association, developer and community group plans for each neighbourhood; creating more joined-up strategic regeneration in contexts where multiple tenures, owners and interests overlap, collide and conflict to produce stalemate.[13] In this new Housing Strategy, stock

11 Merrifield, "Them and Us: Rebuilding the Ruins in Liverpool".

12 Quoted in Merrifield, "Them and Us: Rebuilding the Ruins in Liverpool", p. 61.

13 Inside Housing Awards, "Good Practice in Partnership Working: Liverpool Strategic Housing Partnership for the LIFE Model", *Inside Housing* (12 Nov. 2004).

transfer to housing associations was promoted as the "only realistic option".[14] At its heart was the so-called 'LIFE model', which aimed to rationalise inner-city neighbourhoods into five distinct zones, or 'areas of opportunity' (sound familiar?) assigning one lead housing association to each. This was a response to the confusion of too many agencies operating in one area duplicating processes. Under the LIFE model, each housing association would assign itself a clearly defined role within each area, following L-I-F-E: Lead in an area; Influence what happens; Follow by collaborating with others; or Exit where presence is minimal. In Granby, as for the entire L8 postal district, Plus Dane—then the host organisation of CDS—became the Lead association and began developing plans for holistic neighbourhood management, working more closely with the council to plan redevelopment. Winning an *Inside Housing* award in 2004, the logic of the LIFE model was such that

> Without the LIFE model, the council, private developers and other partners would have had to consult, negotiate and collaborate with around 40 associations operating across the market renewal pathfinder area. Residents and other stakeholders would be confused by the range of partners and effective delivery of the programme could be hampered.[15]

This is where the monolithic logic behind HMR Pathfinders can be seen to derive. The impetus for strategic demolition-and-rebuild schemes in particular zones of empty homes was already beginning to emerge in Liverpool Council thinking as far back as the early 1970s, with the creation of monopoly regeneration zones for housing associations in General Improvement Areas and Housing Action Areas and later given greater coherence as a joined-up policy initiative in the Liverpool Strategic Housing Partnership and the LIFE model. This constructed the operational muscle tissue ready to be fully flexed once HMR funding was secured. Liverpool led a group of northern city councils to lobby central government for funding intervention in failing housing markets. Early reports commissioned by Liverpool council recommended that Liverpool's inner city could be a pilot for government funding of housing market restructuring, becoming one of the largest recipients of funding when HMR Pathfinders were launched in 2002.[16]

The rationale for HMR was radical in its multi-scalar focus on regional market restructuring, bringing together and rationalising the confusing

14 Richard Kemp, then Executive Member for Housing, quoted in Holmes, *A New Vision for Housing*, p. 131.

15 Liverpool Council's group manager for neighbourhood services, quoted in Inside Housing Awards, "Good Practice in Partnership Working".

16 Cocks and Couch, "The Governance of a Shrinking City".

number of previous and ongoing projects. An HMR manager working with Liverpool Council at the time explains:

> We'd been here before, we just keep coming back—Housing Action Areas, General Improvement Areas in these areas years ago, all these government-funded regen' schemes back in the '70s and '80s, then Neighbourhood Renewal Areas, New Deal for Communities, ERDF [European Regional Development Fund]—there were all sorts of regeneration schemes, all looking at their own little bits, but there was never this massive comprehensive approach to dealing with a whole area, looking at doing something quite radical in terms of transforming areas.

This is where HMR came in. Once given the green light, Liverpool was in the perfect position to get a head start and hit the ground running. The 'areas of opportunity' formatted by the LIFE model were straightforwardly translated into ZOOs. The monolithic, abstract nature of redevelopment implemented through ZOOs—and the regeneration zones within them—was not necessarily a bad thing; it was a means by which public authorities and their partners could rationalise space and render manageable an otherwise confusing array of different agents and interests in a complex regeneration process to achieve practical results in the most simplified, efficient and effective way possible. However, the approach appeared to favour certain ways of working that ran counter to residents' lives and foreclosed all other possibilities that may have produced better results. Smaller-scale, more experimental, piecemeal, incremental or participatory approaches were all but suppressed by this singular focus on preferred developer and housing association partners and the preference for large-scale zoning and land banking. Moreover, when working in concert with other, more pernicious logics, this visited what can only be described as violence upon the residents and built environment of Granby. Here, amongst other mistreated neighbourhoods across Merseyside, HMR has been a deeply traumatic experience for those who have stayed on to resist it. Whilst the violence has not always been direct (e.g., the use of physical force)—although it has in some cases been so, in the instances of forcible removal from their homes of a minority of resistant residents—it has nonetheless always been keenly felt by people and place, accumulating and intensifying slowly over time.

Living through Hell: On the Violence of Managed Decline

Many residents of the Granby Triangle were glad to move out of their crumbling homes and into housing newly built by HMR; others were not. In Anfield—an ex-HMR neighbourhood now home to Liverpool's other successful urban CLT, Homebaked—demolition was more widely supported by the local community.[17] In the Granby Triangle, however, the building stock was generally seen to be of a much higher architectural quality. Many believed the council was needlessly demolishing good housing as part of the large-scale zoning conditions required by the Pathfinder partners for profitable development—or else as part of a long-term punitive strategy for the 1981 Uprising and subsequent Granby Residents Association anti-demolition campaigning. Having evicted most remaining public tenants from housing association stock before its transfer into council ownership for consolidation, only those defiant homeowners—those with the security of tenure and embattled commitments to place—remained to resist HMR.

Despite the full weight of the grant coalition set against them, Granby residents pushed back successive attempts to demolish the four remaining streets of the Granby Triangle. The council had for years tried to buy out these defiant homeowners with arguments about the structural condition of properties, deemed too unsafe to inhabit. One common claim was that the bay windows—striking architectural features of larger properties—were 'structurally unsound', that they were coming away from the wall and therefore a health and safety danger. Official surveys recommended that these bays be pulled down and bricked in, but residents challenged this, seeking an independent assessment, which advised the bays could indeed be 'tied-in' thereby saving the houses and confirming suspicions that the council was hell-bent on demolition. One of the most dramatic confrontations came in 2011 when residents engaged in picketing and direct action to blockade Cairns Street with cars against approaching bulldozers. They alerted the local press so that the resulting stand-off was publicised[18]—a successful strategy that further galvanised the spirit of resistance. The council eventually earmarked for demolition the two end houses, numbers 67 and 69 Cairns Street. Residents organised a peaceful protest outside the buildings as they were scaffolded. These represented the first ever instances of direct action to challenge demolition in the Granby Triangle.

Despite modest numbers, around twenty residents armed with banners and placards picketed numbers 67 and 69 and prevented contractors from entering the houses to carry out demolition. This attracted further coverage in the *Liverpool Echo.*[19] Several activists super-glued locks shut and painted

17 Hugh Ellis and Kate Henderson, *Planning Out Poverty: The Reinvention of Social Town Planning* (Town and Country Planning Association, 2013).

18 Tom Duffy, "Peaceful Protest on Toxteth Street Forces Demolition Men to Down Tools", *Liverpool Echo* (12 July 2011).

19 Gary Stewart, "Anger as Toxteth Granby Triangle House 'Damaged' by Contractors", *Liverpool Echo* (29 Sept. 2011); Tom Duffy, "Set Back for Granby Four Streets Trust after Builders' Early Start", *Liverpool Echo* (14 July 2011).

scaffolding with 'anti-vandal paint'—an ironic signifier of what they saw as "civic vandalism". But the builders beat them to it, arriving before sunrise to begin stripping out interiors and, in the process, causing structural damage to adjoining property 65 scheduled for refurbishment. A council spokesperson dismissed it as "unfortunate" collateral damage.[20] Residents accused the builders of intentionally damaging the structure to leave no choice but demolition. Private contractors employed by the grant coalition partners were seen to mistreat, damage and thereby make amenable for demolition housing that they were actually tasked with securing against crime and weathering for possible future refurbishment. I was told by a number of activists that they had witnessed workmen throwing bricks through wooden floors—to "test their strength"—collapsing into cellars and thereby helping bring about the very degradation they were employed to prevent. Such contractors strengthened one thing only: the case for demolition. This put paid to local efforts to save 65–69 Cairns Street.

This was a trend repeated again and again by private contractors for the remaining unoccupied terraces. A longstanding resident-activist recounts to me the actions of a private contractor hired by local housing association LHT:

> As soon as people left, they bricked them up from the inside—so if you looked from the street, they had all this oozing kind of concrete—then they walked outside and smashed all the windows, leaving you with jaggy bits of glass.

By bricking up the windows, the contractors were able to secure—against crime, squatting and the elements—houses which were already in a dangerous state of disrepair through wilful neglect. But to remaining residents it revealed the assumptions made about their neighbourhood, left in a visually vandalised condition as a scar for the community daily to endure. The same resident continues:

> I think it shows that you actually despise the people who are living here, that you don't even rate them as fully human; because it's what you'd do if there was nobody there isn't it? It's what you'd do if it was like an old military site, say, or somewhere that nobody lived.

The violence enacted was most acute in instances where—particularly reported in Anfield—the bricking up of houses was initiated on the very same day residents were moving their belongings out. In direct response to the bricking up of voids, locals subverted these images of violence through artistic expression (Figure 4). Colourful pigeons carved out of wood perched, in various poses, on window ledges to brighten up the bleak view and,

20 Stewart, "Anger as Toxteth Granby Triangle House 'Damaged' by Contractors".

Figure 4 Subverting "target hardening" with artistic symbols of hope.

perhaps, point to a brighter, alternative future for the neighbourhood. The most prominent window infills of grey breezeblocks were boarded over and emblazoned with messages of hope and resilience: "DON'T GIVE UP!" An enduring graffito reads "GAMES (PLEASE)"—a playful subversion of conventional signs banning ball games and a symbol of the carnivalesque spirit imbuing Granby's activism.

New Heartlands' rather heartless approach to securing empty properties nonetheless appears in accordance with guidelines in the Council's 'Living Through Change' programme for HMR delivery. This aimed "to make clearance areas and their surrounding area, safe, secure, clean and well managed", through what was called 'Target Hardening', "fitting extra security measures (e.g., doors, locks, etc.) to occupied properties and around the clearance areas"; and 'Enhanced Void Security', "ensuring that empty properties are appropriately secured to reduce the risk of vandalism and anti-social behaviour".[21] Such impersonal, abstract and technocratic language emphasises the principles of bureaucratic rationalisation, safety and security over any aesthetic and psycho-social effects on existing residents who, unsurprisingly, refer to the programme as 'Living through Hell'. With official policy written in such terms, underhand practices of invoking—often actively performing—structural damage to make the case for the bulldozer was a familiar story in Granby.

Shortly before their dissolution, the Granby Residents Association was told by the council that their base in a disused office on one of Granby Street's corner buildings was likewise structurally unsafe. They were consequently evicted, leaving them without a headquarters from which to plan campaigns. Just as with the technical argument for the bay windows, many residents believed this to be a lie, an excuse to suppress any possible resistance to demolition plans. This suspicion was confirmed by the fact that the very same office space was later offered as a base—without any extra work to make it safe—to the builders working on the redevelopment of Beaconsfield Street for Plus Dane. Incidentally, this is the same building that SNAP had originally rehabilitated from a ruin into the Granby Centre, with various functions as a community anchor over the years: as a Housing Aid Centre, and later as a Community Resource Centre with a neighbourhood police station based there, known locally as the 'cop shop'. More recently, in 2014, the cop shop became home to a weekly 'drop in' surgery run by Plus Dane to provide residents with up-to-date information about how some of the four streets were being regenerated, following the adoption of the CLT vision, and to share memories and views about the area's historical development. Such a sudden turnaround taken by housing associations and the council—from a situation where all alternative ideas were asphyxiated through legalistic suppression to one in which residents were openly invited to comment and contribute to new plans for rehabilitation—represents a radical shift in perspective. So what changed?

The 2008 global financial crisis effectively pulled the plug on large-scale, well-funded state-led regeneration programmes like HMR. In 2011, the incoming Conservative Coalition government, under its austerity agenda,

21 Liverpool City Council, Housing Market Renewal in Liverpool Annual Report 2006/07 (Liverpool City Council, 2007), p. 28.

prematurely cut short HMR, abandoning almost the very concept of urban regeneration policy.[22] For some buildings, 2011 came just a little too late. Whilst campaigners saved the four streets—their layouts and most housing—some demolition could not be stopped. The elegant southern terrace of Ducie Street (its remaining terrace is depicted on the front cover) was demolished in preparation for redevelopment only to find little funds forthcoming after the withdrawal of central government funding. Some refurbishment work had also already been completed—the facade of Beaconsfield Street's southern terrace retained as a preserved shell for otherwise new buildings behind—but most of the area was simply left to crumble into dereliction, still in council ownership but without the funds for either demolition or refurbishment.

Fortunately, 2011 was also the year that residents in Granby began to dream big—when a radical new vision for the neighbourhood, shared by a loose local alliance of activists, social financiers and architects, was coming together in the shape of the Granby Four Streets Community Land Trust. This was an institutional vehicle intended to drive forward community-led rehabilitation rather than profit-led demolition, for the common ownership of land and democratic management of perpetually affordable homes for local people. Granby CLT, formally established as an organisation in 2011—just like its counterpart Homebaked CLT—has proven a great success in turning around Granby's fortunes. In 2013, the Granby Triangle had 128 vacant boarded-up houses and shops, with around 60 households occupied.[23] By 2019, only one of the four streets, Ducie Street, remained derelict, possibly too far gone to save, whilst Cairns Street and Jermyn Street have been almost completely refurbished and repopulated. The next section narrates the background of how the CLT came into existence to transform Granby.

Putting the T into CLT; Finishing the Work that SNAP Started

Granby residents had fought vigorously against demolition plans since the 1990s, mostly under the auspices of the local homeowners' organisation, the Granby Residents' Association. Conflict intensified with the arrival of the more systematic and well-funded HMR Pathfinder, with Granby located in the City Centre South ZOO, allocated to preferred developer Lovell in partnership with preferred housing association Plus Dane. During the anti-demolition campaign, a national Empty Homes Agency campaigner, John Earnshaw, was invited to present ideas about potential rehabilitation solutions. John helped establish in 2007, as its first chair, the Granby Community Partnership, the first formal communication channel between council and community since the

22 Dave O'Brien and Peter Matthews, *After Urban Regeneration: Communities, Policy and Place* (Policy Press, 2015).

23 Assemble, *The Granby Four Streets* (HD Social Investments, 2013), p. 4.

1981 Uprising. The Granby Residents Association entered into agreement with the council and Lovell to build 70 new homes and remodel 165 existing homes, but this angered other residents. The council agreed to fund the community to the annual tune of £10,000, which residents used to research their own vision for the area through fact-finding site visits and conferences as well as funding various community activities such as a regular local newsletter, *The Jangler*.

All this attracted the attention of local groups. A small but influential collective of idealistic young professionals, students and creatives looking for empty homes to retrofit for an ecologically sustainable mutualised co-op—amongst them Ed Gommon, Marianne Heaslip and Gemma Jerome, organised initially as the Northern Alliance Housing Co-operative and later rebranded Terrace 21—tried to convince Granby residents to adopt their co-op idea. Ronnie Hughes (a former senior manager at LHT turned community organiser and acclaimed Liverpool blogger)[24] became increasingly involved in helping the community channel divergent creative energies into a common vision. This sudden injection of people and ideas created what many have characterised as tense internal politics. It was into this fray that the CLT idea was first floated by a leading Granby Residents Association member, Dorothy Kuya. Born and bred in L8 and deeply embedded in the oldest black community in the country, Dorothy was actively involved in race equality and black cultural history throughout her life, becoming the first Community Relations Officer on Merseyside in the 1960s—seen as "Liverpool's greatest fighter against racism and racial intolerance".[25] She was also a lifelong member of the Communist Party and a tireless campaigner for the Granby Residents Association—her house on Jermyn Street was amongst those she was fighting to save from demolition. Before she sadly passed away in 2014, Dorothy helped introduce the CLT idea into the community whilst in contact with John Earnshaw, a freelancer who, by virtue of his work with Granby, was to become a technical advisory consultant for the National CLT Network.

The introduction of so many ideas, however, created a split in the community between a co-op and a CLT faction. This contributed to the dissolution of the Granby Residents Association. So too was the Granby Community Partnership officially disbanded, in 2010, after residents became increasingly frustrated with the council's broken promises and inaction over considering alternatives whilst empty homes were literally falling in. But the CLT idea stuck and a small group of committed activists became the key protagonists in driving it forward.

24 Ronnie's photo blog 'A Sense of Place' is a great resource on Granby and Liverpool's housing history more broadly: https://asenseofplace.com/.

25 David Fleming, Director of National Museums Liverpool: www.liverpoolmuseums.org.uk/about/mediacentre/2014/dorothy-kuya-memorial.aspx. See also Louis Julienne, "Dorothy Kuya—Obituary", *Nerve Magazine* (14 Jan. 2014): www.catalystmedia.org.uk/archive/issues/misc/articles/dorothy_kuya.php.

These mostly women homeowners associated with the city's artistic and creative milieu—Eleanor Lee, Hazel Tilly and Theresa MacDermott amongst others—helped move the campaign on from reactive anti-demolition protests towards more proactive claims of ownership over the neglected, disinvested and largely vacant streets. Out of a state of despair—tenants evicted, properties boarded-up, streets collecting rubbish, blight setting in—they set about cleaning the streets, clearing rubbish, seeding wildflower meadows on vacant land, painting house frontages with colourful artistic murals and bringing garden furniture and potted plants out onto pavements and into the roads.[26] The centre of these insurgent acts of 'guerrilla gardening' was Cairns Street, where most of the green-fingered activists lived. Their vision was to turn the Granby Triangle into the 'Green Triangle'. As early as 2008 'That Bloomin' Cairns Street' won an 'outstanding award' in the Royal Horticultural Society's 'North West Street in Bloom' competition.

Working in parallel with the guerrilla gardening, a council-funded adult education project about ecology and horticulture called 'Growing Granby' resulted in a nearby vacant plot of land being entrusted to local residents on a short-term lease by the new local housing association Liverpool Mutual Homes, for a community garden and allotments. Growing Granby is distinguished from the more spontaneous acts that have transformed the streets themselves into the Green Triangle, according to one guerrilla gardener, "because we work in public space, not behind railings on private land". Such radical collective action has inspired ideas for a 'DIY People Plan' reimagining Granby as a 'Backyard Commons'.[27] What has actually emerged is more of a 'front garden commons' spilling out onto the street. The conscious transplanting of the greenery, domestic furniture and intimate spaces of the home into public space to share it with others I have characterised previously as working *between boundaries*—spatial and legal—constructed by the ownership model and which separate the public from the private.[28] This represents what Nick Blomley calls "creative acts of resistant remapping".[29]

Putting Granby firmly on the map is its monthly street market. Since its inception—kick-started with the £10,000 council funding but organised

26 For photos of the Granby Four Streets over this period of transformation, see https://asenseofplace.com/collections-of-posts/the-story-of-granby-4-streets/ and https://assemblestudio.co.uk/projects/granby-four-streets-2.

27 Jean Grant, "Backyard Commons", in Rob MacDonald, ed., *DIY City* (Liverpool University Press, 2011), pp. 51–59.

28 Matthew Thompson, "Between Boundaries: From Commoning and Guerrilla Gardening to Community Land Trust Development in Liverpool", *Antipode* 47.4 (2015): 1021–1042.

29 Nicholas Blomley, "Un-Real Estate: Proprietary Space and Public Gardening", *Antipode* 36.4 (2004): 614–641.

voluntarily by local residents—the market has become a symbol of resistance, a self-sustaining community hub for small-scale economic and cultural activity, and something of a local legend, attracting people from all over Liverpool and beyond (see Figure 5). On the first Saturday of every month, stalls populate the street, selling everything from second-hand books to daily essentials, with live music and diverse dishes freshly cooked in a festival atmosphere. This DIY experiment is a tentative move towards regenerating Granby through community control over the means of social reproduction. Such 'guerrilla' or 'insurgent' urbanism[30] began to attract influential supporters. One such ally, Erika Rushton—Neighbourhoods Director at Plus Dane at the time who would go on to become a Granby CLT board member and then its chair; a self-styled 'cultural economist' centrally involved in socially innovative urban development projects across Liverpool—put it like this, when I interviewed her in late 2013:

> The thing that most impressed me was that, you know, actually that area has had between 25 and 30 years of engagement, consultations, and master plans and competitions to find the best developer who's going to save everybody … And actually what a few particular women and a couple of guys there did is they stopped going to the engagement meetings, they stopped being consulted; they started sweeping their street, painting the tinned up houses so they had something nicer to look at, planting flowers and the like—which is where we got involved as an organisation, I suppose, helping them do some of that … Then the market started as a one-off, and now attracts two hundred people a time over the course of a day. The idea that you can get two hundred people in the middle of a derelict street in Liverpool on a wet afternoon running up to Christmas is pretty phenomenal—and none of that is about what will happen to their houses; that is all about people in a locality having a relationship with each other and making something happen for the better. So that's what I'm supporting.

This underlines a general feeling—felt in Homebaked, too—that the CLT model is merely a vehicle for something deeper, those acts of commoning embodied by the guerrilla gardening and street market. Owning houses via a CLT was only ever a means to an end for many such activists. At the same time, there arose from guerrilla gardening and the street market a collective desire and hope for something more substantial and durable in institutional form. This began to take shape in November 2011, when Granby Four Streets CLT was officially established as a legal entity, providing campaigners with the organisational front and credibility required to enter more serious

30 Kurt Iveson, "Cities within the City: Do-It-Yourself Urbanism and the Right to the City", *International Journal of Urban and Regional Research* 37.3 (2013): 941–956.

Figure 5 Granby Street Market relocated to Ducie Street during Cairns Street renovation, 2015.

negotiations with the council over the future of their neighbourhood. Not long after, however, in early 2012, the council put the four streets up to tender—welcoming the best bids from private developers and housing associations—and entered into long negotiations with a private development company, Leader One, effectively shunting the CLT off the negotiating table.

Carrying forward the logic of HMR—the compartmentalisation of Liverpool into distinctly bounded ZOOs and 'regeneration zones' each with their own preferred developer—the council sought a single identifiable organisation to hand full responsibility over for regenerating the four streets. Thus the entire area was offered up for tender to the highest bidder. The council's apparent reticence to test out alternatives and engage in smaller-scale, finer-grained, experimental approaches—a hangover from HMR thinking—seemed to arise as much from a fear of uncertainty as from the ideological influence of the ownership model. Irrespective of their rationale, council officers were not willing to listen to alternative proposals and the CLT had little choice other than to approach Leader One to propose a partnership in delivering affordable housing—an idea the company seemed initially to entertain. When council negotiations with Leader One eventually collapsed around a year later under suspicions of corruption, it left in its wake a policy vacuum—inviting a number of variously competing or cooperating alternative approaches to fill the space. The Leader One deal imploded under unreasonable demands for the council to underwrite any losses: effectively to privatise profit and socialise risk. In contrast, the alternatives were all, in different ways, socially innovated approaches emanating from civil society to *rehabilitate* rather than demolish and redevelop the four streets.

For the first time the council entered into a more serious conversation with local residents and set up a steering group to explore the possibility of public asset transfer. However, at the same time, the council announced its own 'Homes for £1' scheme—its so-called 'homesteading' plan—giving away houses for a nominal pound to be renovated through self-help sweat equity on the proviso that certain conditions were met. Homesteaders must live in the house for at least five years without sub-letting and invest capital to match a state-backed low-interest loan. CLT campaigners now had a new competitor and recount the great difficulty in getting their ideas—cleverly rebranded 'community homesteading'—taken at all seriously by the council. For all the strengths of homesteading as a small-scale solution to the empty homes problem, the council appeared more at home with handing the area over to private developers or individual homeowners—even at considerable public expense—than with considering more financially and socially sustainable options in collective housing alternatives.

Working alongside the CLT was the co-op. Terrace 21 was so named by its members to reflect aspirations to recreate 'terraced housing for the 21st century'. They hoped to retrofit to extremely high ecological standards some of the CLT-owned houses and manage these cooperatively through a Mutual Home Ownership Society (MHOS).[31] The idea of a MHOS is to create a more egalitarian distribution of housing costs through mutual aid such that each resident pays a fixed affordable percentage of their income on rental shares in the scheme—no more than 35 per cent of net household income in the case of Terrace 21—so that poorer members are subsidised by richer: from each according to their ability to each according to their need. Designed to work as a key complementary component of CLTs, the MHOS model has been developed by CDS Co-operatives to circumvent the problem of leaseholder enfranchisement: leasing buildings from the CLT, which ultimately protects the land from private buy-outs. Terrace 21 were inspired by LILAC (Low Impact Living Affordable Community) in Leeds, the UK's pioneering MHOS development.[32] LILAC, however, is not coupled with a CLT, so Granby Four Streets is to be the UK's first demonstration project of the CLT–MHOS model.

31 See www.ukmhos.weebly.com and Pat Conaty, Johnston Birchall, Steve Bendle and Rosemary Foggitt, *Common Ground—for Mutual Home Ownership: Community Land Trusts and Shared-Equity Cooperatives to Secure Permanently Affordable Homes for Key Workers* (New Economics Foundation and CDS Cooperatives, 2003).

32 Paul Chatterton, "Towards an Agenda for Post-Carbon Cities: Lessons from Lilac, the

Without other successful examples to evidence—and lacking the legal clarity of private freehold—asset transfer was therefore a difficult case for Terrace 21 to make to any public body whose responsibilities lie in protecting the public interest. The choice to adopt the MHOS model was influenced by their dealings with Leader One, when co-op activists had originally approached Leader One to propose a partnership on behalf of the CLT. A co-founder of Terrace 21 tells me how it was Leader One representatives, during their negotiations with the council, who first suggested to him that "the council isn't interested in having a co-operative there. If you can make it like some kind of ownership thing, then we might be a bit more interested!" A mutual home ownership society, with its semantic associations with classic, private, individual homeownership—despite the actual workings of the model being more akin to a co-op than its name suggests—thereby became preferable as a brand to leverage support from otherwise hostile gatekeepers.

It was at this point that the CLT was approached by a mysterious social finance company called HD Social Investments (later rebranded Steinbeck Studio) backed personally by John Davey, "the mystery millionaire" as CLT members playfully described him before his identity was more publicly revealed. This self-styled 'libertarian economist' and former stockbroker from Jersey was working with Xanthe Hamilton, a filmmaker and the founding director of the innovative social investment vehicle Steinbeck Studio, which was to manage Davey's capital. Hamilton was on the search around the country for socially worthwhile projects in which to invest finance capital for a small return and came across Granby through auspicious links with SAVE Britain's Heritage via local urbanist Jonathan Brown—an interest piqued by the residents' entrepreneurial spirit breathing life back into the faded Victorian grandeur around them. Xanthe, who would go on to work closely with the CLT as a board member, then persuaded the mystery millionaire Davey to invest a £500,000 interest free loan which, according to Xanthe, "unleashed [Granby CLT's] grant-writing power".[33] Indeed, by November 2016, the CLT had accessed a total of £900,000 of grant funding in addition to the half million interest-free loan from Steinbeck Studio. This strategy of zero- or very low-interest social investment was described by CLT activists as "philanthropy at four per cent return", in reference to the early housing association trusts of the nineteenth century known as 'five per cent philanthropy orgs'.[34] With investment via Steinbeck Studio coupled with their successful application to two national grant schemes, the government's Empty

UK's First Ecological, Affordable Cohousing Community", *International Journal for Urban and Regional Research* 37.5 (2013): 1654–1674.

33 Quoted in Stephen Pritchard, "Complexity, Uncertainty and Scalability: How Assemble's Granby 4 Streets Won 2015 Turner Prize", Colouring in Culture Blog, 2016: http://colouringinculture.org/blog/assemble-complexity-uncertainty-scalability#_ftn4.

34 Malpass, "The Discontinuous History of Housing Associations in England".

Homes Fund and that of the Nationwide Foundation, each worth £125,000, CLT activists were now well positioned to acquire houses from the council.

In a presentation given at the London Festival of Architecture 2016, entitled *Granby 4 Streets: The Ideals of Specificity and Scalability in a Social and Architectural Endeavour*, Hamilton describes the five models of regeneration that were, around 2013, "all attempting to exploit [the] swampy ecology of funding, law, insurance and so forth" to find a viable solution for Granby's rehabilitation.[35] One was the 'Homes for £1' scheme the council had been trialling nearby, which utilised sweat equity and personal investment but at great public subsidy; another was the co-operative scheme emerging around Terrace 21, which could work with the CLT as one of its tenants. A third was that of the local housing associations such as Plus Dane who had huge capital leveraging power but whose professionalised development processes proved the most expensive. Fourth was the CLT itself, the democratically governed organisation representing the community and able to win grants but which, according to Xanthe, lacked "finance or technical managerial skills" although it was a "welcoming committee for other models". Finally, a fifth model was Hamilton's own Steinbeck Studio—a "social investor-backed private developer scheme" with a "pot of ready money" and highly networked into professional and artistic circles but ineligible for grants—the perfect complement to the CLT. The genius—and ultimate success—of the CLT was in bringing all these otherwise competing factions together around a common vision with the CLT as its anchor.

Together, the CLT, Steinbeck Studio and Terrace 21 are working as joint partners to realise the community-led vision: a tight-knit partnership that aims to share the assets and the workload involved in such a complex project by providing a range of specialist skills and interests. This has also helped convince the council of the project's viability and social value. Within the partnership, the CLT is both an interest group itself and the ultimate structure under which all other stakeholders are organised: the overarching umbrella institution intended to acquire legal ownership of all the land for long-term collective stewardship, with the use of buildings leased out to partners and residents. Of the 27 initial houses, the CLT has taken on ten itself to rent out at affordable sub-market rates, in addition to acting as stewards for the local area as a whole, recently completing 'Our First 10 Homes', with first tenants settling in. Terrace 21 are in the process of finalising the asset transfer of five houses, which they will retrofit and manage as an MHOS co-op under CLT stewardship. Steinbeck Studio initially hoped to refurbish and internally restructure the twelve larger and grander houses on Ducie Street to provide a mix of one- to five-bedroom market-rate houses that will help subsidise the rest; but long-term structural damage to the properties and indecision over

35 Quoted in Pritchard, "Complexity, Uncertainty and Scalability: How Assemble's Granby 4 Streets Won 2015 Turner Prize".

their fate have all but scuppered this plan. Importantly, the CLT vision for the entire neighbourhood has been adopted by development partners, Plus Dane and Liverpool Mutual Homes, who have refurbished—or rebuilt meticulously to the same design specification, in cases where structural damage was too great—all the remaining houses across the four streets.

One important piece of the puzzle remained: who would do the design and construction for the CLT? Through Xanthe Hamilton's creative networks the CLT found its architects: an innovative London-based architecture and design collective renowned for their hands-on DIY approach to regeneration, appropriately called Assemble.[36] In 2013, Steinbeck Studio commissioned Assemble to write a persuasive design statement—a beautifully illustrated brochure locally lauded for its ingenuity—setting out a vision and practical plan to acquire and refurbish 27 of the 128 vacant boarded-up properties as a mix of affordable homes, as part of a long-term vision to rehabilitate the 113 other empty homes and revive the neighbourhood's economic backbone, Granby Street, as the bustling shop-filled high street it once was, with plans for community-owned enterprise and facilities.[37] Assemble's design statement proved critical in persuading the council to consider the scheme as a viable and attractive option. In it they explain their method:

> The three strands of our vision are bound together by a hands-on approach for delivery that builds on the enterprise, initiative and commitment that the community had shown over the last twenty years ... We seek to maximise local employment and involvement in the construction process. Our approaches are based around simple, accessible methods of construction that can be delivered locally—where the physical act of rebuilding is not only a way of boosting the local economy but a public act that offers residents a direct hand in shaping the area's development.[38]

Since setting up shop on site in Granby, Assemble has undertaken a pioneering do-it-together approach to the rehabilitation of the CLT houses they have named 'community homesteading'. This was partly inspired by Assemble's previous work across the UK, such as the Cineroleum in Clerkenwell, London, a disused petrol station that was transformed into a cinema by hundreds of volunteers working together in a self-initiated, experimental design and construction process. Like much of their work, this was an experiment in creative reuse of an obsolete site but also in the spontaneous and improvised

36 Oliver Wainwright, "The Street That Might Win the Turner Prize: How Assemble Are Transforming Toxteth", *The Guardian* (12 May 2015).

37 See https://assemblestudio.co.uk/projects/granby-four-streets-2.

38 Assemble, *The Granby Four Streets* (HD Social Investments, 2013), p. 26.

collective learning process of building together. It was also inspired by a white paper Xanthe and leading Assemble architect Lewis Jones wrote together in which they coin 'community homesteading' as a concept specifically for Granby—to "expand the houses for a pound model to a larger chunk and community rather than individual ownership".[39] Assemble's vision takes the logic of the self-help do-it-yourself homesteading approach utilised in the council's parallel 'Homes for £1' project but applies it more socially so as to bring together the accumulated skills and wisdom of the community through collective action. During renovation, Lewis Jones and other Assemble members lived on site and worked closely with residents to renovate their own and others' homes, training up local people who can then use their skills for do-it-yourself refurbishment of further houses. The idea is that once Assemble move onto their next brief the regeneration becomes self-sustaining. Through this method, the CLT houses on Cairns Street have by all accounts been beautifully redesigned; the window rendering on each individual facade painted in different shades of bright colour—juxtaposed starkly against the standardised terrace opposite renovated by Liverpool Mutual Homes. Construction costs are much lower than their housing association counterparts: the previously built Plus Dane houses on Beaconsfield Street cost £109,000 per unit and the Liverpool Mutual Homes £120,000, while the CLT aims to spend just £75,000 per house.[40]

Notwithstanding palpable success, the choice of community homesteading as a label is not quite so straightforwardly positive. Assemble's design statement is illustrated with a stylised photograph of Victorian barn-raising.[41] Influenced by the barn-raising traditions of North America and the homesteading of settlers going west creates problematic connotations, perhaps, for a multicultural inner-city neighbourhood in which indigeneity is claimed by various ethnic groups subject to a new kind of settler-colonialism in the form of arts-led gentrification. Despite all the creative interventions they have initiated, there is certainly a sense amongst some more longstanding residents that the trendy newcomers—Assemble and Terrace 21 included—do not possess quite the same right to place as they do. This tension between rights based on longevity of inhabitancy (occupation and biographical attachment to place) versus rights derived from productive contribution to place (improvements made through active labour) will not be an easy issue to resolve in the CLT's formalised property relations and housing allocations policy. Such conflicting claims between original occupation/appropriation and ongoing

39 Quoted in Pritchard, "Complexity, Uncertainty and Scalability: How Assemble's Granby 4 Streets Won 2015 Turner Prize".

40 Figures from a presentation at the northern launch of the National CLT Network's Urban CLT Fund hosted by Homebaked in Liverpool, 2014.

41 Assemble, *The Granby Four Streets*, p. 27.

contribution/improvement run deep in debates around common property and indigenous land rights.[42] It is also a sensitive issue for the global CLT movement to address, particularly in settler-colonial contexts such as the USA, Canada and Australia, as evident in its leading advocate John Emmeus Davis' eventual decision, upon reflection, to drop his original idea of entitling the updated edition of his classic *Community Land Trust Reader* as *"This Land is Ours"*.[43] In Granby, there is a definite presumption among residents that the local black community are its original or indigenous inhabitants: possessing a strong cultural identity firmly rooted in a particular history and geography and strengthened by the adversity associated with the '81 Uprising. How the CLT works to represent and express these ownership rights will be a defining issue of its future.

The CLT's stewardship role has the potential to negotiate these tensions. It has not only brought otherwise competing development partners together but also diverse local people from across traditional cleavages—notably class, race and religion—to produce what is arguably a "politics of space", in which a common spatial vision for place overcomes class politics and unites in broad consensus otherwise divergent property interests.[44] CLT membership extends throughout the L8 postal district, beyond the immediate Granby Triangle, and so the CLT recognises its scalar contributory relationship with surrounding urban areas. Members meet regularly to discuss CLT affairs and democratically elect representatives onto the trust management board, whose membership of twelve periodically rotates, with tripartite representation of three main groups—member residents; the wider local community; and key stakeholders. The latter third include representatives from the council, housing associations Plus Dane and Liverpool Mutual Homes, as well as crucial financial and technical expertise in development. The diverse black community are also actively engaged as stakeholders. The Men's and Women's Somali Groups each have board representation, as does the Steve Biko Housing Association, established in 1982 to provide local black people access to social housing in the context of racial discrimination, now helping develop and deliver the CLT housing allocations policy. Those social housing tenants displaced by HMR, meanwhile, are represented in the wider community third. A large part of the popular mandate for the CLT model—despite some tensions emerging within the community—is its capacity to incorporate multiple tenure types, integrating divergent property interests, and its democratic trust governance structure, enabling wider stakeholder

42 Nicholas Blomley, *Unsettling the City* (Routledge, 2004).

43 A fact imparted at a public seminar given by Susannah Bunce on Canadian CLTs in October 2019, London.

44 Mark Purcell, "Neighborhood Activism among Homeowners as a Politics of Space", *Professional Geographer* 53.2 (2001): 178–194.

participation for long-term place stewardship for wider community benefit over resident-member benefit alone.

Trust is the magic ingredient holding the entire CLT endeavour together. It relies on trust that the council will not cynically take advantage of community aspirations for self-governance to offload public service responsibilities; on the trust of local people, who need to feel included in order to give consent and democratic legitimacy; on trust between members engaging in collective governance; on trust placed in CLT Board members to represent the interests of other members fairly; and ultimately on trust in the community trust itself, as responsible 'steward' of public assets for future generations. Gaining council support, as the principal landowner and gatekeeper, was essential to realise the CLT partnership's plans, which hinged on acquisition of the properties. Yet this proved somewhat difficult in the context of a long, complicated history of mutual mistrust between council and community, first flaring in the 1981 Uprising, and intermittently threatening to paralyse collaborative decision-making. Residents still feel a powerful sense of resentment and injustice about the council's demolition plans, says a prominent resident-activist: "People past and present who live here feel that their property has been stolen from them, I mean really quite powerfully feel that the area has been stolen from quite a tight-knit community, so actually a CLT is quite symbolic in returning ownership to the community".

The moral vocabulary of theft is used in two senses: individual homes 'stolen' by compulsory purchase and forced eviction, and a more collective sense of loss of shared history and community ties. The reappropriation of houses via the CLT was for many residents and activists a necessary but not sufficient condition for realising a broader project of reclaiming community control over their neighbourhood after decades of mistreatment, as Erika Rushton (then working for Plus Dane) attests:

> I think what the residents really wanted was to wrestle some control back over the wider area and have some say in its stewardship going forward. I think the CLT may give them that, but I think that it's also providing a means of saying, "Well, you can have ten houses because that's all you can afford, now have them and that's your lot!" And actually they never set out wanting any houses; what they wanted was to be entrusted with the future of that area. Sitting here as part of an organisation [Plus Dane] and looking at it you think, "None of the rest of us have done a good job of it for the last thirty years so why on earth wouldn't we trust the residents? Why would you trust them less than housing professionals after thirty years of that?"

The CLT is seen as a symbolic reappropriation of place: reclaiming personal homes and community space stolen by the council and protecting against future demolition threats. Such an oppositional position, however, posed additional barriers to negotiating a mutually satisfactory solution. From the council perspective, the burden of proof lay firmly on the CLT to demonstrate its social responsibility to manage assets and to convince local government of the merits of transferring public assets to an untested community-owned organisation. A Granby CLT activist frames the problem thus:

> We have to prove that we can do something before people trust, because that issue of trust goes both ways—local residents don't trust the city council, the city council don't trust local residents to do anything other than kick up a fuss ... Hopefully that would get easier, breaking down the barriers that have been built up over the last ten years with HMR; and a certain fear at the council level—just trusting people to do the best for the neighbourhood—doesn't really seem to be there. I think it's there now with some of the councillors but it's still not there with all of the officers. That's an institutional culture thing, which I expect takes decades to change.

So how to explain the relatively swift shift in council policy if not institutional culture? Part of this was no doubt their sensing of the winds changing in the national policy landscape. Government funding was increasingly being made available for community self-help and empty homes refurbishment, as part of the Conservative's localism agenda, as opposed to grander programmes like HMR. Transitional funding, which had been made available to HMR Pathfinders to finish off work already started, was by now drying up. The Leader One deal then also evaporated. That left the council in the sticky situation of having hundreds of boarded-up empty homes on its balance sheet, just sitting there as liabilities, without the funding or ideas forthcoming for their transformation into assets. Until, that is, the council was given a little push finally to take the leap by a surprising piece of positive press. In May 2015, Assemble were shortlisted for the Turner Prize, specifically for their work with Granby CLT—the first time an architectural design studio has ever been nominated.[45] This brought a huge amount of favourable though unexpected media attention and publicity to Granby Four Streets. Later that year, the project won—the first time a housing or architectural intervention has ever done so. And awards beget awards. Following in the footsteps of the Eldonians, Granby Four Streets CLT was shortlisted as a finalist in the 2016 UN World Habitat Awards. Also in 2016, the social innovation foundation NESTA recognised Granby as one among fifty 'new radicals'—radically transformative "projects, which, if scaled, could transform the lives of millions of

45 Wainwright, "The Street That Might Win the Turner Prize".

people, and offer us a glimpse of a different kind of society".[46] More recently, the New Economics Foundation think tank puts Granby CLT on its 'new economy map' of 'inspiring projects' in its *Change the Rules* campaign.[47]

Assemble and CLT activists have capitalised upon this media frenzy by establishing a social enterprise specialising in the creative production of architectural ceramics based on Assemble's Turner Prize-winning interior designs for the CLT houses. Assemble, led by Lewis Jones, have set up an on-site workshop in a disused corner building on Granby Street, now selling ceramics to international buyers, using the Turner Prize exhibition as a platform to showcase their distinctive, elegant aesthetic. The rationale, design ethos and historical background behind the Granby Workshop is laid out in what is partly a product catalogue and partly a chronicle scrapbook produced collectively by Assemble, residents and fellow travellers—myself included, writing on the conceptual and historical origins of the CLT model.[48] The Granby Workshop was initially a pilot project for creating value out of the very business of the regeneration process, employing local people in experimental manufacturing processes—paid positions as well as volunteers—to design and make furniture, house fixtures and architectural features, using reclaimed materials recycled from the CLT houses themselves. As a social enterprise, profits are reinvested to support programmes to engage local young people (aged 13 to 18) in creative, practical projects. Assemble's great investment in Granby has attracted others to follow suit. There are already signs of economic recovery on Granby Street, now the permanent fixture for the ever-growing street market, with new businesses (such as a hairdressers and an eatery) opening up for the first time in decades—the first step in the long-term plan for its revitalisation as a cultural and retail artery.

The Turner Prize victory has also helped the CLT win large grants for further redevelopment. The four grand three-storey corner buildings framing Cairns and Granby Streets (Figure 4) have suffered considerable structural damage—one of them falling in entirely—but will now be reconstructed and brought back to life with the financial support of Power to Change, the Co-operative Foundation and Homes England (the quango formerly known as the Homes and Communities Agency and, before that, the Housing Corporation). The CLT are in the process of engaging their members and local residents in participatory design workshops to establish what exactly the community wants the CLT-owned four corner buildings eventually to house. Ideas have ranged from housing, shops, cafés, co-working spaces and

46 NESTA chief executive, Geoff Mulgan, 'Meet the 2016 New Radicals', NESTA Blog, 6 July 2016: www.nesta.org.uk/blog/meet-the-2016-new-radicals/.

47 New Economics Foundation, *Change the Rules*: https://letschangetherules.org/map/granby-4-streets.

48 Assemble, eds, *Granby Workshop Catalogue 2015*.

community enterprise to public space. A prestigious grant of almost £250,000 was procured from Arts Council England for Assemble to transform two of the houses on Cairns Street—too dilapidated to save—into the Granby Winter Garden and Common House. Combining an urban garden, meeting space, a studio for creative activities and a 'spare room' to host artists-in-residence as well as paying guests, as a kind of 'cooperative Airbnb', the Winter Garden is intended as another source of self-sustaining revenue for the CLT in years to come. Its first artist-in-residence has been announced as Nina Edge, a prominent local artist and leading activist in the adjacent campaign to save the Welsh Streets from demolition, who has worked with local people, horticultural experts and Assemble to transform the two terraces into a beautiful indoor garden opening the full height of the building up to a glass roof, from which a chandelier refracts sunlight onto subtropical plants and greenery.

In all these many ways, Granby Four Streets comes full circle on the holistic approach set out by SNAP. Assemble's innovative and immersive technique of community homesteading is a conduit for local socioeconomic and political empowerment, bringing diverse groups together around a hands-on project and cultivating new relationships, habits and networks of cooperation and mutual support which may help sustain practices of commoning conducive to CLT governance in the long run. We can trace this approach back to the participatory design processes innovated by the likes of CDS for the new-build co-ops and, in turn, to SNAP. Interesting parallels abound. Just as SNAP activists inspired the development of Britain's first rehab co-ops, so too has Granby CLT forged an alliance with a local eco-housing co-op, Terrace 21. SNAP reimagined regeneration as a holistic endeavour, integrating physical rehab and environmental improvements with social, health, education and employment programmes; likewise, the CLT vision is for an interrelated process of empowering local people, developing their skills through 'do-it-together' training programmes, and improving more than just housing by providing new employment opportunities and enhanced green public spaces. With such obvious spatial and historical as well as social and philosophical connections between the two projects—SNAP mapping directly onto CLT boundaries and originally saving the four streets from demolition—it is little wonder that CLT activists have drawn on SNAP as a source of inspiration. Some of the leading activists (notably, former CLT board member and community organiser Ronnie Hughes) have begun to position the CLT as its contemporary heir, reading the original SNAP report as a rich repository of ideas and historical evidence; they are starting to believe that, in Ronnie's words, "We're finishing the work that SNAP started!"

From Success to Failure: A Great British Property Scandal

Little Klondyke in Bootle provides a fascinating, though tragic, counter-example of how the power of financial interests and abstract logics trumped community aspirations, which ultimately failed to save the neighbourhood from demolition and redevelopment. This is a very different place to Granby. Located in the metropolitan borough of Sefton, several miles north of Liverpool city centre, the area suffers from economic isolation far more viscerally. Like the renowned Welsh Streets adjacent to the Granby Four Streets in L8—home to controversies surrounding the planned, though recently thwarted, demolition of Beatles drummer Ringo Starr's birthplace—Little Klondyke was built by Welsh economic migrants, with roads named after Edith, Eleanor and Marion. And, like the Welsh Streets, it became one of the most notoriously contested neighbourhoods in the New Heartlands Pathfinder, one whose residents fought back against extreme measures to evict them.[49] Likewise, Little Klondyke became one of the main features in various television documentaries about HMR, notably Channel 4's *Great British Property Scandal*, for which celebrity architect George Clarke filmed in the area in February 2012. He then became involved in the local anti-demolition campaign that for some years successfully stalled demolition plans with the critical support of two national housing and conservation charities. Throughout the reign of HMR, the Empty Homes Agency and SAVE Britain's Heritage ran a tireless ten-year national pro-refurbishment campaign in opposition to the demolitions of the New Heartlands Pathfinder. "These charities", explains Jonathan Brown, one of SAVE's most vocal campaigners, "helped link the disparate local anti-demolition groups across northern England to national media support and opened up lobbying routes to MPs and government ministers".[50] Most famously, SAVE had been centrally involved in the campaign to save 440 terraced houses in the Welsh Streets from demolition—in their successful strategy of buying the two-up two-down in which Ringo Starr was born and using their legal resources to challenge compulsory purchase as well as helping bring the case to Public Inquiry in 2014. With involvement of these expert interests, activism in the Little Klondyke evolved into a more forward-looking campaign for a CLT alternative. The Empty Homes Agency had experience with developing a do-it-yourself 'homesteading' model in Stoke-on-Trent, whilst SAVE were connected to comparable events in Granby through Brown's interest in the CLT campaign there. The idea for a CLT came together just in time to put in a bid for the government's Empty Homes

49 Marc Waddington, "88-Year-Old Bootle Woman Evicted from Her Home to Make Way for the Bulldozers", *Liverpool Echo* (9 Mar. 2012).

50 Jonathan Brown, "Why Were the Four Streets Emptied out Anyway? A Granby Back Story", in Assemble, eds, *Granby Workshop Catalogue 2015*, p. 11.

Fund Community Grants Programme in April 2012. This was a detailed plan for refurbishment of 121 homes and restoration of a Welsh Presbyterian Church.

The application was written with the help of the Maritime Community Development Agency, established in 1993 as the only organisation dedicated to community development in Sefton and, since 2003, involved in anti-HMR campaigning. Here, anti-demolition sentiments were much more about socio-economic survival than architectural heritage. Household income in Bootle is still today amongst the lowest in the UK; residents are unable to afford the 'affordable rents' of the new HMR-built properties—some increasing by as much as 100 per cent on what was offered before. Owner-occupiers' compensation for losing their homes often equated to only 50 per cent of a comparable new build; many owner-occupiers were forced to become housing association tenants following compulsory purchase of their homes under HMR. The CLT plan therefore aimed to provide truly affordable housing for local people and was closely aligned with other campaigns against austerity, welfare reform and the 'bedroom tax'. It was primarily driven by one particular well-known local activist, Juliet Edgar, who also stood in local council elections around the same time, as an anti-bedroom tax candidate. Juliet was the lynchpin pulling in all the partners, writing grant applications and making things happen.

Their fully costed scheme included street visualisations and detailed architect drawings of proposed layouts and redesigns, with internal remodelling of housing to suit diverse local needs. The initial proposal was for refurbishment of 'Little Wall', with long-term plans to take on the entire area as Little Klondyke CLT. In June 2012, they received a positive response from the then Department for Communities and Local Government regarding their application, which amounted to over £5 million of government grant to kick-start the project. The task now was to convince the council and galvanise the wider community. The first step towards this goal was the organisation of a scoping day with a fete and information stall for local residents to get a flavour of what a CLT could do for their neighbourhood. This was funded by the National Community Land Trust Network—providing up to £5,000 seed funding per project—and run by John Earnshaw, the Empty Homes Agency and CLT Network Advisor who had worked with Granby in the early stages to set up the Granby Community Partnership. Bad weather, however, dissuaded many residents from attending and the campaign since struggled to attract community support. Earnshaw also helped organise a conference trip to Preston for activists to learn more about the model. However, there were simply not enough local people involved to run the project from the grassroots. John insisted the project required twelve volunteers—to get things set up and to constitute an effective CLT board—but he waited in vain for a month for activists to find the numbers. Thus the project was driven through the passion of Juliet Edgar with too little input from others, which even she acknowledges: "We need to ensure there's a market [demand] there, and we haven't done that yet. We haven't had time to do it". Part of the problem was that, by this point, almost all the houses had been emptied of residents, scattered across the borough, difficult to reconnect. Granby was lucky enough to have a solid core of homeowners to push their project on to success; Little Klondyke lacked this stable tenure group. Another part was the sheer lack of resources compared with Granby and Homebaked, which, as I explore below, sprung from a well-funded Liverpool Biennial public arts project.

Activists were nonetheless slowly but surely building connections with those people who had been decanted into new houses who said they would like to return and get involved in the CLT. Moreover, discussion had begun with Bellway—the preferred developer for this ZOO—who were potentially interested to become a partner in the project as the development agent for refurbishment. The real barrier was the council. Not only did the £5 million government grant require final council approval but also more sustained municipal support for an area facing severe blight, as a representative from the Empty Homes Agency impressed upon me:

> I think they would have needed more support than just simply an approval letter—a helping hand from the council. Approval is not just a letter saying, "Okay yeah you can"—the support is how they release land to them, all sorts of resources, not just financial.

Before the Empty Homes Fund bid went in, activists tried to contact Sefton Council several times to arrange a meeting to discuss the CLT possibility, now that HMR had withdrawn from the area. Yet they were confronted by a hostile attitude. Despite this being just an early feasibility discussion to gauge interest, activists were requested to produce comprehensive documentation of their business plan and a twenty-year strategy before the council were even willing to speak with them. The council eventually sent a formal response, which activists and their partners alike thought "troubling" for being so "incredibly dismissive" of the idea. I asked Alan Lunt, then Strategic Director for the Built Environment at Sefton Metropolitan Borough Council and signatory of the letter, to participate in this research or at least comment on Little Klondyke but I was likewise met with refusal. Participants believe that the council was firmly set on "something bigger" and more lucrative than a community refurbishment project. Their real intentions are revealed in the tactics employed in acquiring and securing local properties.

The council acquired the chapel—then derelict and badly damaged by arson attacks—following its last church service in March 2008 and a diminishing local Presbyterian congregation.[51] It was in the council's interests to

51 Liverpool Echo, "Klondyke Welsh Presbyterian Chapel Can Be Demolished, High Court Rules", *Liverpool Echo* (25 July 2013).

demolish the chapel to make way for large-scale redevelopment, but prior approval submissions were required before any demolition could legally commence. CLT activists led by Juliet Edgar made regular check-ups of the area to make sure no unlawful demolition occurred. One evening they discovered contractors were already pulling down the Victorian church building before they had been made aware of prior approval. SAVE Britain's Heritage were called in and had their lawyers serve legal papers that very night to the demolition contractor and Sefton council. This, however, did not prevent the contractors from finishing the job. It was not just the church, Juliet recalls, which was targeted by such practices:

> We served on the Friday; they continued with the demolition on the Saturday. I think it was by one o'clock Monday the council agreed to stop. Guess what happened on Monday night? Huge fire in some of the properties. Coincidence? So since the day that we filed that legal action, I think it was Monday 29th January [2013], until something like mid-August, there were fires all the time. I was constantly getting phone calls ... We were just documenting the lot of them, and that was part of the evidence that was presented at the High Court. So I do blame them, absolutely, this is the battleground. It's a war. I mean all that time, there'd never been any fires ...

SAVE lawyers took the council to court in a high-profile judicial review over the demolition of the church, arguing against the 'salami-slicing' of the chapel, as if it were separable, from its historical neighbourhood context.[52] Sefton insisted that retaining the chapel was part of its original plan but that had to change due to health and safety implications of its derelict condition and partially collapsed roof.[53] Ultimately, SAVE lost the court case. Without the chapel as a community anchor—and with many of the properties structurally unsound from fire damage—all hopes of establishing a CLT to rehabilitate rather than redevelop the neighbourhood were lost.

52 SAVE, "SAVE Britain's Heritage Newsletter October 2013" (SAVE Britain's Heritage, 2013): www.savebritainsheritage.org/news/newsletters.php.

53 *Liverpool Echo*, "Klondyke Welsh Presbyterian Chapel Can Be Demolished, High Court Rules".

CHAPTER 12

Technocratic Experiment or Experimental Utopia?

Not all local authorities were so dead set against community-led alternatives. In Kensington, on the eastern edge of Liverpool city centre, council officers flirted briefly with the idea of a CLT before quietly dropping it. Although this experiment never really took off with the local community, it is an interesting story to tell, if only for the insight into council thinking in the aftermath of HMR. In some sense, Kensington is not unlike Granby in being one of the more multicultural areas of the city with some truly magnificent Victorian architecture that likewise—and rather controversially—came under the bulldozer's shadow cast by HMR. It was also a very poor area suffering from multiple deprivation and arguably in need of state intervention. It was thus the object of New Labour's New Deal for Communities (NDC), their flagship programme for tackling the central issue of 'social exclusion' through a more joined-up and multi-sectoral approach that incorporated health, crime and education, for instance, as well as housing.[1] Kensington Regeneration—the largest of 39 NDC partnerships across the country—was set up in 2000. The NDC came to an end in 2010 but regeneration work was continued by a successor body, Kensington Community Interest Company. HMR, a more straightforwardly housing-led regeneration policy, had been working in parallel with the NDC until its cancellation in 2011. An independent regeneration consultant was brought in by the council, through their connections with other HMR Pathfinders that had commissioned CLT options studies, and was asked to work with Kensington CIC on exploring the prospects for a CLT succession vehicle.

The potential of the CLT model for regeneration of declining neighbourhoods had caught the attention of various agencies and regeneration partnerships in the early 2000s, just as HMR was getting formulated. As NDC partnerships were being wrapped up, regeneration professionals were searching for ways to sustain the gains made and engage communities after

1 Paul Lawless, Michael Foden, Ian Wilson and Christina Beatty, "Understanding Area-Based Regeneration: The New Deal for Communities Programme in England", *Urban Studies* 47.2 (2009): 257–275.

the funding dried up—for instance, the Shoreditch NDC's scoping study for a 'Community Equity Trust' as a potential succession vehicle.[2] Had this materialised, it would have amounted to a kind of top-down, policy-driven CLT, as opposed to community-led. At the same time, Charlie Baker, a Manchester-based co-op activist and regeneration consultant at URBED (Urbanism, Environment, Design) Ltd, was thinking about ways to adapt the UK-based CLT model—developed by advocate-researcher Bob Paterson at Community Finance Solutions in Salford University—to work in an HMR Pathfinder context. In their masterplan for the Werneth-Freehold HMR area commissioned by the Oldham Local Strategic Partnership in Greater Manchester, URBED first introduced the notion of a CLT as an alternative vehicle for refurbishment of terraced housing—in contexts where rehabilitation over demolition was considered a viable and desirable possibility by HMR Pathfinders.[3] This alternative route to regeneration through HMR was incorporated as a key potential option in Community Finance Solutions' practitioner's guide on CLTs.[4]

The CLT idea was gaining currency and fast becoming fashionable as an option considered by HMR partnerships looking for new ideas. An HMR manager for Liverpool recalls how when she worked for Salford Council (in Greater Manchester) the HMR team seriously explored the option of a CLT in Pendleton: "a way of trying to leverage some more money into that area" as an alternative to the planned Private Finance Initiative bid which remained "really hard to make stack up financially". This plan was even included as a case study in a Community Finance Solutions guide on urban CLTs[5] but ultimately never taken forward. Yet the research gathered on the options study—and others like it—helped create a "buzz" around the concept as well as to lay some preliminary groundwork for seeing it delivered as a viable institutional vehicle. The same HMR manager explained to me how her experience with the Salford project and exposure to URBED ideas helped seed the CLT idea in Liverpool; she put the council in touch with the consultant who would pitch the CLT idea in Kensington. Interest in the CLT idea came from four council officers from different departments, whose motivations are described by the consultant thus:

2 Stephanie Saulter, Alison Masterman and Anna Eagar, *The Community Equity Trust: A Report on a Community-Based Self-Funding Urban Regeneration Model Developed by the Shoreditch Trust* (The Shoreditch Trust, 2008).

3 URBED, *Werneth Freehold: A Masterplan for Housing Market Renewal* (Oldham Local Strategic Partnership and North West Development Agency, 2004).

4 Community Finance Solutions, *Community Land Trusts—A Practitioner's Guide* (University of Salford, 2007).

5 Community Finance Solutions, ed., *Placeshaping: A Toolkit for Urban Community Land Trusts* (University of Salford, 2008).

> It was buzzy; they were looking for a vehicle to go forward; they were thinking ahead to succession vehicles because they knew the thing [HMR] was going; and they wanted a forum to actually be able to grab everything, pull it together.

Employed by Kensington Community Interest Company (CIC)—the successor body of Kensington Regeneration after the NDC was wound up—and with an initial budget of £10,000, the consultant ran a series of workshops, focus groups and presentations with the community about the theory behind a CLT, receiving a generally warm reception:

> I floated the idea several times that if you can early on in the regeneration process do a sort of red line around the finally agreed geography of the place, and then set up a CLT and move all the publicly available land and allow anything that's compulsory purchase or voluntary purchase to move into the CLT; you then put an asset lock on, where any money that is made—whether the "profit" is real or not—gets locked in; and the residents have got a lot of collective control over the whole regeneration process, over what to build and the mix of properties and the rest of it—well, residents have often shown a lot of interest in this.

The proposal, initially presented in a confidential report to the board of Kensington Regeneration CIC, was for Kensington CLT to be incorporated as a legacy body, covering an area delineated by the NDC boundaries, to take over assets currently held by the CIC in order to tap into legacy funding opportunities.[6] A total of 21 sites or properties were identified in the scoping study as suitable for inclusion in the CLT, including an estimated 180 new homes to be built on land that had already been cleared by HMR. Membership of the CLT was envisaged as being open to a variety of groups in the local area. The Kensington Regeneration Board—a small group of stakeholders and experts overseeing the process—were generally receptive. The real challenge came in convincing the much larger community stakeholder group. This resident-facing group of about 30 was intended to represent the community in the NDC area. They effectively controlled the process; their prior approval was required to sign anything off in the Kensington Regeneration Board. Early on in the participatory process, the consultant encountered resistance from the central steering committee of the board, who were the principal brokers of meetings with residents' groups. This central steering committee was composed of vocal activists not necessarily speaking for the entire community

6 Housing Consultancy Ltd, Private and Confidential Report to Board of Kensington Regeneration: Proposal to Establish a Community Land Trust (2008). Source: private correspondence.

but with real commitment to the area and strong political ideologies driving their volunteering. The first hurdle was a negative experience of a CLT conference in London in April 2008, to which the community representatives were invited to go on the suggestion of the council officers. Organised by Community Finance Solutions, the conference was aimed broadly at the professional class of architects, planners, lawyers, social investors, housing managers and movement advocates who were there to discuss the technicalities and challenges of developing CLTs in changing regulatory and political climates. The resident delegation thought they were going to, in the words of the consultant, "meet fifty or a hundred other residents in similar situations, so they could exchange notes" but came away daunted by the technical language, "quite freaked out by the industrial size of the intelligentsia".

As the process progressed, it was clear council officers were getting cold feet too. Whilst the initial invitation to explore a CLT came from middle management it soon drew the attention of senior directors who began, according to the consultant, to "mess things up because they really did not want to be giving up control or loss of budgets, and they wanted to recycle some of the profits they were going to make into other places, thinking 'Liverpool big pot' rather than Kensington". Had the homeowners not reneged on their initial enthusiasm, the CLT may well have been killed off anyway by the territorialism of some high-ranking council officers, seeing the CLT as "taking part of their empire". The official council offer of support of the principle of the CLT was nonetheless, as recorded in the Kensington Regeneration Board report, "caveated by the need to ensure the existing legal agreements with its partners are not infringed", referring directly to the lucrative redevelopment contracts in place between the council and its preferred ZOO developer, Bellway, to redevelop failing housing markets in line with HMR guidelines.[7] The independent consultant had conversations with Bellway, who were relatively amenable to the possibility of a CLT, on the proviso that they maintain contracts for refurbishment work. The report to the Kensington Regeneration Board explicitly stated that "Kensington CLT would be able (subject to funding) to purchase completed properties, but not to act as development agent in its own right"[8]—thereby assuring the council and developer that the development agreements would remain unthreatened. A major point of contention, then, was the loss of potential revenue for developer, council and housing association alike; each standing to make a 'profit' from the government grant investment into HMR for acquisition, demolition and reconstruction. The council would profit from the sale of land to the developer and higher tax receipts from more affluent housing; the developer from the sale of new homes;

7 Quoted in Housing Consultancy Ltd, Private and Confidential Report to Board of Kensington Regeneration, p. 10.

8 Housing Consultancy Ltd, Private and Confidential Report to Board of Kensington Regeneration, p. 10.

the housing associations from higher rent revenue streams and higher value stock against which to leverage further private capital. This is one rationale behind the formation of grant regimes or coalitions in shrinking cities: to profit from 'land banking'—capitalising on cost differentials secured through CPO acquisition at deflated market prices and resale at post-regeneration revalorised prices.[9]

Although land banking provides some clue to the puzzle of Kensington CLT's non-establishment, the campaign appears to have been ultimately thwarted by fractious internal politics between the three main tenure groupings. The homeowners were the driving force behind the CLT. These residents had deep stakes in the area; many were lifelong inhabitants with the time and motivation to get deeply involved in the regeneration process and, just as in Granby, help defend their houses from HMR demolition threats. Kensington was the area that attracted perhaps the most critical academic and media attention in terms of anti-demolition campaigning highlighting the controversial impact of HMR in Liverpool.[10] The fundamental barrier to the further development of the CLT came, according to the consultant who sat in countless homeowner forums as part of his engagement exercises, when

> The leaders and shakers of the homeowners, the "heads above the parapet" people, suddenly realised "Whoops! Membership is open to everybody, not just us"; and although I was able to shape the support to give the homeowners a little bit of preferential representation, it was when they suddenly realised that vote for vote at the AGM all the private tenants, all the housing association tenants—and they particularly hated the short-term, private-sector tenants—outnumbered them. What killed it in the end was the different resident constituencies.

Homeowners saw the other two tenure groupings as differentially deserving or capable of participation and inclusion in the CLT scheme—a kind of "tribal elitism". In these debates, housing association tenants were favoured as 'proper residents' over private tenants on the basis of longevity and permanence of residence. The lead housing association in the area was a subsidiary of Riverside called 'Community Seven', rebranded due to prevailing resident hostilities towards Riverside in the area. The tenants were generally sceptical of Riverside and would have supported the CLT transfer. Although Riverside could lose

9 Matthew Cocks and Chris Couch, "The Governance of a Shrinking City: Housing Renewal in the Liverpool Conurbation, UK", *International Planning Studies* 17.3 (2012): 277–301; Gordon MacLeod and Craig Johnstone, "Stretching Urban Renaissance: Privatizing Space, Civilizing Place, Summoning 'Community'", *International Journal of Urban and Regional Research* 36.1 (2012): 1–28.

10 Anna Minton, *Ground Control: Fear and Happiness in the Twenty-First-Century City* (Penguin, 2012); Chris Allen, *Housing Market Renewal and Social Class* (Routledge, 2008).

potential revenue, it had a history of co-op development behind it as MIH, and ambitions to support future collective housing, demonstrated most recently by their seeding of new-build co-op housing to Langrove Co-op at cost.

A bigger barrier was presented by homeowners' perceptions of private sector tenants. Kensington had experienced a similar trajectory to Granby: deteriorating Victorian terraces and falling property prices with short-term speculators and slum landlords moving into the area to make a profit on the difference between, on the one hand, purchase and maintenance costs and, on the other, rents accruable through housing benefits. The gap in the rental market filled by these landlords tended to be for those people who for whatever reason could not secure a tenancy with a registered provider: recently arrived immigrants who needed a cheap short-term tenancy at short notice or those evicted from housing association tenancies, often with a history of anti-social behaviour or minor criminality. Established homeowners felt threatened by the newcomers—with their different tenurial interests—outnumbering them and potentially taking control of the democratic decision-making process that governed CLT land. The dominance of the 'heads above the parapet' people in the consultation exercises, coupled with their control of the community stakeholder group which ultimately decided outcomes, meant that the voices of other tenure groups—and indeed other homeowners below the parapet—were excluded from the discussion. The independent consultant is adamant that "if Kensington had been emptied of all except for the homeowners, there'd be a community land trust there today". Such a perspective (albeit only one side to a complex story) does suggest one of the main factors for success in Granby was the relative absence of private sector tenants and the consequent opportunity for remaining homeowners to control the process as a relatively coherent domestic property class. It also reveals the dark side to collective housing in enabling tribal exclusivity, especially when internal democracy is not fully opened up to wider publics. Where every effort is made to engage *all* local residents and tenure factions in the process of building a collective alternative, when a democratic participatory process is written into the narrative from the outset, the results are very different. This is nowhere better exemplified than Homebaked, whose background in an earlier experiment in Anfield I explore next.

Dereliction-by-Design and Transatlantic Knowledge Transfer

Like Granby, Anfield had, in the first part of the twentieth century, been a relatively prosperous, "more appealing suburb" benefiting from Liverpool's economic pre-eminence, but, from the late 1970s, began to suffer from the knock-on effects of decline of the docks, with a weakening local economy, falling population and greater housing vacancies and dilapidation.[11] By the

11 Alan Southern, "Local Economy Anfield: Elite Premier League Football and Localism", *Local Economy* 29.3 (2014): 195–212 (p. 202).

new millennium, the ward was arguably in much worse condition than Granby, at least in terms of socioeconomic metrics: 60 per cent of the ward was within the most deprived 10 per cent of areas in the country (according to Indices of Multiple Deprivation) in a local authority consistently ranked the highest or second-highest most deprived in the country since 2000.[12] Despite various local community groups and initiatives being recipients of previous regeneration programmes—notably EU Structural Funds 'Pathways to Integration'[13]—by far the most significant intervention to arrest decline has been the Anfield/Breckfield HMR initiative, designated in 2002, which aimed to inject £40 million to £50 million of public money to lever in a further £300 million of private sector investment.[14] Contrary to the popular media image of HMR—as universally despised by the local community it foists redevelopment upon without due consultation[15]—plans for demolition in Anfield were widely welcomed.[16] Even before HMR was rolled out parts of the local community had supported demolition. In 1999, the Anfield Breckfield Community Steering Group, formed as an alliance between two neighbourhood councils involved in EU Pathways to Integration, worked with the city council and Liverpool Football Club to produce a report in 2002 that advocated the demolition of over two thousand homes. The 2002 community plan led to the formal Neighbourhood Renewal Assessment that would form the basis for securing HMR funding and official declaration of the Renewal Area in 2005, after which the Community Steering Group was replaced by the Anfield Breckfield Partnership Forum, which sought to place the community at the centre of regeneration decisions.

Yet such planning forums appeared only to keep the community at arm's-length from decision-making whilst providing a legitimating screen for the real power players. Since 2000, Liverpool Football Club has unilaterally developed a series of plans for the redevelopment of their stadium in the heart of Anfield—each entailing substantial damage to surrounding streets.[17]

12 Hugh Ellis and Kate Henderson, *Planning Out Poverty: The Reinvention of Social Town Planning* (Town and Country Planning Association, 2013).
13 Richard Meegan and Alison Mitchell, "'It's Not Community Round Here, It's Neighbourhood': Neighbourhood Change and Cohesion in Urban Regeneration Policies", *Urban Studies* 38.12 (2001): 2167–2194.
14 Ellis and Henderson, *Planning Out Poverty: The Reinvention of Social Town Planning*.
15 Rowan Moore, "Liverpool Biennial—Review", *The Guardian* (23 Sept. 2012); Owen Hatherley, "Liverpool's Rotting, Shocking 'Housing Renewal': How Did It Come to This?", *The Guardian* (27 Mar. 2013); Charles Clover, "Nightmare on Lime Street", *Daily Telegraph* (21 May 2005); Steve Doughty and Liz Hull, "Prescott's Plan for Housing 'Is Social Cleansing'", *Daily Mail* (25 May 2007).
16 Ellis and Henderson, *Planning Out Poverty: The Reinvention of Social Town Planning*.
17 Southern, "Local Economy Anfield: Elite Premier League Football and Localism".

The wider neighbourhood suffers in general from a bipolar local economy catering to the transitory needs of football fans over local residents, exacerbated by the club's noticeable lack of reinvestment back into the community. The indecision of Liverpool FC to settle on any one stadium redevelopment scheme and their failure to consult with surrounding property-owners and other residents has led to much local hostility, as well as hesitation from new businesses to invest in the area. As a result, the immediate streets around the stadium—now partly cleared or else renovated—were blighted for many years up until the stadium's recent expansion. Other areas in Anfield have likewise been cleared by HMR or, following its cancellation, post-HMR council-led regeneration plans for 'Anfield Village'. Some residents have fought hard against HMR—framed as a policy of 'dereliction by design'—and, in turn, campaigned for a CLT alternative, which has evolved into Homebaked and its family of community businesses today. However, prior to this community-led experimentation, the CLT idea was first mooted for Anfield in a lesser-known, aborted technocratic experiment led not by an anti-demolition grassroots group but by one of the very same housing associations involved in the HMR Pathfinder and thanked (contemptuously in Figure 6) for delivering dereliction by design. This provides an illuminating background to the limelight focused on Homebaked.

After years of successive regeneration partnerships between the council, housing associations and community forums, as well as a series of plans for the redevelopment of Liverpool FC's stadium, an alternative plan was being developed by Arena Housing. Since 1999, Arena had been the single largest housing association in Anfield—gaining Lead LIFE status as preferred housing association partner in HMR delivery. Arena is another example of commercial expansion necessitating disconnection from place, having formerly been Liver Housing Association, merging with Grosvenor Housing Association in 2002, and now incorporated into Your Housing Group. At an early stage of the community planning process with the Anfield Breckfield Partnership Forum, Arena floated the idea of seeding some of their housing stock as a kind of 'community endowment', over which a resident-led subsidiary of Arena would have overall control for the use of revenues for community benefits and capacity-building.

Arena's interest in finding ways of utilising assets for self-sustaining community benefit led to its application for a Knowledge Transfer Partnership (KTP) with the University of Liverpool Management School. In 2006, the KTP successfully secured funding for an Associate, a dedicated worker based in both partner organisations to explore solutions with local tenants. A study tour to the USA was organised in 2007, to learn about the more established American CLT model and bring back ideas for transfer to the Liverpool context. This was attended by eleven delegates from tenant associations and universities as well as Arena. A key event was the (American) National CLT Network's Annual

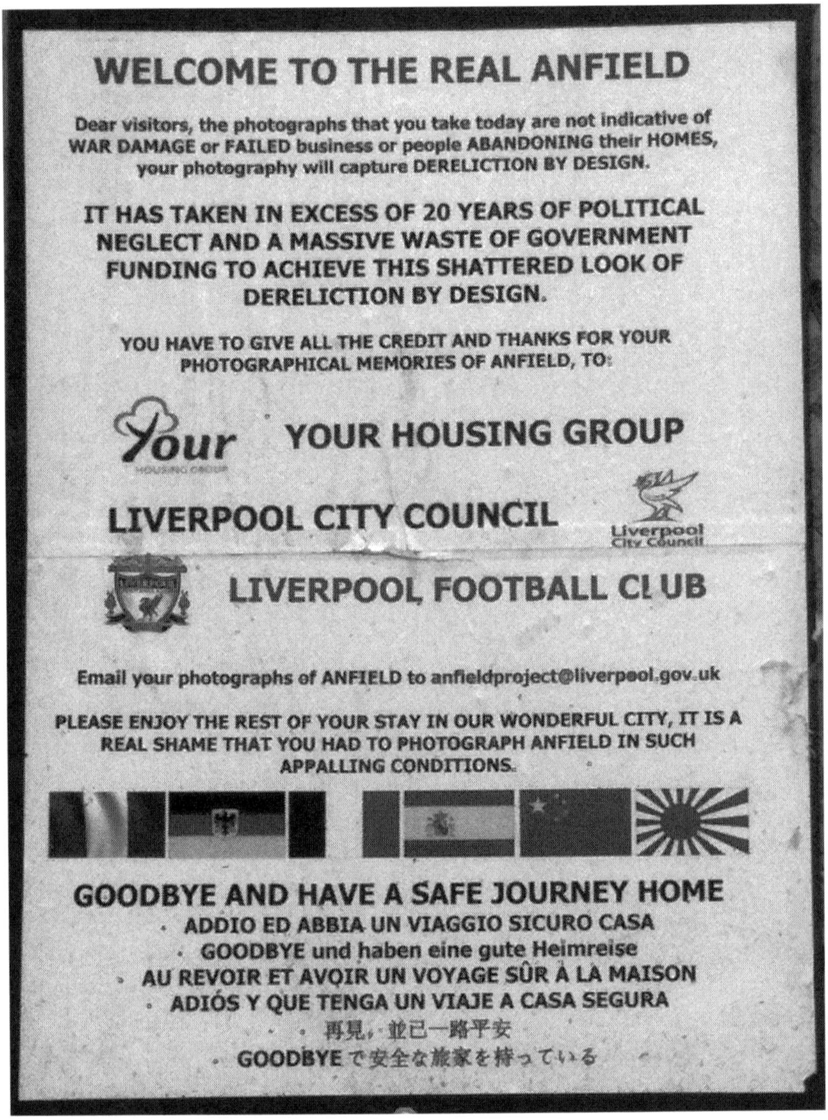

Figure 6 Dereliction by design:
irreverent Scouse wit on display in Anfield.

Conference in 2007 in Minneapolis, which included site visits to local CLTs. The findings of the tour were disseminated to the wider community as a report, seeking to "form part of the narrative of the story of Anfield and Breckfield which began in 1999 and is among other things the story of a quest for social justice in regeneration".[18] The report records the revelatory moments shared by professional and community representatives alike over the radical potential of the CLT model for securing long-term community control:

> It was during a workshop discussion at the conference about what we mean by "perpetuity", the debate touching, for example, on the concept of a 99-year lease and then on the implications for CLTs of having to expand to survive—what might this mean over 200 years? Then one of the delegates said, "When I think about perpetuity, I think about churches". This wasn't meant in an evangelical sense ... but that the CLT estate, and the role of that estate, has the potential to endure down the centuries, capturing and preserving community heritage on community land.[19]

Despite the study tour capturing the imaginations of delegates, this unusual experiment in collective housing development ultimately failed. According to critical assessments published by some of the researchers involved in the study visit—notably Udi Engelsman, Alan Southern and Mike Rowe[20]—this failure is attributed to the top-down nature of the project, too constrained by formal processes and organisational agendas to find its 'soul' in the community. The driving seat of the project had been filled by Arena from the beginning; their motivations were to develop a prototype housing management scheme that would reduce organisational operating costs and eventually enable the community to manage stock in self-financing ways. The KTP Associate was then contracted to 'sell' the idea to the community through extensive consultation, as a mutually beneficial proposal with many potential gains for both parties.

Arena's tenants were initially keen on the idea of community control of assets and generation of revenues for community use; but appetite was less than expected. Independent of the council, HMR and Arena, the KTP Associate's role was to bring these interests together for the co-construction of knowledge in CLT innovation. However, the council, though willing to negotiate over the possibility, was ultimately reluctant to be associated with

18 Peter Bevington, Community Land Trusts—Learning from the USA: An Account of the KTP/Arena Housing Group Research Visit to the United States to Learn about the Community Land Trust Model and Its Potential Transferability to Anfield and Breckfield, Liverpool, 9–18 Oct. 2008, p. 3.

19 Bevington, Community Land Trusts—Learning from the USA, p. 6.

20 Udi Engelsman and Alan Southern, "Knowledge Transfer in Regeneration: Is It Feasible and Can the Community Benefit?", *Journal of Urban Regeneration and Renewal* 4.2 (2010): 147–157; Udi Engelsman, Mike Rowe and Alan Southern, "Community Land Trusts—A Radical or Reformist Response to the Housing Question Today?", *ACME: An International E-Journal for Critical Geographies* 15.3 (2016): 590–615.

the project, whilst Arena Housing was internally divided over the benefits of shedding properties to community ownership. Through this process, some residents became fatigued and alienated by years of seemingly purposeless and overtly bureaucratic consultation. Housing officials became more interested in the CLT idea as a way to cut costs and produce efficiencies in their organisation rather than for radical redistribution of land and power, keeping residents at arm's-length in decision-making, regarding them "mainly as a means to secure resources, for their own organisational agendas".[21] As a result, the community became increasingly reticent to get involved in what was seen as a managerial operation. This case highlights the limits of professionalised, top-down, state-led approaches to collective housing that are focused on "exploring new ways to deploy capital more efficiently", to "prevent further degradation of an asset base".[22] However, participating professionals from Arena report a different story: that it was generally supported by community leaders and eventually folded only due to difficulties in securing the necessary state funding for a large-scale CLT scheme. Moreover, the KTP is recognised as having "opened up new opportunities for political agitation"[23] and establishing vital connections and new networks of knowledge transfer between successful CLT initiatives in the USA—such as Dudley Street in Boston and Cooper Square in New York—and the emerging CLT campaigns in Liverpool, not least the project that was to evolve into Homebaked.

Homebaked: Brick by Brick, Loaf by Loaf, We Build Ourselves

Just like their counterparts in Granby, Homebaked activists are using the CLT model as a platform to innovate a participatory, embedded and holistic approach to local economic development. Over years of negotiations with Liverpool City Council to acquire a terraced row for redevelopment as affordable homes and a revitalised high street of community businesses—now coming to fruition—Homebaked CLT has become a neighbourhood hub for Anfield and a citizen platform for co-designing interventions in the built environment and local economy.[24] Homebaked are perhaps most famous for their namesake cooperative bakery and café that act as the sister or partner organisation to the

21 Engelsman, Rowe and Southern, "Community Land Trusts—A Radical or Reformist Response to the Housing Question Today?", p. 602.

22 Engelsman, Rowe and Southern, "Community Land Trusts—A Radical or Reformist Response to the Housing Question Today?", p. 600.

23 Engelsman, Rowe and Southern, "Community Land Trusts—A Radical or Reformist Response to the Housing Question Today?", p. 600.

24 For photos of Homebaked and the surrounding neighbourhood as the project evolved, see https://asenseofplace.com/collections-of-posts/homebaked-anfield/.

CLT. Homebaked bakery is a co-op that makes award-winning pies, employs many local residents, runs various skills courses, subsidises wholesome food for people in poverty, provides space for therapeutic and sharing activities around baking, cooking and growing and likewise acts as a meeting place and socioeconomic anchor. In 2018, the umbrella organisation Homebaked CLT completed its first affordable homes—a four-bedroom shared flat for young people above the bakery—with plans to rehabilitate the entire terraced row soon to be realised. Although providing affordable housing has always been an ambition, Homebaked is focused on a wider agenda of community business incubation and high street regeneration.

Importantly, the CLT and bakery trade as separate legal entities—the CLT is registered as a Community Interest Company (CIC) whilst the bakery is a Community Benefit Society (BenCom), a relatively new legal form of cooperative that privileges wider community benefit over member benefit. This enables the CLT to operate as the landlord; the bakery its first and foremost tenant. This makes Homebaked an unusual CLT for having a commercial as opposed to a residential tenant. In the first few years, Homebaked bakery effectively comprised the 'resident-tenant' representatives on the CLT board; in future, these positions will be increasingly filled by residents of the CLT-developed housing. Some members feel that Homebaked CLT should be renamed Hometrust in order to distinguish it from Homebaked bakery, to avoid further conflation between the two and to symbolise what the CLT is all about in its emerging role as a community anchor, business incubator and catalyst for holistic urban regeneration. Nonetheless, both organisations are part of the same Homebaked "family", which has recently come to include the Homegrown Collective (an urban food growing project, craft microbrewery and community pub, evolving out of earlier ideas for Homefarm and Homebrew) as well as other spin-offs such as Homesquare, a revitalised public space for gardening, food growing and outdoor and cultural activities. Together as a united project, the Homebaked family intends to revitalise Anfield—in their prefigurative imagery—*brick by brick, loaf by loaf, seed by seed*, via an immersive, incremental, participatory slow-build method of community development.

Right from the outset Homebaked had a powerful political agenda. It began as a public arts project commissioned by the 2010 Liverpool Biennial, whose organisers invited internationally acclaimed Dutch artist Jeanne van Heeswijk to visit Anfield in 2009 and work with local residents on a participatory art initiative to address the effects of HMR on lived experience. Out of her initial interactions with local residents and artists, Jeanne created *2Up2Down*—a community-led design project to reimagine the terraced house, the traditional two-up two-down with its two rooms each on two storeys, and, by extension, to reimagine the future of the area as a whole. The slogan at this juncture was: 'Housing is the battlefield of our time and the house is its monument'.[25] The aim was, first, to protect the area from top-down urban renewal programmes like HMR and, second, radically to transform place through collective alternatives. 2Up2Down was, stated its website in 2012, "a way for local people to 'take matters into their own hands' and make real social and physical change in their neighbourhood".[26] This was an explicitly radical, politically motivated project taking public arts funding to pursue something more akin to action-research or community activism aiming for radical redistribution of land and power to traditionally marginalised communities. Discourses like the right to the city, urban commons and direct democracy are central to the design philosophy of Jeanne van Heeswijk, who calls it "radicalising the local" and believes "communities should co-produce their own futures".[27]

The ambitious political agenda is augmented by a distinctive artistic approach that utilises performative, participatory and interactive methods to create a very different kind of socially engaged, co-produced artwork.[28] This places it, rather ambiguously, within the field of social practice[29]—an intriguing connection I explore in the Epilogue. Central to this effort was Britt Jurgensen, a theatre and performance artist and longstanding local resident, who directed and co-scripted some of the early artistic initiatives and has been one of the main contributors to the ongoing development of the CLT. Initiatives included 'The Anfield Home Tour' in the 2012 Biennial, an intensive urban tour of the area with narration by local residents, and a performative conversation as part of the Future City exhibition in 2013.[30] Such artistic events set the tone for Homebaked being as much about the learning process of experiencing, remembering and narrating change as the urban change itself. Story-telling has indeed been valuable to 2Up2Down, helping build a national reputation and media platform.

That being said, artistic rendering has always only ever overlaid strong foundations in local people creating home-grown, community-led solutions to problems produced by the state and market. The project was founded and driven from the beginning by a committed core of passionate locals born and bred in Anfield (Angela McKay for one) whose families have grown up over the course of their involvement in the project. Greater resident

25 Jeanne van Heeswijk and Britt Jurgensen, "We Are Here to Stay", *Stages: Liverpool Biennial* #1, Future City (2014).

26 Homebaked CLT, "2Up 2Down", 2012: www.2up2down.org.uk/.

27 Heeswijk and Jurgensen, "Introduction", *Stages: Liverpool Biennial #2*.

28 Tim Jeeves, "Performance, Participation and Questions of Ownership in the Anfield Home Tour", *Stages: Liverpool Biennial* #2, Homebaked: A Perfect Recipe (2014).

29 Claire Bishop, *Artificial Hells: Participatory Art and the Politics of Spectatorship* (Verso, 2012).

30 Heeswijk and Jurgensen, "We Are Here to Stay", *Stages: Liverpool Biennial #1*.

involvement gained momentum through a participatory design process with forty young people from the area, which gradually expanded to include adults who were affected by HMR and whose housing needs and desires were expressed in the evolution of the project. The process was facilitated by Marianne Heaslip, an architect from URBED—the progressive urban design and research consultancy based in Manchester that first mooted the idea of an urban CLT as an alternative to and component within an HMR Pathfinder area, in Oldham, Greater Manchester.[31] Heaslip had never used participatory techniques before this project but adapted URBED's 'Building for Change' modelling toolkit that was usually used to get adults to remodel their neighbourhoods—a contemporary equivalent of the 'planning for real' exercises developed by CDS for new-build co-ops. Marianne explained to me how her interest in these issues was piqued by her architecture diploma thesis on the design process in community architecture, for which she compared the Eldonians with the pioneering development of Byker Wall in Newcastle and Manchester's exemplar co-op, Homes for Change, in Hulme. Through the likes of Marianne we can trace a lineage from the design democracy infusing the 1970s new-build co-op and community architecture movements to the social engagement going on in Homebaked and Granby today. As well as a historical link, there is also a spatial connection—with Granby, on the other side of Liverpool, where Heaslip is also an activist campaigning for Granby CLT as part of Terrace 21.

During this initial community engagement period, the 2Up2Down project team were looking for a terraced block for residents to work with and redesign as community-controlled affordable housing, but negotiations with the council and development companies failed to produce results: "They're all charmed by the idea but don't seem to want to give an inch of territory back to the community".[32] 2Up2Down eventually became grounded in the neighbourhood in 2011 when they took over the lease of a newly vacant bakery in the heart of Anfield, which then became a base for community meetings and participatory design activities. The Mitchell's Bakery—founded in 1903 and known as 'The Pie Shop' by football fans from all over the world—is located literally over the road from Liverpool FC, opposite the stadium main entrance. However, Mitchell's was earmarked for demolition as part of HMR, and began to lose custom as residents were emptied from the surrounding streets such that, eventually, its custodians—who were by then in their seventies—accepted the deal offered by the council to buy them out. HMR was prematurely cancelled

31 URBED, *Werneth Freehold: A Masterplan for Housing Market Renewal* (Oldham Local Strategic Partnership and North West Development Agency, 2004); Community Finance Solutions, ed., *Placeshaping: A Toolkit for Urban Community Land Trusts* (University of Salford, 2008).

32 Heeswijk and Jurgensen, "We Are Here to Stay", *Stages: Liverpool Biennial #1*.

shortly afterwards but the designation for demolition remained in the council's effective continuation of the redevelopment plans. The Mitchells retired without compensation and closed the bakery, which then became vacant.

Symbolically, the bakery is a cornerstone of the community, and 2Up2Down capitalised on this cultural history to create hype around the project. The bakery was initially used merely as a meeting place for workshops, but then local people began dropping in to ask workshop participants when they could buy bread again. This inspired the vision to reopen the bakery, thereby becoming the central focus of community efforts to reimagine the neighbourhood. With a temporary lease from the Mitchells, the 2Up2Down team set about rehabilitating the bakery and selling bread again to locals. In these early days, the baking of bread, cakes and pastries was crowd-sourced from various local residents who each used their own kitchens to bake delicious goods for sale in the café—quite literally home-baking, thus inspiring the name 'Homebaked'. The clever branding conjured up slogans that would prove to be very marketable, such as the most famous one emblazoned across the building itself: 'brick by brick, loaf by loaf, we build ourselves'. At around this time, artist-activist Nina Edge from the Welsh Streets—and now Granby Winter Garden's artist-in-residence—brought bread to the bakery in a self-made bag that she labelled: "Rise up Anfield".

Initially financed through voluntary home-baking backed by Biennial funding, Homebaked later ran a successful online crowd-sourcing campaign through Kickstarter called 'An Oven at the Heart of Anfield' to raise the capital for a new bread oven and renovate the kitchen and café area. Over four hundred people donated a total of £22,000. When the renovated co-op bakery opened in 2013, there still remained a compulsory purchase order on the building but—in true Scouse anarcho-entrepreneurial style—they decided to open for trading anyway and, by doing so, slowly but surely proved the concept to the council. The original business plan was to sell bread wholesale to other businesses and use the profits to subsidise food for locals, but this gradually evolved into a focus on pies as it became clear that football fans in particular constituted a big untapped market. Today, Homebaked is famed for its pies and turns a surplus largely on sales made on match days as well as contracts to cater for corporate events, including for Liverpool FC.

The co-op bakery represented just one piece of the puzzle. An overarching organisation was needed to take on the community ownership of the building in which the bakery was housed and, indeed, develop the broader aims of providing affordable homes and regenerating the local economy. By this point, residents and activists had already been discussing which organisational form would be suitable for incorporating the project as a legal entity. It was eventually decided—after "a steep learning curve … trying to find out about alternative models of co-owning and managing land and houses"—that the CLT model was best suited to community asset acquisition, "because it allows genuine community ownership of the organisation".[33] When asked about their choice of the CLT model, Homebaked activists cited its suitability in the new policy and regulatory landscape created by the 2011 Localism Act as well as emerging social investment opportunities. But, digging deeper, it is clear that the connections between members of Homebaked and those of Liverpool's other successful CLT project in Granby, as well as with the ideas being tested out by URBED, were just as important. Moreover, as outlined above, prior to grassroots experimentation the CLT idea was first mooted in Anfield in the knowledge transfer partnership led by Arena Housing. A senior figure within Arena Housing—one of the study tour delegates and leading proponents of Arena's CLT proposal—reportedly presented his findings to some of the Homebaked activists early on in their campaign, thereby helping seed the CLT idea. He has also been a key source of professional support and advice for Homebaked over the years, offering up (what is now) Your Housing Group's resources and expertise for use by activists, who attest to the critical importance of such professional assistance.

At first the council was deeply sceptical of the CLT, despite official backing from the Liverpool Biennial, a particularly powerful and influential partner in getting the project off the ground. In 2013, just when the bakery was due to open, the council drew up new development plans for what it was initially renaming "Anfield Village", but failed to include Homebaked in the masterplan, still marking the terrace for demolition. Caught in a limbo until the lifting of demolition threats, local resident-activists Jayne Lawless, Angela McKay and Britt Jurgensen began meeting with public officials and representatives, including councillors and their then local Labour MP Steve Rotheram (now 'Metro Mayor' for the Liverpool City Region) to lobby for Homebaked to be included in the new masterplan. As the streets behind them were cleared of houses, Homebaked set about adapting their plans to the new policy landscape and proposed a scheme for redeveloping the terrace to the council. During this transitional period of continued uncertainty, Homebaked were, rather gallingly, forced to give back £50,000 of government grant money they were unable to spend on developing new housing above the bakery due to the lack of a secure lease on the property preventing their attaining match-funding or a mortgage. In 2014, after countless meetings (for which activists took along home-baked pies) the council eventually began to see the value of the project and offered an informal agreement to retain and refurbish the terrace. In 2015, the council signalled its interest in a high-density, new-build development; Homebaked embarked on a participatory design process in which a 'local core design team' of members and other residents commissioned architects, working with them intensively over several months to create a multi-storey scheme

33 Heeswijk and Jurgensen, "Introduction", *Stages: Liverpool Biennial #2*, p. 4.

of 40 flats above a row of shops. However, due to low land prices and too little grant funding at the time—notwithstanding a £10,000 grant from the National CLT Network helping fund the design and viability assessment—it struggled to stack up financially. Since then, the council has dropped its insistence on new build in favour of a rehabilitation approach. Today, the council positively celebrates Homebaked as one of the anchors of Anfield's regeneration and a demonstration project to potential investors. By 2018, council officers were inviting Homebaked to deliver presentations at council-run property investment events hosted at Liverpool FC.

What possibly explains such a turnaround? A turning point was marked in 2016, when the CLT won a big grant from Power to Change to redevelop the flat above the bakery, on the argument that third-party backing will finally unlock the bakery asset from the council and leverage further funds. By 2017, multiple strands were coming together. Homebaked had secured a "meanwhile lease" from a local housing association for the residual green space adjoining the terrace. What was to become the Homegrown Collective started running landscaping and urban farming courses and created a community garden christened Homesquare (or Hometurf as some like to call it), host to a temporary outdoor cinema and various 'street' parties. This became a demonstration project of how the neighbourhood's green space could be transformed if residents were given the power to decide and do. It shares with Granby's guerrilla gardening the experimental, do-it-together spirit of 'insurgent' urbanism and aspirations for claiming a 'right to the city'.[34]

A big milestone was achieved in 2018 when the CLT completed its first homes—the four-person shared apartment above the bakery. Crucially, this provides Homebaked with a more substantial rental revenue stream with which to fund activities, pay for staff and become independent of grant income. As a participant-observer on the CLT board, I played a part in thinking through the rationale and in the difficult task of drawing up the allocations policy. Hatched in response to some informal local market research, the idea was to provide affordable rooms for young people (aged 18–35) living or working locally who were in housing need and would otherwise be at the mercy of predatory private landlords. We were targeting Generation Rent with a personal stake in the area. When deciding on criteria for selecting tenants, we consulted Granby CLT and North West Housing Services (who shortly afterwards took on the management and maintenance contract for the flat). One criterion, other than need, was to be the contribution tenants envisaged making to the community. For instance, a number of the flat's very first tenants were already employed as bakers downstairs in the co-op bakery (making those early morning starts so much easier).

Completing the flat marked the moment the CLT proved itself capable of delivering community-owned affordable housing in a way that creates social

34 Iveson, "Cities within the City: Do-It-Yourself Urbanism and the Right to the City".

value. The flat was refurbished through a bespoke apprenticeship scheme for young people interested in learning skills and gaining experience in construction, resulting in a beautifully crafted apartment with ample shared living space, a terrace at the back and many original architectural features brought back to life. As a symbol of viability and a tangible demonstration project showcasing the vision for the wider neighbourhood, more local residents have been drawn into the design process for the next phase. In order to be eligible for new funding for community-led housing from Homes England to develop the remainder of the terraced row on which the bakery sits, the CLT had to partner with a registered housing association—and so it entered into partnership with Your Housing (formerly Arena). The plan is to develop the nine remaining terraces into eight homes, from traditional three-bed family houses to one- and two-bed apartments—all owned and managed by the CLT and retrofitted to high environmental standards with roof-based solar panels installed and constructed through a local apprenticeship programme. Homebaked have secured planning permission and the council has granted them a lease to begin the rehabilitation work of the terraces; once complete, the freehold will be transferred from the council into community ownership. Homebaked bakery is extending its café space into the downstairs of the neighbouring terrace to become more of a hub and offer additional community services such as debt advice. At the other end, adjoining Homesquare, its sister organisation the Homegrown Collective is creating a community business for growing hops and brewing, with space out front for pop-up businesses and cultural activities. In true Homebaked style, the final design was the result of five intensive participatory workshops with twenty local people, with Marianne Heaslip appointed as architect. Site visits to Granby Four Streets and other like-minded projects also helped with inspiration.

Securing help and support from professional bodies has played a pivotal part in Homebaked's success. Just as the Biennial stepped back from the project, handing over responsibility to local residents, the latter gained the support of key gatekeepers, including Ann O'Byrne, then Cabinet Member for Housing. Activists also attracted the interest of other powerful actors in the city region, not least John Sutcliffe, who managed one of the largest surveying firms and sat on many prominent boards, including Homebaked's as its chair (until he sadly passed away in 2017). As a result of this ability to network, gain allies and project a positive image, Homebaked has received a great deal of interest from academic and activist networks and the national as well as local press.[35] Homebaked are just as adept at promoting their brand

35 Rowan Moore, "Liverpool Biennial—Review", *The Guardian* (23 Sept. 2012); Lynsey Hanley, "This Is How We Can Solve the Housing Crisis—One Home at a Time", *The Guardian* (13 Aug. 2012); Rachel Pugh, "'This Is Not about Gentrification': The Pie Shop Reviving an Anfield Street", *The Guardian* (19 Apr. 2017).

image and selling themselves, as they excel at baking and selling the pies that have won them national awards—in particular for their 'Scouse Pie'. From origins in artistic narration, the Homebaked team have continued to use media—particularly social media—to their advantage, becoming a recognised success story in community-led housing and arts-led regeneration.[36] Perhaps because of this, alongside the less visible or recognised harder graft going on behind the scenes—of tirelessly engaging in community meetings, developing new business plans, conducting design workshops, learning about building contracts, applying for planning permission, writing grant applications, ad nauseam—Homebaked has also been very successful in securing large grants from various sources, notably Power to Change and the Esmée Fairbairn Foundation. In fact, both the bakery and the CLT have each received substantial Power to Change funding, which is very unusual for two organisations in such close proximity—one for business development, the other housing development.

Whilst the bakery has achieved business success very quickly with significant local social impact—employing some twenty people by 2017 and spending over £160,000 a year on salaries and £100,000 with local suppliers—the CLT has been slower to realise self-sufficiency, due to the complex property-based nature of the project. Until the new housing envisaged for the terraced row is inhabited and bringing in a sustained flow of rental income, the CLT must rely upon grants and the small, subsidised rent from the bakery alongside the shared apartment. Moreover, it depends largely upon volunteers and a number of temporary contract staff, employed on a fixed-term part-time basis. These staff have been invaluable to the success of the project, all working much longer hours than their contracts stipulate. To say this is more about love than money would be an understatement. There is a growing sense in the organisation, however, that such civic volunteerism is unsustainable in the long run, as it relies unfairly on committed individuals to give up so much of their time for a project that is becoming increasingly complex and labour-intensive. This raises questions over just how replicable or sustainable the model actually is. In neighbourhoods where these capabilities are less in evidence—as in the tragic case of Little Klondyke—this is all too starkly written in a very different fate.

But Homebaked was never simply fated to succeed. Success here is the result of gruelling graft, patience and perseverance. Recent progress made with redeveloping buildings and green space is just the start—the material embodiment—of a far-reaching vision to reimagine and transform life in Anfield. At its heart, this is about changing place, and the way we live and interact with each other and the urban environment. Throughout the

36 Sue Bell Yank, "2Up2Down/Homebaked and the Symbolic Media Narrative", *Stages: Liverpool Biennial* #2, Homebaked: A Perfect Recipe (2014).

participatory design process, the question framing all other interventions that residents, activists and fellow travellers kept asking each other was *what does it mean to live well?* This resonates deeply with the asset-based community development approach of the community economy[37] and solidarity economy[38] movements—where the emphasis is placed on well-being and qualitative use values over quantitative measures such as jobs created or income generated. The latter are still important to Homebaked—in fact, they are common answers given by local people when asked what it means to live well—but the focus is on the *quality* of those jobs and the *relationships* that that income nourishes as it circulates through the local economy.

Seeing Liverpool's Housing History through a Bifocal Verb–Noun Lens

In all the various cases of CLT experimentation in Liverpool—both successes and failures—the issue of *democratic* control over land and assets, in response to the financialisation of land in the new urban question, is the issue of overriding importance. It is the issue that framed the failure of schemes in Kensington, Anfield and Little Klondyke (where, in some cases, residents felt they were not being given the control promised by council and housing association officers and, in others, the state ultimately did not want to give control away) just as much as it motivated successful campaigns in Homebaked and Granby. Unlike rural CLT initiatives in Britain, these urban CLTs are distinctive for privileging democratic control of land, housing and economic assets. The CLT model is just a means to an end: utilised as an institutional platform for gaining such community control. This point is made best by a CLT activist:

> What's really important in both Granby and Anfield is the democratic control of land and assets, which is when a CLT comes into its own ... as compared with the rural context where it's more about affordability a lot of the time. Here it's definitely more about democratic control, because people feel like they want the government to see that people have not been listened to all the time; that they can do it themselves, even though the government should have been doing it all along.

It is not only desires for democracy that motivate CLT campaigns. In all the diverse cases of CLT experimentation—successes and failures—residents and

37 Ethan Miller, "Community Economy: Ontology, Ethics, and Politics for Radically Democratic Economic Organizing", *Rethinking Marxism* 25.4 (2013): 518–533.

38 Peter North and Molly Scott Cato, eds, *Towards Just and Sustainable Economies: The Social and Solidarity Economy North and South* (Policy Press, 2017).

activists have *reacted* against some external threat to dwelling in place. If we wish to move collective alternatives on from being a merely bespoke, isolated solution found in reaction to a contextualised problem to one constituting a newly democratic mainstream, we need first to identify the outlines of the dominant system that reproduces such problems. The distinction between the hegemonic system for housing and regeneration and the counter-hegemonic alternative gestured at by the Liverpool co-ops and CLTs can be glimpsed through the lens of John F.C. Turner's metaphor of seeing housing as a verb or a noun. This is made manifest in Liverpool's history—we can trace its shape in the divergence between large-scale top-down housing-led approaches and smaller-scale, bottom-up collective housing alternatives. This concluding section to Part IV is a retelling of this history through this dialectical lens of housing seen as a noun and a verb, as dead labour and everyday life, as material object and social process.

Top-down property-led approaches tend to focus on the noun-like quality of dwelling, which all too often blinds policymakers from its verb-like dynamics. Whilst much of the justly called 'slum housing' cleared by Liverpool City Council was in dire need of replacing, this created a problematic precedent in successive state programmes for targeting the housing itself as the object of renewal efforts rather than deeper systemic processes and socioeconomic issues at the root of dilapidation and poor conditions. The slum-clearance programme aimed to rehouse residents in modern tenements, tower blocks and houses, mostly built out on the city's periphery. But providing people with all the latest amenities in clean, spacious, safe environments was necessary but not sufficient to improve quality of life and, in fact, too often destroyed the delicate web of social relations that knitted communities together and provided the socioeconomic safety nets and systems of mutual aid and solidarity so important in times of hardship and precarity. Moreover, post-war slum clearances were conducted by the municipal authorities with such fervour as to help tip the inner city into a seemingly inexorable spiral of decline. Whilst similar programmes have posed problems for many post-industrial urban areas of the global rust belt, this has been especially acute for Liverpool—a city that has lost half its population in half a century. Thus the city's housing question morphed into what I have called the neighbourhood question.

Repeated down the decades is a narrow focus on material *dwellings* (seen as a noun) to the detriment of the social relations that animate the activities of *dwelling* (as a verb). Deteriorating conditions in council-managed terraces and tenements were made worse by the political circumstances of Liverpool's so-called 'lost decade' of 1973–83, during which minority Liberal administrations pursued a policy of municipal housing retrenchment: putting a halt to all new council-housebuilding, and switching budgets into the voluntary and third sectors; leading to massive growth in dilapidated 'hard-to-let' properties and a huge waiting list. Liberal motivations were part commendable commitments to the principle of dweller control and part politicking strategy to disarm the Works Department—the city's heavily unionised housing maintenance division, whom the Liberals believed were too powerful, inefficient, bureaucratic and wasteful of public resources. Ironically, by fervently supporting the co-op and housing association movements as alternative means to resolve the housing question, the Liberals only exacerbated it, and paved the way for their demise, through the populist Militant backlash.

For all the Militant-led council's admirable ambitions to reappropriate the means of social reproduction and resolve the housing crisis of the 1970s through a massive £350 million programme of council house building, their Urban Regeneration Strategy was strangely fixated on the type of housing it built rather than its relation to wider socioeconomic processes. Influenced by Alice Coleman's 'design disadvantagement' theory, URS architect Tony Byrne became seduced by a kind of design determinism in which the figure of the inter-war semi-detached suburban house was fetishised as the ideal design for his renewal of council housing. Militant's monomania elevated their housebuilding programme as the answer to many of Liverpool's problems: by socialising the ownership and management of housing, and striking partnerships with big developers, thereby creating new jobs, the council hoped to tackle the worsening unemployment problem as well as inject desperately needed investment into declining neighbourhoods and reverse deteriorating housing conditions for those thousands then stuck on waiting lists or in dilapidated tenements.

We see history repeat itself with HMR in the twenty-first century—curiously similar outcomes from seemingly divergent ideologies. With homes emptying and many neighbourhoods left abandoned, the local state was forced to act: HMR renewed the state's commitment to large-scale intervention in the urban environment after decades of retreat—only with a neoliberal twist. In neoliberalism's assault of individualisation and atomisation on the social relations of state and society, self-interest trumps the common good and private profit triumphs over common wealth. The idea of collectively governing shared resources as a commons appears increasingly alien in this ideological context. The growing dominance of markets in urban policy thinking is evident in the narrow focus of HMR—concocted as a bespoke intervention in 'failing housing markets'. By focusing on the functionality of the market and the exchange value of the housing product—rather than the health of the urban environment or the welfare of inhabitants—HMR seemed to usher in a new urban question, one concerned with the commodification and financialisation of land.

Much like Militant's URS, too much of the energies unleashed through HMR were directed towards treating the surface symptom of a deeper structural problem. Whilst HMR's initial objective of restructuring housing markets was in certain respects forward-thinking in taking as its object the wider systemic structure of regional housing markets, this expansive rationale was soon distilled down to the narrow issue of housing type and design. The reasons for this mission drift are complex and highly political—caught up, as I explained in the previous chapter, in increasingly financialised incentive structures governing housing associations since the 1988 Housing Act. Put simply, because HMR followed an abstract logic of markets and exchange, the problem was successively reformulated and reframed as one of housing 'products' competing for the attention of upwardly mobile 'consumers' in a residential 'market of position'—an expression of the incursion of logics of abstraction and commodification into housing regeneration policy. Terraced housing was deemed to be unpopular and therefore unviable by HMR researchers owing to its low market price, and so the solution was found in replacing it with a new product, reflecting consumer choice, rather than improving wider systemic factors, such as employment, education, health and environmental quality. The terraced house was thereby vilified as 'obsolete'—internalising the responsibility for complex socio-spatial structural problems into the terraced house itself.

In thus fetishising the housing itself over the activities that produce and enliven it, property-led (or noun-like) approaches to regeneration thereby do more damage than first meets the eye. The comprehensive renewal mentality shared by the Slum Clearance Programme, URS and HMR acts to 'thingify' the flow of space,[39] by focusing in on the end-product, the final design, over the process of getting there—neglecting the lived space of inhabitants in favour of abstract visions of planners and technocrats. They tend to obfuscate the interactive connection between dweller and dwelling. The political potential of collective alternatives resides in protecting and democratising that connection.

With contestation over demolition provoked once more by HMR, the seeds of housing activism had reason to grow again—this time in the shape of CLTs. What activists in Granby and Homebaked were quick to realise—just as the Eldonians did before them—was that upgrading the materiality of housing alone would not be enough. This insight is acknowledged even by leading figures in HMR management. A former regional director of the Housing Corporation and managing director of a neighbouring HMR Pathfinder acknowledges that:

> You have to try and make sure that housing is linked into other forms of socio-economic regeneration ... And if I think a mistake was made in the work that led to Housing Market Renewal, well, it should have been called "Market Renewal"; because housing in a sense may stabilise, may

39 Andy Merrifield, "Place and Space: A Lefebvrian Reconciliation", *Transactions of the Institute of British Geographers* 18.4 (1993): 516–531. For a Lefebvrian critique of HMR's American counterpart, HOPE VI, see Jones and Popke, "Re-Envisioning the City: Lefebvre, HOPE VI, and the Neoliberalization of Urban Space".

> stop decline, but in itself it will not be enough to promote economic wellbeing. You have to have other things that go alongside it. That's where the Eldonians were clever.

Yet there is something about the demonstrable materiality of large-scale property-led development that maintains its hegemony: it produces quantifiable, relatively rapid and visible results. With the increasing infiltration of abstraction into urban renewal policy—in the target-driven, performance-measured, market-led and evidence-based approach to designing and evaluating interventions—large-scale housing-led schemes are able to attract large pots of funding from government and the EU, as well as demonstrate their outputs in measurable terms: number of houses demolished, built, refurbished etc. This becomes an almost self-verifying, reinforcing logic, in that greater quantities of demolished and completed homes validate the initial outlay, but also bring additional investment and secure the financial interests of the major stakeholders—the council, housing associations and developers—that constitute Liverpool's 'grant regime'. To justify further investment, the grant regime must demonstrate need through evidence of further housing dereliction and socioeconomic malaise. Facing fiscal austerity—with decreasing resources from central government to resolve growing socio-spatial problems—municipalities like Liverpool are experiencing increasing pressures to exploit the 'rent gap' as an alternative source of revenue.[40]

Despite pulling in huge amounts of government funding into the city, HMR and other schemes like it fail to embed this capital in place or within the social space of the neighbourhoods in need of investment. Instead, much of this capital is siphoned off into the pockets of the various public and private partners comprising the grant regime. This was put to good use in some instances, such as recycled back into basic public services, as a means of cross-subsiding falling council budgets in times of austerity. However, it generally failed to leave a lasting trace in the neighbourhoods themselves, nor did it build the kind of durable socio-spatial infrastructures for the slow and steady work of regeneration once state funding dried up. We can see the shortcomings of housing-led redevelopment all too clearly in the case of HMR: when funding was cut, neighbourhoods were left like "war zones", according to former Lib Dem Leader of Liverpool City Council, Warren Bradley, who has publicly recognised the limitations of this abstract, monolithic housing-led approach to the neighbourhood question:

> You can't rip the heart of the community and promise them something in 15 years' time. ... We announced six renewal areas, and in

40 Hamish Kallin and Tom Slater, "Activating Territorial Stigma: Gentrifying Marginality on Edinburgh's Periphery", *Environment and Planning A* 46.6 (2014): 1351–1368.

> hindsight we should have done it one by one. Completing one area and then moving onto the next. … We should have landscaped areas so that people didn't feel they were living in a war zone. … The big challenge is going to be to sustain communities in areas where we have announced renewal.[41]

Unrealised opportunities to utilise the CLT model within HMR delivery to 'lock in' capital investment and recycle surpluses locally—in a more self-sustaining and self-sufficient method of regeneration that does not require continued top-up public funding—would have represented a paradigm shift from hierarchical dependence on the state towards local autonomy in which regeneration becomes self-generating, building its own momentum from an initial state investment.

HMR was part of a broader trend. By the turn of the millennium, Liverpool had become very talented at playing the 'regeneration game': demonstrating deprivation in order to secure public funding from the EU and central government that could then be multiplied by grant regime partners. The effect on people and place, however, was equally impactful. Declining inner-city neighbourhoods like Anfield have been stuck for a long time in a self-defeating mindset of proving to authorities the severity of local deprivation and the need for external assistance. Born-and-bred local resident, artist and Homebaked co-founder Jayne Lawless (whose father Jimmy sat on the CLT board) describes the dampening, deadening effect this can have on self-esteem and collective identity:

> There was a big pot of gold … In order to access this pot, the area had to tick so many boxes in the magical world of deprivation. So suddenly, we were told all the time that we were from this deprived area. And we were like "I'm not deprived. I don't feel deprived. We have food and clothes, both parents work. How am I deprived?" But the more you feed that in: "You're poor, you're this, you're that", you watch the standards drop; everything seemed to drop, and it took about ten years, but they finally ticked that last box they needed to tick, and that was that.[42]

This is a troubling example of the power of performativity: how the conceptualisations and categories used to analyse socio-spatial conditions can adversely reshape place in their own image.[43] Whilst the regeneration game

41 Quoted in David Bartlett, "Council Leader Warren Bradley: We Ripped Heart Out of Liverpool Communities", *Liverpool Echo* (26 Apr. 2010).

42 Jayne Lawless, quoted in Jeeves, "Performance, Participation and Questions of Ownership in the Anfield Home Tour", p. 7.

43 Manuel B. Aalbers, "Do Maps Make Geography? Part 1: Redlining, Planned Shrinkage,

is no doubt a laudable alternative to managed decline as a response to the neighbourhood question, it too enacts a certain cynical opportunism with respect to place—a cynicism which gets inscribed into the urban fabric. Conversely, Granby and Homebaked CLTs are perhaps the first initiatives of the last few decades positively to assert pride and a celebratory outlook: demonstrating to potential members and investors alike their extraordinary power to effect urban transformation through creative grassroots interventions. By redescribing place in a more positive light, they may well begin to 'perform' that space into being. Seen as a pair, Homebaked and Granby represent a paradigm shift from conventional regeneration programmes. A large part of this shift is to do with time and the nature of learning. Local resident, activist and founder of the Homegrown Collective Sam Jones describes it as a logic of resilience:

> The hard-won cumulative victories and long-term asset-building that is framed in every aspect of the activities of Homebaked ... is a slow and risk-laden process. ... Homebaked has itself understood the importance of slow learning and cumulative change through this longitudinal model. ... This open and long-term modality has been a difficult commitment to retain in the face of the urgency, and even desperation, that characterises the needs of the local residents of Anfield as regeneration strategies shift and change and continue to threaten not only Homebaked but also their own homes.[44]

It is in Granby we find this most viscerally embodied. Granby's grassroots practices are essentially imagined collective claims that actively take ownership over neglected and derelict public space. Working without permission from the council, these guerrilla gardeners engage in everyday acts of commoning: bringing the domestic, intimate spaces of their homes out into the public streetscape, sharing it with others, and creating a distinctive hybrid community garden that mixes domesticity, privacy, communality and public openness—bearing the hallmarks of an 'actually existing commons'.[45] In blurring and working in the liminal space between the spatial and legal boundaries of the ownership model, such insurgent acts are informal and

and the Places of Decline", *ACME: An International E-Journal for Critical Geographies* 13.4 (2014): 525–556; Brett Christophers, "Wild Dragons in the City: Urban Political Economy, Affordable Housing Development and the Performative World-Making of Economic Models", *International Journal of Urban and Regional Research* 38.1 (2014): 79–97.

44 Samantha Jones, "Becoming Homebaked", *Stages: Liverpool Biennial* #2, Homebaked: A Perfect Recipe (2014).

45 Efrat Eizenberg, "Actually Existing Commons: Three Moments of Space of Community Gardens in New York City", *Antipode* 44.3 (2012): 764–782.

unrecognised forms of ownership: an 'imagined proprietorship'[46] or an 'un-real estate'[47]—highlighting ownership as an active process of human doing, a verb, as well as a passive entitlement to an inert object. Enacting collective housing alternatives does not simply amount to a change in legal title securing redistribution of entitlements over land—but is vitalised by commoning: breathing life into institutional formulas. As Peter Linebaugh remarks on common property: "think first not of title deeds, but of human deeds".[48] Just as housing is not simply an object but also an activity, so too is property not a thing or possession but an active social relation, performed through embodied practices. Commoning in Granby cuts across political and social distinctions among residents, who have forged common bonds despite diverse world views through communal cleaning, planting and tending. Nonetheless, these practices are largely confined to a small number of remaining homeowners, highlighting how, as Linebaugh imparts, "Commoning is exclusive inasmuch as it requires participation. It must be entered into. ... This is why we speak neither of rights nor obligations separately".[49] This suggests that commoners need to reach outwards to wider publics to achieve any kind of democratic legitimacy or broader social justice.

In this way, collective alternatives such as Granby and Homebaked CLTs embody what Lefebvre called 'experimental utopias'—an incremental, embodied, performative approach to transforming social relations in the here and now, not some distant future, by staying close to "its implications and consequences on the ground".[50] Lefebvre distinguished 'utopian' (concrete explorations of the possible in everyday life) from 'utopist' (abstract, transcendental visions of an ideal city) which tend towards authoritarianism in their prescriptions.[51] The dialectic between temporal openness and spatial closure—between verb-like and noun-like aspects—marks a creative tension within any utopian project, not least Homebaked. A playful temporary art installation fronts the terrace row whilst it awaits rehabilitation. On each boarded-up window on the first floor are stencilled big colourful letters that read: N-O-W-H-E-R-E. According to artist Daniel Simpkins, this invites

46 Nicholas Blomley, "Un-Real Estate: Proprietary Space and Public Gardening", *Antipode* 36.4 (2004): 614–641.
47 Carol Rose, *Property and Persuasion: Essays on the History, Theory and Rhetoric of Ownership* (Westview Press, 1994).
48 Peter Linebaugh, *The Magna Carta Manifesto: Liberties and Commons for All* (University of California Press, 2009), p. 45.
49 Peter Linebaugh, *Stop, Thief!: The Commons, Enclosures, and Resistance* (PM Press, 2014), p. 15.
50 Henri Lefebvre, *Writings on Cities* (Wiley-Blackwell, 1995), p. 151.
51 David Pinder, "Reconstituting the Possible: Lefebvre, Utopia and the Urban Question", *International Journal of Urban and Regional Research* 39.1 (2013): 28–45.

its *mis*-reading as NowHere—a playful reference to Thomas More's original coinage of the word utopia out of the Greek *ou-topos* meaning 'no place' or 'nowhere' as a pun on the similar word *eu-topos* or 'good place'. This double-vision creates a jarring juxtaposition, as Simpkins implies:

> The word "nowhere" is also in stark contrast to the language of "place making" used by city planners, architects and estate agents who attempt to offset the soullessness of generic urban developments through naming, branding and marketing aimed at creating a false sense of something unique and special.[52]

Little encapsulates this better than the generic HMR regeneration zone billboards thrown up across the city—formatted in standardised script from Granby to Anfield, which could be anywhere or nowhere at all. The taglines gesture vaguely at 'creating neighbourhoods for the future'—not for the present. Paradoxically, 'creating' suggests an active doing in the present—it assures us action is happening now to regenerate these neighbourhoods—but with an ever-receding time horizon, created for the end-user in some distant, abstract future. This assumes a division between the makers and users of urban space—what sociologist Fran Tonkiss calls the 'fallacy of the end-user'.[53] Here, development becomes abstracted from its context and current inhabitants excluded from the production process. The abstract time horizons of neoliberal urban policy, a little like revolutionary socialism—both more 'utopist' than utopian—tend to privilege the future, and the future end-user, over the present. Fortunately, the HMR billboard has been replaced by NOWHERE. If we squint, instead of seeing NoWhere we might just glimpse NowHere. What better way of signifying utopian transformation in the here and now; the immanent sense of prefigurative change; the dialectics of temporal urgency and spatial determinacy? No better way of demonstrating arrival, presence, proprietorship: *now we're here to stay*.

52 Quoted in *Becoming Homebaked*, timeline developed by Britt Jurgensen for 'Trainings for the Not-Yet' Exhibition, Utrecht, 14 Sept. 2019 to 12 Jan. 2020: www.bakonline.org/program-item/trainings-for-the-not-yet/.

53 Fran Tonkiss, "Austerity Urbanism and the Makeshift City", *City: Analysis of Urban Trends, Culture, Theory, Policy, Action* 17.3 (2013): 312–324.

Part V
Conclusion

CHAPTER 13

Reconstructing Public Housing (History)

In September 2018, during the Labour Party's annual national conference in Liverpool, its then leader Jeremy Corbyn took time out of his busy schedule to pay a special visit to Granby. After meeting various residents, who gave him a tour of newly inhabited CLT-owned homes and relayed the story of how they saved them from near total destruction to transform the four streets into a flourishing community-owned neighbourhood, Corbyn had this to say:

> Granby Four Streets is a blueprint for what the rest of the UK could look like under a Labour Government. These homes, once empty, are now filled with life. This community, once abandoned, is now rebuilt. When you give communities democratic control over their local economy and community, real change can happen. When we go into Government, we won't just take power, we'll give it back.[1]

That a Labour Party Leader was so supportive of a community-led project—all too often in the not-so-distant past associated cynically with the Tories' so-called 'Big Society' localism—is surprise enough. That this project for democratic local control was hailed as a "blueprint" for governing the country is truly remarkable. Corbyn's—and Corbynism's—support for Granby Four Streets signalled not only a significant realignment in political direction for the left wing of the Labour Party but also for how we (re)conceive a democratic-socialist state and the provision of public services, not least public housing. This has big implications not just for the UK but internationally too. Notwithstanding news of their resounding electoral defeat on Friday the 13th of December 2019, Corbyn's Labour Party had been widely held on the Left, especially across the Atlantic and in continental Europe, as one of the last-remaining bastions of political hope in an otherwise gloomy global landscape marked by rising reactionary populisms, proto-fascisms, neo-colonial state capitalism and corporate-controlled digital feudalism. The rise of Corbynism mirrored comparable developments in Spain, where the left-populist party Podemos is just one part of an emergent

1 Joe Thomas, "Corbyn Hailed This Liverpool Community as a 'Blueprint' for His Vision of the UK", *Liverpool Echo* (24 Sept. 2018).

counter-hegemonic historic bloc built on the back of the Indignados anti-austerity mass social movement and new municipalist projects such as Barcelona en Comú, the radical citizen platform leading a global movement of Fearless Cities[2]—representing two wings of a multi-scalar counter-offensive to financialised neoliberalism and austerity urbanism. In the UK, if not quite so developed as in Spain, an institutional infrastructure for new policy ideas generation and implementation—a potential Mont Pelerin Society for the Left[3]—is coming together at the national level, including new media and political education organisations like Novara Media and The World Transformed, campaign and community organisers such as the New Economy Organisers Network (NEON) and new think tanks such as Autonomy and Common Wealth. Moreover, just as housing (as a social right of citizenship) has been a central concern in Spanish municipalist movements—(Barcelona en Comú draws its energies from cooperative housing movements and anti-eviction activism combating the foreclosure crisis)[4]—so too in the UK is the notion of public housing back on the agenda. At the municipal scale we see a great deal of experimentation in different forms of public housing from diverse actors. Local authorities are building council houses again, for the first time in decades—more on which below. Activists, housing practitioners and action-researchers are forging coalitions of support for collective housing alternatives, such as Greater Manchester Housing Action's Housing Futures research partnership, which makes the case to Greater Manchester's devolved city-regional government for the social value of community-led alternatives.[5] So too does housing play a key part in the fashionable municipalist model developed for Preston, where local mutualised housing associations are enrolled as anchor institutions and the development of community land trusts for the provision of community-owned affordable homes is a major priority.[6]

So how does the new economic policy thinking orbiting Corbynism—at the moment when Corbynism, now without Corbyn, evolves into its next iteration—depart from the Labour Party of the past, the party of centralised socialism, top-down national ownership of the economy, comprehensive

2 Bertie Russell, "Beyond the Local Trap: New Municipalism and the Rise of the Fearless Cities", *Antipode*, 51.3 (2019): 989–1010.

3 Nick Srnicek and Alex Williams, *Inventing the Future: Postcapitalism and a World without Work* (Verso, 2015).

4 Melissa García-Lamarca, "From Occupying Plazas to Recuperating Housing: Insurgent Practices in Spain", *International Journal of Urban and Regional Research* 41.1 (2017): 37–53.

5 Richard Goulding, *Housing Futures: What Can Community-Led Housing Achieve for Greater Manchester?* (Greater Manchester Housing Action, 2019).

6 Matthew Thompson, "What's so new about New Municipalism?", *Progress in Human Geography* (2020): 1–26: https://doi.org/10.1177/0309132520909480.

urban renewal and mass public housing? Answers can be gleaned from Labour's seminal *Alternative Models of Ownership Report*,[7] written in 2017 by policy thinkers drawn from the cooperative movement, think tanks specialising in community-led local economic development and research institutes interested in remunicipalisation and democratisation of public services. The report laid out a vision for what a democratically owned and socially just economy might look like. Although it focused on economic forms of ownership, it also cited as vital components of a democratised society the housing cooperative movement, mutualised housing associations, community land trusts and mutual home ownership societies. Granby Four Streets CLT's holistic approach to local economic development has been characterised in this vein—at the risk of journalistic overreach, riffing on the portmanteau Corbynomics—as 'Granbynomics'.[8] Corbynomics was the result of the Labour Party's so-called 'institutional turn'—a radical reorientation in policy thinking towards cultivating the new institutions (CLTs and co-ops amongst them) capable of bringing about "a bold transformation of the British economy organised around ownership, control, democracy, and participation".[9] Whether Corbynomics survives Corbyn is beside the point; this recent shift in Labour Party thinking is just one manifestation (and personification) of a deeper political and intellectual current calling for democratising and, after decades of neoliberal dismantling, *reconstructing* public ownership.[10]

It is in this spirit I have written this book—as an intervention in reconstructing the recent history of public housing. Whilst the popular narrative renders it as the rise and fall of monolithic municipal housing, I have sought to construct an alternative account that mines the subterranean seam of experimentation with collective housing alternatives. This possible pathway towards Public Sector Housing 2.0 or Mark II—tentatively undertaken in Liverpool but ultimately not travelled—could nonetheless provide the conceptual building blocks for reconstructing public housing today and in the future, for a system of provision refounded on cooperative practices and collective ownership. But this is about more than just reconstructing public sector housing; it is about renewing political optimism in democratic socialist—and *utopian*—alternatives to a broken system. Since Marx and Engels first

7 Labour Party, "Alternative Models of Ownership" (Labour Party, 2017): http://labour.org.uk/wp-content/uploads/2017/10/Alternative-Models-of-Ownership.pdf.

8 Julia Rampen, "Granbynomics: How Liverpool Is Building a New Economic Model", *New Statesman* (17 Oct. 2019).

9 Martin O'Neill and Joe Guinan, "The Institutional Turn: Labour's New Political Economy", *Renewal* 26.2 (2018): 5–16 (p. 5).

10 Andrew Cumbers, *Reclaiming Public Ownership: Making Space for Economic Democracy* (Zed Books, 2012).

caricatured utopian thought as idealist and insufficiently materialist, utopian housing projects of various pedigrees—from anarchist to state-technocratic—have been 'put on trial'.[11] Emerging from the long decades of derision for anything remotely utopian, during which the End of History and There is No Alternative postured as common sense, with critical-theoretical analogues in 'post-politics'[12] and 'capitalist realism',[13] the balance of forces are finally shifting and, in this Gramscian interregnum when the old is dying and the new cannot be born, there is renewed appetite for exploring what Erik Olin Wright described as 'real utopias'—actually existing alternatives that respond to historical material conditions of suffering and injustice and which transform power relations, incrementally and experimentally, to broaden and deepen possibilities for meaningful democracy.[14]

The collective housing alternatives explored in this book are each, in their own limited and contradictory ways, real utopias. They were all born out of conditions of urgency, of needs left unmet by the state and market; radical new spaces invented out of a pragmatic will to survive in the face of adversity. Closing the gaps opened up by the abstraction and fetishisation of space under capitalism—gaps within the dialectic of the 'thingness' and 'flow of space',[15] its noun-like and verb-like qualities, between material outcome and creative process, between producer and consumer—is the real utopian potential of collective housing alternatives.[16] They attempt to reconnect the producer and user of housing by utilising and cultivating the skillsets, passions, energies and imaginations of current residents—not some abstract target consumer population who may or may not materialise. This is the realm of Lefebvre's 'experimental utopia'—concrete explorations of the possible in everyday life[17]—in which inhabitants themselves, the street-level innovators as opposed to modernist planners or visionaries, concretely shape spatial projects through the testing out by trial and error of experimental material practices, guided by ambitious political visions but rooted in local knowledge and practical wisdom. Experimental utopias tentatively created by co-operators, commoners, community homesteaders, guerrilla gardeners and revolutionary

11 Alice Coleman, *Utopia on Trial: Vision and Reality in Planned Housing* (Hilary Shipman Ltd, 1985).

12 Japhy Wilson and Erik Swyngedouw, eds, *The Post-Political and Its Discontents: Spaces of Depoliticization, Spectres of Radical Politics* (Edinburgh University Press, 2014).

13 Mark Fisher, *Capitalist Realism: Is There No Alternative?* (Zero Books, 2009).

14 Erik Olin Wright, *Envisioning Real Utopias* (Verso, 2010).

15 Merrifield, "Place and Space: A Lefebvrian Reconciliation".

16 I explore these arguments in greater depth in Thompson, "Contesting Dilapidated Dwelling".

17 David Pinder, "Reconstituting the Possible: Lefebvre, Utopia and the Urban Question", *International Journal of Urban and Regional Research* 39.1 (2013): 28–45.

recipe-makers thus tend to transform space endogenously in the here and now, through immanent and immersive methods that are *intense* (not future tense); foregrounding collective property claims as an active 'doing' rather than a passive entitlement, thereby renewing a sense of dwelling as social activity as well as material object.

In sum, this book is about trying to see in collective alternatives a real utopian potential to transform public housing and urban economies. It is about making the commons a foundation of a renewed public sector; about making the foundational economy, of which housing is an intrinsic part, a more democratic domain. It is about democratising and making more socially responsive and collectively beneficial what is arguably the most foundational component of personal and public life: the activity (and materiality) of dwelling. This is a vision by no means shared by all those involved in the projects I have studied or all those I interviewed—although it is implied in the words of many. They have drawn for me the coordinates of a new, alternative system of doing housing, regeneration and urban governance and I have joined up the dots. There is thus real utopian potential to combine the best of the co-op, community development trust and CLT models to create an alternative system of public housing provision and urban governance that may one day, with the right political and institutional support, begin to challenge the hegemony of private property rights and market-oriented, property-led approaches to regeneration.

In this opening chapter of the concluding part, I first return to some of the theoretical political-economic concerns with which I introduced and framed the book, focusing on the power of collective housing alternatives as Polanyian counter-movements and as articulations of the commons in relation to the state and capital. Next, I revisit the three guiding questions structuring the book—the Housing, Neighbourhood and Urban Questions—before highlighting the contradictions manifest in co-ops and CLTs entailed by their (to adapt a phrase from the black feminist poet Audre Lorde) *using the master's tools to dismantle the master's house.*[18] This helps frame subsequent reflections, in chapter 14, on (re)constructing historical narrative through story-telling and myth-making. Here, I explore the dialectic between event and process: the initial spur to action of fighting for collective alternatives in dramatic political campaigns set against their ongoing management and governance through bureaucratic procedures. Next, I consider the myth of Liverpool exceptionalism—whether Liverpool's Cooperative Revolution is an exceptional, one-off occurrence inextricably bound up with the city's unique socioeconomic conditions and cultural identity or, conversely, whether something similar can be replicated elsewhere. In arguing for the latter, I then analyse in finer detail

18 Audre Lorde, "The Master's Tools Will Never Dismantle the Master's House", in *Sister Outsider: Essays and Speeches* (Crossing Press, 1984), pp. 110–114.

what, precisely, were the factors for its emergence in Liverpool; identifying the individual ingredients in the 'recipe for revolution' (to borrow a phrase from Homebaked[19]) as a means for concocting similarly potent cocktails elsewhere. Engaging further with drawing out generalisable lessons from this particular history, in chapter 15 I consider how the task of replication and expansion of housing commons may be achieved through institutional design. The aim here is to advance our understanding of how we might redesign state institutions and prefigure new institutional infrastructure for the reconstruction of public housing through the cooperative coordination, replication and scaling of collective housing alternatives, without sacrificing their radical roots or democratic socialist potential. In short, how might we, rather counterintuitively, build a bureaucracy from below? Finally, in an extended Epilogue, I reflect upon the trilingual translating required of successful campaigners between different registers of communication with fellow activists, with the wider public and with powerful gatekeepers—what activist-writer Dougald Hine calls "Inward", "Outward" and "Upward" languages—where I delve deeper into the power of language and representation for expanding housing commons. Finally, through this lens, I reflect upon Granby's Turner Prize achievement and consider the social, cultural and political implications of the artistic representation of public housing experiments in Granby and Homebaked as forms of socially conscious, politically performative works of art.

In, Against and Beyond Public Housing

In this book I have purposefully represented mutual housing societies, co-operatives, co-housing, community development trusts and CLTs as types of what I call collective housing alternatives for precisely this reason: to emphasise their proximity to public housing, as an *alternative* to state-led provision; foregrounding their capacity to reimagine and reconstruct public housing in more democratic directions, and to establish collective or common ownership of land and assets as a bulwark against commodification and enclosure of the commons. This perspective helps us move beyond bounded definitions of their belonging strictly within communities or civil society as implied by the conventional term 'community-led housing' and highlights, contra 'collaborative housing', their potential to challenge and transform rather than collaborate with capitalism. Although this conceptualisation has been shaped by specific reference to the British context, the concept of institutionalising a 'non-state public' form of housing is applicable to many other

19 Sue Potts, *Homebaked—Impact Report: Recipes for Revolutions* (Homebaked, 2014): www.biennial.com/files/pdfs/3216/140509-final-homebaked-impact-report-suepotts.pdf.

national contexts—as has been recently explored in the case of Denmark[20]—and is intended to resonate internationally.

Collective housing movement-building—in Liverpool and elsewhere—has always been a highly transnational and globally interdependent phenomenon. Cooperative housing is a story of travelling ideas and mobile technologies originally exported from Britain to Scandinavia and back again,[21] spreading out across central and southern Europe where co-ops have really taken root, and now growing through cross-pollination of projects from all over the world. American-founded CLTs were inspired by anti-enclosure philosophies from India and England before being exported across the global North and South.[22] In an increasingly globalised capitalism, collective housing projects are fighting similar threats of accumulation by dispossession. Sharing ideas, learning from each other and developing transnational and inter-urban networks of mutual support and cooperative exchange will only become more salient in the years ahead.

Collective housing alternatives can be understood in Polanyian terms as a counter-movement counteracting the tendencies of capitalism to dis-embed the market from its social foundations in society and commodify land and other common resources. CLTs and co-ops can thus be conceptualised as institutional innovations that attempt to de-commodify land (in the realm of social reproduction) just as worker-owned co-ops do so for labour (in the sphere of production) and community-owned banks and building societies do so for money (in the circuit of exchange). In this sense they are part of an alternative system to capitalism, part of a distinctive social economy rooted in histories of voluntary association, mutualism, anarchism, cooperativism and guild socialism, and defined by the (Polanyian) logic of reciprocity in contrast to the opposing logics of (market) exchange and (state) command. The reciprocity of the social economy combined with the most progressive elements of the state—its powers of redistribution—together maintain social solidarity against the alienation, atomisation, competition and dispossession wrought by capitalism.

Yet the collective housing alternatives explored in this book have rarely remained within the domain of social reproduction—they are about more than just housing. The Eldonians have cleverly utilised the Community Development Trust model to realise their vision of becoming a self-regenerating community—transforming ex-industrial derelict land into a popular

20 Lorenzo Vidal, "Securing Social Gains in, against and beyond the State: The Case of Denmark's 'Common Housing'", *Housing, Theory and Society* 36.4 (2018): 448–468.

21 David Clapham and Keith Kintrea, "Importing Housing Policy: Housing Co-operatives in Britain and Scandinavia", *Housing Studies* 2.3 (1987): 157–169.

22 Tom Moore and Kim McKee, "Empowering Local Communities? An International Review of Community Land Trusts", *Housing Studies* 27.2 (2012): 280–290.

and sustainable urban village collectively controlled by the community, with many positive multiplier effects on local job and business creation and the surrounding environment. Like the Eldonians, Granby and Homebaked have gone beyond just housing to harness collective housing alternatives for local economic development. In Granby, ambitions to revitalise Granby Street as a local retail and cultural artery have already begun to materialise, with new businesses opening up for the first time in decades and plans afoot to install the market in more permanent form. Homebaked have created a community anchor in the co-op bakery, now considered a central keystone in the council's wider regeneration vision—attracting inward investment and football fans to spend their money locally. Now with additional philanthropic funding and the backing of the council, Homebaked are rehabilitating their entire terraced row and nurturing a family of like-minded community projects and enterprises—Homebaked bakery and the Homegrown Collective amongst them—brought together around the common goal of revitalising and democratising the local economy.

Collective alternatives are also part of the foundational economy—a more recently formulated concept informed by a Polanyian perspective. It describes that sphere of economic activity traditionally associated with unproductive tax-supported public services, but which can be reconceived, following the Foundational Economy Collective,[23] as the most socially valuable and highest-employment-generating part of the economy fundamental to all other (re)production. It provides those essential foundations for human and societal flourishing such as health, education, transport, energy, water, food and, last but not least, housing. This thinking suggests *all* housing is a matter of public interest. Many nation-states recognise this by funding or subsidising almost all tenures, including private rental and owner-occupation, either through tax relief, monetary policy, indirect grants or more direct provision. In Britain, dwellers are incentivised to buy a house by various tax benefits; 'buy-to-let' property investment is likewise encouraged; and housing benefit, once paid directly to councils or housing associations, is increasingly diverted to private landlords who profit at public expense.[24] This apparent privatisation and marketisation belies the fact that the state still subsidises a large proportion of housing costs—in large part due to the housing question—because the market, under financialised capitalism, creates artificial scarcity amidst plenty. In some sense, then, all housing is public—funded publicly through redistributive taxation, delivering social value for the good of society as much as for the individual citizen. Collective housing models such as co-ops and CLTs

23 Foundational Economy Collective, *Foundational Economy: The Infrastructure of Everyday Life*.

24 Stuart Hodkinson, Paul Watt and Gerry Mooney, "Introduction: Neoliberal Housing Policy—Time for a Critical Re-Appraisal", *Critical Social Policy* 33.1 (2013): 3–16.

must be understood in this sense before we even begin to look at those special characteristics that contribute to the more delineated notion of public housing as a social right of citizenship.

Yet at the same time as highlighting these important connections with 'the public' I have sought to dissociate collective housing alternatives from the public–private dualism—the ownership model—that pervades property relations under neoliberal capitalism. Here, the notion of the public is reduced to the domain of the state—the Leviathan—as regulator of public space, manager of public services and sovereign arbiter of property relations, serving private interests in exclusive ownership of land and other commodities critical to the accumulation of capital. The commons attempts to 'unsettle this settlement'[25] by constituting a different conception of the public, one predicated on an expansive public sphere of participation, interaction, interdependence and cooperative self-governance. As legal and organisational articulations of housing commons, collective housing alternatives prefigure a way out of the 'Leviathan logic'[26] ordained by Hobbes and since suffusing (neo)liberal society—in the characteristics they share with emerging digital peer-to-peer and platform technologies, as I have argued in greater depth elsewhere.[27] Such configurations tend to short-circuit the inter-mediating forces of state power and capital that currently structure social relations; they tend to replace the Leviathan logic of citizens related to each other ultimately only by virtue of their shared vertical relationships with the state with an alternative way of structuring human relations that privileges the more direct and horizontal ties of mutual aid, co-operation, solidarity and reciprocity. By embodying these values and practices within their institutional structures, co-ops and CLTs, alongside other articulations of the commons, move us in this direction even if, in reality, under conditions still dominated by the state and capital, they rarely live up to their real utopian potential.

Working within the ownership model, actually existing commons—like all real utopias—are neither free from contradictions nor immune to power relations. They are essentially pragmatic compromises made within a hostile legal landscape that attempt to express common relations in institutional form. As common property regimes for *housing,* they are complex hybrid social spaces: combining the privacy of the home with more cooperative social relations for the democratic governance of land. They must necessarily construct their own walls and boundaries—as collective but no less exclusive enclosures—in

25 Nicholas Blomley, *Unsettling the City* (Routledge, 2004).

26 Jeremy Gilbert, *Common Ground: Democracy and Collectivity in an Age of Individualism* (London: Pluto Press, 2013).

27 Matthew Thompson, "Playing with the Rules of the Game: Social Innovation for Urban Transformation", *International Journal of Urban and Regional Research* 43.6 (2019): 1168–1192.

order to protect the commons against the more pernicious enclosures of capital and private property. They do this in different ways. Co-ops operate *with* the concept of ownership as forms of 'collective private ownership',[28] whilst CLTs attempt to move beyond ownership towards the distinctive concept of stewardship, which has the potential to transcend the problem of inward-facing exclusivity associated with co-ops through a more transparent, open and publicly accountable trust structure involving a broad base of stakeholders and the wider community—and not just member-residents. We can see this at play in both Granby and Homebaked CLTs. Stewardship is rooted in the classical CLT model's founding concept of trusterty, which understands land—like all fictitious commodities as originally conceived by Polanyi—as a free gift from nature and therefore something entrusted to all of us and not rightfully owned by any one person.

Of all counter-movements, collective housing alternatives are unique in dealing directly with land and property. That land is a fictitious commodity is an important point for understanding the political potential—as well as ethical roots—of collective housing movements. It is 'fictitious' because unlike a 'real' commodity it is not produced by human labour, pre-existing in nature, yet is artificially presented as a commodity for sale on the market. Moreover, because its value is almost entirely created not through the actions of any particular landowner but through its relationality, locational advantage and countless interactions between multiple actors across society, it is part of our common wealth, whose fruits are justly shared and governed by all. Of all the fictitious commodities—land, labour, capital—land is arguably the most foundational—as it provides the necessary space and natural resources for all production to occur—for both the reproduction of human life and the production of (capitalist) value. Writing in *The New Enclosure*, critical geographer Brett Christophers reminds us of its special qualities: it is a fixed, finite, permanent, immovable, non-reproducible and legally excludable yet easily divisible and universally valuable good, defined by natural monopoly, making it the perfect vehicle for the distribution and store of value, as collateral underwriting debt and credit, and an object of speculative investment for future capital gains.[29] These qualities place land—and all that it supports, not least housing—at the heart of capitalist accumulation and contestation. Moreover, as global capital has exhausted its capacities for productive reinvestment of surplus capital, it has turned towards financialisation of common, public and natural assets as a kind of spatial fix to crises of profitability elsewhere in the system, entailing aggressive speculative investments and accumulation by dispossession in what Harvey has

28 Charles Geisler and Gail Daneker, *Property and Values: Alternatives to Public and Private Ownership* (Island Press, 2000).
29 Brett Christophers, *The New Enclosure: The Appropriation of Public Land in Neoliberal Britain* (Verso, 2018).

argued is the defining feature of our contemporary capitalist epoch.[30] This is the New Urban Question animating the contemporary double movement—the movement towards commodification of land, including via state-led regeneration programmes, such as HMR in Liverpool, facilitating public–private harvesting of urban land value differentials, and the counter-movement of resistance from society, such as collective housing activists deploying community land trusts as institutional tools to resist commodification.

The state has historically played a central role in both the fictitious commodification of land—alongside labour and capital—and counter-moves against it. The state has been instrumental in coordinating and accelerating the expansion of market exchange—its genesis is inseparable from the early development of capitalism through enclosure of the commons, colonial plunder and extraction. Liverpool's housing history attests to this: the Irish Potato Famine which brought so many refugees to Liverpool, into crowded slums by the docks, thereby seeding the conditions and the culture for collective action, was a by-product of the British state's violent capitalist-colonial practices in Ireland. The municipal state acted, eventually, to ameliorate some of these appalling conditions through health and sanitation legislation and building amongst the world's first public housing. The national state was harnessed alongside local authorities in the counter-movement against the market through massive state-funded programmes of comprehensive urban renewal and council house building, including the funding of co-ops in Liverpool. This is the state logic of redistribution being put to work for the development of reciprocity. Yet state motivations were often deeply ambivalent: state financing for public housing following the First World War was designed to absorb the labour of five million military-trained returning conscripted workers and avoid their disaffection, as an "insurance against Bolshevism and revolution".[31] Thus we should approach the state cautiously as neither friend nor foe, not as a unitary entity serving capitalism—as some anti-capitalists tend to see it—but as an ambivalent field of social relations governing a complex set of fiscal, regulatory and legal tools that can, under the right political conditions, be re-engineered for developing housing commons.

Most recently, the state has been commandeered to serve capital. Since the neoliberal discrediting of state intervention from the late 1970s, public provision has been recommodified, outsourced through public–private partnerships, and austerity administered from the centre, leaving local government to pick up the pieces and seek to resolve the crisis in social

30 David Harvey, *Limits to Capital* (Verso Books, 2007).

31 Parliamentary secretary, quoted in Neil Gray, "Spatial Composition and the Urbanization of Capital: The 1915 Glasgow Rent Strikes and the Housing Question Reconsidered", in Neil Gray, ed., *Rent and Its Discontents: A Century of Housing Struggle* (Rowman & Littlefield, 2018), pp. 49–67 (p. 52).

reproduction, most visibly in rising homelessness and destitution, wrought by economic liberalisation. The privatisation of public land has been a primary—if, until recently, relatively invisible—flank in neoliberalisation. Since 1979, around 10 per cent of Britain's total land has been privatised by the state, including council housing—that is approximately half of all the publicly owned land when Thatcher came to power, estimated at around £400 billion in today's value, representing by far the biggest public sell-off.[32] Most of this has gone to private individuals and corporations; some, especially in recent years, sold off to developers by cash-strapped councils to pay for statutory services. Bucking this trend, a growing number of local authorities are experimenting with arm's-length 'special purpose vehicles' to act as developers of new public stock—Liverpool City Council's new municipal housing company was established in 2019 and named, rather appositely, Foundations. Such instruments are an ingenious means of bypassing legal constraints on council borrowing powers hitherto preventing their sourcing finance to build new homes as well as circumventing Right to Buy legislation once built. However, they have been critiqued for leveraging public assets to build for-profit market housing as well as non-profit social housing as a means to generate alternative sources of revenue to cross-subsidise austerity-squeezed public services such as health and social care.[33] In other words, with one hand they stoke the fire of financialisation, asset inflation, speculation and privatisation whilst, with the other, protect public services from those very same flames. Though this may end the direct privatisation of public assets effected through the public–private partnerships of previous modes of roll-back and roll-out neoliberalism, it is still a process of commodification, albeit one municipalised, undertaken by municipalities themselves.

Thus we can understand the state dialectically as a problematic institutional ensemble embroiled in a history of ongoing capitalist-colonial dispossession and extraction, enrolled in upholding elite class interests and accorded an ultimate mandate on the almost untrammelled use of violence whilst, at the same time, recognising it as the only social structure of sufficient scope and scale capable of protecting, supporting and expanding that common sphere of collective life resisting the logic of capital. The task, then, is not to reject the state wholesale but to reimagine and redesign its contours—using cooperative

32 Christophers, *The New Enclosure*.
33 Joe Beswick and Joe Penny, "Demolishing the Present to Sell Off the Future? The Financialisation of Public Housing in London", *International Journal of Urban and Regional Research* 42.4 (2018): 612–632; Brett Christophers, "Putting Financialisation in Its Financial Context: Transformations in Local Government-Led Urban Development in Post-Financial Crisis England", *Transactions of the Institute of British Geographers*, 44.3 (2019): 571–586.

principles as a template—or to prefigure an entirely different kind of state.[34] What might this look like in practical terms? A concomitant alternative to public–private partnerships resides in public–common partnerships whereby the state engages associations of commoners, such as co-ops and CLTs, in mutually beneficial partnerships to democratically govern public and common goods. Common Wealth, one of the new think tanks building a policy infrastructure for the Left, has recently published a report on the subject,[35] proving particularly influential in struggles for collective control over community assets and ex-council housing estates in London, and providing inspiration for reimagining state institutions for the development of collective housing alternatives. These are the kinds of institutional innovations that may work symbiotically with co-ops and CLTs to reconstruct public housing in the twenty-first century—ideas which I explore in greater depth in the final chapter.

How to Answer the Housing, Neighbourhood and Urban Questions?

If collective housing alternatives can be understood in Polanyian terms as part of a counter-movement against commodification, in Marxian terms such "solutions to the social question"[36] tend to be interpreted more critically—as too utopian or simplistic to contend with the incredibly complex problem of capitalism. Engels' original formulation of the housing question—that there can be no isolated solution to persistent material deprivation, class inequalities and uneven urban development so long as the capitalist mode of production persists—is one not easily addressed by co-ops or CLTs acting alone, at least not within the terms set by Marx and Engels. Although they framed the problem too narrowly as one of *material* deprivation, failing to foresee that the state could (and did for some time in some European countries) effectively resolve much housing poverty through public provision, particularly in the inter-war and post-war periods, their rendering remains relevant today. No sooner had the state provided good quality public housing in one locality than did the problem of deprivation appear elsewhere—especially if we trace these displacements globally. As

34 Davina Cooper, "Prefiguring the State", *Antipode* 49.2 (2017): 335–356; Davina Cooper, Nikita Dhawan and Janet Newman, *Reimagining the State: Theoretical Challenges and Transformative Possibilities* (Routledge, 2019).

35 Keir Milburn and Bertie Russell, *Public–Common Partnerships: Building New Circuits of Collective Ownership* (Common Wealth, 2019): https://common-wealth.co.uk/Public-common-partnerships.html.

36 Marx, quoted in William Clare Roberts, *Marx's Inferno: The Political Theory of Capital* (Princeton University Press, 2017), p. 23.

per Engels' thesis, isolated solutions to the housing question merely displace and reproduce the issue in different locations.

Working within these parameters, community development trusts and CLTs can play an important role in addressing what I have called the neighbourhood question—how to resolve the socio-spatial concentration, reproduction and displacement of multiple deprivations within specific neighbourhoods, wrought through uneven urban development, as evident in Liverpool. Whereas state-led solutions (comprehensive inner-city renewal and the construction of outer estates and new towns) focused on material improvements and failed adequately to embed in place new opportunities for individual and collective economic development and community self-governance—leading to the reappearance of symptoms—collective alternatives can act as anchors for recovery. However, they too cannot prevent the displacement of symptoms elsewhere. Only by creating a more systematic, comprehensive coverage of collective alternatives across *all* neighbourhoods threatened by capital flight can the neighbourhood question be more effectively addressed; and for this we need institutional infrastructure and scalar coordination.

Conventional state attempts to tackle the housing and neighbourhood questions—comprehensively clearing inner-city slums and constructing council housing or renewing the market for housing through public–private partnerships like HMR—have revealed new problems of deprivation related to social and cultural needs in the inadequacies of modernist renewal and distant bureaucratic landlordism. Resolving the (material) exploitation of the tenant–landlord relation is not enough; public housing also needs to deal with (cultural) alienation and (socio-spatial) exclusion. This is where collective alternatives can achieve more than traditional state-led forms of provision in terms of what public housing, at its most utopian and politically ambitious, was once intended to accomplish. They can reconnect the producer and user of housing and attempt to resolve the alienation and exploitation inherent to capitalism via collective democratic control over the means of social reproduction and, by extension, production.

Liverpool's co-ops have helped protect tenant-co-operators from material exploitation/deprivation (through the economic security of collective ownership, promoting education, skills learning and new employment), from alienation/disconnection (through the process of democratic design, self-build and ongoing cooperative management), from socio-political exclusion (through the collective empowerment of campaigning, inspiring renewed engagement in electoral politics and securing greater political representation in city decision-making) and from spatial displacement (through security of tenure of collective ownership). By taking control of housing assets and the surpluses generated by rents, the 1970s co-ops have effectively become mini welfare states, collectivising risks and rewards amongst members by, for instance, using co-op surpluses to provide funds for residents to go on skills training or further education courses, helping many find jobs or routes into higher education. Today, the low, below-market rents that they offer for co-op members enable many to pursue creative, political and caring vocations and civic volunteering that creates social value but little exchange value—the kind of endeavours that were once subsidised by the dole—including developing more collective alternatives.

Whilst Liverpool's experiment in cooperative housing was ultimately unable to provide a comprehensive answer to Engels' housing question—partly for structural limitations of the cooperative model in challenging the dominance of capital; partly for contextual factors such as sectarianism and urban decline combining with the exclusivity of the co-op model; partly for the co-op movement being prevented from further growth by exogenous political events—it has, in the various modest ways outlined above, provided a partial, localised, isolated solution to Liverpool's housing crisis and, interestingly, a defence against urban decline, which, if sufficiently scaled up and supported by the state, might constitute an answer to today's urban question. Co-ops represent a possible cell structure for a more cooperative state and society—a template for the larger-scale cooperative ownership and management of public housing and other common resources as a workable alternative to our current marketised or previously more statist systems.

Collective alternatives have proven more effective than state-led forms at protecting publicly funded housing commons from being (re)commodified by the market—partly because they are better insulated from the vagaries of electoral politics governing the fate of state-led provision which has, through a cross-party penchant for privatisation, been residualised and marketised into social housing. The trust structure and asset lock of CLTs especially are useful instruments capable of preventing such a trajectory if utilised for any future renewal of public housing. CLTs may even work in combination with co-ops—as we see in Granby—as their stewards, providing protection from co-optation by the state or commodification by capital. The CLTs are designed for the long haul—slowly to revitalise areas of longstanding decline through incremental, iterative and cumulative participatory design and reconstruction methods—so although perhaps too embryonic to evaluate success, there are already tentative signs of their power to address the neighbourhood question in particular. Bringing residents on board is a painstaking process that requires great effort and patience. Like the Eldonians, they have sought to move beyond just housing to tackle wider socioeconomic regeneration. Whereas the new-build co-ops were pro-demolition, the CLTs are anti-demolition; the focus has moved from housing to wider neighbourhood concerns, reflecting broader shifts from the housing question to the urban question.

An interesting, and problematic, aspect of both Homebaked and Granby is the relatively blank slate with which they started—the loss and opportunity presented by years of local depopulation and forced eviction—to reconstruct a community from the ground up, redefining and reshaping place in the image of a distinctively bohemian, and perhaps exclusive, habitus. Unlike the earlier, more community-driven co-op campaigns, the CLTs are the product of a minority of remaining homeowners and politically oriented activists from near and far. A great deal of work has been put into community organising for both projects, to gain the trust of the wider community and galvanise more active participation from more than just the most vociferous residents. Through their CLT governance structures, Granby and Homebaked have the potential to do more than what the Eldonians have achieved in terms of democracy: to establish an open neighbourhood forum or a public arena for the coming together of disparate local groups to discuss common issues and debate the future of the area; as a 'politics of space'[37] uniting people in deliberation around shared spatial issues, cutting across traditional class, ethnic and religious cleavages. The CLT model's tripartite trust structure, with democratic representation of a broad constituency of local residents as well as other stakeholders, combined with its ability to own land and property assets for the benefit of the wider community—and not just members, as in the case of co-ops—places Granby and Homebaked in a potentially powerful position to take on the role of democratic governance as well as stewardship; as 'meso-scale governance shims'[38]—a term borrowed from joinery to describe a 'wedge' inserted between two existing modes of governance, the household and local government.

The especially strong—if not unique—focus on democratic control in the Liverpool CLTs is largely a product of global capital's locational see-saw depressing the political economy of Liverpool—a shrunken city scarred by capital flight and 'failing' housing markets where affordability, unlike for most other areas of CLT activism in the UK, such as inner London or rural hotspots, has never really been a big problem. The biggest problem for residents of Liverpool has been in acquiring democratic control in order to determine the fate of their neighbourhoods in the face of overweening political forces pushing for their 'managed decline'—either by arch-austerians seeking to speed the 'natural' *autotomy* of a diseased part of the body politic drained of the lifeblood of capitalism or, once it is realised that the state has the leverage to tilt the see-saw, by neoliberal opportunists repackaging people's neighbourhoods as 'zones of opportunity' (ZOOs) to capitalise on the rent gap. At the same time, the relative lack of demand from capital has left a vacuum in development pressure, providing the opportunity and opening up the space for social innovators to imagine and experiment with something different.

37 Mark Purcell, "Neighborhood Activism among Homeowners as a Politics of Space", *Professional Geographer* 53.2 (2001): 178–194.

38 Olivia Williams and Joseph Pierce, "Inserting Scales of Urban Politics: The Possibilities of Meso-Urban Governance Shims", *Urban Geography* 38.6 (2017): 795–812.

This makes Liverpool an interesting laboratory—a socially experimental field—for testing out new ideas and 'isolated solutions', which, if successful in combating capital in one place, might then be replicated elsewhere in the global counter-movement.

Engels' central rebuttal of Proudhon's argument—that is, the tenant–landlord relation is not tantamount to the labour–capital relation, but merely a secondary reflection of the primary contradiction of capitalism—now rests upon less clear-cut a distinction than it used to. Feminists have long argued that this distinction between production of value in the workplace and its ultimate source in the hidden abode—in the life-encompassing field of social reproduction—is mostly a matter of perspective, of accounting measures, of where we draw the line. Yet this distinction—however arbitrarily drawn it may have been by Marxists down the decades—has by now almost completely dissolved in the FIRE economy (Finance-Insurance-Real Estate) of globalised capitalism in which housing is no longer secondary but one of the primary commodities fuelling capital accumulation. This is an economy in which value is produced and extracted at almost every moment in the cycle, not just at the point of production as the labour theory of value holds. This re-centres housing in struggles against capital. Struggle in and around the workplace—through syndicalism, trade unions or political parties—still matters; but it is no longer even the primary point of contestation. Any wins for the labour movement in protecting wages or gaining a greater share of the surplus created in the realm of production are siphoned off through fictitious rent inflation and compounding interest imposed by an increasingly powerful and bloated capitalist class coalition of landowning and financial interests through their use of ever more sophisticated financial instruments in the realm of consumption—and especially housing. Rentier capitalism is fast delivering the 'urban revolution' Lefebvre prophesied in how value is harvested under capitalism.[39] The extension and intensification of the digitally mediated planetary urbanisation of capital blurs the boundaries between primary and secondary contradictions, between production of commodities and the social reproduction of human beings and social support systems. Housing is not only a field of social reproduction; it is increasingly a site of production of surplus value through the commodification of land and property as real estate. This explains why we are caught in a counterintuitively perpetual 'housing crisis'.[40]

Class decomposition muddies the waters still further. Since neoliberal reforms of the 1980s, such as the Right to Buy, the proletariat (all of us who sell our labour power for survival) has become increasingly enmeshed and interdependent with capital through credit and rising (until very recently)

39 Henri Lefebvre, *The Urban Revolution* (University of Minnesota Press, 2003).

40 David Madden and Peter Marcuse, *In Defense of Housing: The Politics of Crisis* (Verso, 2016).

owner-occupation. Owner-occupiers have serious financial stakes in escalating property price inflation, not least in order to fund retirements in an era of imploding social security, asset-based welfare and a social contract overstretched to breaking point. Employee and private pension pots are otherwise entangled in speculative property investments worldwide. Real estate now provides the foundation, the collateral, for most global financial trading—"the commodity which underpins all wealth held in the known 'universe of securities'".[41] Credit advanced for (real commodity) production is therefore made dependent on investments in (fictitious) real estate. At the same time, homelessness, dispossessions and deprivations are on the rise as a result of the fictitious bubble economy squeezing so many out of accessing affordable housing and, in periodically crashing, causing debt defaults and foreclosures. Land and housing have become a central battleground over value in ways which Engels could not have foreseen. Gaining collective control over property has always been an important part of contesting capitalism—founded, as this system is, on the state-enforced ideology of private property ownership—but is proving an increasingly important part of contending with the new urban question, the contemporary incarnation of the housing question.

Nevertheless, Engels has a point. Co-ops and CLTs will always be plugged into global circuits of capital so long as capitalism remains the primary mode of production. They rely on the dead labour of previous rounds of production—the old houses they seek to renovate—or, if building anew, they remain dependent on extractive industries to source bricks and mortar through complex global value chains woven through layers of exploitation. However successfully they act to transform the tenant–landlord relation—and however deeply capital penetrates the secondary circuit of land and property for new sources of profit—there will always be underlying processes, often hidden from view, through which housing and its value is created through the exploitation of other human beings and the plunder of non-human nature. Engels suggested that the only possible resolution of the housing question was the revolutionary overthrow of capital via the seizing of the means of production by the proletariat as a socialist transition to communism. But class decomposition makes it far less clear how the lines will be drawn; (almost) everyone now has skin in the game (at least in the UK). If we wait for the Revolution, we will be waiting quite some time. In the meantime, and in the interstices, collective housing alternatives are building, slowly but surely, a bridge between everyday life and systemic transformation, a bridge between ends and means. Channelling utopian desires into more practical tasks such as property transfer negotiations with the council is seen, by one activist working with Homebaked, as a kind of 'pragmatic radicalism'—an interesting

41 Louis Moreno, "Always Crashing in the Same City: Real Estate, Psychic Capital and Planetary Desire", *City: Analysis of Urban Trends, Culture, Theory, Policy, Action* 22.1 (2018): 152–168.

analogue to Colin Ward's brand of 'pragmatic anarchism'.[42] Whether we call it pragmatic anarchism, radical reformism or real utopian experimentalism—such an approach treads a cautious middle ground between the two false binaries polarising the all-or-nothing revolutionary logic of Engels' housing question. That bridge leads us to the commons. Our only hope to escape capitalist incorporation is through a process of outward and inward expansion of the commons, countervailing and, perhaps, eventually superseding capital.

It is no accident that the commons as an idea is being rediscovered just as neoliberalism and new forms of accumulation by dispossession are becoming so entrenched. This post-capitalist alternative has ancient roots in the concept of commoning—a customary way of life for many before acts of enclosure were enforced by the early modern state and brought capitalism into being through primitive accumulation. Commoning helps us see the dialectical nature of commons as both material resource and social practice—a dialectic into which I have delved by following John F.C. Turner in seeing housing as both noun (material object) and verb (social process). Understanding collective housing alternatives as acts of commoning helps us do two things. First, a focus on commoning situates housing commons within political economy as just one—albeit foundational—part of a broader and deeper global eco-socialist struggle over social reproduction, for wresting control of the means of reproducing human and non-human life itself out from under capital. As various autonomist and feminist Marxists remind us,[43] capitalism is parasitical on human life (and non-human nature) but there is always a social surplus remaining after extraction of surplus value, dynamic energies that can never be totally captured or enclosed, the life-force of the commons.

Second, it moves our attention beyond campaigns for the protection and preservation of existing commons onto the novel terrain of producing new commons. Rent strikes, for instance, have been an important tactic in the struggle to protect our housing commons—some, notably the Glasgow Rent Strike of 1915, preceded the development of public housing by putting pressure on political representatives to put the right policies in place.[44] Strikes effectively quell the flow of capital going to private and public landlords—and thereby break the circuit of rentier capitalism. In this regard, they represent what I

42 Stuart White, "Making Anarchism Respectable? The Social Philosophy of Colin Ward", *Journal of Political Ideologies* 12.1 (2007): 11–28.

43 Silvia Federici, *Re-Enchanting the World: Feminism and the Politics of the Commons* (PM Press, 2019); Massimo De Angelis, *Omnia Sunt Communia: On the Commons and the Transformation to Postcapitalism* (Zed Books, 2017); Michael Hardt and Antonio Negri, *Commonwealth* (Harvard University Press, 2009); John Holloway, *Crack Capitalism* (Pluto Press, 2010).

44 Neil Gray, *Rent and Its Discontents: A Century of Housing Struggle* (Rowman & Littlefield, 2018).

have characterised as *reactive* rather than *proactive* forms of commoning—a distinction variously expressed by scholar-activists as 'maintaining' versus 'expanding' the commons[45] or 'defensive' versus 'offensive' commoning.[46] Although rent strikes play a part in Liverpool's collective housing history, in this book I have sought to highlight more offensive forms of commoning aiming to produce new housing commons, to create new circuits of the common. In some sense, Liverpool's history is a story of defensive commoning—from rent strikes and anti-displacement campaigns against the Slum Clearance Programme of the 1970s to anti-demolition campaigning against HMR in the 2000s—transforming, through the very process of struggle, into offensive modes of commoning, from new-build co-op development to guerrilla gardening and CLT projects.

Reflecting findings from other examples of housing commons in cities around the world, such as in Copenhagen and Montevideo,[47] Barcelona[48] and Washington DC,[49] Liverpool's collective housing alternatives began as pragmatic responses to some threat or crisis, motivated by the necessity of securing decent affordable housing, only slowly evolving into a more widespread political consciousness around 'collective dweller control'.[50] Although democratic control over community assets, including but not limited to housing, became the abiding issue for Liverpool's urban CLTs—as opposed to more material housing conditions, as it was for the co-ops—what initially catalysed CLT activists to action was the demolition threat posed to their homes by HMR, which came to signify a general lack of control over the future of their neighbourhoods, decided undemocratically without their consent. It is doubtful whether such ideological commitments and institutional transformations would have ever crystallised in Liverpool were it not for the initial spur to action—the urgency and desperate need of communities, responding to exogenous shocks and crises, resorting to extraordinary measures to defend their right to dwell in place. This raises questions: how

45 Amanda Huron, *Carving out the Commons: Tenant Organizing and Housing Cooperatives in Washington, DC* (Minnesota Press, 2018).

46 Tim Joubert and Stuart Hodkinson, "Beyond the Rent Strike, Towards the Commons: Why the Housing Question Requires Activism That Generates Its Own Alternatives", in Neil Gray, ed., *Rent and Its Discontents: A Century of Housing Struggle* (Rowman & Littlefield, 2018), pp. 185–200.

47 Lorenzo Vidal, "Cooperative Islands in Capitalist Waters: Limited-Equity Housing Cooperatives, Urban Renewal and Gentrification", *International Journal of Urban and Regional Research* 43.1 (2019): 157–178.

48 García-Lamarca, "From Occupying Plazas to Recuperating Housing: Insurgent Practices in Spain".

49 Huron, *Carving out the Commons.*

50 Colin Ward, *Tenants Take Over* (Architectural Press, 1974).

do we move from the particularities of people and place to more generalisable movements; from *reactive* bespoke campaigns, precariously dependent on civic volunteerism, to *proactive* systematic development of collective alternatives? In short, how do we expand, offensively, whilst maintaining, defensively, our housing commons?

In mirror-image of Marx's circuit of capital, theorists of the commons are beginning to sketch out a 'circuit of the common'.[51] If the commodity is the cellular form of capital, then commons—that is, any good or value produced to be shared rather than accumulated—are the cell form of the common. In the capital circuit, money is used to buy labour power and means of production to produce commodities which, in turn, are traded on the market for more money, some of which is invested for further accumulation. Money begets commodities begets more money than before. In the common circuit, money is no longer the mediator of the process of expansion, which is, instead, voluntarily self-directed by associations of commoners who come together to harness and govern common resources or common wealth to produce commons. Common wealth and associations beget commons beget associations and common wealth. The final conversion is not money but the reproduction of commons, understood as associations of commoners (such as co-ops and CLTs, and their practices of commoning) and common resources (community-owned housing). Any 'surplus' of common wealth or value created in the process is shared for expanding the common circuit.

Association, cooperation and connections *between* associations of commoners, through expanded reciprocity, are the key conduits of this circuitry. In the case of cooperatives, it is little surprise that cooperation between cooperatives is deemed a pivotal governing principle of the global movement. If cooperatives are to survive in a world market dominated by capital—as "cooperative islands in capitalist waters"[52]—they must engage each other in alternative exchange relations and networks of solidarity through the development of integrated cooperative supply chains and alternative global circuits of value. It is extremely difficult, however, to create common circuits of value entirely autonomous from capital when there are so many diverse inputs, labours and materials that go into its production and reproduction—as in the case of housing. When movements for the commons are still relatively weak, sporadic, disconnected and few and far between—as in the case of housing commons—the onus on building these connections is all the more urgent, for in the meantime they remain exposed

51 Greig de Peuter and Nick Dyer-Witheford, "Commons and Cooperatives", *Affinities: A Journal of Radical Theory, Culture, and Action* 4.1 (2010): 30–56; De Angelis, *Omnia Sunt Communia: On the Commons and the Transformation to Postcapitalism*.

52 Vidal, "Cooperative Islands in Capitalist Waters: Limited-Equity Housing Cooperatives, Urban Renewal and Gentrification".

to short-circuiting by capital and are in many ways made reliant on capital's own conduit—that is, money.

What role for the state in all this? The state is clearly a key player in the circuit of capital—as creator of new markets, issuer of currency, underwriter of public and private debt, regulator of production, consumption and exchange and facilitator, generally, of capital accumulation. Although the commons may appear anathema to the state as envisioned under capitalism, the state may also play a role in facilitating the circuit of the common. As Harvey has likewise argued, theorists of commons governance—from liberals to Marxists—recognise the need for some kind of overarching nested scalar structure to connect and coordinate the activities of localised commons and redistribute resources between them to ensure socio-spatial justice.[53] This need not take the form of the state as we know it, but some kind of state-like institutional structure is useful nonetheless. Following Massimo De Angelis' interpretation of systems theory for commons-building,[54] we can conceptualise the development of housing commons and the broader expansion of the circuit of the common as supported by reimagined state institutions—public–common partnerships, for instance—as a kind of 'structural coupling' in which an emergent system of commons can access and harness the complexity and resources of state systems to its own advantage.

What might this look like in practice? In their Common Wealth report, scholar-activists Keir Milburn and Bertie Russell present public–common partnerships less as a fixed institutional blueprint than a set of principles. Three are notable: joint enterprise, in which ownership and governance is shared equally by the state (such as a municipal council) and a common association (such as a co-op or CLT) as the two principal parties on the board of democratically elected directors; joint capitalisation whereby the state agency contributes the majority of funds and underwrites those provided by the common association, such as crowd-funding, charitable grants and membership fees; and distributed democratic control of surplus value. The last suggests that surplus value created by public–common partnerships gets reinvested to support the incubation of other commons projects and their development through further public–common partnerships, thereby transforming surplus capital into common use value to "create an ever-expanding movement of de-commodification and collective democratisation".[55] In accepting that the state contains powerful tools (albeit fashioned primarily for capital) and that the state apparatus can be re-engineered to strengthen the circuit of the common over capital, the question becomes *how*—a question

53 David Harvey, *Rebel Cities: From the Right to the City to the Urban Revolution* (Verso, 2012).

54 De Angelis, *Omnia Sunt Communia: On the Commons and the Transformation to Postcapitalism*.

55 Milburn and Russell, *Public–Common Partnerships: Building New Circuits of Collective Ownership*, p. 16.

I address in more practical policy terms in the final chapter on "building a bureaucracy from below".

Using the Master's Tools to Dismantle the Master's House

If it is true that "The master's tools will never dismantle the master's house",[56] the master's tools nonetheless radically shape and discipline the slave in any master–slave dialectic. Money and the state are the two master mediators of capitalist social relations. In being necessarily mediated by the state and money, co-operatives and CLTs—like all other tools wielded by commoners—face the constant threat of co-optation and incorporation into state and market logics. Max Weber famously described the modern trap of ratcheting bureaucratisation and instrumental rationalisation of society as the 'iron cage'—an image since borrowed by institutionalists to describe the process of 'institutional isomorphism': the creeping correspondence of individual (especially embryonic) organisations to the tools, procedures and values that dominate and homogenise organisational fields.[57] This process is especially problematic for insurgent organisations attempting to transform emergent fields whose operating principles are still being fought over—such as social entrepreneurs and social innovators in the social economy.[58] Organisational fields which are relatively inchoate, which attempt to insert themselves into institutional ensembles and which pose a potential threat to those ensembles, are placed under enormous pressure to comply with the rules of the game, especially as they attempt to resist bureaucratisation and marketisation. There are always huge incentives in mimicking the behaviours, processes and organisational forms of the dominant players and the main funders of the field, to morph into their image, to become isomorphic with state bureaucracy and capital.

The story of professionalisation and commercialisation of housing associations on Merseyside over the past several decades, their becoming increasingly embroiled in accumulation by dispossession and state regulation of social housing, is an exemplary case of institutional isomorphism. The challenge for collective housing alternatives—if they are to avoid the fate of the housing associations—is to grow by 'going viral'[59] rather than scaling up; to coordinate multi-scalar activities through confederated structures of democratic rather

56 Lorde, *Sister Outsider: Essays and Speeches.*

57 Paul J. Dimaggio and Walter W. Powell, "The Iron Cage Revisited: Institutional Isomorphism and Collective Rationality in Organizational Fields", *American Sociological Review* 48.2 (1983): 147–160.

58 Alex Nicholls, "The Legitimacy of Social Entrepreneurship: Reflexive Isomorphism in a Pre-Paradigmatic Field", *Entrepreneurship: Theory and Practice* 34.4 (2010): 611–633.

59 Tom Moore and David Mullins, "Scaling-Up or Going Viral? Comparing Self-Help

than bureaucratic governance; to harness their existing legal powers to resist commodification, such as asset locks, and innovate new forms of legal constitution when such tools lose their power to resist capital; and to use the resources of the state and the mediums of money and markets only sparingly whilst developing alternative self-funding mechanisms and means of circulating the common.

Disciplined by isomorphic pressures towards bureaucratisation, largely dependent on the capital circuit for resources for survival and, at the same time, struggling to expand the circuit of the common—collective housing alternatives must be excellent shape-shifters, able to adapt flexibly to suit the requirements of different gatekeepers and powerbrokers whilst staying true to original principles. This shape-shifting ability—restated in the metaphor of communicating inwardly, upwardly and outwardly to suit different audiences—is the subject of the Epilogue. In this language game, constructing institutional structure around a project is necessary in order to gain the trust of stakeholders, attract funding, simplify decision-making and codify vision and strategy into workable day-to-day procedures, thereby enabling the reproduction of values. Movement and institution, verb and noun—*constituent* power and *constituted* power—form a difficult dialectic. In this there is a constant interplay between creativity and codification. In seeking to establish codifications for the endurance and replication of projects over time, we run the risk of diluting, paralysing and fossilising into inflexible bureaucratic structures the informal, spontaneous and creative energies animating radical collective action. The challenge becomes one of expressing and sustaining the original energies through and within—not outside of—codified structures. These constitutions of power must be flexible and open enough to allow for adaptation and learning through their periodic reimagining and reengineering by constituents—yet stable and legible enough to maintain continuity and legitimacy. Just as radical legal theorists such as Davina Cooper are taking a more creative approach to reimagining the state[60]—as an institutional structure amenable to being transformed through performative and prefigurative practices—so too can collective housing constituents become more proactive in reinventing the legal and organisational models that channel their energies towards common goals. They must avoid fetishising CLTs or co-ops—or any other model—as somehow the end in itself whilst recognising their performative power, if continually (re)designed in the right way, to enact new worlds and defend against entrapment within the iron cage of rationalisation and commodification. There is always a risk in becoming complacent

Housing and Community Land Trust Facilitation", *Voluntary Sector Review* 4.3 (2013): 333–353.

60 Cooper, Dhawan and Newman, *Reimagining the State: Theoretical Challenges and Transformative Possibilities*; Cooper, "Prefiguring the State".

about the power of models to embody and enact social change; the fate of the Eldonians' development trust EGL—its mission drift, commercialisation and collapse—provides a salutary lesson.

That being said, so long as the master's house remains the principal source of subsistence and shelter and the main measure of value, the master's tools remain the only instruments to hand by which to forge new tools that *can* do the dismantling. Co-ops and CLTs have been forged out of a compromised reconfiguration of the master's tools, as imperfect institutional articulations of a housing commons that each in their own specific way promotes a bespoke bundle of common and individual rights in relation to property as presently conceived under capitalism. For instance, the CLT model appears to strike a more even balance than the co-op model, perhaps, between individual and collective property interests: safeguarding individuals' rights to a share of equity, which can be tweaked according to context. The contradictions created for commoners in appropriating the master's tools—when counteracting circuits of value, capital and common, come into contact—is illustrated by more than one conundrum facing the CLT movement in particular. To recap: according to the classic American model that has become canonical internationally, CLTs separate the ownership of land from that of any improvements upon it, notably buildings. This enables the community—present and future residents—to hold the land in trust through a form of stewardship; whilst the buildings themselves—homes or businesses—can be leased or 'owned' by individuals according to covenants that govern things like resale or lease value. But the CLT's ownership of the land is at best abstract and nominal. In practice, occupants of the buildings enjoy full use rights to the property except for just one specific right—the right to exchange for market value, which is curtailed by CLT covenants. The notion that the land under the buildings can somehow be abstracted from its social use and 'owned' by the CLT is a total fiction—for owning land means enjoying the full bundle of rights, from protection against eviction to the ability to dispose of it on the market, which the model forbids CLTs from doing. Thus a group of American scholars[61] are beginning to reconceptualise the CLT model as a 'fiction' which "buries" the rights usually associated with property ownership, in that they cannot actually be exercised by actors. By explaining its operations within the conceptual scaffolding of the ownership model, the CLT 'shores up' the private property relation and, by the same token, speaks in the language—wrought by the master's tools—that people accustomed to property rights will understand. Its focus on land as an organising device is

61 Joseph Pierce, Richard Kruger, Azadeh Hadizadeh Esfahani et al., "Ownership Is a Habit of Mind: How Community Land Trusts Expose Key Consensual Fictions of Urban Property", *Urban Geography* (forthcoming).

both its greatest weakness (in terms of transforming property relations) and its greatest strength (in communicating an idea that may otherwise seem so alien to aspiring homeowners).

A further contradiction resides in how land and housing are valued in CLTs. How can the CLT set rents and resale prices, or indeed borrow money for further development using its land 'assets' as equity, if the CLT-owned share of the property bundle—the land abstracted from the building—is ultimately unrealisable as exchange value? If the entire premise of the CLT idea is to take land off the market *in perpetuity*, how can any market value be attached to its assets? A potentially fatal flaw in this 'dialectic of value' is that whilst low-income residents are helped to realise a form of homeownership within a CLT, they are at the same time prevented from realising the equity of their investments elsewhere, owing to the discrepancy between their equity share in the CLT—whose value is decoupled from the market to ensure security of tenure—and the general rise in property prices in local, national and international capitalist markets.[62] For low- and middle-income people alike, this 'liquidity trap' may amount to a kind of spatial entrapment. Only the large-scale expansion of CLTs through institutional coordination—and their connection and cooperation with other movements for the common—can resolve such seemingly intractable problems. Such contradictions underline the curious fact that when people enter into a contract with a CLT, what they are 'buying into' is not the property value of the capitalist market so much as a narrative about a different way of conceiving and distributing value. Capitalism has some powerful ideological buttressing shoring up its own conception of value as commodity form—from folkloric tales and popular historical narratives to scientific 'discoveries' such as the tragedy of the commons. It is to the utility of narrative as a tool for the outward expansion of the common circuit for housing (partly through reflection on what it has done—and continues to do—for capital) that I now turn.

62 Sarah Ilene Stein, "Wake up Fannie, I Think I Got Something to Say to You: Financing Community Land Trust Homebuyers without Stripping Affordability Provisions", *Emory Law Journal* 60.1 (2015): 209–249.

CHAPTER 14

On (Myth) Making History

Narrative, story-telling and myth-making may help sustain collective energies in making the difficult transition all collective housing alternatives must make if they are to succeed—that from the exciting events punctuating political struggle to the more mundane, complicated work of building new institutional processes; moving "from the 'military' administration to the 'civil' one" once the campaign has been won.[1] Writing about the curiously interwoven phenomena of Brexit and Englishness, journalist James Meek presents two myths bound up with English national identity, Robin Hood and St George—a juxtaposition that might shed some light on this transition. The Brexiteers' narrative of 'taking back control' of British sovereignty from a 'bureaucratic', 'elitist' and 'anti-democratic' European Union through the victory of a popular referendum is likened to the event of St George slaying the dragon with one fell swoop of his sword. In contrast, the myth of Robin Hood—stealing from the rich to give to the poor in an ongoing, incremental process of vigilante redistribution—appears to better represent "slow, complicated, boring Robin Hood-like achievements such as the National Health Service, progressive taxation and universal education" but which "yield in the folk-narrative of England to St George-like releases".[2] Meek puts it succinctly: "Robin Hood is a process; St George is an event … Robin Hood is justice; St George is victory". Just as the event of Brexit is contrasted in this way with the process of post-war welfare state institutionalisation, so too can the victorious campaigns to reclaim a housing commons in Liverpool be likewise juxtaposed with the subsequent struggle to build institutional structures for the long-term survival, growth and replication of collective alternatives. Whilst "the slaying of the dragon is quick, easy to remember, and easy to celebrate", Meek remarks, the ongoing process of institutionalisation is "slow, complicated, boring".

Whatever we think of the politics of Brexit—and I draw no direct comparison here with the substance of radical housing politics—Meek's analogy nonetheless provides some interesting lessons for understanding the institutionalisation of

1 Alan McDonald, *The Weller Way: The Story of the Weller Street Housing Cooperative* (Faber & Faber, 1986), p. 203.

2 James Meek, "Brexit and Myths of Englishness", *London Review of Books* 40.19 (2018): 17–20 (p. 17).

collective housing alternatives. Focusing on St George-like events over Robin Hood-like processes makes for a more exciting and dramatic narrative. It enlivens the telling of history with characters, drama, battles between enemies and victories against all odds; but it tends to simplify, personify and dramatise history and, therefore, necessarily misses other, more complicated, perhaps more boring but also more important aspects of the story. This is evident in how I conjured my own mythic tale of a grand battle between two forces—seeing housing like a noun or like a verb: between technocratic comprehensive redevelopment and democratic collective alternatives—with obvious connotations of good versus evil, of allies and enemies. But if we see St George-like events and Robin Hood-like processes as part of a dialectical whole rather than as distinct entities, it is clear that I have focused more on the first counterpart of this dialectic—on the eventful and almost mythic beginnings of collective housing alternatives—than on their ongoing institutionalisation. Liverpool's history demonstrates that campaigns flow from proactive, disruptive and often extra-legal attempts to claim a common right to place. The Weller Street Co-op asserted their right to stay together as a community against the council policy of slum clearance and rehousing. The Eldonians likewise refused displacement, and occupied Portland Gardens during council attempts to municipalise the co-op. Langrove initiated an occupation against demolition, and so too did Granby residents resist the bulldozers through direct action. These were all campaigns about gaining popular democratic control, some kind of sovereignty, from an overbearing authority, albeit one located at the scale of the local state rather than supra-national level. They are all great stories of fights won against the odds. However, the long-term survival and viability of collective control over the means of social reproduction is, in all these cases, dependent on the construction of new institutions to incubate and support such practices as well as on state support to authorise and finance community acquisition of land and recognise its legal ownership. The campaign battle itself only commences the longer-term struggle to build institutional durability. As Billy Floyd is reported to have proclaimed at the carnivalesque street party celebrating the Weller Street's completion of their cooperative scheme in 1982: "This is not the end, it's the beginning".[3]

Myth-making is all too often overlooked in its power to communicate and replicate like a meme the enduring value and meaning of any counter-hegemonic movement, not least cooperativism and commons, in galvanising popular and political support and in keeping the co-operative spirit alive amongst co-operators long after the campaign struggle is over. Following political theorist William Clare Roberts' exploration of the socialist, communist and mutualist myths and discourses that animated Marx's writing of *Capital*, we can define myths as

3 Gibson, *Counterweight: The Neighbourhood Option*, p. 23.

> the stories we tell ourselves and one another to make shorthand sense of the world. They are not true in the way that science is, but that is neither here nor there. They are action-guiding, meaning-giving, and their truth or falsity is an ethical and political question, not merely an epistemological one.[4]

We need new myths that can help transform what seems ideologically impossible today into real possibilities tomorrow—'demanding the urban impossible' as Chatterton encapsulates it.[5] Liverpool has a particular penchant for myth-making. Its foundational myth as a city of radicals helps narrate its rich history of collective action—more on which below. But it does not mean that collective alternatives cannot happen anywhere else. In order to move beyond the confining perspective of people and place—beyond colourful characters and one-off St George-like events—we need stories that tap into the popular imagination, speak to shared experience and inspire a new common sense.

Liberal and neoliberal protagonists know this all too well. Take, for instance, the myth of the commons. In *The Tragedy of the Commons*, Garrett Hardin presents the concept of property as the only logical solution to the tragic inevitability of the 'free-rider problem', in which unowned and unmanaged resources available to all are said always to result in overuse and underinvestment owing to self-interested short-termist competitive individualism—with a strict choice between distribution of private property rights or public ownership by state management. Hardin is hardly original—the myth can be traced back as far as Aristotle's philosophical concept of the distribution of care, in which humans were said to be more careful with things they can call their own than with those owned in common. There is a performative power to this myth: the assumed root cause of the tragedy of the commons—selfish individualism—is better seen as a symptom of the successful transmission of such powerful parables buttressing the hegemony of private property. The lack of counter-narratives or popular myths that tell positive stories about the commons is all too evident. Nick Blomley quips: "the tragedy of the commons ... is less its supposed internal failures than its external invisibility".[6]

Hobbes' *Leviathan* represents another powerful (neo)liberal-propagated parable that has successfully permeated our collective consciousness. The state of nature that Hobbes imagined as defining human existence before the invention of the sovereign state to arbitrate a 'social contract' was one in which, without the protection of the Leviathan and the tacit collective agreement to be governed by its rules, life was notoriously 'solitary, poor, nasty, brutish, and

4 Roberts, *Marx's Inferno: The Political Theory of Capital*, p. 33.

5 Chatterton, "The Urban Impossible: A Eulogy for the Unfinished City".

6 Blomley, *Unsettling the City*, p. 8.

short'. That this tale has embedded itself deep within our cultural fabric as to make the need for a powerful state to rule over us appear intuitively obvious—so much so that the social contract has become the conceptual starting point for all subsequent Western political philosophy working in the liberal tradition, from Rousseau to Rawls—says more about the ideological power of this fable than it does about its historical accuracy. Communitarians and anarchists such as Kropotkin have long contested this narrative by telling another story—a myth in mirror image—in which humans are said to have lived in relatively peaceful, materially abundant and highly co-operative self-organised tribes in which mutual aid, gift relations and reciprocity predominated over hierarchical command or exchange relations and that it was, in fact, only with the consolidation of the Leviathan in the emergence of empires and nation-states that violence, war, competition and brutal domination became such common facets of human existence. The historical record suggests the reality is rather more complicated; that these tendencies existed concurrently. Recent anthropological and archaeological evidence attests that parasitical state-like bureaucracies emerged in ancient agrarian societies in order to measure, coordinate, collect and appropriate the mass harvesting of grains to supply surpluses.[7] Outside of this hegemony, pre-agrarian humans adopted radically different social arrangements depending on the seasons, allowing authoritarian structures within small bands to predominate at certain times, during hunting for instance, whilst gathering together in very large numbers to form temporary, self-organised, horizontally governed proto-city-states during times of feast and plenty.[8] This suggests several things: that our pre-agrarian ancestors were more adept at flexibly adapting their institutional arrangements to changing contexts and adopting different social roles within such structures; that egalitarianism is not the mainstay of small tribes or communes, which can be just as authoritarian and dominating as states; and that egalitarian city-states were commonplace long before the advent of bureaucracy or capitalism. The corollary is that we can relearn the lost art of institutional innovation and flexibility; that libertarian socialism at the scale of the state is a real possibility under the right conditions.

The Left—especially the radical revolutionary Left—has been pretty good at conjuring myths too. We might see Engels' argument in *The Housing Question* as belonging to that powerful mythological tradition presented as scientific socialism and depicting the proletarian takeover of the state through insurrectionary action as the only way to defeat capitalism and inaugurate communism—the very same tradition that inspired so many violent revolutions across the world and established the authoritarian Soviet Union. Whilst

7 James C. Scott, *Against the Grain: A Deep History of the Earliest States* (Yale University Press, 2017).

8 David Graeber and David Wengrow, "How to Change the Course of Human History (at Least, the Part That's Already Happened)", *Eurozine* (2 Mar. 2018).

we can say that Marxist mythology had powerful material and social effects on the world, it is also true to say that it has not always created a better world nor, indeed, brought about anything resembling post-capitalism—only a highly centralised, productivist and undemocratic form of state-socialism nonetheless participating in the capitalist world economy. The Revolution as envisaged by the Leninist strain in Marxist thought is much like St George slaying the dragon. It is a strategy that foregrounds the event itself as the end goal without due consideration of how to sustain its energy after the clamour and fervour is depleted. It would appear that the Left is much better at inventing complex yet compelling mythologies about the structural power of capitalism and the ultimate futility of any attempt to make capital impotent—short of slaying the proverbial dragon—than it is at creating utopian visions that both inspire and sustain incremental action in the here and now.

Engels' dramatisation of the Marxist myth through the characters of Proudhon and his fellow anarchists—rendering them as little more than utopian dreamers—has done untold damage to the task of resolving the housing question as well as to the intellectual coherence, political cohesion and tactical success of the Left, broadly conceived. In an early chapter in his unfinished work *Acid Communism*, the late cultural theorist Mark Fisher provides insight into how the Left has been riven with division by such misguided myth-making—in ways we can trace through Liverpool's history of cooperative housing. Fisher describes the two leftist foes of democratic socialism or libertarian communism—what could just as easily apply to the co-operative movement and its two successive opponents, Liverpool Council's labour organisation, the Works Department, and, later, the Militant Tendency-controlled administration:

> The first obstructive figure of the left was the complacent steward of Cold War organised labour or social democracy: backward-looking, bureaucratic, resigned to the "inevitability" of capitalism, more interested in preserving the income and status of white men than in expanding the struggle to include, this figure is defined by compromise and eventual failure.
>
> The other figure—what I want to call the Harsh Leninist Superego—is defined by its absolute refusal of compromise. According to Freud, the superego is characterised by the quantitatively and qualitatively excessive nature of its demands: whatever we do, it's never enough. The Harsh Leninist Superego mandates a militant ascesis. The militant will be single-mindedly dedicated to the revolutionary event, and unflinchingly committed to the means necessary to bring it about.[9]

9 Mark Fisher, *K-Punk: The Collected Writings of Mark Fisher (2004–2016)* (Repeater, 2018).

Whilst the first allegorical figure is perhaps too caught up in slow, boring, complicated bureaucratic procedures to remember the point of galvanising moments of resistance to the collective struggle for transformation, the second is so fixated on the revolutionary event itself that he (again, probably a man) misses the importance of practice. This is just another formulation of the dialectic of means and ends. The promise of collective housing alternatives lies in treading an alternative path between these two extremes—a radical reformism that shuns compromise but prizes cooperation. For collective alternatives to flourish, we need a refocusing of the ends and means in campaigning and institutionalisation. Engels' housing question will not be resolved without the slow, complicated, boring work of cultivating Robin Hood-like practices of commoning and institutions for the commons that may prefigure a post-capitalist future from within 'the cracks of capital'[10] by working 'in, against and beyond the state'.[11] Working within the state to move beyond it speaks to a myth that economic geographer Andy Cumbers identifies amongst commons advocates—the myth of civil society. Here, the imagined possibility of radical autonomy for the commons from state-capitalism rests on the liberal myth of the abstract separability of the domains of state, market and civil society when in reality they cannot be separated as all are interrelated. Power works relationally, *through and between* these relations, not as some entity that can be possessed in isolation. If the commons does indeed transcend these oppositions, then housing commons are to emerge and to be cultivated in the spaces in between.

From Heroic Event to Boring Bureaucratic Process

The art of myth-making seems to run against the grain of (whilst remaining deeply embedded within) our modern mentalities. Max Weber charted how modernity entailed a disenchantment from superstitious, mythical, spiritual and heroic ways of seeing the world and, through the Enlightenment, their secularisation and rationalisation into scientific and bureaucratic systems.[12] In *The Utopia of Rules*, David Graeber follows Weber to present bureaucracy as the neutral, transparent and value-free form of regulation and administration which defines modernity and, importantly for my argument here, appears to be diametrically opposed to the heroic, mythic and folkloric societies of the pre-modern periods that went before it. Bureaucracy as an 'ideal type' is stripped bare of all notions of heroism, chivalry, honour, valour, ritual, custom, magic and the epic battles between good and evil that

10 Holloway, *Crack Capitalism*.

11 Andrew Cumbers, "Constructing a Global Commons in, against and beyond the State", *Space and Polity* 19.1 (2015): 62–75.

12 Karl Löwith, *Max Weber and Karl Marx* (Routledge, 1993).

seem to have marked ancient and medieval societies and, instead, embodies distinctly bureaucratic codes—there are the principles of value-free, rule-bound neutrality (disavowing notions of good and evil); indifference (that the rules are the same for everyone, the law is indifferent between persons and their characteristics); regularity and predictability (that actions by the state are routinely and evenly applied across events of a similar kind); mechanical operation (that actions are taken not according to stories or human interpretation but through machine-like detachment) and, lastly, transparency (rules are supposed to be clear, uniformly expressed, and accessible to all).[13] Whilst bureaucracy pertains to a certain comforting routine and assurance in being treated equally and transparently by the Leviathan—a 'utopia of rules'—it also entails a certain amount of disillusionment and alienation.

There is certainly a sense in which the phenomenon of 'post-development blues'—the deflation experienced by so many participants in Liverpool's co-op movement as the excitement of campaign victory dissipated and the reality of managing and maintaining a housing development set in—involves a disenchantment and disillusionment from the world as it once was, animated by collective spirits, as bureaucratic routines replace more dynamic events. Juxtaposing exciting events and boring institutional processes captures something intractable standing in the way of developing collective alternatives from sporadic campaigns into durable institutions. Much of the tailing off of individual commitments to collective dweller control can be attributed to the inevitable burn-out and anti-climactic come-down from the intensity of the struggle. But keeping the original participants interested in the ongoing development of co-ops and CLTs is not the only issue. Not only are routine jobs more mundane, technical and laborious, but the people doing them inevitably change, as some people move on, older are replaced by younger generations and—to invert a criticism levelled at the Eldonians—revolutionaries do eventually retire, just like the rest of us. The second and third generations of the Liverpool co-op member-residents do not have personal memories of severe housing need—they lack the life-defining experience of solidarity in struggle—which helped motivate the first generation to manage co-ops directly. Much of the voluntary 'heavy-lifting' required—financial, staffing, facilities management, repairs, allocations, legal services—is complex and demanding, not to mention 'boring', so it is understandable why residents are happy to offload these responsibilities onto trained specialists such as NWHS. For these reasons, the creation of folktales and myths about the collective struggle remains important for transmitting the value of cooperation down the generations.

Myth-making, however, can be dangerous. Campaigners can all too easily become intoxicated by their own mythologies—with potentially poisonous

13 David Graeber, *The Utopia of Rules: On Technology, Stupidity, and the Secret Joys of Bureaucracy* (Melville House, 2015).

consequences. This is precisely what happened to Weller Street: they got so carried away with their own self-asserted image as pioneers of radical autonomy that they alienated other co-ops, their potential allies and partners, leading to the collapse of their independent secondary agency before it even really got going. They got so drunk on the narrative they had constructed of their independence and autonomy (their motto, as Alan McDonald described it, was 'professionals on tap, not on top!')[14] that they overlooked the fact that CDS were instrumental in their success. They created an origin story that denied the role of their 'mother' co-op, who they then disowned, even attempting 'matricide'. Similarly, Granby CLT may have succumbed to the power of their own myth of 'do-it-yourself' insurgent urbanism. Their history of successfully challenging the council, preventing HMR demolition and taking ownership over the four streets through direct action, coupled with the resourceful culture of guerrilla gardening and experimentation with commoning has led to a celebration of amateurism and activism over expertise and professionalism. This 'cult of the amateur' has only been fuelled further by Assemble's involvement (none of the collective is RIBA qualified) and the Turner Prize endorsement of their self-styled amateurism—their unconventional, anti-professional and distinctively experimental methods of engaging people in architecture and urban design. Such a celebration of amateurs was very much in evidence in the Weller Street Co-op, too. One of their many mottos, in Tony Gibson's account, proudly proclaims that "Professionals built the Titanic. Amateurs built the Ark".[15]

Residents do, indeed, generally know better than experts about the nature of their own neighbourhood and housing needs; the successes of the new-build co-ops and the CLTs alike are testament to that. Arrogant rejection of professional knowledge, however, can lead to poor results. In Granby, this has had implications for the project that suggest professional expertise is not to be so easily dismissed. For instance, before they can begin retrofitting, Terrace 21 are currently awaiting the legal transfer of their allocated houses from the council—a decision that rests with Homes England (the quango formerly known as the Homes and Communities Agency and before that the Housing Corporation). This decision hinges on the removal of a covenant that stipulates the buildings cannot be transferred out of public ownership owing to the public subsidy, not least through HMR, that has been invested in them over the years. It is the regulatory remit of Homes England to ensure that state-funded assets are being disposed of in the public interest. Whilst Terrace 21 are waiting, Granby CLT has simply gone ahead with the renovation of their properties (likewise subject to this covenant) without consent—doing as they have done countless times before. There is a certain sense in which

14 McDonald, *The Weller Way*.

15 Gibson, *Counterweight: The Neighbourhood Option*, p. 113.

this is an admirable 'can do' attitude to gets things done by transgressing bureaucratic and legal boundaries. Yet there is also a feeling, shared by some observers and fellow travellers, that such bold action is not always guided by deliberate intention but often done out of ignorance, owing perhaps to the lack of specialist construction and legal knowledge among Assemble and the CLT. Indeed, the mythology built up around campaigns—particularly when emphasising the heroic activist or amateur architect—can have detrimental impacts on relationships with professionals and experts who are critical to the success of inherently complex projects in the built environment. What is needed, therefore, is not a complete renunciation of professionalism but a new kind of professional that integrates an amateur do-it-yourself attitude and democratic approach with expert knowledge.

As society becomes increasingly bureaucratised, myths—through dialectical association—maintain an even greater hold over our collective consciousness. For Graeber, this explains the recent resurgence in grand mythic and mystical tales, magical realms and fantasy worlds in literature, cinema and gaming that we see in such popular cultural phenomena as *Game of Thrones*, *Harry Potter*, *Lord of the Rings*, *Dungeons and Dragons* and *The Lion, the Witch and the Wardrobe*. (Recall that Narnia is used as an image to convey the mystical world of 'Eldonia'.) Even fantasy sci-fi worlds set in a distant future such as *Star Wars* conjure up a lost heroic past, pitting the evil and thoroughly bureaucratic Galactic Empire against the romantic figures of The Resistance. Graeber also cites the strange confluence of mythic or heroic narrative devices within archetypally bureaucratic contexts as further evidence of the tightening grip of bureaucracy—*Sherlock Holmes*, *James Bond*, countless American cop shows, even *Harry Potter*, all present heroes working within more confined, ordinary bureaucratic settings of law enforcement, state espionage or boarding schools. The growing popularity of such cultural forms is, claims Graeber, largely explicable as "an attempt to imagine a world utterly purged of bureaucracy, which readers enjoy both as a form of vicarious escapism and as reassurance that, ultimately, a boring, administered world is probably preferable to any imaginable alternative".[16] (Hence *utopia* of rules.) Interestingly, the Terrace 21 co-op in Granby was originally named the Northern Alliance Housing Co-operative by its founder Ed Gommon as a subtle nod towards the Rebel Alliance of *Star Wars*.[17] Asked why they rebranded it Terrace 21, leading members suggest it was partly because it had become commonly abbreviated to NAHC and "NAHC sounds too officious and bureaucratic!"

16 Graeber, *The Utopia of Rules: On Technology, Stupidity, and the Secret Joys of Bureaucracy*.
17 Ed's greater inspiration was the Afghan freedom fighter Ahmad Shah Massoud, the Lion of the Panjshir and leader of the Northern Alliance against the Taliban. The original vision for the Northern Alliance Housing Cooperative was for a rebel network of rehab co-ops across northern cities hit by HMR.

The dialectic of heroic event and bureaucratic process presented here—and in the myths of St George and Robin Hood—speaks to a number of tensions latent within movements for collective housing alternatives. One is an apparent incompatibility between bureaucratic organisation and democracy, as articulated by Weber and other social theorists such as Robert Michels. Michels' 'iron law of oligarchy' holds that the need for organisational leadership inevitably leads to the creation of a bureaucracy controlled by an undemocratic elite—those we might now call technocrats—who govern on claims to expertise that therefore disavow direct popular participation. We can see these tendencies at work in Liverpool where processes of professionalisation have led to the bureaucratic co-optation and dilution of democratic values. A 'tendency to oligarchy', argued Colin Ward,[18] following Michels, operates within all forms of human organisation; co-ops and CLTs—conceived as institutionalisations of a housing commons—are certainly not exempt. For instance, we see a tendency towards abstraction in the Eldonian model—with a growing gap between ends and means as the project has scaled up. Very little active direct participation from residents in the decision-making and management of their housing means the village is run more like an efficient community-based housing association or parish council than a mutual. Residents treat the management of their housing and environment as a service provided to them as of right rather than a co-produced benefit of collective self-government.

A big question left unanswered by collective housing advocates (myself included) hangs on whether deep engagement really matters. Should declining levels of participation in the cooperative self-management of housing be seen as a problem or, conversely, a mark of success? What if, for instance, the efficiencies of scale produced by the Eldonians (or, by extension, the municipal state) mean that residents are freed to engage in other worthwhile activities for which they may be better suited, and which may have a deeper social value and political impact than the mere management of housing? How does this change our assessment of Eldonia the 'nanny state'? Is there not a sense in which the bureaucratisation of (public) housing as a universally provided, efficiently delivered, transparently regulated service would allow for the freeing up of our imaginations and energies for other, more worthwhile activities like the pursuit of knowledge, care and love or the arts, crafts and sciences? This depends, perhaps, on whether one thinks of the design, construction and maintenance of housing as an intrinsic part of the art of living, a craft in itself, or as a means to an end, a mere administrative burden.

It is worth dwelling on the tension between professionals and residents—bureaucracy and democracy—running through attempts to construct collective housing alternatives. In cases where this relationship had not been cultivated with enough care and consideration, we see deleterious results. Liverpool's

18 Ward, *Anarchy in Action*.

1970s co-ops were much better than the Eldonians at inculcating participation and cooperation within their smaller communities, but their exclusionary and inward-facing 'waggon train' urban designs produced a problematic legacy. Where professionals had a good relationship with their client co-op (as in the case of architect Bill Halsall and Weller Street) they produced arguably more successful urban designs. But where these two forces clashed rather than co-operated (as in the case of the council town planner confronting the will of Leta-Claudia Co-op) the results have been less sensitive to the tried and tested principles of the urban design discipline, such as public openness, legibility, permeability and connectivity.

Bureaucracy and expertise are important brakes on darker tendencies latent within heroic or parochial perspectives on the world. Defensive designs were not so much a spatial expression of the co-op model as they were a popular response to Liverpool's threatening environment marked by deprivation, dilapidation, crime, sectarian violence and state-led displacement. Many co-ops turned their backs on the city, setting a trend as exemplars of defensible space that would inform the policy development of secured-by-design. Such defensive (sub)urbanism created spatial divisions in an already divided city: splintering Liverpool's urban environment and ramifying the sense of parochialism and disconnection, as "a city of a thousand villages" (a common phrase said of Liverpool) sharply divided between localist neighbourhoods. It risks adding new layers to a history of sectarianism: producing isolated clusters of 'militant particularisms',[19] incapable of drawing strength from cooperation and solidarity, and disconnected from the wider struggle for urban land reform. Communication, mutual learning and movement-building are made all the more difficult by such a context.

These lessons garnered from the juxtaposition of mythic event and bureaucratic process highlight a number of implications for movement- and institution-building. First, it suggests the need to create and embed within new institutional forms the bureaucratic procedures and governance processes that will ensure the long-term reproduction of practices of commoning and common management of housing as the founding members and original activists are, over time, succeeded by future generations. Second, it highlights that institutional structures need to be developed that are capable of countering uncooperative tendencies embedded in histories of sectarianism, mistrust of authorities and urban angst in order to instil new practices of cooperation, mutual aid and solidarity amongst those whose experience tells them otherwise. Third, it suggests we need to make the bureaucratic tasks of such institutions as collectively governable, legible and meaningful as possible

19 David Harvey, "Militant Particularism and Global Ambition: The Conceptual Politics of Place, Space, and Environment in the Work of Raymond Williams", *Social Text* 42 (1995): 69–98.

so that member-residents can do it themselves. At the same time, we need to ensure that professional expertise is built into coordinating structures from the outset. How can we (re)configure an institutional infrastructure to support the development of expertise, close the gap between professionals and residents and make the former more accountable to the latter—to create an institutional infrastructure that is more democratic? In short, how do we go about *building a bureaucracy from below*? Before attempting to answer this question, I want to consider one more salient myth that raises the issue of replicability.

The Myth of Liverpool Exceptionalism

Approaching collective housing development through the lens of myth-making has one last lesson to teach us. It is very tempting to mythologise this history of collective housing experimentation as a product of Liverpool's unique cultural character—its 'exceptionalism' as a 'city of radicals' oft-suggested to be 'in but not of England'. Such a reading of history would emphasise the particularities of people and place—foregrounding Liverpool's unusual socio-geographical position at the crossroads of continents and its unique historical traditions—in explaining why the city became host to these events and movements. How might such a myth be constructed? It would start by building on the 'foundational myth' of Liverpool as a radical, revolutionary city—the 1911 strike and the anarcho-syndicalism that infused its culture of political militancy, whose legacy was arguably the Trotskyist Militant Tendency.[20] Tony Lane, amongst others, claims anarcho-syndicalism had a subtly pervasive impact on Liverpool culture and urban politics: first seeping into land-based industries via anarchic seafarers regularly moving between different occupations, who "in their wake left traces of their experience and habits of mind"; eventually infusing into broader community-based action over council housing as the "democratic moment, born and then nurtured in the workplace, took wing and outflew its origins".[21]

We can see the spirit of Liverpool's distinctively anarchic, firebrand politics embodied in some of the more politically motivated co-op campaigns—Weller Street, Leta-Claudia, Thirlmere, the Eldonians and Langrove—in their bolshie challenge to local authority plans for rehousing, and the pride of place given to direct action in their repertoire of contention. Critical in driving forward these campaigns were strong community organisers and charismatic leaders. Their figureheads tended to be authoritative and powerful men—the likes of Billy Floyd and Tony McGann—who, as we have seen, were so often characterised in terms of heroic acts of war fought

20 Ball, "'Militant Liverpool' as Liverpool Exceptionalism: The Rise, Fall and Character of the City Council, 1983–1987".

21 Lane, *Liverpool: City of the Sea*, pp. 116, 135.

against the council. Here we are back in the realm of St George. Most of the co-op organising, however, was done by women through established neighbourhood networks. Later co-ops were even more female-led, especially in Kirkby, galvanised by mostly young single mothers seeking better housing conditions for their families. Thus we can trace another strand of influence in Liverpool's exceptional growth of co-ops to the traditionally 'matriarchal society' of many of its neighbourhoods.

The influence of place-based radicalism may have been fairly direct: coming through certain residents' contact with syndicalist practices in their work on the docks and factories and experience with local trade unionism. There was also perhaps a more circuitous route at play here: anarchist ideas transmitted through families and social networks down the generations to the children of workers involved in direct action. These 'children of the revolution' may have come into contact with radical ideas during their university years of the 1960s, graduating to become those architects, co-op developers and community workers so ideologically committed to cooperativism and who were critical in making the movement. Architects such as Tom Clay for Neighbourhood Housing Services and Bill Halsall for CDS and MIH co-ops are excellent examples of this generation of young radicals, exposed to new ideas in participatory design at university and through their formative work with SNAP, which provided them the tools and inspiration to innovate new models of democratic neighbourhood regeneration in their work with rehab and new-build co-ops respectively. So too were co-ops a kind of political school for member co-operators. Countless working-class residents were empowered by their experience of campaigning to find jobs or to pursue further education for the first time; many others were politicised and radicalised by the process and stood for local election. The influence on Liverpool politics of key councillors—invariably Labour—who cut their teeth in co-op campaigning is palpable. Phil Hughes of Weller Street was instrumental, as Chair of Housing following the deposal of Militant, in securing the future of Langrove Street Co-op, then threatened by Tony Byrne's plans to expand Everton Park. One of Langrove's principal resident-activists, Jane Corbett, is still going strong today, at the time of writing, as Assistant Mayor of Liverpool and Mayoral Lead for Fairness and Tackling Poverty.

Likewise, a large number of the housing managers working with CDS, MIH and LHT were schooled in co-op development. Some have retained their passion for co-ops even as their organisations have mutated into large commercialised bureaucratic behemoths. Riverside (formerly MIH) now working with Langrove to support the development of the first co-op on Merseyside in decades, for instance, would not have been possible were it not for key advocates still working—now in positions of power—within the organisation. In the 1970s, a significant proportion of this new ideologically driven class of urban community professionals came not from Liverpool but from around the country, and even internationally, attracted to the city by its radical reputation, including Paul Lusk from Oxford and Jack McBane from Canada. Thus a virtuous cycle of radical innovation was spun in Liverpool through the 1960s and 1970s: momentum generated by the city's history and reputation attracting innovators from elsewhere, brought into contact with the last remnants of working-class anarcho-syndicalism and the young heirs of this tradition, to co-produce a brief surge of cooperative activism.

We then see a direct thread—embedded in place and local practices—between the co-ops and the subsequent CLT activism several decades later. Many of the vociferous local activists campaigning against HMR were themselves involved in earlier instances of Liverpool radicalism: those leading resistance in Granby had cut their teeth on various forms of activism, such as a women's housing co-op, a radical printing press and voluntary housing action in the 1970s. In Granby, the idea for a co-op, which led to exploration of the CLT model, was originally mooted by, amongst others, Ed Gommon—a longstanding member-resident of one of the early rehab co-ops in L8, Alt Co-op, and the son of one of the leading architects of the new-build co-ops who helped design Hesketh Street and Shorefields as part of the practice Innes Wilkin Ainsley Gommon. This young professional inherited a great deal from the co-op movement to become something of an enthusiast, and the founding member of the Northern Alliance Housing Co-operative, Granby CLT's partner co-op now known as Terrace 21. In Granby we can see the direct lineage from SNAP and the new-build co-op movement to the fruition of the contemporary CLT campaign. Activists there are "continuing the work that SNAP started".

Liverpool's CLT movement, therefore, does not just draw on the rich repository of radicalism embedded in place but so too on another, deeply intertwined Liverpudlian tradition: the borrowing of ideas from across the globe. The idea for Homebaked as a cooperative bakery was largely sourced from Dutch inspiration and the international experience with co-op models embodied in the artist-activist Jeanne van Heeswijk. The CLT idea was first introduced to Anfield by Arena's KTP American study tour, whose participants—community representatives, academics and housing professionals—diffused their new knowledge locally in ways which would inform the later campaign to establish a CLT as part of Homebaked. Terrace 21 co-op activists in Granby sought advice from the academic researchers on the KTP study tour, disseminating the CLT model to Granby, where it gained the approval of residents, winning out over an alternative vision for a purely cooperative scheme.

In these many ways, Liverpool's CLT movement has evolved as a product of place: the descendent of a distinctively local co-op tradition, coming to fruition through the creative collision of ideas from elsewhere. This process of travelling ideas can be likened to that for mobile policies, in which buzzy new models for urban policy such as creative quarters or enterprise zones are mobilised by public professionals and private consultants plugged into global circuits of fast policymaking.[22] Only, with the collective housing models brought to Liverpool, these more alternative ideas are mobilised by a variety of different actors, through slower, more circuitous and sporadic routes—South American self-help traditions via John F.C. Turner and Colin Ward, for instance—reassembling in Liverpool, where they mutate through exposure to local radical traditions—themselves the result of earlier global mobilisations, not least Spanish anarcho-syndicalism—to construct novel assemblages in Homebaked and Granby. These collective alternatives are made up of material practices in participatory planning techniques, developed locally though derived globally, as well as more contemporary ideas associated with claiming the right to the city and reclaiming the urban commons arriving from Europe and the USA. The importance of place to the development of collective housing alternatives in Liverpool is therefore as much a function of Liverpool's international connectedness and hybrid relationality—as a mongrel maritime city made up of bits from elsewhere—as it is the city's distinctive historical-geographical context and cultural character.

The neat narrative I have just sketched of Liverpool as especially fertile ground for collective housing alternatives to take root may well help identify and link together some of the key characters and cultural characteristics that brought all this into play where and when they did but, if we rely too heavily upon such a reading of history—a reading that plays too much into mythological renderings of Liverpool's exceptionalism as a uniquely radical city—it does real damage to the notion that such movements can be replicated and grown elsewhere. If we wish to see collective housing models grow into a counter-hegemonic alternative system of delivering public housing and urban governance—one which can seriously rival and eventually supplant the dominant system of private property and state–market relations—we need to move beyond such particularistic explanation and think in clearer terms what the essential factors are in developing the movement on a more generalisable scale.

Recipes for Revolution: From Cultivating Local Delicacies to Sourcing Essential Ingredients

As I suggested in the prologue, a large part of my interest in delving into the reasons behind the co-op movement's growth is to understand how a certain set of factors came together to produce Liverpool's so-called Co-op Spring or Cooperative Revolution in order to impart insight into the necessary

22 Cristina Temenos and Tom Baker, "Enriching Urban Policy Mobilities Research", *International Journal of Urban and Regional Research* 39.4 (2015): 824–827.

ingredients and possible trajectories of future collective housing movements. Everyone I interviewed was asked why they thought it was Liverpool, of all places, that became host to one of the most vital housing co-operative movements in British history, and why this happened when it did. Almost all interviewees, many of whom were personally involved in Liverpool's co-ops, said something similar: that "it was just of the moment". Other responses were similarly elusive: that "a set of circumstances" peculiar to inner-city Liverpool of the 1970s had made it "ripe for development"; that "a confluence of factors had come together to make it happen" or a "cocktail enabled it to occur" or, alternatively, "a combination of mutual interests" coalesced at the right time and the right place. Others grasped for more elaborate metaphors: the movement was said to "blossom briefly under this kind of political spotlight, showered with money to develop co-ops, but only for a very short time, until the heavens closed again". But all these responses seem to beg the question; they leave the answer tantalisingly hanging.

What are the specific components which make up this 'cocktail', this 'confluence of factors'? From the history I have traced in this book, we can straightforwardly identify seven basic ingredients: (1) housing need amongst communities left unmet by the state and market translating into collective desires for alternatives; (2) strong leadership and social organisation within these communities to lead and organise campaigns; (3) dedicated activists and professionals committed to cooperative principles supported by secondary support networks based locally; (4) availability of cheap and vacant land to develop or empty housing in need of refurbishment; (5) local political will and policy support from council officers; (6) a benign funding and legislative regime at the national scale; and (7) place-based cultural traditions of political radicalism and experimentation with alternatives upon which to draw.

These seven factors align very closely with the coordinates mapped out by Johnston Birchall in his enquiry into the 'hidden history' of cooperative housing in Britain.[23] Like my interviewee above, Birchall employs a horticultural analogy, conjuring a naturalistic, pre-modern image of housing, to distinguish between the seeds, soil, cultivation, environment and climate required for co-ops to take root and blossom: housing needs left unmet; cooperative models that work in practice; charismatic promoters or 'cultivators'; a favourable legal and financial environment; and a conducive psychological, ideological and political climate. Similarly, Homebaked plays on a baking metaphor to suggest the right "recipe for a revolution" with ingredients listed under step-by-step points like 'Find the Correct Oven', 'Set the Right Temperature', 'Use Locally Sourced Ingredients', 'Kneed [sic] with Care' and 'Understand your

23 Birchall, "The Hidden History of Co-operative Housing in Britain"; Birchall, *Building Communities the Co-operative Way.*

Customer'.[24] Evoking the sphere of social reproduction as a key site of struggle, such a baking analogy was employed in Homebaked's early days by co-founder Fred Brown (who is no longer with us):

> Taking the time it needs is a recognised and vital part of the baking process, next to applying heat to produce the best results. Give it the time, give it the resources and try not to prescribe. We nurture each other. As the dough rises, we rise.[25]

Heeding Fred's cautions over being too prescriptive, we might nonetheless ask: what were the essential ingredients in the recipe for Liverpool's Cooperative Revolution? We can see how Liverpool's co-op movement only ever grew amidst relatively conducive financial and legal conditions as well as a favourable political and ideological climate. The 1974 Housing Act and its amendments by key co-op advocates in the heart of the Labour Government—notably Harold Campbell and Reg Freeson—created a hospitable legal and financial environment at the local level. Cultivators were forged in the fire of radical political action of the late 1960s and early 1970s—the second cycle of contention set in motion against capitalist mass consumption and state bureaucracy. This radicalism infused idealistic professionals and urban communities alike. Innovative organisations and practices—like CDS and participatory design processes—were cultivated in this period. A whole ecosystem emerged: multiple development agencies, 'mother' co-ops, competed with each other to spawn daughter co-ops amongst communities with the collective desires to address their housing needs. As these offspring grew in number, strength and confidence, they began to self-organise and create new grassroots organisations, such as the Merseyside Federation of Housing Co-operatives, which in turn provided support to enable further growth and replication.

Fast forward to the twenty-first century and the cataclysmic global economic crash of 2008 ('the strange non-death of neoliberalism')[26] and its political fallout in 2011 ('the year of dreaming dangerously')[27] have precipitated an ideological climate with both new opportunities and new challenges for experimental projects aimed at transformative change. Just as 1968 inaugurated the long decade of the 1970s in which ideas from the counter-culture

24 Sue Potts, *Homebaked—Impact Report: Recipes for Revolutions* (Homebaked, 2014): www.biennial.com/files/pdfs/3216/140509-final-homebaked-impact-report-suepotts.pdf.

25 Quoted in *Becoming Homebaked*, timeline developed by Britt Jurgensen for 'Trainings for the Not-Yet' Exhibition (2020): www.bakonline.org/program-item/trainings-for-the-not-yet/.

26 Colin Crouch, *The Strange Non-Death of Neo-Liberalism* (Polity Press, 2011).

27 Žižek, *The Year of Dreaming Dangerously*.

and the New Left fomented a period of contention and experimentation with new forms of social organisation, including collective housing alternatives, so too can we see similar signs of rupture and transformation in the efflorescence of social movements in the wake of 2008. Nonetheless, it is clear that much has changed since the cooperative heyday of the 1970s. Neoliberalism is still stubbornly stumbling on, if only as a zombie.[28] Neoliberal values have seeped into almost every pore of society; private homeownership ingrained in the national psyche. Public housing—like all things public—has long been in retreat, replaced by a watered-down version called 'social housing'. Public service provision has been privatised and outsourced to quasi-governmental organisations, such as housing associations, or wholly for-profit private consortiums. *Government* has splintered into a fragmented form of *governance*. 'Community' has become a buzzword in urban policy—part of a new localism of offloading welfare responsibilities onto citizens themselves.

As forms of social innovation, collective alternatives have emerged in this context from civil society organisations and social movements outside the state, in reaction to state and market failure, yet are increasingly caught up in a dense web of governance arrangements and actors—across public, private and third sectors—often working at cross-purposes, but sometimes collaboratively and cooperatively in state-funded projects. The state once played a more direct and central role in this process of social innovation, at least in Liverpool. SNAP was a council-commissioned action-research project run by the voluntary housing campaign group Shelter, using state funding to deliver its radical participatory agenda. The co-op movement was effectively bankrolled by central government, via the Housing Corporation, and promoted locally by the Liberal-led council. The Eldonians received unprecedented political and financial support from Thatcher's government. But these sources of support have become increasingly indirect and circuitous—mediated through a confused web of governmental agencies, quangos, arm's-length financial intermediaries, charities, foundations, banks, social investors and private companies. Homebaked was commissioned by Liverpool Biennial, itself funded by a range of state agencies, including Liverpool Council, the Arts Council for England and the EU, and also Peel Holdings, the Merseyside-based private consortium with huge investments in Liverpool's infrastructure and speculative development. Granby has relied on philanthropic capitalism in the shape of social finance from an ex-stockbroker 'mystery millionaire'. The idea for a CLT in Liverpool was first tested out by a large commercialised housing association in Anfield and a state-funded regeneration partnership in Kensington. What all these examples demonstrate is the increasingly complex crossovers, permeable boundaries and multiple enmeshments between grassroots groups and professional companies, housing associations and charities as

28 Crouch, *The Strange Non-Death of Neo-Liberalism.*

well as local and national state actors in the innovation of potentially transformative—but all too often co-opted and compromised—collective housing alternatives.

So how did we get here? The 1988 Housing Act effectively put paid to any further co-op development, causing existing co-ops to "wither on the vine" as one interviewee likened it. The Act placed great pressure on small-scale charitable trusts like CDS, LHT and MIH to expand through mergers, acquisitions and stock transfers—dropping their titular place identities and morphing into placeless commercialised concerns: Plus Dane, Onward Homes, Riverside. Through this process, the place-based system of dedicated secondary development agencies all but dissolved—subsumed within corporate agendas tied to generating exchange value above all else. Committed co-operators working within Plus Dane, after its takeover of CDS, disbanded to reincarnate a secondary organisation in the form of North West Housing Services, which now offers professional support to both Homebaked and Granby as well as most remaining co-ops on Merseyside but which, as I argue below, lacks the democratic impetus for collective alternative development.

Aside from NWHS, the organisations that evolved out of the co-op agencies are now too implicated in large-scale profitable redevelopment—as evident in HMR—to be of much service to CLTs. Homebaked has been lucky enough to have at their disposal the professional contacts and experience of Liverpool Biennial. Granby has been fortunate in finding a social investor to back the project not just with financial but also with cultural capital, helping bring Assemble to the neighbourhood. In the past, these processes of procurement and selection of architects and agents would have been facilitated by CDS et al., but today depends upon the personal connections of activists in a snowballing process of trial and error. Both Granby and Homebaked are privileged by a broad range of professional involvement, but Little Klondyke was not; part of the reason for its failure was the lack of social capital and professional know-how to draw upon. Both Homebaked and Granby have drawn upon advice from independent consultancies, such as Locally Made and URBED, as well as from the national umbrella organisation, the National CLT Network. The other major players are SAVE Britain's Heritage and the Empty Homes Agency, two national campaign organisations with particular ideological interests in conserving architectural heritage and promoting the reuse of empty homes respectively. These two groups have supported CLTs not necessarily as mutual experiments for affordable housing but as instruments conducive to the realisation of their own, albeit related, agendas (the Empty Homes Agency is committed to community self-help, of which CLTs are a significant component). The central involvement of partisan single-issue charities in the development of Liverpool's CLT movement suggests just how far collective housing development has fallen from its height, standing on the shoulders of the state in the 1970s, when co-ops were generously state-funded and systematically developed by a bespoke professional infrastructure.

After 2011, with a renewed localism agenda and funding opportunities for self-help, the premature abandonment of HMR, coupled with slowly changing attitudes in the council, the essential ingredients for collective housing growth began to mix again, only to leave lingering the bad taste of austerity. In a public talk at an academic housing conference in Liverpool in 2016, Ann O'Byrne, then Liverpool Council Member for Housing and political supporter of Granby and Homebaked, revealed the logic behind the council's continued preference for large-scale redevelopment schemes over small-scale community-led projects. Conservative government-led fiscal austerity had entailed 58 per cent cuts to the city's budget, leaving the council little choice—if they wished to protect essential public services from any further cutbacks, to avoid compounding the untold harm already afflicted on thousands of vulnerable people—than to make up the shortfall from other sources. The main alternative method of revenue generation left open to the council is property-led regeneration: selling public land to developers for large capital receipts and then procuring higher council taxes from the more affluent housing built in place of low value terraces—an admission of exploiting the rent gap through state-led 'gentrification by stealth'.[29] Austerity urbanism thus opens with one hand a window of opportunity for small-scale alternative solutions while slamming it shut with the other—forcing the hand of the council to maintain the hegemony of large-scale housing-led development rather than support collective alternatives. This sheds new light on the reasons why Sefton council—similarly hard-hit by austerity—was so indisposed to accept £5 million of central government funding to support Little Klondyke CLT. Austerity urbanism and neoliberalism thus pit potential allies—municipal authorities and collective alternatives—against each other. As alternative forms of public provision, CLTs must now compete with councils and housing associations for control over increasingly scarce public resources.

Collective housing alternatives today risk exposing themselves to unwanted responsibilities for delivering public services on the cheap—and falling through the 'trapdoor of community'.[30] This may be a backdoor route to further privatisation and cutbacks in public services, which are offloaded onto communities, and justified through such discourses as sustainability, self-sufficiency and especially resilience—tacitly promoting community capabilities to defend against structural forces by maintaining the status quo rather than achieve any kind of radical transformation. By reproducing such discourses,

29 Bridge, Butler and Lees, *Mixed Communities: Gentrification by Stealth?*; Kallin and Slater, "Activating Territorial Stigma: Gentrifying Marginality on Edinburgh's Periphery".

30 Steve Herbert, "The Trapdoor of Community", *Annals of the Association of American Geographers* 95.4 (2008): 850–865.

collective alternatives ironically play into the hands of neoliberal austerity. This was certainly the stance of Militant, who saw co-ops as a threat to socialism. Indeed, the values of entrepreneurialism, creativity, self-reliance, flexibility, experimentalism and do-it-yourself initiative so central to Granby CLT and Homebaked—as experimental utopias—are at the same time the values treasured by 'roll-with-it' neoliberalisation: the normalisation into everyday life of enterprise and self-governing capabilities.[31] Granby and Homebaked might be framed as the unwitting agents of austerity urbanism: taking up the slack in a paralysed development model and filling the gap left by the retreating state to reuse derelict housing productively when all else has failed. They may pave the way for the next wave of speculative property development to hit Liverpool after its long decline: rescuing desirable architectural assets from near-destruction, valorising the land and environment through painstaking unpaid voluntary labour—civic volunteerism—and attracting social financiers, artists and architects in nascent waves of gentrification. Yet we must remember that these projects grew out of a community's passion for place and radical ideals; they were not foisted upon them by the state seeking to offload responsibilities. In the cases where this did happen (such as with Kensington's and Anfield's failed experiments) tenants actually resisted the imposition of the CLT idea and rejected the narratives presented to them, which at base were about operational costs and organisational efficiencies. There is perhaps an inbuilt safeguard against neoliberal exploitation of communities within the CLT model: to get it going, residents really have to want to do it.

No less dangerous is an associated tendency for individual projects to pursue a kind of competitive vanguardism—encouraged by neoliberal discourses of austerity localism and community resilience. This risks fragmenting an already fragile CLT movement in Liverpool—dividing and conquering projects before they can be connected through networks of mutual support. To move towards a strategy of mutual 'resourcefulness' rather than self-reliant 'resilience', for which critical geographers Danny MacKinnon and Kate Derickson have argued,[32] the co-op and CLT movements in Liverpool need to build bridges between individual projects and develop those supportive infrastructures and 'enabler' organisations promoted by the likes of John F.C. Turner and embodied by CDS in the late 1970s and later by the Merseyside Federation of Co-ops. It is vital, however, as I argue below, for such enablers—or any kind of bureaucratic structure—to be grounded in the democratic decision-making of grassroots movements.

31 Roger Keil, "The Urban Politics of Roll-with-It Neoliberalization", *City: Analysis of Urban Trends, Culture, Theory, Policy, Action* 13.2–3 (2009): 230–245.

32 Danny MacKinnon and Kate D. Derickson, "From Resilience to Resourcefulness: A Critique of Resilience Policy and Activism", *Progress in Human Geography* 37.2 (2013): 253–270.

If the local state is no longer in a position to help develop institutions for collective alternatives as it was perhaps better placed to do so in the 1970s—and is, in fact, so systematically weakened by a central state apparatus turned against local government by political forces hell-bent on displacing the debts of neoliberalism, via devolved austerity, such that there are more immediate and stronger incentives to work *against* the development of collective alternatives, not least for its own survival—then alternative institutions must be constructed from the ground up. At the same time, the state should not be altogether abandoned. An all-too-common knee-jerk response, particularly among radicals associated with the commons, is to reject the state entirely for its complicity with and takeover by capital and to build alternatives outside its institutional walls. But as we have seen in the historical rise and fall (and recent rediscovery) of the foundational economy—first with municipal socialism in the 1890s and later with post-war institutions such as the NHS—the state is very much amenable to be harnessed for interests and causes other than capital; that its relative receptivity in this regard comes in waves shaped by cycles of contention and their structural undercurrents. Reforming the state and reshaping its institutions to the benefit of collective alternatives, then, is an important—and possible—task to be undertaken alongside incubating social innovations in the cracks of capitalism. So, how do we go about this dual strategy of building alternatives outside the state whilst simultaneously attempting to reinvent the state from the inside? What are the tools available in the current conjuncture that can generate momentum for a new wave of collective alternatives?

CHAPTER 15

Building a Bureaucracy from Below

What would a bureaucracy for the democratic development of collective alternatives look like? If Public Sector Housing 2.0 never quite took off in the 1970s, how might it do so today? If we recall that a housing commons is both a material resource pool (e.g., common land) and a set of social practices (commoning)—both noun and verb—then we need institutions that can, on the one hand, provide resources for specialist advice and acquire land and housing for (re)development and, on the other, cultivate practices of commoning through education. Education and a supportive infrastructure are fundamental if we are to see collective alternatives developed more proactively by others than those already interested ideologically or motivated by reaction to need left unmet. In short, we need agencies that can offer resources for housing development and professional support and complementary organisations that can provide education, skills training and platforms for communication, co-operation and knowledge sharing. For the 1970s co-op movement, these two functions were delivered by an institutional structure comprising a national body, the Housing Corporation, which coordinated state funding, and local secondary organisations, like CDS, which offered professional support and education to co-ops. What was good—and not so good—about this set-up? And why has it proven ultimately inadequate to enable the institutionalisation of an autonomous and democratic movement?

First, there are reasons to be wary of a centralised bureaucracy such as that enabling the 1970s co-ops. Modern bureaucracies arose through violent imperial plunder and domineering colonial conquest, with the tools and techniques used to map, categorise, control, subjugate and ultimately exploit a given territory and its people, as much as they did by any supposedly public-spirited attempt to provide a peaceful, rational, trustworthy system of governance.[1] The Housing Corporation is an interesting example of how bureaucratic and colonial forms of administration are bound up together in troubling ways, as one co-op development worker remarked to me:

> Part of its function was to give employment to ex-colonial civil servants coming out of a newly independent … coming from Nigeria, to the

1 William Davies, *Nervous States: How Feeling Took over the World* (Jonathan Cape, 2018).

> Housing Corporation! So you had these people who were pro co-op working in it, but you also had these ex-colonial civil servants, you know: "The natives don't want to cooperate!" When I started in the late '70s, there was a guy doing registration, the local officer of the Housing Corporation, he had a great grey handlebar moustache and saw his job of doing registration as health kit inspection … There's something quite colonial about the whole Housing Corporation ethos: going in "civilising the natives", empowering them, although "empowering" was not in the vocabulary back then.

This underlines the need to build a bureaucracy from below—to put democracy first wherever they conflict. Nonetheless, bureaucracies like all social structures are composed of multiple and contradictory parts and the localised system of support emerging in Liverpool in the 1970s, whilst financially tied to the Housing Corporation, was shaped more by the instincts of anarchist, self-build and community architecture movements. Without the extensive support of co-op development agencies acting as secondary or 'mother' co-ops, Liverpool's cooperative revolution would never have begun. SNAP was seminal in setting up the first rehab co-ops: revolutionising community planning methods, providing the basic tools for further experimentation and demonstrating how rehab could be delivered as an effective alternative to demolition. Neighbourhood Housing Services and CDS were both incredibly important to the development of the rehab and new-build movements respectively. The reason CDS proved viable where Neighbourhood Housing Services did not was its strategy to build its own houses to provide an asset base and continuous rental stream to cross-subsidise new-build co-op projects, which were very resource-intensive despite generous Housing Corporation HAG funding.

There are lessons here for building an institutional infrastructure from below—the need to secure an asset base and a sustainable source of revenue independent of the state. CDS embodied the role of 'enabler' promoted by John F.C. Turner in his recommendations for an autonomous system of self-help housing, supported by state-funded infrastructure. It was an early example of the intermediaries identified as so important to the contemporary growth of self-help housing and CLTs, either through 'scaling up' or 'going viral'.[2] In either case—arborescent growth or rhizomatic replication—key intermediaries or secondaries offer essential education, training, communication, guidance and support. Yet there is a great danger that professional organisations exploit unequal power relations for their own ends. Though there were certainly suspicions amongst Weller Street residents that CDS

2 Moore and Mullins, "Scaling-Up or Going Viral? Comparing Self-Help Housing and Community Land Trust Facilitation".

were taking them for a ride, participant testimony suggests CDS was committed to promoting dweller control, pushing against financial and legal constraints. Experimental socio-material practices like participatory planning techniques—innovated in partnership with architects such as Bill Halsall—were the result of CDS stretching its organisational capabilities to the limit and taking risks by investing heavily in untested methods in the hope of producing lasting social value. While CDS played a central role, other organisations were also pivotal—not least LHT and MIH. Indeed, competition between secondary co-ops and service providers was a fundamental factor in social innovation: paradoxically furthering the possibilities for cooperation within communities through competition at higher scales driving up standards and providing choice. This suggests a monolithic, centralised, one-size-fits-all structure is ill-suited to the plural forms of collective alternatives.

Dormant, Not Defunct: Self-Funding the Next Co-Op Spring

Following its demise through the 1980s, there are good reasons why now is the moment to rebuild a city-regional institutional infrastructure. As one observer told me, the cooperative spirit in Liverpool is "dormant" rather than "defunct"; another, that the city "still has that ferment feel about it" despite the fact that "we haven't got the money to play with now". This may be about to change. Many participants believe that the time has come, that co-ops are now at a critical threshold, on the cusp of a new phase of expansion having accumulated a large asset and resource base in the intervening fallow period. A curious implication of the 1988 Act rent reforms was unintentionally to create the opportunity for co-ops to make large surpluses. Their modest mortgage repayment schedules had been originally calculated on the basis of very low rents, the 'fair rents' set by the 1974 Act. The 1988 Act, however, replaced these with 'assured rents', generally much higher in order to pay for ongoing costs in the absence of HAG funding. Any new tenants coming in after 1988, therefore, would be paying assured rents, and, as turnover escalated, co-ops found it easier to pay mortgage and other costs, pocketing increasing surpluses. The co-ops are now, as one member revealed, "coming out of the other end" of the dormant period, having repaid debts, with potentially considerable "reserves to enable them to now start to develop new homes". Collectively, liquid assets are estimated to be well into the millions—at least £21 million—just sitting in individual co-op bank accounts. If these co-op reserves could somehow be made available to those currently campaigning for alternatives, there may be a CLT Uprising to match the Co-op Spring.

When CDS merged with Plus Dane, it came under the regulatory purview of the Housing Corporation, which put pressure on Plus Dane to utilise this untapped asset base—"to get them sweating their assets"—as a means to leverage funding for further development. This may account for CDS's break with Plus Dane, due to its dependence on Housing Corporation grants and allocations for developing its social housing portfolio, with an incentive to follow the top-down mandate to divert co-op surpluses into new development. Legally, the surpluses are owned securely by the co-ops, but whilst managed under the auspices of Plus Dane they were at risk of being co-opted. By becoming independent as NWHS, this enabled the safeguarding of co-ops from any potential asset-stripping. Previously, CDS had been registered with the Housing Corporation, which enabled the organisation to build its own houses and develop an asset base, against which to leverage private capital for expansion. Although this was the foundation that assured the early viability of CDS, in contrast to Neighbourhood Housing Services, such a logic has since driven the 'empire building' of the big housing associations. NWHS is now sitting in a unique position as financial manager and advisor for the majority of Liverpool co-ops, with the potential to reincarnate the initiating secondary role of CDS for a possible co-op revival. For this to occur, NWHS needs to persuade their co-op clients of the efficacy of pooling surpluses together and investing this resource into new co-op development. The process of setting up a collective fund coordinated by NWHS is under way. The idea is to pool capital reserves in a central pot which could then provide grants and low-interest loans for new or existing groups to develop new co-operative housing. This would be self-sustaining patient capital that is financially beneficial for cooperative development and which would not seek to make a profit, only to replenish the 'solidarity fund' over the long term such that contributing co-ops do not lose their initial investments.

However, it is unclear whether NWHS has the capacity, incentive or commitment to drive the wider renewal of the co-op movement on Merseyside. By all accounts, NWHS provides a good service in supporting co-ops and now CLTs but, like CDS before it, the organisation has its own prerogatives, which while aligning quite closely with collective alternatives are very much distinct. NWHS, like all professional secondary organisations not owned by their members, has an incentive to make money like any other business, to push their own professional agenda and, above all, to present themselves as an indispensable intermediary for the successful operation of the co-ops. Secondaries have the perverse incentive—whether realised or not—to keep their members (or, rather, 'clients') in the dark about their operations, to prevent co-ops from deliberating amongst themselves or from seeing ways in which they could pool resources and share knowledge more directly without recourse to a professional organisation. Without democratic underpinnings, such an organisation may do more to divide and rule co-ops than bring them together in strength and solidarity. In many ways, then, professional secondary organisations like NWHS, CDS, MIH and Neighbourhood Housing Services all embody a state-like Leviathan logic in that they act to maintain relations between members only via their shared vertical relationship with the secondary. This is no way to build a democratic movement. The professional expertise of secondaries is vital to movement-building but needs to be made the servant of the movement. In short, the secondary should be the client of the movement, not vice versa.

Liverpool's co-op movement requires a democratically governed city-regional federated structure to negotiate with local government, to communicate its values to wider publics, to facilitate knowledge sharing and source professional expertise, to pool resources between individual co-ops in order to coordinate funds for further development, to undertake education and training for new and existing members and to provide the kind of democratic arena for the grassroots cultivation of a movement. The development of such networks and federations is fundamental to one of the seven founding principles of cooperativism, building on the original five values of the Rochdale Pioneers and enshrined by the International Co-operative Alliance in 1966—that of *cooperation among co-operatives.* Conduits for cooperation had originally been put in place by CDS, who suggested the establishment of the Merseyside Federation of Co-ops, which for some time provided a fruitful arena for collaboration, knowledge sharing, resource pooling and mutual learning. However, the Federation disbanded in the early 1990s, after the generous state funding of co-ops inaugurated by the 1974 Act (which had helped pay for Federation activities) had finally come to an end and its members became increasingly detached from movement-building or cooperative education. Radical Routes, a nationwide grassroots network of around 40 housing co-ops, worker-owned co-ops and social centres working explicitly towards radical social change, provides an interesting alternative template for emulation. Promisingly, Radical Routes have begun to research possibilities for pooling resources for renewed co-op development, in a similar though more universal and bottom-up vein to NWHS in Liverpool—what they call the 'co-op cluster' model.[3] Re-establishing a member-based and democratic federation of Merseyside co-ops needs to go hand in hand with establishing a fund organised through a co-op cluster if we are ever to see the revitalisation—and not merely diluted expansion—of the movement.

Perhaps unsurprisingly for their relative youth, CLTs have a far less mature dedicated secondary infrastructure. The National CLT Network works closely with its members to provide advice, directing them to resources and funding opportunities and coordinating activities between regions as well as lobbying government for legislative reform and public programmes. But there are communication gaps between the Network, based in London, and their members in various localities—a gap that is now being bridged by regional 'umbrella' CLTs. However, such umbrellas operate at regional scales

3 Radical Routes, "Co-op Clusters: Roundtable Report" (2018): www.radicalroutes.org.uk/publicdownloads/Co-opClusters_report_lowres.pdf.

often covering several counties; unlike the co-op movement, no substantial secondary infrastructure has (yet) emerged at the urban or city-regional scale, except for tentative signs in London. East London CLT, established in 2007 as the very first urban CLT in the UK, a little ahead of Granby and Homebaked, and since evolved into an enabler organisation, London CLT, which incubates new CLTs across the capital. It was set up by London Citizens, part of Citizens UK, a powerful and well-resourced body of community organisers and civic volunteers who have been instrumental in campaigning for and delivering East London CLT at the St Clements hospital site and now further 'sister' sites in other boroughs.[4] Unlike a secondary co-op organisation, London CLT operates almost as a franchise, maintaining legal control over each additional CLT they help establish. It is a highly effective model of development built upon the expertise and organisational capacities of London Citizens although, increasingly, questions over local autonomy and democracy simmer beneath surface successes. Nonetheless, there is an opportunity in Liverpool to imitate this model whereby Granby and Homebaked work together to help create new CLTs with their expertise or else establish an entirely independent enabling organisation to do so.

But it is no use thinking inside the silo of just one collective housing model or only the Liverpool city region; we need to develop such structures at a larger scale, between regions and across all collective housing movements, so that co-ops and CLTs, alongside others, are linked together by mutually beneficial common infrastructure. Communication gaps and missed opportunities for cooperation between collective housing movements currently exist. Individual movements will be much stronger by working together if they too, just like individual projects, share knowledge, pool resources and forge political alliances. Greater coordination in the development of different models is now gaining momentum in the UK. There are signs of this with the coming together in 2017 of the national umbrella organisations for CLTs, co-housing and co-ops to host jointly, for the first time, the National Community-Led Housing Conference, mirroring the UK government's £300 million Community-Led Housing Fund, running until 2020.[5]

Lessons might be learned from London—the only other city in Britain with an established co-op sector and a growing CLT movement. Here, various organisations have come together to establish the London Community-Led Housing Hub, a resource and advice centre for all kinds of community-led housing. This is financially supported by the Mayor of London and several borough councils, coordinated by the National CLT Network, the

4 Bunce, "Pursuing Urban Commons: Politics and Alliances in Community Land Trust Activism in East London".

5 Mullins and Moore, "Self-Organised and Civil Society Participation in Housing Provision".

Confederation of Co-operative Housing and UK Cohousing and, crucially, hosted by CDS Co-operatives, the original London-based secondary organisation from which sprung Liverpool's CDS. Together, NWHS and CDS Co-operatives are the only two independent secondaries in the country; the latter is the larger, owning around a thousand co-op homes across London and managing 45 co-ops with around two thousand homes. The Hub's offer of financial and technical support to any community group interested in housing themselves is underpinned by an inclusive ethos that attempts to transcend traditional movement divides and silo-thinking such that, in the words on their website,[6] "a determined and enthusiastic group of people is more important than any theoretical model". This has the potential to go a long way towards galvanising a more cohesive and cooperative meta-movement of collective housing alternatives in ways which share resources and knowledge between co-op, CLT, co-housing and other like-minded movements.

Interestingly, it was CDS Co-operatives who really pushed and lobbied for the establishment of the London Community-Led Housing Hub, which demonstrates the potential importance of NWHS in doing something similar in Liverpool and the north-west. Indeed, Greater Manchester Combined Authority has recently invited NWHS to trial an enabling hub in Manchester, influenced by policy-relevant action-research into community-led housing.[7] To this end in Liverpool, Power to Change are working with some of the exemplar organisations they have funded (notably Granby and Homebaked, two of their favourites nationally) as well as NWHS to help set up an 'enabler hub' for the city. Yet this charitable trust, endowed by the Big Lottery Fund with money raised from national lottery ticket sales to support neighbourhood regeneration through community enterprise, is on a ten-year time-limited programme and whose networking reach is limited to those organisations they have funded, overlooking the larger localised ecosystem of collective alternatives. This underlines how, in the current absence of progressive state funding or consistent coordination from above, we need a new system of support constructed from below with self-sustaining resources generated by collective alternatives themselves.

In sum, Liverpool's recent history of co-op movement renewal spells out a number of lessons for broader collective alternative institutionalisation. It points to how investments made in assets such as land and housing will one day mature for harvesting for the reinvestment in new growth—if only the governance structures and cultures of co-operation among co-ops can be (re)constituted. So too does it make clear the dangers of institutional capture by the state, capital and professional agendas: had CDS/NWHS remained under Housing Corporation regulation they would have been

6 https://www.communityledhousing.london/.

7 Goulding, *Housing Futures: What Can Community-Led Housing Achieve for Greater Manchester?*

forced to leverage 'their assets' for indiscriminate social housing construction without consideration of cooperative values, and one of the movement's key independent resources would have been lost to the state and its neoliberalised conception of public housing development. Nonetheless, it also articulates the essential role of the state and the ambiguous relationship collective housing alternatives maintain with the public sector. In this case, the assets now potentially providing a new source of growth for an autonomous cooperative movement were originally the product of state investment—the substantial public funding for the purchase, planning, construction and maintenance of new-build co-op housing. Likewise in the case of Granby and Homebaked CLTs, their ownership of property assets—a critical factor in their economic viability—is only thanks to the council. It is in this sense that we must see collective alternatives as a bridge between the common and the public—as a potential site for the renewal of public housing and the transformation of the state more broadly.

Realising Municipal Dreams

Of all community anchor organisations in Liverpool, the Eldonians have shown how a community development trust model can generate surpluses for more self-sustaining regeneration and urban governance—albeit one with massive initial state investment—providing a starting point for how the state system might be redesigned. Commentators writing in 1988 made some interesting divinations of government intentions for funding the Eldonians:

> Perhaps they would like to see—in Liverpool and elsewhere—a city run by a federation of development trusts on the lines of the Eldonians' prototype, with government funds being coordinated by a Task Force … The city council could then be allowed to wither away.[8]

This Marxist phrase was said, rather sardonically, of a context in which the central state was centralising political control, stripping the local state of economic powers and shutting down socialist dissent—from the ousting of Militant from Liverpool City Council to Thatcher's abolishment of the radical municipal socialist Greater London Council. While we must be wary of any strategy to allow city councils to wither away—at least in the current conjuncture of neoliberal austerity—there are some interesting lessons here for renewing a municipalism centred on collective alternatives. First, it recalls the SNAP final report recommendations for a "task force under the Cabinet Office" to coordinate a decentralised Urban Programme of metropolitan

8 Cowan, Hannay and Owens, "The Light on Top of the Tunnel", p. 63.

development agencies.[9] Any mention of 'Task Force' summons images of a highly technocratic and unaccountable structure of quangos coordinated by a central state unresponsive to local democracy. We must remain cognisant of the need to embed democracy in any such multi-scalar structure. But if we read it in a more politically expansive light, it conjures the anarchist vision for decentralised self-governing city-regions, composed of community-controlled associations and connected through a democratic federated structure through the subsidiarity principle—envisioned by the likes of Kropotkin and the eco-socialist Murray Bookchin, whose ideas on libertarian municipalism we can trace through the new municipalist movement emerging globally.[10]

Grassroots groups and collective alternatives across inner-city Liverpool are beginning to discuss the development of a local political manifesto for urban transformation inspired by the new municipalist movement Fearless Cities[11] and which they are tentatively calling Fearless Neighbourhoods.[12] Thus we might follow their lead in taking inspiration from the recent resurgence of municipalism in cities around the world, including Preston in the UK. Here, a Labour-led council administration (with strong links to its sister Cooperative Party and the wider cooperative movement) is experimenting with new policy approaches around developing the foundational economy through collective alternatives.[13] Borrowing ideas from Cleveland in the USA as well as the Mondragon Corporation in Basque Spain, the largest and most successful federation of worker-owned co-ops in the world, the so-called Preston model harnesses the spending powers of anchor institutions—those place-based and locally embedded (that is, *anchored*) organisations with important civic and social functions, often the mainstays of the foundational economy—for local economic development and the stimulation of new co-operative enterprises and collective alternatives. The idea is that procurement and commissioning and the supply chains of participating anchor institutions—which include universities, hospitals, housing associations, local authorities, county councils, police constabularies, Further Education colleges and school trusts—are redirected towards local social enterprises, especially worker-owned co-ops, so that contracts for cleaning, catering, marketing, construction and the like go to firms that, as much as possible, employ local labour, are governed democratically and reinvest surpluses within the locality for the generation of social value over private profit. This is a two-pronged approach: bending

9 McConaghy, *Another Chance for Cities: SNAP 69–72*, p. 207.

10 Thompson, "What's so new about New Municipalism?".

11 Russell, "Beyond the Local Trap: New Municipalism and the Rise of the Fearless Cities".

12 Jurgensen, 'Trainings for the Not-Yet' Exhibition (2020): www.bakonline.org/program-item/trainings-for-the-not-yet/.

13 Thompson, "What's so new about New Municipalism?".

institutional spend to create local demand for goods and services—for which public housing provision is well suited—coupled with meeting that demand by stimulating local supply through the incubation and development of the cooperative movement and social enterprise sector. Another strategic flank is the development of community land trusts to take on underused private or public assets for community benefit. Preston's is a nascent model of how the local state can be retooled for the gestation and institutionalisation of collective alternatives as part of an economy reoriented to the foundational.

Building on these new municipalist foundations, we can see how an architecture for collective alternatives—in public housing, urban regeneration and neighbourhood governance—might take shape. Anchor institutions operate at a relatively large scale—with civic functions that stretch across an entire municipality, metropolitan area or wider region. At a more localised scale, 'community anchor organisations' can do for deprived neighbourhoods what anchor institutions do for economically depressed cities like Preston or Liverpool.[14] They may take on a coordinating or mediating role for contracts and commissions that smaller individual co-ops and social enterprises seek with anchor institutions; act as hubs for a whole host of community activities, from meeting places to food growing and street markets; provide incubation space and expertise for social entrepreneurs and start-ups; and an arena for democratic deliberation between otherwise unconnected diverse members of the wider community. Community development trusts like the Eldonians and CLTs like Granby and Homebaked are well-placed to adopt this community anchor function. In the USA, such collective alternatives have been likened to 'governance shims'[15]—a new layer of governance wedged between community and local authority—to emphasise the important role they may play in cities of the future, as democratic stewards of place. That these are common property regimes—that is, they hold land and community assets in trust, protecting these from market predation through an asset lock whilst enabling participatory decision-making over their use—represents an important and under-recognised potential civic function in democratic urban governance.

These ideas are not all that new. There is a long-established Community Development Corporation sector in the USA, with roots in 1960s radicalism but since becoming a ubiquitous feature of urban North America with a large number of organisations operating today across a diverse range of local

14 Matthew Thompson, Vicky Nowak, Alan Southern et al., "Re-grounding the City with Polanyi: From Urban Entrepreneurialism to Entrepreneurial Municipalism", *Environment and Planning A: Economy and Space*: 1–24: https://doi.org/10.1177/0308518X19899698; James Henderson and Christopher McWilliams, "The UK Community Anchor Model and Its Challenges for Community Sector Theory and Practice".

15 Williams and Pierce, "Inserting Scales of Urban Politics".

economic development activities.[16] They were once seen as "the crucial coordinating agent" of the three domains of production, consumption and exchange in an alternative system of community-based development, overseeing the activities of CLTs, credit unions, consumer and worker cooperatives.[17] Although most do not function in their fullest, most radical capacity and have been subject to co-optation and mission drift from radical community control towards more operational service delivery as part of the shadow state, community development corporations nonetheless provide important lessons for how similar institutional forms may be developed in the UK in answer to the neighbourhood question.

The neighbourhood question forces us to consider scale. Collective housing alternatives are very energy-intensive and complicated to coordinate at a sufficiently large enough scale to address the urban-economic problems of a city the size and nature of Liverpool or, indeed, to provide the necessary strategic oversight to link together and avoid duplication of diverse small-scale projects all operating in a piecemeal fashion. This is one of the reasons why conventional regeneration programmes like HMR adopt a more abstract, professionalised and uniform approach—for the efficiencies and simplicities that come with economies of scale. Nonetheless, HMR went too far in this direction. There is no necessary reason why HMR funding could not have been channelled into a diversity of CLT projects, as suggested by URBED and tentatively explored in Kensington to no avail. A more balanced, hybrid combination needs to be innovated so that resident-led, locally responsive, publicly accountable and resourceful projects can develop—supported and coordinated by larger-scale enabling bodies, like community development corporations but with greater grassroots engagement.

Democratically governed and publicly accountable community development corporations could replace HMR Pathfinders and other such public–private partnerships in the next round of state-led urban regeneration, if and when austerity urbanism releases its stranglehold. After democratic voting and deliberation in a local area have established the need and desire for state intervention, any resulting community development corporation would need to be statutorily protected so that long-term housing restructuring programmes cannot be simply switched off halfway through their cycle by the whims of electoral party politics, as happened in the case of HMR, but are instead controlled locally through democratic structures. This would enable a more sustained 'investment mode' of state funding—the state as 'friendly investor', as one interviewee put it, rather than drip-feeder of sporadic grants. The

16 DeFilippis, *Unmaking Goliath*; Bruyn and Meehan, *Beyond the Market and the State: New Directions in Community Development*.

17 Bruyn and Meehan, *Beyond the Market and the State: New Directions in Community Development*, p. 16.

culture of grants is counterproductive for the long-term regeneration of areas, as it encourages competitive bidding, vanguardism and vulnerable dependence on civic volunteerism as well as on government and philanthropic hand-outs. When combined with competitive tendering of public sector assets, this leads to a monumental waste of resources, as potential co-operators are pitted against each other in a zero sum game, resulting in time wasted, unrealised ideas and exhausted creativity for all but the winning bidder. More collaborative processes of public tendering would allow competing visions to be explored in creative dialogue.

This brings us back to the issue of funding. As we know, the 1970s co-ops were funded through a state-led system of grants centrally coordinated by the Housing Corporation. Since then, we have seen the dismantling and splintering of governance and funding mechanisms for collective alternatives and the wider social economy such that a number of intermediaries have patchily filled the gaps between centralised funders and local projects. Big Society Capital—which, since its establishment in 2012 by the Conservative Coalition government, has been one of the biggest providers of social investment (loans to social enterprises including CLTs), awash with dead people's dormant bank accounts and match-funding from the big four retail banks—has struggled to reach or attract enough applications from deserving beneficiaries at the local level.[18] For instance, Access (the Foundation for Social Investment) exists fundamentally to find more effective ways to distribute funds from Big Society Capital as well as grants from the Big Lottery Fund to those that need them—and takes a slice of the pie in the process. A tangled competitive ecosystem of private consultants and quasi-public intermediaries has thus sprung up—what some in the field liken to a "non-profit industrial complex", a trend accelerated by the 'Market Stalinism'[19] of the New Labour years and the ongoing 'bullshitisation' of jobs in an economy increasingly exhausted of meaningful and socially (re)productive work.[20] There is a real need to reform this confusing, exploitative and wasteful system of social investment for one that provides patient capital and grants attuned to project needs, democratically coordinated through city-regional Solidarity Funds, such as that potentially emerging amongst the Liverpool co-ops with or without NWHS. If we are to work towards the replacement of this irrational centralised system by a democratically federated municipalist structure of self-governing collective alternatives through the incremental and prefigurative contracting of different social, economic and institutional relationships—how can we speed up this

18 Leslie Huckfield, *The Rise and Influence of Social Enterprise, Social Investment and Public Service Mutuals, NCIA Inquiry into the Future of Voluntary Services*, Working Paper 3 (National Coalition for Independent Action, 2014).

19 Fisher, *Capitalist Realism: Is There No Alternative?*

20 Graeber, *Bullshit Jobs: A Theory*.

transformation of the state? How can we help reinvent the state from the inside—as the councillors and co-operators in Preston suggest it can be done? To unleash the self-expansive dynamic of the circuit of the common, we need to genetically reengineer the DNA code underwriting its cell form, those legal models that constitute CLTs and co-ops.

Recoding the DNA of Collective Alternatives

It is not only the tools of the local state that require reinvention; the central state and its legislative apparatus are vitally important, too, for the development of collective alternatives. The Labour and Cooperative Party councillors retooling the armoury of the state in Preston are the Reg Freesons and the Harold Campbells of our day—but where are the cooperative advocates and innovators operating at the national level? We need legislative reform comparable in potency to the 1974 Housing Act to work alongside new municipalism. We also need new legal codes. If we see co-ops and CLTs as the cell structure comprising the body of the movement (with secondary enabler organisations as the organs, perhaps) then the legal models through which collective alternatives are constituted represent the DNA code. The legal form of collective alternatives defines their capabilities and limitations and determines the stream of benefits and costs that flow to such organisations from the state and capital. The role of bureaucracy and of technocrats resides in creating, defining and arbitrating the codes that determine the specific social, political and economic powers of collective alternatives. What do these codes look like in practice? In the UK, the legal DNA of co-ops was the Industrial and Provident Society, up until 2014, after which, due to legislative reform, this was recoded as either a Co-operative Society or Community Benefit Society (BenCom). Urban CLTs, meanwhile, are generally established as Community Interest Companies (CICs), the favoured form for social enterprise inaugurated by the Companies Act 2004. However, for all the benefits of the CIC legal form, more radical community enterprises—Homebaked and Granby CLTs included—associate it with the co-optation and instrumentalisation of the social economy by New Labour and its Third Way agenda of instilling a business mentality in projects for social inclusion and redistribution.

An alternative to forming as a CIC is to be a charity—a Charitable Incorporated Organisation or, perhaps, a Company Limited by Guarantee. CIOs in particular are more established charitable forms with roots in philanthropy and voluntary association—overseen by the national regulatory body, the Charity Commission. Distinguishing charities from CICs is their emphasis on a legally accountable and transparent trust structure governed by trustees, who have greater control over the actions and decisions of any executive staff, including their pay. By contrast, there is nothing to stop social entrepreneurs running a CIC from remunerating themselves however much they like while also claiming non-profit status. The CLT tripartite structure is designed to prevent such aberrations but the legal form it takes will help or hinder its constitutional covenants in different ways. The important factor for CLTs is that the legal form chosen enables an asset lock to prevent profiteering or the flipping of land. Because co-ops come from a different tradition and lack an asset lock, they were, up until the 2014 reforms, inappropriate forms for CLTs to adopt. Co-ops share all surpluses amongst members and while this brings people together around a shared material interest, it also makes the co-op more vulnerable to co-optation. 'Carpet-bagging', as the movement refers to it, occurs when members use co-operative resources for their own private benefit rather than for collective aims, either actively through 'stair-casing' equity shares and then selling for a profit or, more passively, by allowing rents to fall to a minimum and under-occupying properties.[21]

Interestingly, the Co-operative and Community Benefit Societies Act 2014 attempts to tackle some of these issues by splitting the cooperative movement down the middle between those organisations more classically resembling co-ops—Cooperative Societies, which work for the mutual benefit of members—and those that make moves towards trust-like constitutions—Community Benefit Societies, or BenComs, which work for the benefit of the wider community. Unlike traditional co-ops, including cooperative societies, BenComs have the added mechanism of incorporating an asset lock, much like a CIC. At the same time, they maintain a cooperative ownership structure such that members of a CLT constituted as a BenCom are effective part-owners in the endeavour and have a greater stake than they would in the case of being a CIC or charity. In the current context, many philanthropic funding bodies are wary of giving grants to organisations which lack the critical scrutiny of a trustee structure or an asset lock, and it is unclear whether BenComs can attract the same funding from organisations such as English Heritage or The Esmée Fairbairn Foundation as can CICs and Charitable Incorporated Organisations. Nonetheless, BenComs open up alternative avenues of funding that are more grounded in the community. They enable the issuing of community shares—a valuable source of revenue which also engages more people in the ownership of the project. Homebaked CLT have for a while been weighing up the advantages of switching from a CIC to a BenCom legal form. Part of the appeal for Homebaked is that this would allow them legally to pay their trustees, many of whom also do consultancy or part-time project work for the CLT. The BenCom is a good example of a legal innovation which creates new possibilities for CLTs like Homebaked to realise their cooperative values whilst protecting their assets within a trust structure. More innovation—and education—in legal coding is required if we are to see a flourishing of new projects to suit different contexts.

21 Radical Routes, "Co-op Clusters: Roundtable Report", 2018: www.radicalroutes.org.uk/publicdownloads/Co-opClusters_report_lowres.pdf.

Yet all these innovations are ultimately sticking plasters over a fundamentally broken system that lacks the legal or political recognition of common property rights as legitimate forms of ownership. Currently, British law only acknowledges two distinct types of tenure: freehold and leasehold; landlord and tenant—a bipolar separation inherited from feudalism but fiercely guarded under capitalism. As such, the law treats members of collective housing alternatives as essentially tenants or as part-owners, which gives individuals either too much or too little power over their stake. David Rodgers, the former chief executive of England's largest housing cooperative agency, CDS Cooperatives in London, alerts us to the peculiar fact that

> In a housing co-operative a member has a dual relationship with the co-operative, firstly as member with rights to participate in the democratic control of the co-operative's affairs, secondly as a tenant of the landlord co-operative. The two relationships are, legally, entirely separate. In tenancy law the co-operative is as feudal a landlord as any other.[22]

Efforts at reform that are not radical enough—reformist reforms rather than radical reforms—only lead us down into deeper perversities. Ironically, leaseholder empowerment legislation passed to protect tenants from their vulnerable position with respect to ruthless landlords—notably the 1967 Leasehold Reform Act—now threatens the operation of CLTs by empowering members to buy out their share of the scheme and preventing the collective organisation from imposing limits on individual control of equity. The CLT and Mutual Home Ownership Society (MHOS) models, as pursued by Terrace 21 in Granby, are two examples of institutional innovations that have been specifically designed to work within the current polarised system to utilise aspects of freehold and leasehold to create the *effect* of a common property regime. But only with the constitution of a truly cooperative tenure bringing about the complete overhaul of the landlord–tenant binary—a master–slave relation of exploitation and alienation upon which stands the capitalist ownership model—will the institutional space be cleared for commoning to thrive.

If we wish to move beyond forever (re)inventing ever-more sophisticated but ultimately constricted compromises, we need radical legal reform—or revolution. The housing cooperative movement in the UK has been a vocal proponent of tenure reform. David Rodgers has argued—in person as well as in print[23]—for a 'third estate' to complement the two original estates we have inherited from medieval feudalism and to provide the legal basis for common property relations—a legal common property right—as a possible

22 David Rodgers, *New Mutualism: The Third Estate* (The Co-operative Party, 1999).

23 Rodgers, *New Mutualism*.

way to empower tenants from what amounts to a state of feudal dependency. Legislating the 'third estate' would provide the legal protection required for common property institutions, including collective housing alternatives, to maintain their relations of commoning over time. To this end, not only do we need skilled story-tellers and mythologists to conjure new narratives that can capture the popular imagination for the outward replication of collective alternatives—to build the movement alongside the co-operators and commoners themselves—so too do we need social innovators, radical lawyers and socialist legislators to come up with imaginative ways of codifying new institutional and legal (re)forms in order to surmount the multiple problems and contradictions inherent to articulating actually existing commons in, against and beyond the capitalist system of public–private property relations.

Epilogue

Translating Between Inward, Upward and Outward Languages

In a fascinating collection of writings about a community gardening project in Peterborough called The Green Backyard, Dougald Hine's offering—aptly titled "Spelling It Out"—evokes the different languages all such projects must learn if they are to be at all successful. "The *Inward* language", Hine writes:

> is the way that those at the heart of a project make sense of what they are doing, the way of seeing the world that makes it possible. It may be a complex model of how things are and how they could be; it may be entirely intuitive and largely unspoken. It is a creative, living language.[1]

Alongside this 'mother tongue'—spoken by activists, comrades and fellow travellers to craft a common vision and theory of change—Hine identifies two important others, each differing in vocabulary, tone and register, each with their own intended audience and purpose in mind. The 'upward language' is the language of "power and resources: the language of funding applications, the language of those who are in a position to interpret regulations and impose or remove obstacles". In contrast to the living creativity of the inward, this is "not a reflective or a curious language, it is a language of busy people who make decisions without having time to immerse themselves in the realities their decisions will affect …" But it is only through learning the upward language that a community project has any hope of negotiating the challenging terrain of legal constitutions, funding applications, legislative reform, planning approval, professional partnerships and the like.

All the collective housing alternatives explored in the preceding pages have each, in their own way, been defined by their ability to master these two dialectically opposed languages. Speaking only one of them is not enough by itself to ensure survival—inward and upward are complementary parts of a whole just as much as they appear to pull in different directions. It is useless

1 Dougald Hine, "Spelling It Out", in Jessie Brennan, ed., *Re: Development—Voices, Cyanotypes and Writings from the Green Backyard* (UCL Press, 2017): https://medium.com/@dougald/spelling-it-out-ce47d4ea8d9b#.okzjrjw1q.

cultivating a richly woven discourse internally, amongst a small group of avid enthusiasts, if that means the more challenging task of speaking upwards, to the gatekeepers of political support, legal legitimacy and financial resources, is neglected. Without this, collective housing alternatives will wither on the vine. We see this in the case of the failed Little Klondyke CLT—but not for want of trying. By the same token, if all energies are directed upwards, to the detriment of inward fluency, this may well prevent the seed from ever growing or, alternatively, risk the fruit being plucked and discarded before fully ripening. For the former outcome, the two CLTs driven from above by institutional actors, in Kensington and Anfield, are cases in point. The more recent experience of the Eldonians gestures towards the latter. Such institutional capture and extraction of grassroots energies is an ever-present threat posed by conversing in the language of power. Yet campaigners must use the tools of the upward—spatial visions, business plans, professional terminology, construction methods etc.—in order to plan, develop and manage anything at all or, indeed, to negotiate land acquisition from the state, which must be convinced of the community's competency to manage public assets. Campaigns must, to some extent, become fluent in the language of state bureaucracy, market processes and professional mores if they are ever to gain the trust of key gatekeepers and successfully attract essential financial and legal support.

This translation balancing act is made trickier still by the introduction of a third vocabulary—the outward language—in which a project is distilled down to its core essence and articulated to wider publics. In Hine's analogy, this is "the language in which you can explain it to your mum, or to someone you just met in the pub, and realise that they get it—not that they have understood everything about what you're doing, but that something here makes sense and sounds good". Both the inward and the upward necessarily engage in *complexity*, and try to explain, in different ways, how a project might work—either in terms of ideological visions and social theories about the world and how the project intends to change it, or else in the terminology of public policies, government regulations, legal instruments, financial mechanisms and business plans. The outward, by contrast, shuns all such intricacies and pretensions to explain simply, in lay terms, what the project does and why it is at all useful or interesting for everyday life. In Hine's words, it is "not about *how your project works*, it's about *what it does*". Crucially, to distil the complexity of the inward and the upward into an intuitively compelling and attractive idea that can be grasped at a stroke by anybody even vaguely interested, the outward language needs to be concise, straightforward and persuasive. It might work best by analogy and metaphor—employing images that capture concepts in the quotidian and vernacular. This is a discourse that can thrive in media representation and go viral on social media. It is the medium through which a project communicates its significance to the outside world and attempts to gain popular appeal.

Granby and Homebaked CLTs have become well-versed in the outward language. They are each fortunate enough to have powerful linguists in their midst who are talented in the art of representation. The story of Granby has been articulated through an artistic medium by architects Assemble who helped secure popular and political recognition through the Turner Prize. Homebaked was gifted by a simple yet effective image at its heart—the sensually evocative image of home baking—and has used this to craft a compelling brand narrative that has helped catch the imaginations of neighbours and punters, politicians and funders. The outward literature produced by and for Homebaked is conscious of this image. For instance, a piece written for the special issue dedicated to Homebaked in the Liverpool Biennial online journal *#Stages* reveals the third flank in Homebaked's strategy, which might rather read: brick by brick, loaf by loaf, *story by story*, we build ourselves:

> It is very difficult to give up control of the symbolic media narrative in favour of the actual on-the-ground work, because it seems that one may determine the other ...A symbolic counterattack on prevailing narratives, carefully calibrated through self-branding and actualisation, can shift understanding and pave the way for progress, as surely as baking bread or laying down brick.[2]

It is not only individual projects that must utilise the outward language to gain support; the movement as a whole must be canny about the way it presents itself if it is to ever win over the public. One of the biggest challenges facing the expansion of collective housing as a popular tenure of choice—rather than bespoke reaction to need, as it has so often been over its history in Liverpool—lies in convincing potential residents to forfeit some of their equity share and accumulative property rights, for other more intangible benefits in collective control, social justice and security of tenure. The elephant in the room is the system of private property rights under the ownership model, where individual homeownership is ideologically entrenched as the most desirable option—almost a precondition for neoliberal forms of citizenship—and a central strategy of economic security for aspiring homeowners in a period of welfare retrenchment and uncertainty. Collective models, however, require residents to reorient their personal interests towards more collective ends. For this reason, they may be limited to very specific contexts: protecting neighbourhoods from financial speculation or spiralling decline, and securing against the threat of gentrification or state-led displacement. A large part of the challenge is therefore branding: marketing models cleverly so that they swim rather than sink in the discursive mainstream. The Mutual Homeownership Society (MHOS) model used by Granby's Terrace 21 co-op is a good example

2 Yank, "2Up2Down/Homebaked and the Symbolic Media Narrative", p. 6.

of how what is essentially good old-fashioned cooperativism can be rebranded within the ideological parameters of the ownership model.

There is something in the tension between inward and upward languages, in particular, which captures the dialectic at the heart of any attempt to develop and grow a collective housing alternative. One way to represent the growing chasm between inward and upward, activist and professional, civil society and state, is through the metaphor offered up by John F.C. Turner—that housing can be seen from essentially two perspectives: as a noun or as a verb. Whilst the upward language of policy and bureaucracy tends toward abstraction and objectification and is in some sense, therefore, noun-like, the inward, as Hine paints it, "is a creative, living language" and is more at home with the active, unfolding, uncontained flows of everyday life, more verb-like. But this should be seen as a holistic dialectic rather than binary choice. The relatively fluid and spontaneous energy of innovators, activists, campaigners and residents—expressed through, and in some sense already codified by, the inward language spoken amongst them—must be translated into institutional codes if it is to ever get past the gatekeepers to access legal, financial and political help. The challenge of growth, replication and institutionalisation hinges on this tension: between, on the one hand, inspiring, mobilising and sustaining the intense political campaign energy and grassroots practices of commoning that are the lifeblood of collective alternatives and, on the other, the need for legal definition, professional expertise and codification into institutional structures if such alternatives are to reproduce and replicate their practices across space and time. In this tension lies the ever-present danger of projects mimicking and gradually resembling, through institutional isomorphism, their funders, regulators and legislators. Practising the upward language at the cost of sustaining the inward and outward opens the door to co-optation or dilution by more powerful agents and agendas that run counter to original values.

Nonetheless, engaging in the upward world—be that of professionals, politicians, lawyers or local or national state officials—to reconfigure existing vocabularies or invent new words is a critically important and often overlooked aspect of developing collective housing movements. This is the spirit with which collective housing advocates have lobbied for the construction of new legal models and codes for the articulation of their inward visions of an urban commons in the upward language of law and politics. Co-ops and CLTs are not by themselves all that meaningful in upward terms. For this, they must be translated into legal models, such as, in the UK, Industrial and Provident Societies (pre-2014), Community Benefit Societies (post-2014) and Community Interest Companies (since 2006)—each unlocking a number of benefits and powers in various combinations. The way in which collective alternatives choose to express themselves upwardly has real material impacts for their long-term success but so too is the form in which they have been branded, outwardly, important for attracting support. This is the realm in between the inward and the upward, in which actors vie with each other over the popular articulation of collective alternatives. The 'co-operative' and 'community land trust' models are in many ways symbolic distillations in outward terms of ideas emanating from inward languages. They sink or swim depending on their ability to catch the wave of popular imagination.

Part of what makes the collective housing alternatives explored in this book extraordinary is the way in which these three languages—but particularly the inward and upward—have been brought together in such close conversation. It is not just the inward-speaking campaigners doing the talking: upward-speakers play an important role in this narrative too. In the late 1970s, the Liverpool-based co-op development agency CDS was skilled at bridging the gap between the lived space of co-op communities and the professional world of architects and planners: drawing on and developing local skills and practical wisdom, helping residents acquire the knowledge and tools required to take control over the decision-making process, even though the actual development work itself was conducted by professionals. More-responsive housing designs and urban environments that better stand the test of time than much of the surrounding housing built by the municipal or private sector; socioeconomic empowerment of residents to find jobs in architectural and building companies as well as other firms; political mobilisation of campaigners to stand for local election and represent their communities in important council positions—these are some of the benefits derived from this approach, only made possible by intensive exchange between inward and upward languages.

The participatory techniques first tested out by SNAP and later reincarnated in the community homesteading approach innovated by Assemble in Granby are proven ways to close the gap between grassroots innovators and institutionalised experts. Assemble's approach to living on site throughout the development process, in one of the very houses that has since been rehabilitated, is an excellent example of how professionals can get more hands-on in helping residents learn the tools of the trade and necessary expertise as they work, and reside, together in the same space—an innovative method to help bring into closer contact the often antagonistic and disconnected inward and upward worlds. But this is a lot to ask of professionals unused to such immersive practices and extreme time commitments. Assemble are not RIBA-qualified and there is the question of whether they would have such freedom to innovate if they were fully paid up members of the architectural profession.

At the same time, we must acknowledge the serious limitations to cross-fertilisation of the inward and upward. One limit is the appetite or indeed capacity of communities to cooperate with professionals. We can see this in the intense power struggle of Weller Street with CDS. Another limit is the financial self-interest of professionals to remain gatekeepers of specialist knowledge, to protect their privileged status and sustain a mystique around their work in order to be able to keep charging people for it. Here's Weller Street Co-op's Chairman Peter Tyrell recounting his experience:

> These professionals play the word game on you. They start with all these long load of words … There's always that language barrier and that professional mystique which they're not prepared to give away. They always want to hide something from you … They don't want to allow you to have complete and free access to all their knowledge … They give you the impression that they do but it's my experience that they don't.[3]

One final limit may be more fundamental. It remains impractical to incorporate residents completely into the design and development process, for this is extremely complex, involving the multiple interactions of complicated bureaucratic, architectural, legal and financial procedures, each of which have their own forms of expertise honed over years of learning and experience. Do we really expect residents of co-ops and CLTs, often from disadvantaged backgrounds, to upskill themselves in a matter of months? To suggest that residents can rehabilitate or build housing anew through a grassroots self-help approach misapprehends the scale and difficulty of the challenges facing urban neighbourhoods. Assemble, for instance, have attempted to implement such an approach as fully as possible, but have come up against these constraints, and have had to employ professional contractors to carry out the most demanding structural refurbishment work. Collective alternatives rely on an incredibly close engagement between residents and professionals in resource-intensive and time-consuming participatory processes—not least to overcome the inward and the upward languages getting lost in translation.

Hine's analogy also conveys—unwittingly—the great burden placed on the shoulders of collective housing alternatives, forced to be polyglot by the accumulating demands and splintering divisions of neoliberal capitalism. There is massive waste, lost time and missed opportunity in a system set up in such a way as to entail so many failed funding and land acquisition applications by so many different groups all competing to claim from a beleaguered state their collective rights to housing. Everything at the outset seems stacked against them. They must somehow engage in three different worlds, speak three different languages. There is a certain schizoid mentality attendant to changing register between audiences, often at a moment's notice, keeping divergent interests all in play, holding multiple perspectives simultaneously. Speaking inward, upward and outward languages and constantly translating

3 Tony Gibson, *Counterweight: The Neighbourhood Option* (Russell Press, 1984), p. 112.

between them takes a great deal of energy and resources and creates strain for those brave and passionate enough to play the game. But this should not be seen simply as wordplay for its own sake. Such projects have at stake people's livelihoods and dwellings; their ability to live with dignity in the place they call home. If these things are so important, why does the process of securing them have to be so difficult?

Part of the answer, here, might be found in the apparently widening gap between upward and inward languages—between the language of the state and professionals, on the one hand, and the language of activists and citizens on the other. As the capacity of local government has been shattered by central government policy and the onus has moved from the state onto communities, the distance between these two worlds has only widened. Into this gap have stepped a number of professional translators—from activist-artists to community organisers and consultants. Many of those involved in the collective campaigns of the past and the present imparted to me the huge barriers to comprehension upheld by the gatekeepers; how surmounting these barriers seems to have become harder over the years; and that more should be done to speak in a common tongue. What might have been achieved in Kensington, one wonders, were the community representatives, on their first experience of a CLT practitioner conference in London, not so "freaked out by the industrial size of the intelligentsia". Hine hints at the challenge—but also sees hope—in this task of divining the key to the gate:

> You need a guide who is initiated into the relevant version of this language, who knows which words currently act as keys to which doors, what you have to say to have a decent chance of the gatekeepers letting you through. Yet inside these institutions, you are dealing with human beings, so if you can allow glimpses of what matters about your project to show through the filter of keywords, it may just make a difference.[4]

Whilst Hine's analogy of linguistic translation no doubt rings true for many community projects, it resonates especially with grassroots campaigns for (re) claiming the commons. The Green Backyard in Peterborough—for which it was written—albeit a gardening project, bears deep affinities with many of the housing commons that have been reappropriated, defended and created in Liverpool. Indeed, translation is an idea at the core of commoning. In his book on commoning in the city, activist-architect and spatial theorist Stavros Stavrides argues that "the creation of common spaces involves practices of translation that build bridges between people with different political, cultural

4 Dougald Hine, "Spelling It Out", in Jessie Brennan, ed., *Re: Development—Voices, Cyanotypes and Writings from the Green Backyard* (UCL Press, 2017).

or religious backgrounds".[5] The art of translating across differences—of negotiating a common space out of disparate elements—is all the more important for keeping alive the emancipatory and transformative potential of commoning; for sustaining its expansive dynamic and preventing its co-option by the homogenising and flattening forces of capital and bureaucracy, which seek to do all the mediating and keep their subjects passive, in the dark, isolated from one another except by their shared hierarchical relationship to the master code. Stavrides quotes philosopher Jacques Rancière in suggesting "An emancipated community is a community of narrators and translators".[6]

Thus Hine's metaphor also invites us to reflect upon the nature of narration and story-telling—not only for those involved in crafting campaigns in the present but also for those of us concerned with framing and explaining events of the past in ways which may have some bearing on the future. In this book, it was never my intention to speak from the page to policymakers or the gatekeepers of resources and I do not offer here any specific policy recommendations or detailed critique of legislation or regulation. Having said that, much of the material I have included is critical of urban policy discourses and practices (for instance, the argument about the damaging abstraction of HMR and other technocratic forms of urban renewal) and it would be a missed opportunity if this were to be incomprehensible if it ever did reach their ears. Some parts of the history told herein—such as SNAP and the early rehabilitation co-operative movement—might come across as more versed in the technicalities of the upward than the intuitive visions of the inward. For these older histories, it was much harder to track down those residents involved in the original community campaigning—many have moved on, lost touch with the co-ops or passed away. The perspectives of professionals loom larger here, then, than they do perhaps in the more contemporary narratives on the CLTs. I have sought to counter these tendencies by triangulating my interviews with secondary sources, but, like any history, my reading is necessarily a partial one.

Having worked closely with Homebaked and come into personal contact with Granby as well as a few Eldonian and co-op activists, their inward language has no doubt infused my own reading of their history. But I have tried to reach outwards, too. I have tried to translate their inner discourse—"the shorthand expressions and the charged words that build up among a group of people working together to bring about or sustain something that matters to them deeply"[7]—into an explanatory model of the wider housing landscape, the political-economic forces shaping it and how it could be transformed by such alternatives. This is meant to speak to as wide an audience as

5 Stavros Stavrides, *Common Space: The City as Commons* (Zed Books, 2016), p. 43.

6 Stavrides, *Common Space: The City as Commons*, p. 42.

7 Hine, "Spelling It Out".

possible, although I am all too aware of the inevitable compromises at play. The difficulty has come in developing a story that adequately represents the intricacies, complexities and contradictions of the wider social reality within which collective housing alternatives are embedded whilst also keeping an eye on making the language as clear, fresh and relatable as possible so as to communicate outwardly to potential supporters without expert knowledge the meaning of these projects for everyday life.

Artificial Hells, Social Practice and Artistic Spectacle: Who (or What) Is All This For?

Finally, in closing, Hine's analogy spells out more than first meets the eye—or at least than he intended. The focus on linguistic representation in collective alternative campaigning—on the idea of expression, on translation between mediums, on the separation between the presentation of a project and its reception by an audience, on the use of metaphor, on representation in any sense—implies a certain artistic bent to today's activists. Artistic representation is central to both Granby and Homebaked: Granby's Turner Prize victory enters it into a genre of performance art; Homebaked has been driven by artists from the get-go, funded by the Liverpool Biennial arts festival. Indeed, it seems to suggest a certain curatorship—and spectatorship—has come to mark such projects, as if they were conceived first and foremost as aesthetic objects. In some sense, artist-activists have stepped into the yawning space between the inward, the upward and the outward languages emerging as a result of the dismantling of public housing, the splintering of governance, the financialisation of the economy and the atomisation of society.

There is a certain paradoxical sense in which treating housing and regeneration as a verb is to invite its objectification as art, albeit a kind of performance art. This is most clearly visible in the popular rendering and self-expression of Granby and Homebaked as distinctly *artistic*—as well as social and political—projects. Both Homebaked and Granby embody prevailing trends towards participatory art—what has come to be known in the field as 'social practice' alongside a number of associated terms from community arts and socially engaged art to experimental, dialogic, interventionist, research-based and collaborative art. Through citizen engagement in art, social practice is seen to have, argues art historian, critic and theorist Claire Bishop in her provocative critique *Artificial Hells*,[8] performative transformative power in cultivating emancipatory social relations, but so often falls short of the mark. The unwitting progenitor of social practice is the libertarian-Marxist Guy Debord, the founder of the avant-garde Situationist International. Following

8 Claire Bishop, *Artificial Hells: Participatory Art and the Politics of Spectatorship* (Verso, 2012).

Debord's promotion of a radical kind of participatory art to eliminate the spectator's position in a society increasingly dominated by commodities, consumption and spectacle,[9] socially engaged artists attempt to break down the boundaries between creator and spectator and release art from the elitist and consumerist curated space of the gallery to be set free in the street, to interact spontaneously with people and place, for more culturally generative, socially useful and politically potent interventions.

One of the early examples of contemporary social practice identified by Bishop is a project devised in 1999 by Danish arts collective Superspin around collaboration with elderly residents of a high-rise block in Liverpool—one of those earmarked for redevelopment in the Liverpool Housing Action Trust regeneration programme—to create their own community TV and communications channel named *tenantspin*. Supported by Liverpool's Foundation for Art and Creative Technology (FACT), Liverpool Housing Action Trust and Arena Housing (the housing association which would go on to experiment with a CLT in Anfield through its Knowledge Transfer Partnership), *tenantspin* had a big influence on the deepening intersection of urbanism and art in the city. Some of the housing and community engagement professionals working on the project (such as Paul Kelly) would go on to become board members of Homebaked CLT. The project in many ways anticipated—and set the bar for—what was to come via the urban curatorship of Liverpool Biennial, founded in 1998, which has since funded and showcased a number of social practice interventions into Liverpool's housing politics, especially in response to HMR. Bishop points to biennial art festivals as one of the main conduits for social practice—citing their rapid replication across the world (33 new biennials founded in the decade leading up to 2006) as evidence of what she first identified, in an influential essay, as the art world's 'social turn'.[10]

Clearly, social practice thinking has deeply permeated Liverpool's housing activism. Issue #3 of *Stages*, the online journal of Liverpool Biennial, is dedicated to documenting a five-day interactive workshop held in 2014 in which prominent artists, writers, curators and community organisers—including many of those involved in Granby and Homebaked, such as Theresa MacDermott, Sam Jones and Nina Edge, who has received a number of Biennial commissions over the years for artistic provocations on housing demolition and HMR—gathered "to consider how Liverpool Biennial might inhabit its city in more significant ways. … Their starting point was the state of housing in the district of Toxteth, Liverpool 8. … This complex, loaded situation acted as the prompt for a week of research and inquiry".[11] In *Artificial*

9 Guy Debord, *Society of the Spectacle and Other Films* (Rebel Press, 1967/1992).

10 Claire Bishop, "The Social Turn: Collaboration and Its Discontents", *Artforum* 44.6 (2006): 178–183 (p. 178).

11 See www.biennial.com/journal/issue-3/pdf/introduction.

Hells Bishop cites as a globally pioneering practitioner of social practice Jeanne van Heeswijk—the Liverpool Biennial-commissioned creator of *2Up2Down* and co-founder and abiding critical friend of Homebaked.[12] According to her author biography in the special issue of *Stages* dedicated to Homebaked, Jeanne

> embeds herself, for years at a time, in communities from Rotterdam to Liverpool, working with them to improve their neighbourhoods and empowering them to take matters into their own hands, creating an alternative to the urban planning schemes which rarely take embedded culture into account, that are often foisted upon by local authorities. Her work often attempts to unravel invisible legislation, governmental codes, and social institutions, gradually enabling areas to take control over their future. She calls it "radicalising the local" by empowering communities to become their own antidote.[13]

Jeanne is part of a global network of artists, activists, architects, urbanists and critical academics—including David Harvey—linked together through Cohabitation Strategies, a non-profit cooperative for socio-spatial research, design and development, founded in response to the 2008 global financial crash, in Rotterdam—where Jeanne lives and does most of her work. Their mission is to help others claim the right to the city; "to generate socially just and environmentally responsible urban projects by designing and developing diverse socio-spatial strategies".[14] Concluding their seven aims is: "Envisioning new collective urban imaginaries leading to socio-spatial change using creativity and urban play".

All this—however admirable—is by no means unproblematic. Bishop argues that the social turn in art has produced a concomitant ethical turn in art criticism, in which the working process rather than finished product—the *how* over the *what*—is judged on the degree to which it produces transformative processes of collaboration and social impact rather than on the aesthetic merit of the actual artwork. "This emphasis", she writes, "on process over product (i.e. means over ends) is justified as oppositional to capitalism's predilection for the contrary".[15] Here, we begin to see parallels with housing seen as a verb over a noun, a lived experience over a commodity. In a similar way in which it might be asking too much of collective housing alternatives to perform all those political, economic and cultural transformations argued for in this book, for Bishop, the ethical criteria of social practice may stretch

12 Bishop, *Artificial Hells: Participatory Art and the Politics of Spectatorship.*

13 Jeanne van Heeswijk and Britt Jurgensen, "Introduction", *Stages: Liverpool Biennial* #2, Homebaked: A Perfect Recipe (2014).

14 Cohabitation Strategies (CohStra): www.cohstra.org/.

15 Bishop, "The Social Turn: Collaboration and Its Discontents", p. 180.

the function of art too far, may ask just too much of it. In drawing these comparisons, I do not mean to demean the political power of participatory art, collective housing alternatives or their combination—indeed, if Granby and Homebaked are to be framed in this way, I would suggest that they have had a positively powerful impact on people and place—but I do intend to question how this sits next to the traditional purpose of art as ultimately residing in beauty, with aesthetics, not political or social reform. There is clearly a problem with the way in which art, today, has become such a valuable global commodity, reduced to exchange value, yet there is equally cause for concern if art is to be valued only for its use value, its instrumentality, for this would mean reducing it to something else. Oscar Wilde's take on the eternal nature of art—that "all art is quite useless"[16]—throws in doubt the entire premise of social practice. The implication is that, in constructing urban spaces as art works to be collectively crafted, experienced and then consumed in the popular, architectural or academic press, we risk turning them into spectacles and aestheticising—trivialising, even—deeply political issues.

Is this really such a bad thing? Art has long been used as a political tool for highlighting important issues in the public sphere; an age-old debate has engulfed aesthetic theory over the role and function of art in society. Is art's ultimate aim the Beautiful—pure, formal aesthetics divorced from ethical and epistemological concerns—or is the Good or even the True part of its purview too? Recent trends in contemporary art around social practice place political activism centre-stage; art has been weaponised as a tool for social justice, as a platform for speaking truth to power. Granby CLT's Turner Prize nomination, though unprecedented, is not anomalous. For the 2018 award, yet another architectural collective was shortlisted—one likewise unaffiliated to the profession and concerned fundamentally with socio-spatial justice. Forensic Architecture, the Goldsmiths-based action-research agency founded by architect scholar-activist Eyal Weizman and comprising architects, journalists, lawyers and scientists, was shortlisted for film, text and photographs documenting their investigative work into state violence in Palestinian Bedouin communities, which has been instrumental in bringing charges against the Israeli police. Seen generously, Forensic Architecture and Assemble show art at its most politically and socially transformative—art that shocks an audience out of complacency or defamiliarises troubling states of affairs we normally take for granted; art that presents alternatives and possible ways out of societal systems that dominate, demean and dehumanise us.

Looked at sceptically, however, Assemble and Forensic Architecture are part of the polarisation of art as either consumerist entertainment or professional

16 Oscar Wilde, Preface to *The Picture of Dorian Gray*, in Lippincott's Monthly Magazine (1890).

commodity. As they attempt to subvert the 'society of the spectacle',[17] they enact, in the same breath, their own spectacle and thereby help reproduce this society, in darkly comic Situationist style. Their outward framing in the *academese* of social practice and the *art-speak*[18] of the art world acts to alienate and exclude potential supporters and drives a wider wedge between the inward and the outward languages than that existing before. In collective alternatives of the past—Weller Street and the Eldonians, for instance—residents were more straightforward about what they wanted and spoke in more direct, tangible and meaningful terms: of achieving better housing conditions and staying together as a community; of achieving democratic control over decisions being taken and collective ownership of land, houses, shops and enterprises; of winning a war against the council and in defining the terms of debate against middle-class professionals. The permeation of art-speak into more recent interventions can only represent a kind of gentrification of the discourses used inwardly to frame and outwardly to pitch projects to the public and the art world. This is just one aspect of their creeping commodification. The spectacle-isation of Granby—and, in less dramatic ways, Homebaked—demeans the long, hard struggle of resisting the dominance of exchange value over use value and asserting an alternative, more people-focused conception of place-making. It fetishises as a product—a commodity and curiosity—the deeply embedded social process of regeneration. In reifying these projects as outstanding, one-of-a-kind artistic creations, to be sold on the global (socially engaged) art market, we place them in a bubble of exception, depoliticising their power to contest neoliberalism by boxing them off as unthreatening spectacles. Their treatment as such has serious implications for what I have tried to convey as their real utopian power.

For some critics, such as the community arts practitioner and scholar–activist Stephen Pritchard, Granby is the product of auspicious collaborations with globally networked and highly mobile creative professionals and social innovators at the frontier of urban commodification. From this perspective, Assemble's intervention in Granby is "not here used as a form of resistance but rather as an instrument for the neoliberal concept of culture-led regeneration, albeit in more novel forms".[19] It is certainly difficult to argue with Pritchard's assessment that "The extensive and often complexly intertwined experiences of the Granby 4 Streets and Steinbeck Studio teams makes it rather difficult to accept claims that the project was under-skilled or, indeed,

17 Guy Debord, *Society of the Spectacle and Other Films* (Rebel Press, 1967).
18 Andy Beckett, "A User's Guide to Art-Speak", *The Guardian* (27 Jan. 2013): www.theguardian.com/artanddesign/2013/jan/27/users-guide-international-art-english.
19 Stephen Pritchard, "Complexity, Uncertainty and Scalability: How Assemble's Granby 4 Streets Won 2015 Turner Prize", Colouring in Culture Blog, 2016: http://colouringinculture.org/blog/assemble-complexity-uncertainty-scalability#_ftn4.

that it was community-led". Indeed, despite Assemble's (anti)credentials as a trans-disciplinary design collective generalising in cooperative DIY through a self-consciously amateur ethos, they have become a highly successful and sought-after outfit at the vanguard of the arts-led regeneration industry. Catapulted into the limelight so soon after their establishment in 2010, the "dazzling trajectory of this loosely assembled collective of designers and makers", as architectural critic Oliver Wainwright put it,[20] was, according to Pritchard, already very much on display by the time they landed in Granby. Even though the eighteen-strong collective, many graduates of the University of Cambridge, were all still in their mid-twenties and lacked architectural qualifications when nominated for the Turner Prize, they were already the talk of the (arts-led regenerated) town, having delivered a number of significant commissions as a longstanding partner of Create London, a prolific grant funder of social practice projects across east London.[21] Moreover, Assemble were brought to Granby via their connections with Steinbeck Studio's Xanthe Hamilton, who so happens to be the daughter-in-law of Saskia Sassen, the globe-trotting superstar urbanist. Sassen's ideas on world city formation and the 'brutality' and 'complexity' of globalisation, on the global capital flows and complex assemblages that shape planetary urbanisation and produce violent 'expulsions',[22] have helped define the new urbanist zeitgeist. Appositely, the innovative model of social investment-fuelled arts-led regeneration which Xanthe presented at the London Festival of Architecture in 2016—Pritchard quotes her as revealing[23]—was written "for Saskia Sassen".

Writing in the inaugural issue of *Stages* recording the outputs of Liverpool Biennial's Future City forum—alongside an article about Homebaked[24]—Sassen asks the pointed question: where is the "new frontier zone" in our global urban condition? During historical colonial-capitalist and imperial times, she muses, "the frontier was at the edge of the system, but now we're past that kind of edge".[25] In our age of planetary urbanisation, increasingly subsuming everyone and everything within a globalising capitalism, nothing remains

20 Oliver Wainwright, "The Street That Might Win the Turner Prize: How Assemble Are Transforming Toxteth", *The Guardian* (12 May 2015).

21 Create London: https://createlondon.org/about-us/.

22 Saskia Sassen, *Expulsions: Brutality and Complexity in the Global Economy* (Harvard University Press, 2014).

23 Hamilton, *Granby 4 Streets: The Ideals of Specificity and Scalability in a Social and Architectural Endeavour*, 2016, quoted in Pritchard, "Complexity, Uncertainty and Scalability: How Assemble's Granby 4 Streets Won 2015 Turner Prize".

24 Jeanne van Heeswijk and Britt Jurgensen, "We Are Here to Stay", *Stages: Liverpool Biennial* #1, Future City (2014).

25 Saskia Sassen and Irit Rogoff, "What is our Globalised Urban Future?", *Stages: Liverpool Biennial #1*.

outside the all-consuming purview of capital such that the frontier space of encounter, complexity, indeterminacy, experimentation, possibility and conflict has shifted from the colonial edge to the immanent "inside" of capitalist cities, into urban development itself and the spaces in between: "a zone where actors from different worlds have an encounter, an encounter for which there are no established rules". Here, Sassen is translating insights from Marxist urban theory—Lefebvre's ideas on planetary urbanisation and their reinterpretation by Merrifield in *The New Urban Question*—into the neoliberal lingua franca. The new, urbanised Wild West she alludes to—a world of cowboys and speculators in the gold rush economy of rental extraction, property-led creative destruction and gambling on collateralised debt obligations, all competing to "cash in on legalized looting"[26]—has as its corollary those residual, liminal, often derelict 'frontier' spaces intermittently evacuated by capital in which the vacuum left by managed decline is quickly (re)occupied by social innovators and entrepreneurs riding the latest wave of 'roll-with-it' neoliberalisation.[27] Granby is in many respects precisely such a frontier zone—a Zone of Opportunity for diverse opportunists all vying to make *something* (their name, a living, a 'killing'?) out of the differentials and indeterminacies; a ZOO in which to watch the spectacle of 'the latest thing' being performed. On this reading, Assemble's choice of conceptual rendering—community *homesteading*, claiming original/indigenous territory and pushing the boundaries of the urban frontier—reveals more about their celebrated approach than perhaps they are even conscious of.

Pritchard's diagnosis of Granby Four Streets as a frontier zone of capital accumulation and neoliberal intermediation may well be overstated—the upshot of capitalocentric 'strong theorising'.[28] Such an analysis overlooks the foundational role played by grassroots guerrilla gardening in transforming Granby long before Steinbeck Studio or Assemble rocked up to curate the scene, conveniently brushing over the renewed hope and energy that these actors have inspired amongst residents, activists and their supporters. It also fails to recognise that Granby—like the wider city for which it is a microcosm—has always been an 'edgy' intersection of energies on the 'edge' of different worlds,[29] a globally interconnected place of transition and encounter of people from Ireland to the Caribbean, from Somalia to Malaysia.[30] Nonetheless, important

26 Andy Merrifield, *The New Urban Question* (Pluto Press, 2014), p. 73.

27 Roger Keil, "The Urban Politics of Roll-with-It Neoliberalization", *City: Analysis of Urban Trends, Culture, Theory, Policy, Action* 13.2–3 (2009): 230–245.

28 J.K. Gibson-Graham, "Diverse Economies: Performative Practices for 'Other Worlds'", *Progress in Human Geography* 32.5 (2008): 613–632.

29 Steve Higginson and Tony Wailey, *Edgy Cities* (Northern Lights, 2006); John Davies, *Cities on the Edge* (Liverpool University Press, 2008).

30 Tim Bunnell, *From World City to the World in One City: Liverpool through Malay Lives* (Wiley-Blackwell, 2016).

and troubling questions remain unanswered, namely: *who*—or *what*—is Granby Four Streets really for?

In her public statement about becoming the Granby Winter Garden's inaugural artist-in-residence, Nina Edge implies a possible answer:

> Granby people have inspired the world, by digging in and planting themselves a bright future. I'm as pleased as punch to be appointed for the horticultural commission, which will be formed from plants, structures and lighting, inside a house that has been empty for many years. *This is exactly the kind of experimental and creative environment in which new ways of making art can grow.*[31]

There is a sense in which Granby Four Streets has been curated by Assemble to meet the bohemian-bourgeois liberal-ethical gaze—voraciously consumed by expert, amateur and armchair critics alike. Assemble have used the Turner Prize success as a sleek PR campaign for their own work—and who can blame them? Granby has been inadvertently inserted into global circuits of (cultural) capital—part of a circus of urban policy tourism frequented by professionals and students of art and architecture, planning and geography (myself included). Their intervention is part of an emerging assemblage in Liverpool—intersecting with multi-scalar assemblages globally—pushing the city's over-played 'regeneration game' to its logical (exhaustively creative, creatively exhausted) conclusion. Benefiting materially from this new culture-led regeneration industry, this new kind of grant regime, an arts-led grant regime—the latest arm of the non-profit industrial complex—are the countless artists, community arts practitioners, arts organisations, biennials, charities, philanthropic foundations, philanthropists, social financiers, cultural economists, regeneration consultants, think tanks, housing associations, speculative property developers, community engagement professionals, policy wonks, social innovators and urban imagineers, joined by the academics, journalists and art critics who study and evaluate them, all connected in a loosely assembled network of value production and extraction … I could go on. But it is too easy to caricature Granby and Homebaked as 'novel forms' of 'neoliberal culture-led regeneration'. This represents resignation to just one part of the dialectic; social reality is more complex than that. Commodification of housing and neighbourhoods and their enrolment into an arts-led regeneration industry is only one side of the story. That Granby and Homebaked are artificial hells *and* real utopias, at the same time, reflects the dual character of housing as both noun and verb; the dead labour of capital and the dynamic, embodied practices of commoning.

31 Emphasis added. Quoted on Granby CLT's website: www.granby4streetsclt.co.uk/granby-winter-garden/.

Granby's and Homebaked's categorisation as 'art' seems to express a cynical post-political mood that lingers on in spite of recent reopenings in the ideological fissures of neoliberalism better than it does their status as politically transformative projects. They have been showered with art awards and grants not only for charting a new frontier in arts-led commodification but because they disclose something truly beautiful in their design, in their cultivation of vital places and the social relationships that reproduce such spaces. In this way, they are *exceptional*—but their extraordinariness says less about the art world than it does about the inadequacies of urban policy and political economy. That artists have had to step into the gap left by the retreating state when it comes to important political issues like the right to shelter and dwell in a particular place says a great deal about our current conjuncture. If we wish to move beyond this impasse towards the reproduction and replication of such practices—that is, if we wish to see collective housing alternatives more systematically developed—we need to construct the requisite institutional infrastructure. Until we do, they will continue to be sporadically curated and celebrated as novel spectacles. If the value of art is not simply to represent reality but also to provide a counterpoint to it, and thereby invite its transformation, then perhaps this is what the artistic presentation of Granby and Homebaked reveals: a window into alternatives as well as a mirror of the system as it currently looks. Their artistic function is to charm us with a carefully curated alternative approach to urbanism—one that bears aesthetic as well as socio-political appeal—and, by the same token, to shock us with the absurdity of how, under capitalism, we have come to treat dwelling(s) so carelessly.

Bibliography

Aalbers, Manuel B. (2014). "Do Maps Make Geography? Part 1: Redlining, Planned Shrinkage, and the Places of Decline". *ACME: An International E-Journal for Critical Geographies* 13.4: 525–556.

Aalbers, Manuel B., and Brett Christophers (2014). "Centring Housing in Political Economy". *Housing, Theory and Society* 31.4: 373–394.

—— (2014). "The Housing Question under Capitalist Political Economies". *Housing, Theory and Society* 31.4: 422–428.

Allen, Chris (2008). *Housing Market Renewal and Social Class*. Routledge.

Allen, Chris, and Lee Crookes (2009). "Fables of the Reconstruction: A Phenomenology of 'Place Shaping' in the North of England". *Town Planning Review* 80.4: 455–480.

Anderson, Hugh (1984). "Co-op Dividends". *Architects' Journal* (18 July).

Angelis, Massimo De (2006). *The Beginning of History: Value Struggles and Global Capital*. Pluto Press.

—— (2017). *Omnia Sunt Communia: On the Commons and the Transformation to Postcapitalism*. Zed Books.

Angotti, Tom (2007). *New York for Sale: Community Planning Confronts Global Real Estate*. MIT Press.

Assemble, eds (2015). *Granby Workshop Catalogue 2015*. http://www.sharethecity.org/wp-content/uploads/2015/10/15-10-07s-Assemble-Granby-Turner-Prize-Workshop-Catalogue.pdf.

Atkinson, Rowland, Simon Parker and Emma Regina Morales (2017). "Non-State Space: The Strategic Ejection of Dangerous and High Maintenance Urban Space". *Territory, Politics, Governance* 5.4: 443–458.

Attoh, Kafui (2011). "What Kind of Right Is the Right to the City?". *Progress in Human Geography* 35.5: 669–685.

Baeten, Guy (2000). "From Community Planning to Partnership Planning: Urban Regeneration and Shifting Power Geometries on the South Bank, London". *GeoJournal* 51: 293–300.

—— (2001). "Urban Regeneration, Social Exclusion and Shifting Power Geometries on the South Bank, London". *Geographische Zeitschrift* 89.2/3: 104–113.

Bailey, Nick (2012). "The Role, Organisation and Contribution of Community Enterprise to Urban Regeneration Policy in the UK". *Progress in Planning* 77.1: 1–35.

Ball, Jonny (2017). "'Militant Liverpool' as Liverpool Exceptionalism: The Rise, Fall and Character of the City Council, 1983–1987". *Transactions of the Historic Society of Lancashire and Cheshire* 166: 145–186.
Beckett, Andy (2015). *Promised You a Miracle: UK 80–82*. Penguin Books.
Belchem, John, and Bryan Biggs (2011). *Liverpool: City of Radicals*. Liverpool University Press.
Bell Yank, Sue (2014). "2Up2Down/Homebaked and the Symbolic Media Narrative". *Stages: Liverpool Biennial #2*. Homebaked: A Perfect Recipe. www.biennial.com/journal/issue-2/test.
Bentham, Justin, Andrew Bowman, Marta De Cuesta, Ewald Engelen, Ismail Ertürk, Peter Folkman, Julie Froud et al. (2013). *Manifesto for the Foundational Economy*, CRESC Working Paper 131. Centre for Research on Socio-Cultural Change.
Beswick, Joe, and Joe Penny (2018). "Demolishing the Present to Sell Off the Future? The Financialisation of Public Housing in London". *International Journal for Urban and Regional Research* 42.4: 612–632.
Bhattacharya, Tithi, ed. (2017). *Social Reproduction Theory: Remapping Class, Recentering Oppression*. Pluto Press.
Birchall, Johnston (1988). *Building Communities the Co-operative Way*. Routledge.
—— (1991). "The Hidden History of Co-operative Housing in Britain". *Department of Government Working Papers* 17.
—— (1995). "Co-Partnership Housing and the Garden City Movement". *Planning Perspectives* 10.4: 329–358.
Bishop, Claire (2006). "The Social Turn: Collaboration and Its Discontents". *Artforum* 44.6: 178–183.
—— (2012). *Artificial Hells: Participatory Art and the Politics of Spectatorship*. Verso.
Blomley, Nicholas (2004). "Un-Real Estate: Proprietary Space and Public Gardening". *Antipode* 36.4: 614–641.
—— (2004). *Unsettling the City*. Routledge.
Boland, Philip (2008). "The Construction of Images of People and Place: Labelling Liverpool and Stereotyping Scousers". *Cities* 25.6: 355–369.
Bolt, Gideon, and Ronald Van Kempen (2011). "Successful Mixing? Effects of Urban Restructuring Policies in Dutch Neighbourhoods". *Tijdschrift Voor Economische En Sociale Geografie* 102.3: 361–368.
Boughton, John (2018). *Municipal Dreams: The Rise and Fall of Council Housing*. Verso.
Bridge, Gary, Tim Butler and Loretta Lees, eds (2012). *Mixed Communities: Gentrification by Stealth?* Policy Press.
Bruyn, Severyn, and James Meehan (1987). *Beyond the Market and the State: New Directions in Community Development*. Temple University Press.
Buber, Martin (1958). *Paths in Utopia*. Beacon Press.
Bunce, Susannah (2016). "Pursuing Urban Commons: Politics and Alliances in Community Land Trust Activism in East London". *Antipode* 478.1: 134–150.
Bunnell, Tim (2016). *From World City to the World in One City: Liverpool through Malay Lives*. Wiley-Blackwell.

Burgess, Rod (1978). "Petty Commodity Housing or Dweller Control? A Critique of John Turner's Views on Housing Policy". *World Development* 6.9–10: 1105–1133.

—— (1985). "The Limits of State Self-Help Housing Programmes". *Development and Change* 16.2: 271–312.

Castells, Manuel (1977). *The Urban Question: A Marxist Approach*. MIT Press.

CDP (Community Development Project) (1977). *Gilding the Ghetto: The State and the Poverty Experiments*. CDP Inter-Project Editorial Team.

Chatterton, Paul (2010). "The Urban Impossible: A Eulogy for the Unfinished City". *City* 14.3: 234–244.

—— (2013). "Towards an Agenda for Post-Carbon Cities: Lessons from Lilac, the UK's First Ecological, Affordable Cohousing Community". *International Journal for Urban and Regional Research* 37.5: 1654–1674.

Christophers, Brett (2014). "Wild Dragons in the City: Urban Political Economy, Affordable Housing Development and the Performative World-Making of Economic Models". *International Journal of Urban and Regional Research* 38.1: 79–97.

—— (2018). *The New Enclosure: The Appropriation of Public Land in Neoliberal Britain*. Verso.

—— (2019). "Putting Financialisation in Its Financial Context: Transformations in Local Government-Led Urban Development in Post-Financial Crisis England". *Transactions of the Institute of British Geographers* 44.3: 571–586.

Clapham, David, and Keith Kintrea (1987). "Importing Housing Policy: Housing Co-operatives in Britain and Scandinavia". *Housing Studies* 2.3: 157–169.

—— (1992). *Housing Co-operatives in Britain*. Longman.

Clay, Tom (1978). "The Liverpool Co-ops". *Architects' Journal* (5 July).

Cocks, Matthew, and Chris Couch (2012). "The Governance of a Shrinking City: Housing Renewal in the Liverpool Conurbation, UK". *International Planning Studies* 17.3: 277–301.

Cole, Ian (2012). "Housing Market Renewal and Demolition in England in the 2000s: The Governance of 'Wicked Problems'". *International Journal of Housing Policy* 12.3: 347–366.

Coleman, Alice (1985). *Utopia on Trial: Vision and Reality in Planned Housing*. Hilary Shipman Ltd.

Conaty, Pat, and Martin Large, eds (2014). *Commons Sense: Co-operative Place Making and the Capturing of Land Value for 21st Century Garden Cities*. Hawthorn Press.

Conway, Dennis (1982). "Self-Help Housing, the Commodity Nature of Housing and Amelioration of the Housing Deficit: Continuing the Turner-Burgess Debate". *Antipode* 14.2: 40–46.

Cooke, Philip, ed. (1989). *Localities: Changing Face of Urban Britain*. Routledge.

Cooper, Davina (2017). "Prefiguring the State". *Antipode* 49.2: 335–356.

Cooper, Davina, Nikita Dhawan and Janet Newman (2019). *Reimagining the State: Theoretical Challenges and Transformative Possibilities*. Routledge.

Cornelius, John (1982). *Liverpool 8*. John Murray Publishers.

Couch, Chris (2003). *City of Change and Challenge: Urban Planning and Regeneration in Liverpool*. Ashgate.

—— (2008). "Housing Renewal and the Community in a Shrinking City". *Town Planning Review* 79.6: 695–703.

Couch, Chris, and Matthew Cocks (2013). "Housing Vacancy and the Shrinking City: Trends and Policies in the UK and the City of Liverpool". *Housing Studies* 28.3: 499–519.

Cowan, Robert (1986). "Co-op or Cop-Out?". *ROOF* 11.4.

Cowan, Robert, P. Hannay and R. Owens (1988). "The Light on Top of the Tunnel, in Vauxhall Victors: Eldonians Special Issue". *Architects' Journal* (23 Mar.): 37–66.

Cox, Kevin R. (1993). "The Local and the Global in the New Urban Politics: A Critical View". *Environment and Planning D: Society and Space* 11.4: 433–448.

Crabtree, Louise (2018). "Self-Organised Housing in Australia: Housing Diversity in an Age of Market Heat". *International Journal of Housing Policy* 18.1: 15–34.

Crouch, Colin (2011). *The Strange Non-Death of Neo-Liberalism*. Polity Press.

Cumbers, Andrew (2012). *Reclaiming Public Ownership: Making Space for Economic Democracy*. Zed Books.

—— (2015). "Constructing a Global Commons in, against and beyond the State". *Space and Polity* 19.1: 62–75.

Czischke, Darinka (2018). "Collaborative Housing and Housing Providers: Towards an Analytical Framework of Multi-Stakeholder Collaboration in Housing Co-Production". *International Journal of Housing Policy* 18.1: 55–81.

Darcy, Michael (2010). "De-Concentration of Disadvantage and Mixed Income Housing: A Critical Discourse Approach". *Housing, Theory and Society* 27.1: 1–22.

Davies, John (2008). *Cities on the Edge*. Liverpool University Press.

Davies, William (2018). *Nervous States: How Feeling Took over the World*. Jonathan Cape.

Davis, John Emmeus (1990). *Contested Ground: Collective Action and the Urban Neighborhood*. Cornell University Press.

——, ed. (2010). *The Community Land Trust Reader*. Lincoln Institute of Land Policy.

—— (2010). "Origins and Evolution of the Community Land Trust in the United States". In John Emmeus Davis, ed. *The Community Land Trust Reader*, 3–47. Lincoln Institute of Land Policy.

Deas, Iain, Graham Haughton and Stephen Hincks (2014). "'A Good Geography Is Whatever It Needs to Be': Evolving Spatial Imaginaries in North West England". In Phil Allmendinger, Graham Haughton, Jörg Knieling and Frank Othengrafen, eds. *Soft Spaces in Europe: Re-Negotiating Governance, Boundaries and Borders*, 25–44. Routledge.

Debord, Guy (1967). *Society of the Spectacle and Other Films*. Rebel Press.

DeFilippis, James (1999). "Alternatives to the 'New Urban Politics': Finding Locality and Autonomy in Local Economic Development". *Political Geography* 18: 973–990.

—— (2004). *Unmaking Goliath: Community Control in the Face of Global Capital*. Routledge.

DeFilippis, James, and Peter North (2004). "The Emancipatory Community? Place, Politics and Collective Action in Cities". In Loretta Lees, ed. *The Emancipatory City? Paradoxes and Possibilities*, 72–88. SAGE.

Dembski, Sebastian (2015). "Structure and Imagination of Changing Cities: Manchester, Liverpool and the Spatial In-Between". *Urban Studies* 52.9: 1647–1664.

De Peuter, Greig, and Nick Dyer-Witheford (2010). "Commons and Cooperatives". *Affinities: A Journal of Radical Theory, Culture, and Action* 4.1: 30–56.

Dimaggio, Paul J., and Walter W. Powell (1983). "The Iron Cage Revisited: Institutional Isomorphism and Collective Rationality in Organizational Fields". *American Sociological Review* 48.2: 147–160.

Dockerill, Bertie (2016). "Liverpool Corporation and the Origins of Municipal Social Housing, 1842–1890". *Transactions of the Historic Society of Lancashire and Cheshire* 165: 39–56.

Dorling, Danny (2014). *All That Is Solid: How the Great Housing Disaster Defines Our Times, and What We Can Do About It*. Allen Lane.

Edwards, Michael (2015). *Prospects for Land, Rent and Housing in UK Cities*, Foresight Future of Cities: Working Paper. Government Office for Science. www.gov.uk/government/publications/future-of-cities-land-rent-and-housing-in-uk-cities.

Eizenberg, Efrat (2012). "Actually Existing Commons: Three Moments of Space of Community Gardens in New York City". *Antipode* 44.3: 764–782.

Ellis, Hugh, and Kate Henderson (2013). *Planning Out Poverty: The Reinvention of Social Town Planning*. Town and Country Planning Association.

Engels, Friedrich (1972). *The Housing Question*. Progress Publishers.

—— (1992). *The Condition of the Working Class in England*. Penguin Classics.

Engelsman, Udi, and Alan Southern (2010). "Knowledge Transfer in Regeneration: Is It Feasible and Can the Community Benefit?". *Journal of Urban Regeneration and Renewal* 4.2: 147–157.

Engelsman, Udi, Mike Rowe and Alan Southern (2016). "Community Land Trusts—A Radical or Reformist Response to the Housing Question Today?". *ACME: An International E-Journal for Critical Geographies* 15.3: 590–615.

Federici, Silvia (2019). *Re-Enchanting the World: Feminism and the Politics of the Commons*. PM Press.

Fisher, Mark (2009). *Capitalist Realism: Is There No Alternative?* Zero Books.

—— (2018). *K-Punk: The Collected Writings of Mark Fisher (2004–2016)*. Repeater.

Flint, John (2012). "Housing Policy, the Right to the City and the Construction of Knowledge". *International Journal of Housing Policy* 12.3: 253–261.

Foundational Economy Collective (2018). *Foundational Economy: The Infrastructure of Everyday Life*. Manchester University Press.

Fraser, Nancy (2014). "Behind Marx's Hidden Abode". *New Left Review* 86 (Mar.–Apr.).

Freire, Paulo (1970). *Pedagogy of the Oppressed*. Continuum.

Frost, Diane, and Peter North (2013). *Militant Liverpool: A City on the Edge*. Liverpool University Press.

Frost, Diane, and Richard Phillips (2011). *Liverpool '81: Remembering the Riots*. Liverpool University Press.

Fuller, Duncan, Andrew Jonas and Roger Lee, eds (2010). *Interrogating Alterity: Alternative Economic and Political Spaces*. Ashgate.

Fullilove, Mindy Thompson (2004). *Root Shock: How Tearing up City Neighborhoods Hurts America, and What We Can Do about It*. One World/Ballantine Books.

García-Lamarca, Melissa (2017). "From Occupying Plazas to Recuperating Housing: Insurgent Practices in Spain". *International Journal of Urban and Regional Research* 41.1: 37–53.

Geisler, Charles, and Gail Daneker (2000). *Property and Values: Alternatives to Public and Private Ownership*. Island Press.

George, Henry (1879). *Progress and Poverty: An Inquiry into the Cause of Industrial Depressions and of Increase of Want with Increase of Wealth*. Doubleday, Page & Co.

Gibson, Tony (1984). *Counterweight: The Neighbourhood Option*. Russell Press.

Gibson-Graham, J.K. (1996). *The End of Capitalism (As We Knew It): A Feminist Critique of Political Economy*. Blackwell.

—— (2006). *A Postcapitalist Politics*. University of Minnesota Press.

—— (2008). "Diverse Economies: Performative Practices for 'Other Worlds'". *Progress in Human Geography* 32.5: 613–632.

Gilbert, Jeremy (2013). *Common Ground: Democracy and Collectivity in an Age of Individualism*. Pluto Press.

Godin, Benoît (2012). "Social Innovation: Utopias of Innovation from *c*.1830 to the Present". *Project on the Intellectual History of Innovation* 11: 1–52.

Goodman, Robert (1972). *After the Planners*. Simon & Schuster.

Goulding, Richard (2019). *Housing Futures: What Can Community-Led Housing Achieve for Greater Manchester?* Greater Manchester Housing Action. www.gmhousingaction.com/housing-futures/.

Graeber, David (2001). *Toward an Anthropological Theory of Value: The False Coin of Our Own Dreams*.

—— (2015). *The Utopia of Rules: On Technology, Stupidity, and the Secret Joys of Bureaucracy*. Melville House.

—— (2018). *Bullshit Jobs: A Theory*. Allen Lane.

Graeber, David, and David Wengrow (2018). "How to Change the Course of Human History (at Least, the Part That's Already Happened)". *Eurozine* (2 Mar.). www.eurozine.com/change-course-human-history/.

Grant, Jean (2011). "Backyard Commons". In Rob MacDonald, ed. *DIY City*, 51–59. Liverpool University Press.

Gratz, Roberta Brandes (1989). *The Living City*. Simon & Schuster.

Gray, Neil, ed. (2018). *Rent and Its Discontents: A Century of Housing Struggle*. Rowman & Littlefield.

—— (2018). "Spatial Composition and the Urbanization of Capital: The 1915 Glasgow Rent Strikes and the Housing Question Reconsidered". In Neil Gray, ed. *Rent and Its Discontents: A Century of Housing Struggle*, 49–67. Rowman & Littlefield.

Grosskurth, Anne (1985). "Bringing Back the Braddocks". *ROOF* 10.1: 19–23.

Hall, Peter (1997). "Regeneration Policies for Peripheral Housing Estates: Inward- and Outward-Looking Approaches". *Urban Studies* 34.5: 873–890.

Hardt, Michael, and Antonio Negri (2009). *Commonwealth*. Harvard University Press.

Harloe, Michael (1995). *The People's Home?: Social Rented Housing in Europe and America*. Wiley-Blackwell.

Harloe, Michael, Chris Pickvance and John Urry, eds (1990). *Place, Policy and Politics: Do Localities Matter?* Routledge.

Hartman, Chester (1984). "The Right to Stay Put". In Chester Hartman, ed. *Between Eminence and Notoriety: Four Decades of Radical Urban Planning*, 304–318. CUPR Press.

Harvey, David (1989). "From Managerialism to Entrepreneurialism: The Transformation in Urban Governance in Late Capitalism". *Geografiska Annaler* 71.1: 3–17.

—— (1995). "Militant Particularism and Global Ambition: The Conceptual Politics of Place, Space, and Environment in the Work of Raymond Williams". *Social Text* 42: 69–98.

—— (2003). *The New Imperialism*. Oxford University Press.

—— (2006). "Neo-Liberalism as Creative Destruction". *Geografiska Annaler, Series B: Human Geography* 88.2: 145–158.

—— (2007). *Limits to Capital*. Verso Books.

—— (2012). *Rebel Cities: From the Right to the City to the Urban Revolution*. Verso.

Hatherley, Owen (2011). *A Guide to the New Ruins of Great Britain*. Verso Books.

Heeswijk, Jeanne van, and Britt Jurgensen (2014). "Introduction". *Stages: Liverpool Biennial #2*. Homebaked: A Perfect Recipe. www.biennial.com/journal/issue-2/introduction.

—— (2014). "We Are Here to Stay". *Stages: Liverpool Biennial #1*, Future City. www.biennial.com/journal/issue-1/we-are-here-to-stay-.

Heidegger, Martin (1971). "Poetically Man Dwells". In Martin Heidegger and Albert Hofstadter, eds. *Poetry, Language, Thought*, 213–229. Harper & Row.

—— (1978). "Building Dwelling Thinking". In David Farrell Krell, ed. *Basic Writings*, 347–363. Routledge.

Henderson, James, and Christopher McWilliams (2017). "The UK Community Anchor Model and Its Challenges for Community Sector Theory and Practice". *Urban Studies* 54.16: 3826–3842.

Herbert, Steve (2008). "The Trapdoor of Community". *Annals of the Association of American Geographers* 95.4: 850–865.

Higginson, Steve, and Tony Wailey (2006). *Edgy Cities*. Northern Lights.

Hine, Dougald (2017). "Spelling It Out". In Jessie Brennan, ed. *Re: Development—Voices, Cyanotypes and Writings from the Green Backyard*, 58–60. UCL Press.

Hodkinson, Stuart (2010). "Housing in Common: In Search of Strategy for Housing Alterity in England in the 21st Century". In Duncan Fuller, Andrew E. G. Jonas and Roger Lee, eds. *Interrogating Alterity: Alternative and Economic Political Spaces*, 241–258. Ashgate.

—— (2012). "The New Urban Enclosures". *City: Analysis of Urban Trends, Culture, Theory, Policy, Action* 16.5: 500–518.

—— (2012). "The Return of the Housing Question". *Ephemera: Theory and Politics in Organization* 12.4: 423–444.

Hodkinson, Stuart, Paul Watt and Gerry Mooney (2013). "Introduction: Neoliberal Housing Policy—Time for a Critical Re-Appraisal". *Critical Social Policy* 33.1: 3–16.

Hollander, Justin B., and Jeremy Németh (2011). "The Bounds of Smart Decline: A Foundational Theory for Planning Shrinking Cities". *Housing Policy Debate* 21.3: 349–367.

Holloway, John (2010). *Crack Capitalism*. Pluto Press.

Holmes, Christopher (2005). *A New Vision for Housing*. Routledge.

Honeywell, Carissa (2007). "Utopianism and Anarchism". *Journal of Political Ideologies* 12.3: 239–254.

Hook, Michael (1970). "New Homes for Old: A Cold Hard Look at Urban Renewal". *Architects' Journal* (1 July).

—— (1970). "SNAP: Toxteth, Liverpool". *Architects' Journal* (10 June).

—— (1977). "Housing Co-operatives". *Architects' Journal* (29 June).

Howard, Ebenezer (1898). *To-Morrow: A Peaceful Path to Real Reform*. Cambridge University Press.

Huckfield, Leslie (2014). *The Rise and Influence of Social Enterprise, Social Investment and Public Service Mutuals. NCIA Inquiry into the Future of Voluntary Services*, Working Paper 3. National Coalition for Independent Action (NCIA).

Huron, Amanda (2018). *Carving out the Commons: Tenant Organizing and Housing Cooperatives in Washington, DC*. Minnesota Press.

Imbroscio, David (1997). *Reconstructing City Politics: Alternative Economic Development and Urban Regimes*. SAGE.

—— (2004). "Can We Grant a Right to Place?". *Politics & Society* 32.4: 575–609.

—— (2012). "Beyond Mobility: The Limits of Liberal Urban Policy". *Journal of Urban Affairs* 34.1: 1–20.

Iveson, Kurt (2013). "Cities within the City: Do-It-Yourself Urbanism and the Right to the City", *International Journal of Urban and Regional Research* 37.3: 941–956.

Jacobs, Jane (1961). *The Death and Life of Great American Cities*. Vintage Books.

Jacobs, Jane M., and Loretta Lees (2013). "Defensible Space on the Move: Revisiting the Urban Geography of Alice Coleman". *International Journal of Urban and Regional Research* 37.5: 1559–1583.

Jeeves, Tim (2014). "Performance, Participation and Questions of Ownership in the Anfield Home Tour". *Stages: Liverpool Biennial* #2. Homebaked: A Perfect Recipe. www.biennial.com/journal/issue-2/performace-participation-and-questions-of-ownership-in-the-anfield-home-tour.

Jessop, Bob (1990). *State Theory: Putting the Capitalist State in Its Place*. Polity Press.

Jones, Katherine T., and Jeff Popke (2010). "Re-Envisioning the City: Lefebvre, HOPE VI, and the Neoliberalization of Urban Space". *Urban Geography* 31.1: 114–133.

Jones, Samantha (2014). "Becoming Homebaked". *Stages: Liverpool Biennial #2*. Homebaked: A Perfect Recipe. www.biennial.com/journal/issue-2/becoming-homebaked/.

Joubert, Tim, and Stuart Hodkinson (2018). "Beyond the Rent Strike, Towards the Commons: Why the Housing Question Requires Activism That Generates its Own Alternatives". In Neil Gray, ed. *Rent and Its Discontents: A Century of Housing Struggle*, 185–200. Rowman & Littlefield.

Jung, Carl (1961). *Memories, Dreams, Reflections*. Random House.

Kallin, Hamish, and Tom Slater (2014). "Activating Territorial Stigma: Gentrifying Marginality on Edinburgh's Periphery". *Environment and Planning A* 46.6: 1351–1368.

Keil, Roger (2009). "The Urban Politics of Roll-with-It Neoliberalization". *City: Analysis of Urban Trends, Culture, Theory, Policy, Action* 13.2–3: 230–245.

Keiller, Patrick (2013). "The Dilapidated Dwelling". In *The View from the Train: Cities and Other Landscapes*, 51–63. Verso Books.

Keucheyan, Razmig (2013). *The Left Hemisphere: Mapping Critical Theory Today*, ed. Gregory Elliott. Verso.

Kilfoyle, Peter (2000). *Left Behind: Winning Back a Labour Heartland and the Defeat of Militant*. Politico's Publishing.

King, Peter (2004). *Private Dwelling: Contemplating the Use of Housing*. Routledge.

Lane, Tony (1978). "Liverpool—City of Harder Times to Come". *Marxism Today* (Nov.): 336–343.

—— (1981). "Merseyside under the Hammer". *Marxism Today* (Feb.): 18–21.

—— (1986). "We Are the Champions: Liverpool vs the 1980s". *Marxism Today* (Jan.): 8–11.

—— (1997). *Liverpool: City of the Sea*. 2nd ed. Liverpool University Press.

Lang, Richard, and Harald Stoeger (2018). "The Role of the Local Institutional Context in Understanding Collaborative Housing Models: Empirical Evidence from Austria". *International Journal of Housing Policy* 18.1: 35–54.

Lawless, Paul, Michael Foden, Ian Wilson and Christina Beatty (2009). "Understanding Area-Based Regeneration: The New Deal for Communities Programme in England". *Urban Studies* 47.2: 257–275.

Leather, Philip, and Brendan Nevin (2013). "The Housing Market Renewal Programme: Origins, Outcomes and the Effectiveness of Public Policy Interventions in a Volatile Market". *Urban Studies* 50.5: 856–875.

Lee, Roger, Andrew Leyshon, Theresa Aldridge, Jane Tooke, Colin Williams and Nigel Thrift (2004). "Making Geographies and Histories? Constructing Local Circuits of Value". *Environment and Planning D: Society and Space* 22.4: 595–617.

Lees, Loretta (2003). "Policy (Re)Turns: Gentrification Research and Urban Policy—Urban Policy and Gentrification Research". *Environment and Planning A* 35.4: 571–574.

Lefebvre, Henri (1991). *The Production of Space*. Blackwell.

—— (1995). *Writings on Cities*. Wiley-Blackwell.

—— (2002). *Critique of Everyday Life*, vol. 2. Verso.

—— (2003). *The Urban Revolution*. University of Minnesota Press.
Leyshon, Andrew, Roger Lee and Colin C. Williams (2003). *Alternative Economic Spaces*. SAGE.
Linebaugh, Peter (2009). *The Magna Carta Manifesto: Liberties and Commons for All*. University of California Press.
—— (2014). *Stop, Thief!: The Commons, Enclosures, and Resistance*. PM PRESS.
Loney, Martin (1983). *Community against Government: British Community Development Project, 1968–78*. Heinemann Educational Books.
Lorde, Audre (1984). "The Master's Tools Will Never Dismantle the Master's House". In *Sister Outsider: Essays and Speeches*, 110–114. Crossing Press.
Lovering, John (2007). "The Relationship between Urban Regeneration and Neoliberalism: Two Presumptuous Theories and a Research Agenda". *International Journal of Urban and Regional Research* 12.4: 343–366.
Löwith, Karl (1993). *Max Weber and Karl Marx*. Routledge.
Lusk, Paul (1998). "Citizenship and Consumption in the Development of Social Rights: The Liverpool New-Build Housing Co-operative Movement", unpublished thesis, Salford University.
McBane, Jack (2008). *The Rebirth of Liverpool: The Eldonian Way*. Liverpool University Press.
McConaghy, Des (1972). *Another Chance for Cities: SNAP 69–72*. Liverpool: Shelter Neighbourhood Action Project.
McDonald, Alan (1986). *The Weller Way: The Story of the Weller Street Housing Cooperative*. Faber & Faber.
MacKinnon, Danny, and Kate D. Derickson (2013). "From Resilience to Resourcefulness: A Critique of Resilience Policy and Activism". *Progress in Human Geography* 37.2: 253–270.
MacLeod, Gordon, and Craig Johnstone (2012). "Stretching Urban Renaissance: Privatizing Space, Civilizing Place, Summoning 'Community'". *International Journal of Urban and Regional Research* 36.1: 1–28.
Madden, David (2014). Neighborhood as Spatial Project: Making the Urban Order on the Downtown Brooklyn Waterfront". *International Journal of Urban and Regional Research* 38.2: 471–497.
Madden, David, and Peter Marcuse (2016). *In Defense of Housing: The Politics of Crisis*. Verso.
Malpass, Peter (2000). "The Discontinuous History of Housing Associations in England". *Housing Studies* 15.2: 195–212.
Malpass, Peter, and Ceri Victory (2010). "The Modernisation of Social Housing in England". *International Journal of Housing Policy* 10.1: 3–18.
Mars, Tim (1981). "Housing in Liverpool 8". *ROOF* 6.5.
—— (1987). "Mersey Tunnel Vision?". *ROOF* 12.6.
Marx, Karl (1970). *A Contribution to the Critique of Political Economy*. International Publishers.
—— (1973). *Grundrisse: Foundations of the Critique of Political Economy*, ed. Martin Nicolaus. Penguin.
—— (1990). *Capital: Critique of Political Economy*, vol. 1. Penguin Classics.

Massey, Doreen (1984). *Spatial Division of Labour: Social Structures and the Geography of Production*. Palgrave Macmillan.

May, Todd (2008). *The Political Thought of Jacques Rancière: Creating Equality*. Edinburgh University Press.

Medoff, Peter, and Holly Sklar (1994). *Streets of Hope: The Fall and Rise of an Urban Neighborhood*. South End Press.

Meegan, Richard (1990). "Merseyside in Crisis and in Conflict". In Michael Harloe, Chris Pickvance and John Urry, eds. *Place, Policy and Politics: Do Localities Matter?*, 67–83. Routledge.

—— (1999). "Urban Development Corporations, Urban Entrepreneurialism, and Locality: The Merseyside Development Corporation". In Rob Imrie and Huw Thomas, eds. *British Urban Policy: An Evaluation of the Urban Development Corporations*, 64–105. SAGE.

Meegan, Richard, and Alison Mitchell (2001). "'It's Not Community Round Here, It's Neighbourhood': Neighbourhood Change and Cohesion in Urban Regeneration Policies". *Urban Studies* 38.12: 2167–2194.

Meehan, James (2014). "Reinventing Real Estate: The Community Land Trust and the Social Market in Land". *Journal of Applied Social Science* 8.2: 113–133.

Meek, James (2014). *Private Island: Why Britain Now Belongs to Someone Else*. Verso Books.

—— (2018). "Brexit and Myths of Englishness". *London Review of Books* 40.19: 17–20.

Merrifield, Andy (1993). "Place and Space: A Lefebvrian Reconciliation". *Transactions of the Institute of British Geographers* 18.4: 516–531.

—— (1996). "Social Justice and Communities of Difference: A Snapshot from Liverpool". In Andy Merrifield and Erik Swyngedouw, eds. *The Urbanization of Injustice*, 256–285. New York University Press.

—— (2002). "Them and Us: Rebuilding the Ruins in Liverpool". In *Dialectical Urbanism*, 53–73. Monthly Review Press.

—— (2006). *Henri Lefebvre: A Critical Introduction*. Routledge.

—— (2011). "The Right to the City and Beyond: Notes on a Lefebvrian Re-Conceptualization". *City* 15.3–4: 468–476.

—— (2014). *The New Urban Question*. Pluto Press.

Merseyside Socialist Research Group (1980). *Merseyside in Crisis*. Manchester Free Press.

Metzger, John T. (2000). "Planned Abandonment: The Neighborhood Life-Cycle Theory and National Urban Policy". *Housing Policy Debate* 11.1: 7–40.

Midheme, Emmanuel, and Frank Moulaert (2013). "Pushing Back the Frontiers of Property: Community Land Trusts and Low-Income Housing in Urban Kenya". *Land Use Policy* 35: 73–84.

Milburn, Keir, and Bertie Russell (2019). *Public–Common Partnerships: Building New Circuits of Collective Ownership*. Common Wealth. https://common-wealth.co.uk/Public-common-partnerships.html.

Miller, Ethan (2013). "Community Economy: Ontology, Ethics, and Politics for Radically Democratic Economic Organizing". *Rethinking Marxism* 25.4: 518–533.

Minton, Anna (2012). *Ground Control: Fear and Happiness in the Twenty-First-Century City*. Penguin.

Mitchell, Don (2014). "Taking Space". *Stages: Liverpool Biennial* #2. Homebaked: A Perfect Recipe. www.biennial.com/journal/issue-2/taking-space.

Moore, Tom, and David Mullins (2013). "Scaling-up or Going Viral? Comparing Self-Help Housing and Community Land Trust Facilitation". *Voluntary Sector Review* 4.3: 333–353.

Moore, Tom, and Kim McKee (2012). "Empowering Local Communities? An International Review of Community Land Trusts". *Housing Studies* 27.2: 280–290.

Moreno, Louis (2018). "Always Crashing in the Same City: Real Estate, Psychic Capital and Planetary Desire". *City: Analysis of Urban Trends, Culture, Theory, Policy, Action* 22.1: 152–168.

Mouffe, Chantal (2018). *For a Left Populism*. Verso.

Moulaert, Frank (2009). "Social Innovation: Institutionally Embedded, Territorially (Re)Produced". In Diana MacCullum, Frank Moulaert, Jean Hillier and Serena Vicari Haddock, eds. *Social Innovation and Territorial Development*, 11–24. Ashgate.

Moulaert, Frank, Flavia Martinelli, Erik Swyngedouw and Sara González (2005). "Towards Alternative Model(s) of Local Innovation". *Urban Studies* 42.11: 1969–1990.

—— (2010). *Can Neighbourhoods Save the City?: Community Development and Social Innovation*. Abingdon: Routledge.

Moulaert, Frank, and Oana Ailenei (2005). "Social Economy, Third Sector and Solidarity Relations: A Conceptual Synthesis from History to Present". *Urban Studies* 42.11: 2037–2054.

Mullins, David (2010). "Self-Help Housing: Could It Play a Greater Role?". *Third Sector Research Centre*, Working Paper 11.

Mullins, David, and Tom Moore (2018). "Self-Organised and Civil Society Participation in Housing Provision". *International Journal of Housing Policy* 18.1: 1–14.

Murray, Robin, Jeremy Gilbert and Andrew Goffey (2015). "Post-Post-Fordism in the Era of Platforms: Robin Murray Talks to Jeremy Gilbert and Andrew Goffey". *New Formations* 84/85: 184–208.

Nevin, Brendan, Peter Lee, Jenny Phillimore, Alex Burfitt and Lisa Goodson (1999). *Measuring the Sustainability of Neighbourhoods in Liverpool*. Centre for Urban and Regional Studies, University of Birmingham.

Nicholls, Alex (2010). "The Legitimacy of Social Entrepreneurship: Reflexive Isomorphism in a Pre-Paradigmatic Field". *Entrepreneurship: Theory and Practice* 34.4: 611–633.

North, Peter, and Molly Scott Cato, eds (2017). *Towards Just and Sustainable Economies: The Social and Solidarity Economy North and South*. Policy Press.

O'Brien, Dave, and Peter Matthews (2015). *After Urban Regeneration: Communities, Policy and Place*. Policy Press.

O'Brien, Mark (2011). "Liverpool 1911 and Its Era: Foundational Myth or Authentic Tradition". In John Belchem and Bryan Biggs, eds. *Liverpool: City of Radicals*, 140–158. Liverpool University Press.

O'Neill, Martin, and Joe Guinan (2018). "The Institutional Turn: Labour's New Political Economy". *Renewal* 26.2: 5–16. http://renewal.org.uk/articles/the-institutional-turn-labours-new-political-economy.

Ospina, José (1987). *Housing Ourselves*. Hilary Shipman Ltd.

Ostrom, Elinor, Thomas Dietz, Nives Dolšak, Paul C. Stern, Susan Stonich and Elke U. Weber, eds (2002). *The Drama of the Commons*. National Academy Press.

Parker, Simon, and Rowland Atkinson (2020). "Disorderly Cities and the Policy-Making Field: The 1981 English Riots and the Management of Urban Decline". *British Politics* 15: 160–177.

Parkinson, Michael (1985). *Liverpool on the Brink: One City's Struggle against Government Cuts*. Policy Journals Ltd.

—— (2019). *Liverpool Beyond the Brink: The Remaking of a Post-Imperial City*. Liverpool University Press.

Peck, Jamie (2005). "Struggling with the Creative Class". *International Journal of Urban and Regional Research* 29.4: 740–770.

Pierce, Joseph, Deborah Martin and James Murphy (2011). "Relational Place-Making: The Networked Politics of Place". *Transactions of the Institute of British Geographers* 36.1: 54–70.

Pierce, Joseph, Richard Kruger, Azadeh Hadizadeh Esfahani, Olivia R. Williams, James DeFilippis and Deborah G. Martin (forthcoming). "Ownership Is a Habit of Mind: How Community Land Trusts Expose Key Consensual Fictions of Urban Property". *Urban Geography*.

Pinder, David (2013). "Reconstituting the Possible: Lefebvre, Utopia and the Urban Question". *International Journal of Urban and Regional Research* 39.1: 28–45.

Pinnegar, Simon (2009). "The Question of Scale in Housing-Led Regeneration: Tied to the Neighbourhood?". *Environment and Planning A* 41.12: 2911–2928.

—— (2012). "For the City? The Difficult Spaces of Market Restructuring Policy For the City?". *International Journal of Housing Policy* 12.3: 281–297.

Polanyi, Karl (1944). *The Great Transformation: The Political and Economic Origins of Our Time*. Beacon Press.

Power, Anne, and Katharine Mumford (1999). *The Slow Death of Great Cities? Urban Abandonment or Urban Renaissance*. Joseph Rowntree Foundation.

Pritchard, Stephen (2016). "Complexity, Uncertainty and Scalability: How Assemble's Granby 4 Streets Won 2015 Turner Prize". Colouring in Culture Blog. http://colouringinculture.org/blog/assemble-complexity-uncertainty-scalability#_ftn4.

Purcell, Mark (2001). "Neighborhood Activism among Homeowners as a Politics of Space". *Professional Geographer* 53.2: 178–194.

—— (2002). "Excavating Lefebvre: The Right to the City and Its Urban Politics of the Inhabitant". *GeoJournal* 58.2–3: 99–108.

—— (2003). "Citizenship and the Right to the Global City: Reimagining the Capitalist World Order". *International Journal of Urban and Regional Research* 27.3: 564–590.

Putnam, Robert (2000). *Bowling Alone: The Collapse and Revival of American Community*. Simon & Schuster.

Raco, Mike, and Robert Imrie (2003). *Urban Renaissance?: New Labour, Community and Urban Policy*. Policy Press.

Roberts, Peter (2008). "Social Innovation, Spatial Transformation and Sustainable Communities: Liverpool and the 'Eldonians'". In Paul Drewe, Juan-Luis Klein and Edward Hulsbergen, eds. *The Challenge of Social Innovation in Urban Revitalization*. Amsterdam: Techne Press.

Roberts, William Clare (2017). *Marx's Inferno: The Political Theory of Capital*. Princeton University Press.

Rodgers, David (1999). *New Mutualism: The Third Estate*. The Co-operative Party.

Rogers, Ken (2010). *The Lost Tribe of Everton and Scottie Road*. Trinity Mirror Sport Media.

—— (2012). *Lost Tribe: The People's Memories: 2*. Trinity Mirror North West and North Wales.

Rolnik, Raquel (2013). "Late Neoliberalism: The Financialization of Homeownership and Housing Rights". *International Journal of Urban and Regional Research* 37.3: 1058–1066.

Rose, Carol (1986). "The Comedy of the Commons: Commerce, Custom, and Inherently Public Property of Chicago Law Review". *University of Chicago Law Review* 53.3: 711–781.

—— (1994). *Property and Persuasion: Essays on the History, Theory and Rhetoric of Ownership*. Westview Press.

—— (1998). "The Several Futures of Property: Of Cyberspace and Folk Tales, Emission Trades and Ecosystems". *Minnesota Law Review* 83: 129–182.

Russell, Bertie (2019). "Beyond the Local Trap: New Municipalism and the Rise of the Fearless Cities". *Antipode* 51.3: 989–1010.

Sarkissian, Wendy (1976). "The Idea of Social Mix in Town Planning: An Historical Review". *Urban Studies* 13.3: 231–246.

Sassen, Saskia (2014). *Expulsions: Brutality and Complexity in the Global Economy*. Harvard University Press.

Sassen, Saskia, and Irit Rogoff (2014). "What is our Globalised Urban Future?". *Stages: Liverpool Biennial #1*. www.biennial.com/journal/issue-1/what-is-our-globalised-urban-future.

Schwartz, Herman, and Leonard Seabrooke, eds (2009). *The Politics of Housing Booms and Busts*. Palgrave Macmillan.

Scott, James C. (2017). *Against the Grain: A Deep History of the Earliest States*. Yale University Press.

Sheppard, David, and Derek Worlock (1988). *Better Together: Christian Partnership in a Hurt City*. Hodder & Stoughton.

Singer, Joseph William (2000). *Entitlement: The Paradoxes of Property*. Yale University Press.

Smith, Neil (1982). "Gentrification and Uneven Development". *Economic Geography* 58.2: 139–155.

—— (1989). "Gentrification, the Frontier, and Restructuring of Urban Space". In Neil Smith and Peter Williams, eds. *Gentrification of the City*. Allen & Unwin.

Soifer, Steven D. (1990). "The Burlington Community Land Trust: A Socialist Approach to Affordable Housing?". *Journal of Urban Affairs* 12.3: 237–252.

Southern, Alan (2014). "Enterprise, Wealth Creation and Place: A Case Study of the Liverpool City-Region". In Lee Pugalis and Joyce Liddle, eds. *Enterprising Places: Leadership and Governance Networks*, 227–257. Emerald Group Publishing Limited.

—— (2014). "Local Economy Anfield: Elite Premier League Football and Localism". *Local Economy* 29.3: 195–212.

Srnicek, Nick, and Alex Williams (2015). *Inventing the Future: Postcapitalism and a World without Work*. London: Verso.

Stavrides, Stavros (2016). *Common Space: The City as Commons*. Zed Books.

Stein, Sarah Ilene (2015). "Wake up Fannie, I Think I Got Something to Say to You: Financing Community Land Trust Homebuyers without Stripping Affordability Provisions". *Emory Law Journal* 60.1: 209–249.

Sykes, Olivier, Jonathan Brown, Matthew Cocks, David Shaw and Chris Couch (2013). "A City Profile of Liverpool". *Cities* 35: 299–318.

Taafe, Peter, and Tony Mulhearn (1988). *Liverpool. A City That Dared to Fight*. Fortress.

Taplin, Eric (1994). *Near to Revolution: The Liverpool General Transport Strike of 1911*. Bluecoat.

Tarrow, Sidney (1994). *Power in Movement: Social Movements and Contentious Politics*. Cambridge University Press.

Temenos, Cristina, and Tom Baker (2015). "Enriching Urban Policy Mobilities Research". *International Journal of Urban and Regional Research* 39.4: 824–827.

Thompson, Matthew (2015). "Between Boundaries: From Commoning and Guerrilla Gardening to Community Land Trust Development in Liverpool". *Antipode* 47.4: 1021–1042.

—— (2017). "Contesting Dilapidated Dwelling". In Graham Cairns, Georgios Artopoulos and Kirsten Day, eds. *From Conflict to Inclusion in Housing: Interaction of Communities, Residents and Activists*, 199–226. UCL Press.

—— (2017). "LIFE in a ZOO: Henri Lefebvre and the (Social) Production of (Abstract) Space in Liverpool". *City: Analysis of Urban Trends, Culture, Theory, Policy, Action* 21.2: 104–126.

—— (2019). "Playing with the Rules of the Game: Social Innovation for Urban Transformation". *International Journal of Urban and Regional Research* 43.6: 1168–1192.

—— (2020). "What's So New about New Municipalism?". *Progress in Human Geography*: 1–26. https://doi.org/10.1177/0309132520909480.

Thompson, Matthew, Vicky Nowak, Alan Southern, Jackie Davies and Peter Furmedge (2020). "Re-grounding the City with Polanyi: From Urban Entrepreneurialism to Entrepreneurial Municipalism". *Environment and Planning A: Economy and Space*: 1–24. https://doi.org/10.1177/0308518X19899698.

Tilly, Charles (1978). *From Mobilisation to Revolution*. Longman Higher Education.
Tonkiss, Fran (2013). "Austerity Urbanism and the Makeshift City". *City: Analysis of Urban Trends, Culture, Theory, Policy, Action* 17.3: 312–324.
Towers, Graham (1995). *Building Democracy: Community Architecture in the Inner Cities*. Routledge.
Tunstall, Rebecca (2003). "'Mixed Tenure' Policy in the UK: Privatisation, Pluralism or Euphemism?". *Housing, Theory and Society* 20.3: 153–159.
Turner, John F.C. (1972). "Housing as a Verb". In John F.C. Turner and Robert Fichter, eds. *Freedom to Build*, 148–175. Collier Macmillan.
—— (1977). *Housing by People: Toward Autonomy in Building Environments*. Pantheon Books.
—— (1978). "Housing in Three Dimensions: Terms of Reference for the Housing Question Redefined". *World Development* 6.9–10 (Sept.): 1135–1145.
Turner, John F.C., and Robert Fichter, eds (1972). *Freedom to Build*. Collier Macmillan.
Vidal, Lorenzo (2018). "Securing Social Gains in, against and beyond the State: The Case of Denmark's 'Common Housing'". *Housing, Theory and Society* 36.4: 448–468.
—— (2019). "Cooperative Islands in Capitalist Waters: Limited-Equity Housing Cooperatives, Urban Renewal and Gentrification". *International Journal of Urban and Regional Research* 43.1: 157–178.
Wainwright, Hilary (1987). *Labour: A Tale of Two Parties*. Hogarth Press.
Ward, Colin (1973). *Anarchy in Action*. Freedom Press.
—— (1974). *Tenants Take Over*. Architectural Press.
—— (1983). *Housing: An Anarchist Approach*. Freedom Press.
—— (1985). *When We Build Again: Let's Have Housing That Works!* Pluto Press.
—— (1989). *Welcome, Thinner City: Urban Survival in the 1990s*. NCVO Publications.
—— (2002). *Cotters and Squatters: The Hidden History of Housing*. Five Leaves Publications.
Ward, Colin, and David Goodway (2003). *Talking Anarchy, 2003*. Five Leaves Publications.
Wates, Nick (1982). "The Liverpool Breakthrough: Or Public Sector Housing Phase 2". *Architects' Journal* (8 Sept.).
—— (1985). "Co-op Consolidation". *Architectural Review* (Apr.).
Wates, Nick, and Charles Knevitt (1987). *Community Architecture: How People Are Creating Their Own Environment*. Penguin Books.
Webb, David (2010). "Rethinking the Role of Markets in Urban Renewal: The Housing Market Renewal Initiative in England". *Housing, Theory and Society* 27.4: 313–331.
—— (2011). "'Problem Neighbourhoods' in a Part-Linear, Part-Network Regime: Problems with, and Possible Responses to, the Housing Market Renewal Leviathan", unpublished PhD thesis, Newcastle University.
—— (2012). "Conceptualising the Bounded Agency of Housing Researchers: The Case of Housing Market Renewal in England". *International Journal of Housing Policy* 12.3: 315–330.

White, Stuart (2007). "Making Anarchism Respectable? The Social Philosophy of Colin Ward". *Journal of Political Ideologies* 12.1: 11–28.

—— (2011). "Social Anarchism, Lifestyle Anarchism, and the Anarchism of Colin Ward". *Anarchist Studies* 19.2: 92–104.

Williams, Olivia, and Joseph Pierce (2017). "Inserting Scales of Urban Politics: The Possibilities of Meso-Urban Governance Shims". *Urban Geography* 38.6: 795–812.

Wilson, Japhy (2013). "'The Devastating Conquest of the Lived by the Conceived': The Concept of Abstract Space in the Work of Henri Lefebvre". *Space and Culture* 16.3: 364–380.

Wilson, Japhy, and Erik Swyngedouw, eds (2014). *The Post-Political and Its Discontents: Spaces of Depoliticization, Spectres of Radical Politics*. Edinburgh University Press.

Winstanley, Gerrard (2011). *A Common Treasury*. Verso.

Wolch, Jennifer (1990). *The Shadow State: Government and Voluntary Sector in Transition*. Foundation Centre.

Wright, Erik Olin (2010). *Envisioning Real Utopias*. Verso.

Wright, Patrick (1991). *A Journey Through Ruins: The Last Days of London*. Radius.

Žižek, Slavoj (2012). *The Year of Dreaming Dangerously*. Verso Books.

Index

abstraction 15, 50–52, 55, 57, 195–198, 254–255, 298
  see also technocracy; violence
alienation 14, 50–55, 136, 183, 276, 295
alterity 11
  see also diverse economies
amateurism 296–297, 340
  see also expertise; professionals
anarchism 55–58, 169, 269
  anarcho-syndicalism 33, 80, 246, 300–303
  lifestyle anarchism 53, 108, 169
  pragmatic/respectable anarchism *see* Ward
  see also Bookchin; Kropotkin; prefigurative politics; Proudhon
anchor institutions 264, 319–320
  community anchor organisations 138–139, 318–320
Anderson, Joe 153, 155
Anfield 208, 210, 237–251, 256–259, 302, 336
architecture xv, 29, 32, 83, 97, 111–114, 221, 296, 338–340
  Architects' Journal 60, 118
  community architecture 53–54, 82–83, 111, 144, 245
  see also Assemble; design; Royal Institute of British Architects
Arena Housing Association 239–242, 247, 336
  see also Your Housing
art 211, 215, 343, 335–343
  Arts Council England 227, 306
  arts-led regeneration *see* gentrification; regeneration
  socially-engaged art 244, 335–343
  see also design; social practice
Assemble (architects) 296–297, 331–332, 338–342
Atlantic Gateway vision 153
austerity 4, 212, 229, 255, 273–274, 308–310
  see also resilience; urbanism
Australia 11, 183, 191, 223
autonomy 12, 57, 98, 108, 169, 173, 294, 296
  collective dweller control *see* Ward
  local autonomy 138, 256, 316
  user autonomy *see* Turner

baking 246, 304–305, 329
Barcelona 264, 282
Beat poets 33
Beatles 33, 228
Birchall, Johnston 304
  hidden history of housing co-ops xvii, 70–72, 304–305
Bishop, Claire 335–342
Blomley, Nick 18, 215, 291
Bookchin, Murray 319
Borsodi, Ralph 181–182
boss politics 62, 65, 103, 146
Braddock, Jack and Bessie 62
Brexit 289
Brown, Jonathan xi, 219, 228
Buber, Martin 56

bullshit jobs *see* Graeber
bureaucracy 51, 67–68, 77–78, 90, 134, 294–300, 311–312, 332
  building a bureaucracy from below 300, 311–326
  dialectic with democracy *see* dialectics
  see also alienation; technocracy; Weber
Byker Wall, Newcastle 144, 245
Byrne, Tony 109–113, 118–119, 172

Campbell, Harold 72–73, 93, 169, 305, 323
Canada 86, 183, 223, 302
Canning Housing Co-operative 69
capitalism 3, 6–7, 45–53, 56–57, 123–124, 177–179, 185–188, 194, 268–276, 279–284, 293
  accumulation by dispossession *see* dispossession
  capitalist realism *see* Fisher
  commodification 179, 185–190, 194, 253, 268, 273–280, 339, 243
  commodity fetishism 58, 198
  contradictions (primary and secondary) 50–52, 186–188
  fictitious commodities *see* Polanyi
  labour–capital relation *see* labour
  primitive accumulation 7, 179, 281
  reform vs. revolution 42, 46, 51, 55–57, 259, 280–281, 292–294
  use and exchange value *see* value
  see also abstraction; alienation; class; crisis; exchange; exploitation; labour; market competition/failure; Marxism; neoliberalism; post-capitalism; revolution
Castells, Manuel 22, 39–40, 186
  The Urban Question 22, 39–40, 47, 186
Catholicism 119, 140–141, 145–146, 182
  see also sectarianism
charity *see* not-for-profit organisations
  see also philanthropic funding; social economy
citizenship 8, 17, 23, 136, 177, 271, 329
  see also rights
civil society 5, 11, 23–24, 136, 186, 268, 294, 306
class *see* labour; working class culture
  see also creative class
co-housing 6, 13, 169, 268, 316–317
Coin Street Community Builders 139
Coleman, Alice 111–113, 156, 172, 198, 253
collaborative housing 11–12, 268
colonialism 33, 123, 194, 222, 273, 311, 340–341
  British Empire 27, 29–30, 34, 124–125, 273
  colonial origins of the Housing Corporation 311–312
  settler-colonialism 222–223, 340–341
  see also slavery
common ownership co-operatives 51, 71, 74
commons 3, 5, 10, 12–26, 42, 49, 178–180, 184, 215, 244, 253, 257–258, 268–273, 281–284, 287, 291, 294, 330, 333–334
  circuit of the common 283–286, 323
  the common (Hardt and Negri) 12–13, 18
  common property regimes 19, 21, 271, 320, 325
  commoning 136, 216, 227, 257–258, 281–283, 294, 299, 311, 325, 330, 333–334
  enclosure of the commons 3, 5, 7, 13, 15, 45, 178–179, 184–185, 194, 268, 271–274, 281
  public–common partnerships 275, 284

tragedy of the commons 288, 291
see also circuits of value; rights; social movements
communism 51, 280, 292–293
communes 45, 51, 53, 57, 169, 292
Communist Party of Great Britain (1920–91) 108, 214
libertarian socialism/communism 10, 108, 292, 293
community architecture *see* architecture
community asset transfer 139, 144, 218–220, 225, 249, 296
community benefit societies 243, 323–324
community development corporations 138, 320–321
Community Development Projects (CDP) 35, 66–67, 127–128, 156
Vauxhall CDP *see* Vauxhall
community development trusts 41, 128, 138–139, 143, 156, 167, 173–174, 269, 318–320
community economy *see* Gibson-Graham
community enterprise 42, 152, 166, 171, 227, 317, 323
Community Finance Solutions 233, 235
community interest companies 234, 243, 323–324
Community Land Cooperative of Cincinnati 182
community land trusts 9, 178–185, 213, 216–227, 229, 232–237, 239–251, 257–259, 269, 272, 277–278, 287–288, 316
history 178–185
theory 178–185, 287–288
see also community asset transfer; land value capture; stewardship; trusterty
community-led housing 11–12, 249, 268, 316–317
London Community-Led Housing Hub 316–317
community organising 11, 80–81, 170, 173, 278
see also leadership
conservation 148, 228
see also SAVE Britain's Heritage
Conservative Party 31, 35, 62, 64, 70–72, 90–91, 93, 151, 171–172, 212, 225, 308, 322
Cooper, Davina 286
Cooper Square CLT, New York 183, 242
Co-operative Development Services (CDS) 60, 73–78, 81–87, 94–96, 106, 108, 112–120, 134–146, 160–164, 301, 307, 311–317, 331
cooperativism 51, 53, 85, 98, 169, 269, 290, 315
CDS Co-operatives (London) 73–74, 218, 317, 325
Confederation of Co-operative Housing 317
Co-operative Housing Services 72–74
Co-operative Party 70
International Co-operative Alliance 53, 315
see also common ownership co-operatives; co-ownership societies; federations; housing co-operatives; Radical Routes; Rochdale Pioneers; secondary support infrastructure; social movements; tenant co-partnerships
co-ownership societies 13, 70–72
Co-ownership Development Society 70, 72
Corbett, Jane 119–120
Corbyn, Jeremy 263–265
Corbynism 263–265
council housing 4, 8, 27, 30–33, 36, 52–54, 64–65, 89–92, 102, 107–112, 253, 265, 274
residualisation 8, 54, 196, 203, 274
see also social housing
creative class 198
crisis 3, 6–8, 14, 39, 125–126, 178, 186–187, 212, 274, 279, 282

crowd funding 246, 284, 324
Cumbers, Andy 265, 294

Davis, John Emmeus 19, 181, 223
De Angelis, Massimo 10, 284
Debord, Guy 335–336
defensible space 102, 111–112, 156, 299
  see also design; urbanism
democracy 9, 18, 59, 81, 158, 174, 237, 244, 251–252, 266, 271, 278, 282, 284, 290, 314–317, 319, 320–321
  collective dweller control *see* Ward
  democratic socialism 10, 107, 265, 293
  dialectic with bureaucracy *see* dialectics
  economic democracy 12, 51, 265
deprivation 48, 51, 55, 66–67, 136, 178, 185, 232, 238, 256, 275–276
design 97–102, 106, 110–118, 221–222, 226, 298, 331, 337, 340, 343
  democratic/participatory design 59, 82, 113, 144, 149, 156, 162, 170, 222, 227, 245, 247, 249, 301
  design determinism 111, 113, 172, 198, 253–254
  design disadvantagement 110–113, 172, 253
  secured-by-design 156, 170, 299
  'utalitarianism' 84, 97–98, 169
  see also architecture; art
dialectics xix, 15–16, 48, 101, 131, 252, 258–259, 274, 286, 342
  bureaucracy and democracy 158, 298, 312, 319, 314–317
  dialectic of commoning (resource and practice) 15, 281, 311
  event and process 289–290, 294–300
  master–slave dialectic 285, 325
  means and ends 55–57, 294, 298
  noun and verb 15, 18–19, 48, 131, 172, 252, 286, 342
  thingness and flow of space 131, 254, 266
  see also methodology; value
Dingle 62, 79, 87, 118
direct action 28, 33, 80, 118–119, 172, 186, 206, 209, 290, 296, 300
  see also rent strikes; social movements; war
displacement 14, 20, 34, 62, 86, 124, 142, 168, 183, 191, 276
dispossession 5, 7, 13, 124, 179, 194, 280
  accumulation by dispossession 179, 194–195, 272–273
diverse economies 11, 57, 137, 251
do-it-yourself urbanism 53, 216, 221–222, 228, 248, 296–297, 309
  see also insurgent/guerrilla urbanism; squatting
Dudley Street CLT, Boston 183, 242
dwelling 8–9, 14–15, 54–55, 58, 252, 267, 343
  domesticity 45, 49, 57, 78–79, 215, 257
  dilapidated dwelling(s) *see* Keiller
  dwelling vs. dwellings 48–50, 54–55, 172, 198, 252, 254, 267
  privacy 54, 257, 271
  see also dialectics; empty homes; homesteading; squatting

East London CLT 184, 316
Edgar, Juliet 229, 231
Edge, Nina 227, 246, 336, 342
Eldonians 36, 90, 114, 118, 128, 134–135, 139, 140–161, 165–174, 245, 254–255, 277–278, 290, 298–300, 318, 328
  Eldonian Community Based Housing Association 151–154, 158–159, 165
  Eldonian Community Trust 105, 128, 139, 146, 152, 166

Eldonian Group Ltd (EGL) 152–156, 159–160, 165–167, 174, 287
Portland Gardens Housing Co-operative 114, 143–144, 148, 151, 159, 290
self-regenerating community vision 36, 134, 143, 147–148, 152, 154, 161, 168, 170, 172, 269
empty homes 7, 23, 41, 178, 189, 207, 214, 218, 221, 225
see also homesteading; squatting
Empty Homes Agency 206, 213, 228–230, 307
enclosure 3, 5, 7, 13, 15, 45, 178–179, 184–185, 194, 268, 271–274, 281
new urban enclosures 13, 178–179, 194, 272, 274
see also dispossession
Engels, Friedrich 3–4, 29, 39–41, 45–48, 123–124, 180, 185–186, 275–281
debate with Proudhon 40–41, 45–46, 50, 55, 279, 293–294
The Housing Question 3–4, 39–41, 46–47, 123–124, 180, 185–186, 275–277, 292–293
see also Haussmann
Englishness 10, 32, 100, 289
entrepreneurialism 102, 166, 171–172, 219, 246, 309
European Union 34, 37, 238, 255–256, 289, 306
Evans, George 146–147, 150, 152–153, 158
Everton 63, 118–120, 156, 301
exchange 13, 16, 23–24, 137–138, 194, 253, 269, 273, 283–284, 287–288, 321
see also value
expertise 9, 69, 78, 95, 101, 161, 223, 247, 298–300, 315–316
amateurs vs. professionals 101, 161, 296, 298–300, 315, 330–332
see also amateurism; professionals; technocracy
exploitation 13–14, 46–47, 50–52, 136, 276, 280

Fearless Cities 264, 319
see also municipalism
federations 95, 117–118, 305, 309, 315–319
see also secondary support infrastructure
feminism 49, 52, 57, 279
finance 109, 114, 137, 162, 164, 219–220, 233, 246, 274
see also crowd funding; patient capital; philanthropic funding; solidarity funds
financialisation 8, 40–41, 177–178, 253, 272, 274, 335
Fisher, Mark 293
capitalist realism 13, 266
Floyd, Billy 59, 79–81, 94, 146, 290, 300
Fordism 22, 41, 186
Forensic Architecture 338–339
foundational economy 22–25, 169, 267, 270, 310, 319
Freeson, Reg 70–72, 305, 323
Freire, Paulo 119

Gandhi, Mahatma 182
Garden City movement 19, 32, 51, 101, 180
see also tenant co-partnerships
General Improvement Areas 65–73, 207–208
Generation Rent 4, 178, 248
gentrification 14, 124, 182–183, 192, 195, 199, 329
arts-led gentrification 222, 309, 339–342
state-led gentrification 124, 192, 308
see also regeneration; violence
George, Henry 179, 180–181, 185
Gibson-Graham, J.K. 11, 49, 56–57
community economy 11, 137, 251

weak vs. strong theory 57, 341
Ginsberg, Allen 33
Glasgow xvi, 53, 109, 281
Gommon, Ed 214, 297, 302
governance 136, 161–167, 171–172, 182, 223–224, 278, 284–286, 299, 306–326
collective self-governance 97–98, 135–137, 161, 169, 171, 271
meso-scale governance shims 278, 320
see also federations; the state; stewardship
Graeber, David 49, 56, 294, 297
bullshit jobs 49, 322
utopia of rules 294–297
Granby 65–69, 73, 79, 82, 127–130, 132, 140, 196, 199–230, 237, 245, 259, 263, 302
Granby Four Streets CLT 184, 199, 206, 213–227, 251, 254–258, 263, 265, 270, 272, 277–278, 290, 296, 302, 307–309, 329, 331, 335–343
Granby Street Housing Co-operative 69
Greater London Council (1965–86) 139, 318
Grenfell Tower 4
guerrilla gardening 215–216, 282, 296, 341
guild socialism 25, 136, 269

Halsall, Bill 78, 80, 82–83, 86, 97–98, 101, 106, 109, 144, 147–149, 151, 156, 158, 299, 301, 313
Hardin, Garrett 291
Harris, Jackie 116–117
Harvey, David xiii, 40, 171, 179, 186–188, 194, 272, 284, 337
spatial fix 40, 187, 272
urban entrepreneurialism 171–172
Hatherley, Owen 32, 113
Hatton, Derek 109–110, 112
Hatton houses 112–113, 162
Haussmann, Baron 123–124, 195
Haussmannisation 125–126, 194–195
Heaslip, Marianne 214, 245, 249
van Heeswijk, Jeanne 243–244, 302, 337
Heidegger, Martin 54–55
Heseltine, Michael 35, 36, 133–134, 147, 148, 205
Hesketh Street Housing Co-operative 87, 93, 99, 169, 302
Hine, Dougald 268, 327–335
Inward, upward and outward languages 286, 327–335
historical cycles/waves xviii, 87, 168, 170, 179, 300–305, 309–310
see also crisis; place effects; social movements
Hobbes, Thomas 18, 271, 291
Leviathan logic 18, 24, 271, 292, 295, 314
Hodkinson, Stuart 13, 178, 194
Holloway, John 56
Homebaked xviii, 177, 209, 213, 216, 230, 239, 242–251, 254, 256–259, 270, 272, 277–280, 302–309, 316–318, 324, 329, 334–343
homelessness 6–7, 66, 178, 274
homeownership 10, 70, 177, 219, 236, 288, 306, 329
see also property
Homes and Communities Agency 164, 226, 296
Homes England 164, 226, 249, 296
homesteading 218, 222, 228
community homesteading 218, 221–222, 227, 331, 341
horticulture 215, 304
Housing Act (1961) 70
Housing Act (1969) 65–67, 92
Housing Act (1974) 71–73, 92–93, 305, 313, 315, 323
Housing Act (1988) 161–164, 174, 197, 204, 307, 313
Housing Action Areas 67, 73, 92, 204, 207–208

Housing Action Trust (HAT) 162, 336
Housing Association Grant (HAG) 71–73, 77, 112, 312–313
housing associations 5, 8, 11, 68, 71–76, 86, 107, 110, 120, 162–165, 173–174, 193–194, 196–197, 203–207, 212, 220, 223, 239, 285, 306, 314
    stock transfer 4, 8, 73, 162–164, 184, 204–205, 207, 307
housing co-operatives 9–10, 25, 34, 60–122, 144–145, 149, 161–162, 214, 302–305, 315, 325
    hidden history *see* Birchall; Ward
    new-build co-ops 60–61, 76–122, 227, 245, 302, 312
    rehabilitation co-ops 65–76, 218, 227, 296–297, 302, 312
        see also common ownership co-operatives; community benefit societies; cooperativism; co-ownership societies; mutual homeownership societies
Housing Corporation 70–77, 87, 93, 95, 96, 116, 144, 148–149, 151–152, 162, 164, 311–314
Housing Market Renewal 27, 41, 189–200, 207–213, 225, 228–236, 238–239, 243, 245, 253–256, 259, 282, 321
    New Heartlands Pathfinder 193, 196, 212, 228
    zones of opportunity (ZOO) 193, 196, 208, 217, 278, 341
housing question, the 3–4, 39–41, 45–59, 123–124, 180, 185–186, 275–284, 292–293
    tenant–landlord relation *see* tenure
Howard, Ebenezer 19, 180
Howarth, George 108, 115–116
Howe, Geoffrey 35, 129, 133
Hughes, Phil 84, 90, 119–120, 301
Hughes, Ronnie 214, 227
Illich, Ivan 58
institutionalism 20–21, 136–138, 264–265, 268–271, 274–276, 283–286, 289–290, 294, 318–323
    constituted vs. constituent power 286, 292, 330
    institutional innovation 136, 274–275, 286, 292, 318–326
    institutional isomorphism 285–286, 330
    the institutional turn 264–265, 284
    scaling/replication *see* scale (scaling up or going viral)
    see also law; performativity; revolution; secondary support infrastructure; social innovation
insurgent/guerrilla urbanism 216, 248, 257–258, 296, 341
Irish Catholic communities 32, 66, 102, 129, 140–141, 145–146
Irish Potato Famine (1845–47) 30, 61, 140, 168, 273

Jacobs, Jane 54
Jenkin, Patrick 148–150
Jerry-built houses 30, 140, 204
Johnson, Boris 184
Jones, Lewis 222, 226
Jones, Samantha 257, 336
Jung, Carl 33
Jurgensen, Britt 244, 247

Keiller, Patrick 45, 47, 49, 124, 125
    dilapidated dwelling(s) 6, 38, 45, 47, 49, 54, 89, 105, 123–128, 132, 203
Kemp, Richard 90–92, 118, 207
Kensington (Liverpool) 232–237
King, Martin Luther 119
Kinnock, Neil 147
Kirkby 62, 64, 115–118, 173
knowledge transfer 117, 239–242, 247
    see also policy mobilities
Knowsley 64, 108, 114–118, 173

Kropotkin, Peter 18, 292, 319
Kuya, Dorothy 214

labour 19, 48–50, 52, 57, 58, 179, 181, 186, 222, 250, 269, 272, 273, 279, 283, 309
  dead and living labour 252, 280, 342
  labour–capital relation 45–47, 50, 186, 279
  labour movement 33–34, 51, 61, 80, 90–91, 104, 279, 301
Labour Party 32, 61, 65, 90, 103–104, 107–110, 145–146, 147, 172, 263–265
  New Labour 5, 92, 147, 172, 188, 191, 232, 322, 323
land ownership 16, 173, 180–181, 268, 287–288
  see also property
land reform 183, 325–326
land value capture 14, 19–20, 180–181, 272–273
landlords 4, 13, 30, 46, 68, 76, 180, 204, 237, 248, 270, 282, 325
  absentee landlordism 14, 54, 67–68, 183
  public landlordism 54, 183
  see also tenure
Lane, Tony 31–33, 80, 125–126, 300
Langrove Community Housing Co-operative 118–120, 172, 290, 301
law 14–16, 20–21, 77–78, 95, 118, 145, 172, 231, 323–326, 330
  extra-legal activism *see* direct action
Lawless, Jayne 247, 256
leadership (community) 79–81, 87, 98, 116, 142, 146–147, 151, 159, 160, 298, 304
  see also boss politics
Leasehold Reform Act (1967) 218, 325
Lefebvre, Henri 17, 39–40, 51–52, 55, 131, 187, 258, 266, 279, 341
  abstract space xviii, 51–52, 55, 193–198
  experimental utopias *see* utopia
  The Production of Space 52, 131, 254, 266
  Right to the City 17–18, 185, 244, 248, 303, 337
  urban revolution 187, 279
Leta-Claudia Housing Co-operative 86–87, 101, 114, 300
Liberal Democrats (party) 189, 206, 255
Liberal Party 32, 64–65, 72–74, 87, 89–93, 105–109
LIFE model 206–208
Linebaugh, Peter 5, 258
Little Klondyke 228–231, 250, 308
Liverpool 27–37, 60–70, 201–208
  city region 115, 247, 316
  exceptionalism 27–28, 30–33, 300–303
  maritime culture/economy 27–28, 29, 80, 125, 147, 168, 303
    see also seafaring
  radicalism 29–34
  Scouse 28, 97, 240, 250
  tribalism 140–141, 156, 299
  see also anarchism (anarcho-syndicalism); Merseyside
Liverpool 8 (postal district) 38, 65–66, 73, 207, 214, 223, 336
Liverpool Biennial 230, 243–247, 249, 306, 329, 335–337, 340
Liverpool City Council 30–32, 61–66, 69, 72–74, 89–93, 103–105, 149–150, 162–163, 189, 207, 242, 274
  'The Corpy' 30–32, 59, 62, 64, 75, 163, 174, 202
  the lost decade (1970s) 89–91, 103, 167, 252
  Works Department 90–92, 144, 253, 293
  see also Militant Tendency
Liverpool Echo (newspaper) 199, 209

Liverpool Federation of Housing Co-operatives 95, 117
  see also Merseyside Federation
Liverpool Football Club 238–239, 245–246, 248
Liverpool Housing Trust (LHT) 68, 71–72, 86, 114, 163, 203, 210, 301, 307, 313
Liverpool Mutual Homes 163, 215, 221–223
local economic development 35–37, 135–139, 143, 151, 172, 242, 255–257, 265, 269–270, 319
localism 11, 225, 263, 306, 308
  local autonomy 138, 256, 316
  militant particularism 299
  the trapdoor of community 308
  see also community asset transfer
Localism Act (2011) 247
locality debates 134–135
  see also scale
London 31–32, 73, 86, 116–117, 124, 133, 139, 183–185, 220–221, 316–317, 340
  see also Greater London Council
London Citizens 185, 316
London CLT 316
Lorde, Audre 267, 285
Lusk, Paul 60, 81–82, 85, 96, 108, 302

McBane, Jack 140, 143–144, 146, 148, 150, 158, 302
McConaghy, Des 67, 68, 71
MacDermott, Theresa 215, 336
McDonald, Alan 78, 79, 83, 94, 96, 160, 296
MacDonald, Rob 97, 101
McGann, Tony 141–152, 155, 159, 160, 166, 300
McKay, Angela xi, 244, 247
Malaysia 66, 341
managed decline 35, 128–133, 202–204, 208–210, 278
  dereliction-by-design 239–240
  planned shrinkage 131–132
  root shock 132, 203
  urban autotomy 129, 278
  see also shrinking cities; violence
Manchester xii, 30, 124, 153, 233, 245, 264, 317
market competition 85–87, 161–167
market failure 136, 178, 189–198, 306
Marx, Karl 3, 7, 45–46, 48, 50–51, 55, 57, 179, 185, 186, 194, 265, 283, 290
Marxism 17, 21–22, 31, 39–42, 45–52, 55–58, 104, 110, 134–135, 179, 181, 185–189, 194–195, 275, 279, 292–293, 318, 341
  autonomist Marxism 56, 281, 284
  Marxist feminism *see* feminism; social reproduction theory
  see also capitalism; communism; Engels; Lefebvre; Stalinism
Massey, Doreen 134
Meek, James 289
Meredith, Catherine 60, 78, 81, 86, 113
Merrifield, Andy 17, 40, 194–195, 201–202, 341
  The New Urban Question 40, 47, 195, 273, 341
Merseyside 60, 64, 74, 104, 115, 126, 129, 134, 153, 163, 164, 196
  see also Liverpool
Merseyside Development Corporation 105, 114, 118, 147, 150, 205
Merseyside Federation of Housing Co-operatives 117–118, 305, 309, 315
  see also Liverpool Federation
Merseyside Improved Houses (MIH) 68, 71, 72, 86, 115, 164, 120, 143–144, 146, 148, 156, 163–164, 237, 301, 313, 314
  see also Riverside
Merseyside Task Force 36, 133–134, 135, 147–148, 150
methodology (research) xi–xii, xvi–xviii, 39–42, 303–304, 334–335

see also dialectics; story-telling and narrating history
Militant Tendency 36, 90, 103–110, 133, 172, 293, 300
municipalisation of Liverpool co-ops 36, 90, 103–115, 118, 144–145
Urban Regeneration Strategy (URS) 105–114, 119, 253, 254
see also Hatton houses
Mill Street Housing Co-operative 84, 87, 102, 106, 118
Minister for Merseyside 36, 133, 135
mixed communities 92, 191–192
Mondragon Co-operative Corporation 319
money 250, 269, 283–284
More, Thomas 46, 259
Morris, William 180
Mouffe, Chantal 42
multiculturalism 29, 66, 79, 222–223, 232
see also race
municipalism 318–321
municipal socialism 21, 25, 31, 36, 103–110, 133–134, 310
municipalisation 71, 264–265
new municipalism 264–265, 323
see also anchor institutions; Fearless Cities; Militant Tendency; Preston model
mutual homeownership societies (MHOS) 6, 218–220, 265, 325, 329
mutualism 25, 51, 53, 108, 136, 269, 325
mythology 289–300
Liverpool's foundational myth 28, 291, 300
myth of civil society 294
myth of Robin Hood 289–293
myth of St George 289–293, 298, 301
see also story-telling and narrating history
Narnia, The Chronicles of 154, 297
National Community Land Trust
American CLT Network 239–241
Network 9, 183, 214, 229, 248, 307, 315–317
National Health Service 10, 310, 289
Natton, Barry 86, 144
neighbourhood abandonment 38, 41, 127, 189, 204
Neighbourhood Housing Services 69, 72–73, 76, 82, 85–86, 143, 301, 312, 314
neighbourhood life-cycle theory 130–131
neighbourhood question, the 41, 123–139, 170–172, 252, 254–257, 276–279, 320–321
neoliberalism 4–5, 10, 16, 22–23, 56, 133, 171, 177–178, 187, 192, 253, 273–274, 279–281, 291, 305–306, 309–310, 332, 339–343
'roll with it' neoliberalisation 309, 341
networks *see* federations
New Deal for Communities (NDC) 184, 208, 232–234
new towns 32, 35, 52, 62, 64, 115, 125, 132
new urban left 51–52, 53–54, 69, 134, 306
North West Housing Services (NWHS) 161, 164, 248, 295, 307, 314–315, 317, 322
Northern Alliance Housing Cooperative (Terrace 21) 214, 297, 302
not-for-profit organisations 9, 25, 57, 71, 166, 180, 323–324
charities 71, 152, 164, 228, 284, 306–307, 323–325
community interest companies (CIC) 234, 243, 323–324, 330
non-profit industrial complex 322, 342
see also social economy; third sector

O'Byrne, Ann 249, 308
Oldham 233, 245
Owen, Robert 45
ownership *see* homeownership; property; stewardship; theft

Paris 51, 52, 123
Parkinson, Michael 35–36, 89–92
patient capital 314, 322
see also solidarity funds
Peel Holdings 153, 306
performativity 56, 131, 244, 256, 258, 286, 291, 335
see also institutionalism; mythology; prefigurative politics
philanthropic funding 219, 248, 306, 322, 324, 342
see also finance; patient capital; solidarity funds
Piggeries 63, 87
place effects 168, 178
see also historical cycles
planning (urban) 23, 54, 62, 77, 101, 118, 132–133, 149–150, 151–152, 156, 170, 191, 238, 337
'planning for real' participatory techniques 83, 170, 245, 303, 313
see also urban design
Plus Dane 163–164, 207, 212–213, 220–222, 224, 307, 313–314
Polanyi, Karl 16, 23, 269–270, 272, 275
fictitious commodities 272
police brutality 129, 201
policy mobilities 111, 173, 180, 183, 239–242, 245, 269, 302–303, 319
see also knowledge transfer
political education/empowerment 80–82, 84, 116, 120, 137, 170, 264, 276, 301, 331
post-capitalism 11, 13, 57, 281, 293
post-development blues 160–161, 295
post-politics 35, 195, 266, 343
prefigurative politics 11, 55–57, 243, 259, 286
Preston model 264, 319–320, 323
Prince Albert Gardens Housing Co-operative 87, 108
Prince of Wales (Charles) 83, 100, 111, 147
private rental sector 4, 68, 70, 196, 270
procurement/tendering 217, 307, 319, 322
professionals and professionalisation 9, 34, 53–54, 69–70, 76–83, 95, 101, 108, 163, 170, 220, 235, 242, 247, 249, 285, 296–300, 302, 306–307, 311–315, 327–328, 330–334, 338–339
see also amateurism; bureaucracy; expertise; technocracy
property 4–6, 14–21, 24, 40, 45, 177–182, 187, 193–194, 222–224, 258, 267, 271–272, 278–280, 287–288, 291, 318, 325–326, 329
common property regimes 16, 19–21, 258, 271, 287–288, 291, 320, 325–326
the ownership model *see* Singer
property-led development *see* regeneration
property rights *see* rights
proprietorship 20, 258, 259
tyranny of property 180–181
see also real estate
Protestantism 32, 102, 106, 118, 140, 146
see also sectarianism
Proudhon, Pierre-Joseph 40–41, 45–46, 51, 279, 293
public, the 4, 12, 14, 16, 21–25, 271, 338
public–common partnerships 275, 284
public housing 4–5, 13, 22, 60–61, 71, 91–93, 105–113, 265, 267–270, 273, 276–277, 306

public ownership 7–8, 12–13, 22–24, 110, 265, 274, 291, 296, 318–322
public–private dualism 16, 18, 25, 135, 271
public space 19, 215–216, 227, 243, 257, 271
see also foundational economy; procurement; the state

quasi non-governmental organisations (quangos) 71, 133, 226, 296, 306, 319

race 37, 132, 214, 223
racism 35, 128–129, 132, 201–203, 205, 214
Radical Routes 315
Rancière, Jacques 334
real estate 279–280
regeneration 35–37, 65–68, 74, 105, 120, 124–128, 130–133, 143, 170–172, 182, 188–193, 203–208, 212–213, 220, 232–236, 238–239, 254–257, 277–278, 318–322
arts-led regeneration 221–222, 243–246, 250, 257–259, 335–343
community-led development 66–67, 119–120, 127–128, 137–139, 143, 148–154, 220–222, 226–227, 243–244, 248–251, 317
post-war urban renewal 32, 51–52, 115, 124–127, 132, 136, 252
property-led development 35, 133, 172, 189–196, 252–256, 308–309, 341
public–private partnerships 184, 189, 273–275, 306, 321
the regeneration game 36–37, 256–257, 342
see also planning; urbanism
rent gap *see* Smith
rent strikes 34, 63, 64, 128, 173, 281–282
residualisation (council housing) 8, 54, 196, 203, 274
resilience 171, 308–309
revolution 27–28, 42, 51, 55–57, 160, 259, 273, 280–281, 292–294, 300–301
Liverpool's new-build cooperative revolution 59, 94, 99, 160, 303–305
radical reformism 42, 56, 266
urban revolution *see* Lefebvre
rights 5, 14–15, 16–21, 179, 184–185, 222–223, 258, 325
common land rights 6, 18, 185, 179, 222–223, 290
property rights 16, 20–21, 187–188, 291, 325, 329
Right to Buy 4, 8, 92, 111, 274, 279
Right to the City 17–18, 185, 244, 248, 303, 337
right to place 14, 172, 185, 222–223
right to stay put 14, 185
see also citizenship; property
Rochdale Pioneers 315
Rose, Carol 20–21, 258
Rotheram, Steve 247
Royal Institute of British Architects (RIBA) 83, 296, 331
rurality 10, 32, 27, 58, 100, 182, 183, 251
Rushton, Erika 216, 224
Ruskin, John 179–180

Salford 233
Sanders, Bernie 183
Sassen, Saskia 340–341
SAVE Britain's Heritage 206, 219, 228, 231, 307
scale (geographical) 21, 40, 46–47, 124, 134–136, 168, 186, 190–191, 264, 315–316, 320
economies of scale 14, 58, 158, 161, 163, 174, 193, 208, 298, 308, 321

scaling up or going viral 169–170, 277, 285–286, 288, 312–318
see also localism; secondary support infrastructure
Scandinavia 70, 269
Scotland 10, 32
seafaring 33, 66, 300
see also Liverpool (maritime culture)
secondary support infrastructure 69–78, 85, 94–96, 117, 139, 144, 161, 173, 304, 307, 311–317, 323
see also CDS; federations; institutionalism; NWHS
sectarianism 32, 61, 102–103, 106, 118–119, 129, 145–146, 150, 277, 299
Sefton 193, 228–231
self-build housing 11, 53, 57, 83, 312
self-help housing 11, 46–47, 53–54, 57–58, 82, 128, 171, 218, 222, 225, 303, 307, 312, 332
see also empty homes; Empty Homes Agency
self-organised housing 11–12
Shelter 65–66, 68, 118, 119, 306
shelter *see* dwelling
Shelter Neighbourhood Action Project (SNAP) 65–69, 74, 79, 82–83, 92, 127–128, 203–204, 212, 227, 301, 302, 306, 312, 318–319, 331
Sheppard, Bishop David 147, 150
Shorefields Housing Co-operative 87, 102, 106, 118, 302
shrinking cities 124–127, 185, 190, 236
see also managed decline
Singer, Joseph William 16
ownership model 16–20, 215, 217, 257, 271, 287, 329–330
Skelmersdale 62
slavery 29, 178
Slum Clearance Programme 32, 34–35, 37, 63, 64, 65, 74, 76, 87, 125–126, 132, 141, 252, 254
slums 4, 30–31, 52, 59, 61, 63–64, 67, 79, 87–88, 90, 99, 127, 140, 195
Smith, Neil 188, 194
locational see-saw 188–189, 278
rent gap 194, 255, 278, 308
social economy 24–25, 135–139, 269, 285, 322–324
community economy *see* Gibson-Graham
social enterprise 57, 138, 148, 152–153, 167, 171–172, 226, 320, 323–324
social finance/investment 219, 247, 306, 322
social value *see* value
solidarity economy 137, 251
see also not-for-profit organisations; social innovation; solidarity funds; third sector
social exclusion 14, 21, 136, 178, 232, 276
social housing 5, 8, 54, 156, 162, 164, 196–197, 223, 274, 306, 314
social innovation 36, 81, 135–139, 173, 218, 225–226, 306, 313
social movements 17, 50–51, 65, 184, 264, 306
cycles of contention 50–51, 53, 186, 305
movement building 117, 269, 284, 299, 315
see also commons; cooperativism
social practice 244, 335–343
social reproduction theory 49–50, 52, 186, 279, 281
solidarity funds 313–315, 322
see also patient capital
Somali communities 66, 223, 341
Southdene Housing Co-operative 116–117
sovereignty 17–18, 20, 271, 289–290, 291–292
space, the production of 51–52, 130, 134–135, 185–189
dialectic of thing and flow 131, 254, 266
politics of space 223, 278

public space *see* public
spatial fix 40, 187, 272
see also Lefebvre
squatting 13, 57–58, 88, 119, 145
Stalinism 97, 108, 146, 169, 322
Star Wars 297
Starr, Ringo 228
state, the 5, 7–8, 10–12, 15–18, 20, 21–25, 56, 188, 191, 194, 270–271, 273–274, 284–286, 294, 310, 318, 323
Leviathan logic *see* Hobbes
shadow state 71, 321
state-led gentrification *see* gentrification
state theory 21–22, 284, 286, 294
welfare state *see* welfare
see also procurement; the public; quangos; sovereignty; third sector; violence
Steinbeck Studio 219–221, 339–341
Steinberg, Max 87, 106, 116, 147–150
Steve Biko Housing Association 223
stewardship 181–185, 220–224, 272, 278, 287
see also governance; trusterty
stigma (territorial) 35, 130, 196, 201–202, 255–257
Stoke-on-Trent xiv, 228
story-telling and narrating history 244, 265–266, 289–294, 300, 303–304, 334–335
see also Hine; methodology; mythology
sustainability 196, 214, 308
financial 24, 138, 151, 165–166, 168, 177, 218, 250, 313–314
sustainable communities 151, 156, 172, 191–192
see also resilience

technocracy 58, 212, 232–233, 235, 241–242, 298, 318–319, 323
see also bureaucracy; expertise; professionals
tenant co-partnerships 51
tenure (housing) 8, 21, 54, 70, 191, 196–198, 203, 223, 230, 236–237, 325–326
leasehold vs. freehold 181, 218–219, 249, 325–326
security of tenure 14, 209, 276, 288, 329
tenant–landlord relation 46–47, 279–280, 325–326
third estate 325–326
see also land reform; property
Terrace 21 co-operative 214, 218–220, 222, 227, 245, 296–297, 302, 325, 329
Thatcher, Margaret 4, 8, 36, 92, 104–105, 111–112, 119, 129, 133, 139, 147–148, 150–151, 318
theft 50, 105, 224–225
third sector 5, 60–61, 71, 91, 161–164, 252
see also not-for-profit organisations; quangos
Thirlmere Housing Co-operative 86, 87, 96, 101, 114, 300
Toxteth Riots 35, 128–129, 133, 167, 201–202, 205, 209, 224
trade unions *see* labour movement
transnationalism 269
see also policy mobilities
trust/mistrust 79, 81, 95, 119, 146, 165, 167, 201, 224–225, 278, 286, 299, 311, 328
trusterty/trusteeship 180, 181–182, 272, 287, 324
Turner, John F.C. 15, 39, 40, 46, 48, 53, 55, 57–58, 172, 252, 281, 303, 309, 312, 330
debate with Burgess on commodity nature of housing 39, 46–47, 58
housing as a verb *see* dialectics (noun and verb)
resourcefulness 58, 309
user autonomy 40, 53, 57

Turner Prize xv–xvi, 225–226, 296, 329, 335, 338, 340, 342

UN World Habitat 151, 225
uneven urban development 41, 123–125, 134–136, 188, 275–276, 190–191
  locational see-saw *see* Smith
United States of America 33, 111, 130, 132, 138, 180–183, 222, 239–241, 287, 320
universities 80, 82, 166, 233, 239, 301, 319, 340
urban design 99–102, 115, 155–156, 299
  see also design
Urban Question, The 22, 39–42, 51–52, 177–178, 186–187, 275–284
  the new urban question 40, 187–189, 195, 251, 273, 279–280, 341
urbanism and sub-urbanism 10, 99–101, 156, 299, 336–343
  anti-urbanism 32, 10, 100–101
  austerity urbanism 208–209, 264, 321
  defensive urbanism 99–102, 155–156, 198, 299
  radical urbanism 243–244, 336–337
  see also insurgent/guerrilla urbanism; regeneration; rurality; social practice
URBED 233, 245, 247, 307
utopia 42, 46, 55–57, 258–259, 265–267, 275–276, 293
  experimental utopias 258, 266–267, 309
  real utopias *see* Wright
  utopia of rules *see* Graeber
  utopian socialism 3, 10, 42, 45–46, 51, 275

value 7, 14, 19–20, 24, 39–40, 47–50, 181, 194, 197, 251, 272–273, 279–281, 287
  circuits of value 13, 137–138, 283–284, 287
  dialectic of value 287–288
  exchange and use value 7, 17, 48–50, 192, 251, 253, 287–288, 338–339
  social value 50, 137, 166, 264, 270, 277, 298, 319
  see also money
vandalism 66, 99, 111, 119, 155, 209–212
Vauxhall CDP 66, 127, 128, 156
Vauxhall (Liverpool) 31, 66, 114, 127, 128, 140–142, 145–147
Vauxhall Neighbourhood Council 156
Vienna 31–32, 87
violence (state) 192–195, 208–212, 274, 292, 299, 338

war (metaphor) 79, 95–96, 160, 172, 178, 206, 231, 273, 290
Ward, Colin xii, 7, 16, 34, 40, 54–59, 98, 169, 280–281, 298, 303
  collective dweller control 34, 40, 57, 78, 169, 282, 295
  hidden history of housing 53, 57
  pragmatic/respectable anarchism xii, 56, 281
Weber, Max 285, 294, 298
welfare 8, 16, 21–24, 51, 181, 276–277, 289
  see also foundational economy
Weller Street Housing Co-operative 34, 58–59, 60, 74–84, 85–87, 94–101, 116, 117, 119, 146, 158, 169, 290, 296, 300–301, 331–332
Welsh Streets 227, 228, 246
Wilde, Oscar 338
Winstanley, Gerrard 179–180
working-class culture 28, 32–34, 53, 66, 79–80, 108, 169, 192, 198
World Wars 32, 132, 181, 273
  The Blitz 132

Worlock, Archbishop Derek 147, 149–150
Wright, Erik Olin 42, 266
  real utopias 42, 266–267, 271, 280–281, 339, 342
young people 33, 35, 75, 103, 116–117, 153, 226, 243, 248–249, 301
  see also Generation Rent
Your Housing Group 239, 247, 249
  see also Arena